Human Services

Eighth Edition

Human Services

Concepts and Intervention Strategies

Joseph J. Mehr
Illinois Department of Human Services

Allyn and Bacon

Boston ■ London ■ Toronto ■ Sydney ■ Tokyo ■ Singapore

Editor in Chief, Social Sciences: Karen Hanson
Editorial Assistant: Alyssa Pratt
Marketing Manager: Jackie Aaron
Production Administrator: Annette Joseph
Production Coordinator: Susan Freese
Editorial-Production Service: Colophon
Electronic Composition: Graphic World
Composition Buyer: Linda Cox
Manufacturing Buyer: Julie McNeill
Cover Administrator: Brian Gogolin
Cover Designer: Suzanne Harbison

Copyright © 2001, 1998, 1995, 1992, 1988, 1986, 1983, 1980 by Allyn & Bacon
A Pearson Education Company
160 Gould Street
Needham Heights, MA 02494
Internet: www.abacon.com

Between the time website information is gathered and then published, it is not unusual for some sites to have closed. Also, the transcription of URLs can result in unintended typographical errors. The publisher would appreciate being notified of any problems with URLs so that they may be corrected in subsequent editions. Thank you.

Library of Congress Cataloging-in-Publication Data

Mehr, Joseph
    Human services : concepts and intervention strategies / Joseph J. Mehr. — 8th ed.
      p. cm.
    Includes bibliographical references and index.
    ISBN 0-205-31750-2 (alk. paper)
    1. Human services—United States. 2. Social service—United States. 3. Public welfare—United States. I. Title.
    HV95 .M35 2000
    361.973—dc21

                                                          00-041627

Printed in the United States of America

10 9 8 7 6 5 4 3 2   RRDV 05 04 03 02 01

PHOTO CREDITS:
p. 6: Robert Harbison; p. 23: Jerry Cooke/Photo Researchers, Inc.; p. 26: Courtesy of Lyndon Baines Johnson Library Collection; p. 53: Mary Kate Denny/PhotoEdit; p. 75: Robert Harbison; p. 93: Robert Harbison; p. 105: Robert Harbison; p. 111: Alon Reininger/Woodfin Camp & Associates; p. 128: Robert Harbison; p. 155: Will Hart; p. 167: Robert Harbison; p. 205: PhotoEdit; p. 233: Jerry Howard/Positive Images; p. 244: Robert Harbison; p. 246: Leslie Sloan/Woodfin Camp & Associates; p. 288: A. Ramey/Stock, Boston; p. 295: Robert Harbison

In memory of Peter and Elizabeth

Contents

PART III   *Contemporary Strategies*

Preface

As this eighth edition of *Human Services* goes to press, a joining of fiscal conservatism and liberal activism seems to have the United States in its grip. The economic outlook continues to be positive, but both Democrats and Republicans are seeking a balanced federal budget. President Clinton ended his first term by signing a major welfare reform bill into law that substantially reduces the welfare safety net. This comes on top of the Democratic loss of health care reform. There is no doubt that many people in the United States will continue to need helping services.

Being interested in human services means being interested in and committed to finding solutions to the human problems that face people in modern times. These social and psychological problems are extremely complex and require a coordinated and integrated approach. This is what the human services are all about—helping ourselves and helping others to solve problems.

The term *human services* has become an all-encompassing phrase used to label services provided to individuals or groups who, for whatever reason, have failed to be included in the mainstream of the society and culture or who experience the pain and anguish of life in these troubled times.

The field of human services is oriented toward dealing with all major social, psychological, and economic ills. Unfortunately, the dollar resources that exist at the federal, state, and local levels are limited, and it seems unlikely that they will increase greatly in the foreseeable future. This fact has prompted the approach taken in this new edition of *Human Services*—a focus on concepts and strategies that can have a significant impact on human problems in spite of limited fiscal and human resources.

People with the most difficult problems must receive the maximum application of resources if human services is to be a workable concept. Our primary concern must be with those who are most at risk and with the conditions that have brought them to that low point of survival.

The content of *Human Services* reflects this view. The book does not ignore traditional systems for dealing with problem behavior but focuses primarily on newer approaches to human problems that hold promise for the future. These approaches are presented within the framework of human services concepts such as integrated services, recognition of the importance of environment and social institutions, rapid problem solution, and perhaps most important, a new consciousness about the directions in which we need to go in meeting the needs of both client and community.

Part I provides an orientation to and presents a perspective for viewing the field of human services. It examines the development of human services concepts. It distinguishes between integrative and generic concepts of human services and places modern human services in a historical context. Part II focuses on the parameters of the field of human services. This part of the book discusses the roles of human services entry-level professionals and workers and explores human services problems and the boundaries of the field. Part III surveys the strategies that have been used traditionally to treat people in need. It concludes with examples of how human services workers can integrate these approaches into their work and emphasizes the importance of personal relationship factors in all human services delivery systems. Part IV explores the new strategies for helping people in need that are most closely identified with a human services approach. The section concludes with an examination of ethical and legal issues that affect human services workers.

After reading this book, you will have a basic understanding of human services and the prevailing strategies for dealing with the major problems of people in need. You should also be able to understand the most important approaches of professionals in correctional institutions, community mental health centers, mental hospitals, crisis centers, substance abuse service centers, facilities for mentally retarded people, and multiservices centers. In addition, the role functions of human services workers should be clear: what they do, how they do it, and what effect they can have on people in need.

Acknowledgments

I would like to thank those individuals who reviewed the seventh edition of this text and offered useful suggestions: Sharon Eisen, Mott Community College, and Dave Worster, University of New Hampshire. And, once again, I would like to thank the reviewers of previous editions: Ruth E. Andes, Genesee Community College; Sharon K. Hall, University of Houston–Clear Lake; and Thomas Richardson, College of DuPage; Dennis B. Cogan, Georgia State University; Mikel Garcia, California State University at Fullerton; Carol A. Jenkins, Biola University; Tricia McClam, the University of Tennessee; Patrick McGrath, the National College of Education; and Cynthia Crosson-Tower, Fitchburg State College.

1

Human Services

A New Direction

- What is the meaning of *human services?*
- What recent circumstances have resulted in the growth of the field of human services?
- What is meant by *social policy?*
- What are the differences between the concepts of *integration* and *generic human services?*
- What are the ten attributes of generic human services?
- What is a human service worker?

Two New Beginnings

■■ Mary Lynn has always been a good listener. Lately, that talent has been coming in handy. Her best friend called yesterday, sobbing so much that Mary Lynn could hardly understand her. Finally, she pieced together that Judy's husband, Dick, had hit her several times in the ribs and then choked her till she almost blacked out, all because of a late breakfast. Mary Lynn encouraged Judy to let it all out, and Judy did! Judy revealed that her broken arm from "a fall" two years ago was really due to Dick, and this kind of behavior had become frequent since Dick was laid off.

While expressing her concern and understanding, Mary Lynn grew very worried about her friend's welfare. She began to encourage Judy to get help. Judy was adamant that Dick would "kill her" if she brought the topic of counseling up to him. After much coaxing, Mary Lynn convinced Judy to go with her to a women's shelter for advice and help.

Now that Judy was going to get some professional support, Mary Lynn began thinking about how rewarding it was to help her friend. The idea occurred to her that working at the women's shelter must be really worthwhile. Mary Lynn decided to talk to some of the people there about how she could find a career in that field. The community college might even have a training program for it. Mary Lynn vaguely recalled reading in the paper about human service technology. Maybe she would look into that. After all, it's never too late to start something new, even if you're supposed to be old enough to know better!

Human services is a phrase that is often used to group activities that focus on helping people live better lives. In the broadest sense, the human services include formal systems such as government welfare programs, education, mental retardation services, mental health organizations, child care programs, physical health care establishments, and the correctional services of the legal justice system. The phrase also has more specific meanings. Some authors have described its most important feature as a new consciousness among workers and clients in the formal helping systems. Others have focused on human services as a concept that embodies an integrated delivery of services to consumers. Still others have defined it as a sociopolitical movement that has aspects of a subtle revolution. Individual human service workers may focus on one or more of these factors as the most important aspect of human services, depending on their training, experience, and personal goals. The theme that all share is the improvement of quality of living for the neediest members of our society.

What Is a Human Service Worker?

Just as there are two conceptions of the field of human services—the integration concept and the generic concept—there are several possible definitions of *human service workers.*

A human service worker is anyone who is trained or educated in helping activities. This definition fits in with the use of the term *human services* as a broad phrase that subsumes all the established helping professions and helping activities. But this definition would include all members of the traditional helping professions and virtually everyone else who provides helping service to the needy. For our purposes, it is much too broad.

A human service worker is a person who does not have traditional professional academic credentials but who, through experience, training, or education, provides helping services. If human service workers were defined this way, traditional helping professionals would be ruled out. And indeed, although some members of the established traditional professions work from a framework that embodies some of the attributes of human services, many do not. The large majority of traditional professionals maintain a self-identity related to their specific academic training. They do not identify themselves as *human service workers* but as *social workers* or *psychologists,* for example.

The problem with this definition is that, like the previous one, it includes too broad a range of those who provide helping services. It would include volunteers, police, paramedics, helpful and concerned bartenders, and so on. While these people may provide helpful efforts as adjuncts to formal human services systems, there is little utility in a definition that includes them as human service workers.

A human service worker is a trained entry-level professional. The human service worker provides uniquely designed interventions for individuals experiencing emotional, cognitive, and/or social problems. These services are for the purpose of assisting the individual and/or group to achieve the highest level of functioning they are capable of achieving within the context of the society in which they live (Cogan, 1993).[1]

The field of human services and entry-level human service professionals are characterized by a multidisciplinary or interdisciplinary viewpoint, a concern for the whole person, and a recognition that the field of human services can lay claim to a philosophical uniqueness that continues to evolve dynamically (Kronick, 1986; Macht, 1986; Mehr, 1986).

Human services as a field of endeavor, academic discipline, and social science has the potential to become a factor in changing policy toward domestic human conditions that are more supportive of programs designed to enhance the quality of life for all people (Cimmino, 1999). Cimmino describes what he calls three pillars that define human services: advocacy, or valuing individuals and families; research, or raising social and political consciousness; and credentialing, or training students, developing resources, and providing professional support. Human service workers have the potential to contribute something new and different to the helping services—something beyond what the traditional professions have to offer. The human service professional is a new type of worker: a social health generalist change agent, whose actual job title may be only one of the many that fit into the human services field (see Box 1.1).

BOX 1.1   Typical Employment Titles for Human Service Workers

Mental health technician	Case coordinator
Drug abuse counselor	Life skills instructor
Client advocate	Neighborhood worker
Social service aide	Group activities aide
Probation officer	Case monitor
Parole officer	Child advocate
Gerontology aide	Group home worker
Home health aide	Crisis intervention counselor
Mental health aide	Community organizer
Intake interviewer	Community outreach worker
Social work assistant	Community action worker
Psychological aide	Halfway house counselor
Assistant case manager	Rehabilitation case worker
Residential manager	Protective services aide
Case worker	Family support worker
Youth worker	Social service liaison
Residential counselor	Behavioral management aide
Case management aide	Eligibility counselor
Alcohol counselor	Adult day care worker
Activity aide	Social skills trainer

Current Conceptions of Human Services Systems

Some agreement exists about the events that have led to the development of the human services approach, but complete agreement does not yet exist in regard to just what the field is. Some professionals feel that it is a totally new approach to providing innovative services to persons in need. Others describe it as a primarily organizational approach to the delivery of established services that have been developed by the traditional helping professionals. More and more think it is a field with its own concrete identity, comparable to social work or psychology. In the material that follows, the primary current conceptions of human services will be explored.

The two major conceptions of human services place primary emphasis on differing aspects of service delivery problems. The first conception deals mainly with the integration of existing services into a coordinated network at the local, state, or federal level. This has been termed the *human services integration concept*. The second conception, includes the concept of system integration, but it also focuses on the issue of human services as a distinct new field, identifiable by the attitudes of its practitioners and the technologies it uses. This second concept, called the *generic human services concept*, forms the underlying fabric of this book.

Human Services Integration Concept

The primary focus of this conceptualization of human services is its emphasis on integrating the various human services systems under one organizational or administrative system (Gage, 1976; Orlans, 1982). It has sometimes been called the *umbrella agency concept* (see Figure 1.1). It is the simpler of the two approaches and has fewer implications in terms of the types of services offered or the underlying conceptual frameworks. In an early article, March (1968) describes programs under this framework as having the following features: (1) comprehensiveness of services, (2) decentralized facilities located in areas with a high population density, and (3) integrated administration that supports continuity of care from one service element to the next with a minimum of wasted time or duplication of activity. Four models of this type of organization, ranging from simple to complex, have been widely adopted: (1) the information and referral center, (2) the diagnostic center, (3) the one-step multiservice center, and (4) a linked comprehensive network (Demone and Harshbarger, 1974; Sauber, 1983).

A study reported by Parham (1974) gives a working definition for human services integration: "The linking together by various means of the services of two or more service providers to allow treatment of an individual's or family's needs in a more coordinated and comprehensive manner."

A number of state governments appear to be using this conception of human services as an integrated system. To date, Georgia, Florida, Minnesota, and Wisconsin are well on their way toward such a model. The conception appears quite popular, and to some degree evaluation can demonstrate that it has improved the delivery of coordinated services to those in need (Frumkin et al., 1983).

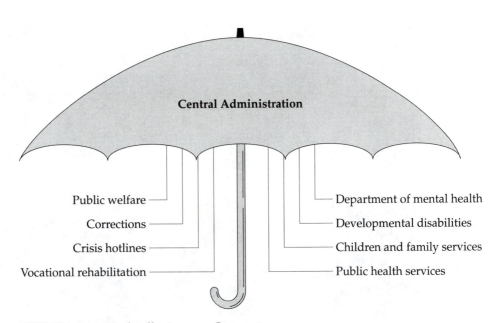

FIGURE 1.1   Umbrella Agency Concept

There does seem to be a major problem in the model's lack of careful attention to the very services it would integrate. That this approach may be "old wine in new bottles" is a real concern.

Unfortunately, in some states, Departments of Human Services have been formed as umbrella agencies with no significant change in how the various subunits do business with each other. At the end of the 1990s, for example, state government in Illinois established a Department of Human Services that integrated little but the upper levels of administrative staff, but had little impact on actual service practice. However, the basic concepts of service integration are unquestionably valid and desirable; in fact, they are an important part of the alternative generic concept of human services.

The Generic Human Services Concept

Even though the term *human services* is often used simply as a substitute for other terms (such as *social services*), it is becoming more and more apparent that human services is in reality a new field. The boundaries between the subspecialties of human services (mental health, corrections, child care, education, welfare, mental retardation, and so on) are becoming less well defined. The common attributes of generic human services become more obvious as those boundaries dissipate.

One well-known educator in human services, Dr. Harold McPheeters, has been involved in the field since at least 1965. In 1989, when asked if there was

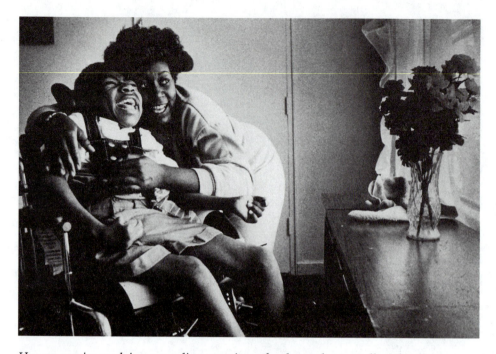

Human service work is a rewarding experience for the worker as well as the client.

something that could be called a human services delivery model, he answered as follows (McClam and Woodside, 1989):

> *I don't know. I feel there needs to be a differentiation of the roles of human services and social work. I feel that human services has much more of an orientation to helping the client in any possible way—being with that client to get the job done to improve that person's functioning. Human service workers do whatever needs to be done—it might be psychological, or it might be assisting with medical needs or social needs. Human service workers are not constrained by any single philosophical orientation or technology. They're much more oriented to helping the client solve a problem with whatever it takes, using a range of biological, social, psychological approaches. They ought to have the ability to deal confidently in all of those areas to help the clients. To me, this generic orientation to getting the job done is philosophically the difference between human service workers and other professions.*

Cimmino (1993, 1999) has moved the concept of generic human services a step further by describing a "social health generalist." Compared with the mental health generalist of the 1960s and 1970s, this idea reflects the need for human service workers in a variety of roles within a rapidly changing social and economic system. The social health generalist role includes a broader knowledge base of a variety of community resources, case management strategies, social policy, and political influences. The social health generalist concept implies a time when separate services subsystems no longer exist and individuals will be helped with all their problems through one comprehensive system based on solutions to problems, rather than many different and unrelated services systems. Such a comprehensive services system would embody characteristics of the generic human services concept, such as the following:

1. Generic human services can be delivered only through an integrated service system.
2. Human services places increasing importance on environment (cultural expectations, here-and-now relationships) as a factor in problems of life adjustment but does not ignore psychological issues.
3. Human services focuses on problem solution rather than on treatment.
4. Human services has a major task of understanding the impact of social institutions, social systems, and the social problems of client-consumers.
5. A major task for human services is identifying and using *experiences* by which people grow, mature, or change.
6. Human service workers are identified by their competencies rather than by level of formal education or type of educational degree.
7. The focus for training human service workers is an emphasis on learning skills, but knowledge is not ignored.
8. The human services system demands evidence that its technologies and approaches *work.*
9. Human services is pragmatic and eclectic. It uses all the things that work in dealing with client-consumer problems.
10. Human services is parsimonious.

It is obvious from this list that human services is not a new science or field of knowledge; it is, however, a new approach to using the understandings and discoveries of the current sciences and professions. Human services, while not antagonistic to the traditional professions, is a new mixture of attitudes, approaches, and behaviors. This will become clearer as we examine each attribute individually.

   1. *Generic human services can be delivered only through an integrated service system.* This concept of the integration of service has been examined more fully earlier in this chapter. The client-consumer *must* be able to obtain all the needed services through the same system if the problem of fragmentation of services is to be avoided. To provide *only* psychological support in the face of concrete problems such as lack of decent housing, no employment, or no social contacts does not deal with the total pattern of problems and is likely to be ineffective.
   Put yourself in the client's place. How would you react if you were an unemployed single parent with two preschool children, living in an unheated three-room apartment, with no money for rent, barely enough food, and no funds to pay for child care so that you could hunt for a job? Would you be angry? Would you

feel hopeless and depressed? A counselor at a mental health center could try to help you with your angry, hopeless, or depressed feelings, but the other problems would still be there. In an integrated service center you would get help for all or most of these problems at the same time: job training; advocacy with the gas company so that the heat could be turned on; help with temporary public aid money, food stamps, and arrangements for child care; and counseling for the emotional problems.

2. *Human services places increasing importance on environment as a factor in problems of life adjustment but does not ignore psychological issues.* Until recently, most of the human services subspecialties focused on the inner person, the psychological dynamics that caused the problem or illness, to the virtual exclusion of environmental factors. The true human services approach seeks an appropriate balance between psychological dynamics and here-and-now factors. Such an approach recognizes that it is inappropriate to deal with personality characteristics or maladaptation until real progress is made on the client-consumer's physical needs, such as food, shelter, and safety. In effect, it is futile to deal with the psychological dynamics of a symptom pattern without first dealing with such precipitating factors as social isolation, loss of employment, or lack of monetary resources. However, once basic needs have been dealt with, the client's behavior, thinking, and feeling can become the focus of his or her concern.

3. *Human services focuses on problem solution rather than on treatment.* The concept of *treatment* implies illness, and a great deal of evidence exists that once begun, many of the traditional treatment systems are virtually interminable. Human services focuses on the development of solutions to real-life problems and the development of the client's problem-solving capacities. This basic process must occur before treatment can be effective. It is conceivable that once the human services problems are dealt with, treatment will be unnecessary.

4. *Human services has a major task of understanding the impact of social institutions, social systems, and particularly cultural diversity on social problems* (see Box 1.2). The problems and processes of the *inner* person are dealt with as well as possible, considering the current knowledge and resources of the traditional professionals: the social worker, psychologist, psychiatrist, and so forth. But these professions have generally ignored a critical area that human services focuses on: the social-institutional environment. This is not to say that the field of human services should ignore the issues of the inner person. These issues are important, and human services must incorporate them into its system; however, the prime focus must be on the problem areas that have not been dealt with. Human services must look for new answers to human problems that can supplement and complement the already widely accepted strategies. These answers are most likely to be in the arena of effects of social institutions, new institutions such as peer groups and consumer groups, cross-cultural issues, community political attitudes, quality of life, social change, and many others.

BOX 1.2   "There She Lies, the Great Melting Pot"

In 1908, as great waves of immigrants arrived, playwright Israel Zangwill's *The Melting Pot* opened in New York. From this play and that era comes the phrase that has been used to characterize the United States—a melting pot of races, cultures, and religions, in which raw resources would be melted down into a new, stronger alloy. Although the metaphor is striking, today the multicultural perspective would advocate a different idea—perhaps a stew, in which many different ingredients create a flavor that is unique, a stew that is less desirable if any ingredient is left out.

Human services in the United States must pay particular attention to a host of issues of culture because of the nation's remarkable diversity. Few other countries have its range of cultural diversity, but many others have at least several diverse cultural minorities to consider.

---

5. *A major task for human services is identifying and using experiences by which people grow, mature, or change.* Even though the traditional helping services are considered to be growth experiences, it is imperative to identify additional experiences of this type, preferably ones that are natural or built into our existing systems (Wilson, 1983). The recent growth of self-sustaining communities of people who were once hospitalized for a mental illness who now provide one another with social and emotional support and cooperate in business ventures for their livelihood is a good example of this process, as are the work-release programs in corrections. Other examples are Alcoholics Anonymous, Synanon, and peer therapy programs (see Rosel, 1983). This process is extremely important in terms of resource use and staffing because the communities are generally self-supporting and require little funding from the tax base.

6. *Human service workers are identified by their competencies (their ability to do things) rather than by level of formal education or type of educational degree.* In current systems, the educational degree is the prime criterion for employment, size of salary, importance, power, and credibility in spite of the relatively well-established evidence that the degree has relatively little to do with ability to work effectively with clients. The tremendous growth in the use of entry-level professionals and studies done on their effectiveness indicate that relatively uneducated staff members can competently perform a large percentage of the tasks currently done by traditional professionals (Hattie, Sharpley, and Rogers, 1984). Human service workers, then, are identified by what they can do, not by how far they went in school or what they studied.

7. *The focus for training human service workers is an emphasis on learning skills, but knowledge is not ignored.* Although a human service worker needs to *know* many things, knowing does not necessarily imply being able to *do*. The focus of education in the traditional fields has been on knowledge rather than on experience and

behavior, with the significant exception of medical training. The current trend, even in the traditional professions, is now toward skills-focused degree programs, such as the doctorate in psychology, which focuses on practical experience rather than on book learning. Because human services focuses on doing, it makes sense that human services training or degree programs must focus on competence-oriented education and training in addition to academically oriented education.

8. *The human services system demands evidence that its technologies and approaches work.* The helping services have often been based on unprovable assumptions and have rarely been evaluated in terms of effectiveness. Does what we are doing really work? A major attribute of human services *must* be valid evaluation and a commitment to act on the results of that evaluation. The delivery of a particular service must be based on its effectiveness in problem solution rather than on the deliverer's *belief* that it is good for the client or on the fact that the deliverer enjoys doing it.

9. *Human services is pragmatic and eclectic. It uses all the things that work in dealing with client-consumer problems.* All too frequently, valid solutions are not used by a system because they do not fit into a set of rigid assumptions about treatment. A case in point is the rejection of behavioral (learning theory) technologies by systems that are predominantly psychodynamic in orientation. Another example is the inclusion of "alternative healing" such as American Indian healing rituals, or other cultural approaches to service delivery, when working with people of other cultural groups. Human service systems employ service delivery approaches on the basis of their proven effectiveness rather than on the basis of theoretical preconceptions.

10. *Human services is parsimonious.* By and large, human services systems are tax supported because they focus on dealing with people who do not have the ability to pay. A major problem has always been that there never seems to be enough tax money to fund complex services for all those who have been identified as needing services (McQuaide, 1983). A compounding factor in most of the traditional systems has been the issue of overtreatment—that is, delivering long-term services to a small percentage of potential clients, which in effect ties up the system and prevents services from being delivered equally to all. A major attribute of human services systems, then, is parsimony—providing a minimum level of effective intervention for the client but avoiding creating in the client an overdependency on services. This approach ensures that the greatest number of client-consumers will receive services.

A good example of this concept is the problem of phobias, or irrational fears. In the traditional mental health services system, a phobic client often is dealt with through psychotherapy. This type of intervention generally is involved and time-consuming, often taking years to effect a relief of symptoms. Techniques developed by behavior therapists can often effect symptom reduction within a few weeks to a few months. In the interest of parsimony, the behavioral techniques would be the service of choice in this case so that more clients could be effectively dealt with using the available staff resources. The concept of parsimony implies delivering effective services to the greatest number of clients possible, through the most efficient use of resources possible (Johnson, 1983).

Social Policy and Human Services

The antecedents of the human services concept did not occur in a vacuum. Those historical developments reflected changing social policies and at the same time were instrumental in leading to social policy changes. All human service workers owe their occupation to current social policies as those policies are codified in the law and governmental rules and regulations.

Social policy refers to principles, guidelines, and concepts that guide a society's actions toward its members, usually formalized as governmental laws, regulations, and rules. In the realm of human services, the most important social policies are usually referred to as *social welfare policies*. Time after time in this text, issues will be raised and social responses will be described that are reflections of current or changing social welfare policies.

To formulate the most effective social policy, some experts believe that a strength-based approach has the most likelihood of success (Chapin, 1995). This type of approach requires a thoughtful identification of the basic needs, with consideration to cultural factors and other issues that may be barriers to meeting those needs. This identification of needs includes a process for negotiation of definitions by the needy group or its advocates. Then, there is a process of identifying ways that the needy currently overcome such barriers (a best practice model); these are the strengths to be capitalized on. Resources for need satisfaction are then identified, and finally policy is formulated. After formulation of the policy and its goals, programs are designed, implemented, and evaluated, always with client and advocate input. Unfortunately, few if any social policies are formulated, promulgated, and implemented in this rigorous manner.

The process by which social policies typically change is much less obvious, less planned, and less focused on client and advocate input. Policies are modified, rejected, or created to meet the perceived needs of society at a particular moment in time, and the perception of what constitutes a need, as we shall see, does change from time to time. The formulation of social policy first requires that social needs be identified. Once needs have been identified, the needs are evaluated for priority. The prioritization of social needs is a complex and difficult task, but one that is clearly necessary when resources are not available to adequately deal with all social needs. That has always been and will always be the case.

There is no absolute scale on which social needs can be ranked. The setting of priorities often depends on citizen advocacy, advocacy by professionals and researchers, and lobbying efforts brought to bear on local, state, and federal elected officials. At any time the priority of competing needs will be advocated by different groups, some of whom will succeed and some of whom will fail.

As some needs are successfully identified as deserving action, policies will be formulated through negotiation by those needs' advocates, the government, and at times through voter referenda. The resulting social policy must then be turned into action.

The action phase of social policy implementation requires the development of specific plans and programs. At this stage, lawmakers, the courts, and governmental bodies begin to interpret what the policy requires. Programs are designed to meet the social need based on interpretation of the more general social policy. Of critical significance at this and later stages of social policy implementation is the availability of local, state, and federal funding. Lack of adequate funding has frequently prevented the effective implementation of sound social policy.

Once social policies are codified through law, rule, and governmental regulation, and programs are developed, funded, and implemented, the tale still continues. Policies and programs are not static; they are continually changing and undergoing modification, not only because we may find new ways of doing things but also because society is ever changing, ever redefining its priorities.

Social policy can also be viewed from the perspective of official policy versus de facto policy. Official policy is the policy that is espoused by the majority, the experts, and the rule makers; de facto policy is the policy in practice. The two are often the same but *may* be different. For example, in the field of criminal corrections, the espoused social policy is rehabilitation of offenders. In actuality, the de facto policy is punishment, which is clear from the limited investment in rehabilitation services and the overwhelming investment of resources in incarceration.

A second example comes from the mental health field. For several decades, the espoused social policy in the mental health sector has been to value community care over the use of hospitalization, and the decrease in state hospital beds has been used to show movement in this direction. However, the de facto policy in mental health has continued to support hospital care for the mentally ill, as evidenced by the dramatic increase in community care hospital psychiatric beds and huge increases in admissions to those settings (Kiesler, 1982, 1992). Thus, there are several variants of social policy in the area of mental health, which over time may evolve into a clearer policy or perhaps remain blurred.

A final example of a de facto social policy is represented by the decade of the 1980s and the first few years of the 1990s, when the conservative Republican administrations of Presidents Reagan and Bush set the tone for the nation. In those years, the threat of economic inflation and then recession and the demands of the cold war resulted in reductions in human services funding in order to reduce federal deficits and at the same time increase defense spending. Through those years, human services fared poorly in competition with policies of military superiority, an image of governmental fiscal responsibility, and promises to the electorate of reduced taxation.

Can human service workers influence social policy? McPheeters (1999) points out that human service workers tend to do little in the area of trying to influence social policy, but those who want social policies that are responsive to their view of what needs to be done will have to be more active in their attempts to influence others, on a variety of fronts. He suggests that each human service worker should become educated on local political issues as well as national issues and should register, vote, talk to legislators, attend hearings, ask to testify on issues of interest, build coalitions with others, and remain committed. Human service workers have an obligation to pursue greater influence in social policy development, and many of the skills that human service workers have or gain are especially well suited to the advocacy role that social policy development requires (Hahn, 1994).

In the 1990s, the social policy issue in the forefront on a national level first appeared to be universal health care. In 1993, the sequential Republican administrations of Presidents Ronald Reagan and George Bush were replaced by the Democratic administration of President Bill Clinton. Although President Clinton recognized the need to reduce the federal deficit and made it a major initiative, he also appeared to see the need for improved public services. His administration was committed to national health care reform, to include increased access for mental health services for all citizens regardless of their ability to pay. Of particular importance for the field of human services was the possibility that this health care reform might include funding both for the provision of mental health services in hospitals and for services in the community for persons with serious and persistent mental illness.

The Democratic administration faced a difficult balancing act: to reduce the federal deficit and stimulate the economy, while at the same time push through health care reform and otherwise improve human services. Success would bring sweeping changes in many human services systems, particularly in mental health. Unfortunately, health care reform at a national level was soundly defeated by a Republican majority in Congress.

In contrast, deficit reduction and welfare reform took priority, and sweeping changes were proposed and signed into law. The changes, pushed by a conservative Republican Congress and signed into law by a centrist Democratic president facing reelection, are focused on dramatically reducing welfare rolls and saving money. It essentially does away with what was criticized as an "almost unlimited entitlement." The new system presumes that able-bodied persons can find jobs that will enable them to become self-sufficient. Failure of a parent—usually a single mother—to become gainfully employed means that she and her child or children lose publicly funded benefits. The plan saves about $55 billion in state and federal expenditures. There is a five-year lifetime limit on welfare benefits, and after two years of benefits able-bodied adults are required to work or risk losing the benefits. Food stamps are kept as a benefit, but able-bodied adults without dependents are limited to three months of food stamps during a three-year period. Most benefits would be denied to legal immigrants who are not citizens and definitely denied to illegal immigrants. These changes affected 12.8 million recipients of Aid to Families with Dependent Children (AFDC) and 26 million Americans who receive food stamps. States are supposed to provide job training and other services to assist recipients in obtaining work. Opponents of the change fear that it will result in great hardship for the poor. They do not believe states will be able to link recipients who are willing to work with employers willing to hire. This change will have vast implications for human services, but we will have to wait for implementation and experience before we fully understand those implications.

Summary

1. *Human services* can be defined as a field that helps individuals cope with problems of a social welfare, psychological, behavioral, or legal nature. Human services is characterized by an integrated, pragmatic approach focusing on problem solution within the client's life space, utilizing change strategies affecting both the internal person and his or her external environment.

2. A human service worker is a trained entry-level professional. The human service worker provides uniquely designed interventions for individuals experiencing emotional, cognitive, and/or social problems. These services are for the purpose of assisting the individual and/or group to achieve the highest level of functioning they are capable of achieving within the context of the society in which they live.

3. Human services has come to be characterized by new attitudes on the part of staff members and an increased emphasis on providing services to the neediest. It focuses on the poor and disenfranchised rather than on groups that have always been able to pay for services.

4. One approach to human services focuses on integrating various service delivery systems under a single administrative organization. This approach has been criticized for not placing enough emphasis on new service methods and technologies.

5. The generic human services approach adds to the concept of integration a focus on the types of methods and technologies used to help people in need.

6. Generic human services share a number of characteristics: integrated services; emphasis on environmental factors; problem solution; understanding of social institutions, systems, and problems; identification of growth experiences; competence of workers; development of skills in workers; evaluation of services; pragmatism and eclecticism; parsimony or efficiency.

7. Social policy consists of principles, guidelines, and concepts that guide social action. It is developed through a complicated process of advocacy and legislative action and is constantly changing in interpretation.

Discussion Questions

1. An important aspect of human services is serving disadvantaged populations. Why?

2. What major problem exists in the integration approach to human services?

3. What are the attributes of the generic approach to human services?

4. In what ways are the integration approach and the generic approach similar? How do they differ?

5. Why do we need a human services approach?

6. What impact might the social policy of welfare reform in the late 1990s have on the future of human services?

Learning Experiences

1. Ask two different community providers to define *human services*. Compare their definitions.

2. Check the ethnic mix of people receiving public financial aid in your community, county, or state. Does it reflect the overall population? If not, try to find out why.

3. Determine whether your community, county, or state has the integrated approach to human services, the generic approach, or neither.

4. Find out who your state legislature representative is, and determine her or his position on welfare reform.

Endnote

1. Definition contributed by Dennis B. Cogan, professor of mental health and human services, Georgia State University, Atlanta, May 1993.

Recommended Readings

Cimmino, P. F. (1999). Basic concepts and definitions of human services. In H. S. Harris and D. C. Maloney (Eds.), *Human services: Contemporary issues and trends* (2nd ed.). Boston: Allyn and Bacon.

Hahn, A. J. (1994). *The politics of caring: Human services at the local level.* Boulder, CO: Westview Press.

Harris, H. S., & Maloney, D. C. (Eds.). (1999). *Human services: Contemporary issues and trends* (2nd ed.). Boston: Allyn and Bacon.

2

A History of Helping

- How long have people offered helping services?
- How did the view that disturbed people are sick affect helping services?
- What three viewpoints about human behavior have developed since the turn of the century?
- What is the social welfare movement?

The field of human services shares with the other helping professions a history that can be traced back into antiquity. The study of the history of helping services illustrates that the type and extent of assistance provided to needy people is dependent on the "self-evident truths" of particular historical periods. Those so-called truths include how a society or culture defines the concept of *needy* and what it considers an appropriate response to human problems.

Suppose, for example, that a person has no livelihood, cannot pay for shelter, food, or clothing, and has no one to provide care or support. For a society to support such a person constitutes a burden on the self-supporting members of the society. The extent to which members of different societies or cultures have viewed that burden as acceptable or appropriate varies widely.

One culture at a particular point in history may hold the belief that poverty is due to laziness, lack of motivation, or poor character and either offer no assistance or grudgingly offer only minimal assistance. Another culture may view poverty as a god's punishment for sin. Assistance requires the person to repent for the sins, and aid may then be offered through a religious organization. A third culture may view poverty as caused by impersonal, uncontrollable external factors. Assistance may be offered willingly because it is believed that poverty could strike any member of the group at any time.

Throughout history, many different beliefs have been held about why people behave the way they do, why they become disadvantaged, whether their problems ought to be of concern to the culture at large, and what ought to be done about them. The history of human services concerns the changing ways in which societies and cultures have organized to deal with the problems of people. At different times, the problems people have posed for society have been ignored, treated harshly, or dealt with in a more humane manner. The type of response has depended on the beliefs held about the causes of problematic human behavior and about the "right" way to deal with those causes and the people who suffer from them.

The Dark Past of "Helping"

In dim antiquity, before the development of written language, we suspect that some helping of others, at least of members of one's clan, did occur. We also know that some so-called treatments were violent, such as trephining—opening a hole in a person's skull to let out the evil spirits that are causing problem behavior. In later eras, as society became more agricultural and complex, particularly in the Near East, written codes of conduct began to be developed. For example, in 1750 B.C., the Babylonian code of Hammurabi covered the gamut from major laws to very detailed regulations for business, labor, wages, and behavior. This code illustrates a harsh approach to the control of human behavior: "If a man break a man's bone, they shall break *his* bone." Yet the code also showed compassion, such as providing for the adoption of orphaned infants.

This mixture of "an eye for an eye" justice and some concern for social welfare is also present in the later writings of Hebraic law. The Hebraic (Jewish) tradition of law, as set down in the Talmud, recognized that people who were disabled or otherwise disadvantaged deserved some assistance (Scheerenberger, 1983). This principle is embodied, for example, in the Hebrew practice of leaving a generous amount of grain unharvested around the fields for the use of widows and fatherless children (Landon, 1986).

The classic Greek and Roman civilizations were an odd mix of enlightened views and harsh conditions. At times, pensions were provided for the disabled, sometimes the needy were given free grain, and some residential institutions were set up for the orphaned children of men killed in battle (Trattner, 1986). But although the Roman philosopher Cicero stated that "Justice commands us to have mercy on all," charity was unusual during the Greek and Roman eras.

Things were not much better during the dawn and adolescence of the Christian era in the West, when belief in the existence of witches and demonology led to persecution of many unfortunate people who were believed to be witches and warlocks.

The Dark Ages was a bleak period, but the Roman Catholic church encouraged some humane institutions. The clergy set up monasteries, many of which became social service agencies of a sort. The income from church lands and donations was used to provide monetary assistance to the worthy poor. Monks and nuns reached out into the homes of some of the poor to provide food, clothing, and succor. By the eleventh and twelfth centuries, secular relief was provided by craft and merchant guilds (guilds were somewhat like today's unions) for destitute members and their families. Religious and lay groups opened hospices that offered shelter and care for weary travelers, orphans, the aged, the sick, and the poor. It was an era of contrasts and inconsistency. During the next 300 to 500 years, punitive attitudes slowly moderated and the first glimmers of the concept of social welfare began to appear.

Social Welfare: Toward a Community Approach

Although history seems to have been marked by inhumane approaches to disadvantaged and problem-ridden people, there have always been people who were charitable toward the less fortunate. Through most of history, charity was given for the benefit of both the needy and the *giver*. Charity was a moral virtue that raised the giver's status and moral standing while helping the needy.

As societies became more complex, simple charity was no longer adequate in dealing with the needy. A major change in perception occurred in the 1500s, when the view developed that civil governments should address the needs of persons through civil legislation. The decline of the church as a ruling body and the erosion of feudal systems led to a growing involvement of civil law and government in human services. In 1536, the Henrican Poor Laws were passed in England. These laws provided for the punishment of beggars and vagabonds but offered civil relief for the "worthy poor." The state assumed responsibility for them, whether they were young, old, disabled, or able-bodied. The laws were expanded in 1601 into what are now known as the Elizabethan Poor Laws. Henceforth, social welfare would be seen as having a dual role: provision of charitable relief and a means toward correcting behavior (Landon, 1986; Romanyshyn, 1971).

Nearly 200 years later, the Industrial Revolution resulted in large concentrations of disadvantaged people in urban areas. To deal with this problem, many public and private institutions were opened. These included workhouses; debtors' prisons; penal institutions; houses for orphans, delinquents, and unwed mothers; and mental institutions. These institutions required workers and helping services to become more formalized. However, their conditions left much to be desired. The concern of some private citizens over these conditions led to a number of attempts at social reform.

The growing numbers of urban poor in a land where wealth was considered a virtue and dependency a vice led to great concern over the problems of social disability. In 1843, a private voluntary organization, the New York Association for Improving Conditions of the Poor, was formed. This group was concerned with the evil effect of poverty on community life but to a large extent saw poverty as the result of irresponsible behavior by those who *became* poor. The needy were seen either as worthy poor (widows, orphans, the sick, in dire straits through no fault of their own) or as unworthy poor (able-bodied persons who had no income because of laziness or character faults). As in previous eras, civil authorities attempted to discourage the "unworthy" from asking for help through the use of shame and humiliation (Landon, 1986). For example, in pre-Revolutionary times the poor were treated as morally deficient. They had to swear to the pauper's oath, and their names were entered on the poor roll exhibited in the city hall or in the marketplace. Local newspapers published the names of all paupers with the amounts of their relief allowances. In Pennsylvania at that time, all members of a pauper family had to wear the letter *P* on the shoulder of the right sleeve.

About the same time that the New York Association for Improving Conditions of the Poor was being formed, one of the first great reformers of social services appeared. Dorothea Dix, a retired schoolteacher, was asked to teach a Sunday school class at the East Cambridge, Massachusetts, jail. She was shocked at the general conditions of prisons and was particularly appalled at the manner in which those who were considered insane were handled. In midwinter, they were huddled in unheated cells, given slop to eat, and untreated for physical illnesses. She began a personal investigation of conditions in jails, debtors' prisons, and asylums across this country, exposing the ill treatment and brutality that had become common.

Dorothea Dix began a series of presentations to state legislatures urging solutions to the deplorable conditions she had uncovered. To the Massachusetts legislature, in 1843, she stated, "I come to present the strong claims of suffering humanity. I come as the advocate of helpless, forgotten, insane and idiotic men and women; of beings sunk to a condition from which the most unconcerned would start with real horror" (Grob, 1994). Her exposés hit a responsive chord with the populace and with legislators, and by the time of her withdrawal from active lobbying for improved conditions, she was directly responsible for the establishment of more than thirty mental hospitals in the United States and Europe. Her main efforts were focused on the plight of the insane, but her reform efforts were also significant in the areas of corrections, education, poverty, and the provision of physical health services to the indigent. In a sense, her efforts at reform foreshadowed the advocacy role of human service workers.

The social welfare movement made major strides in the 1800s and early 1900s. For example, in 1880, the Salvation Army, founded in 1878 by William Booth in England, was imported to the United States. Although a religious organization, the Salvation Army utilized military rank for its members and focused primarily on implementing social welfare programs. It currently works in seventy nations and operates more than 3,000 social welfare institutions.

In the United States, in the 1870s, an economic depression brought great need for charitable relief of a homegrown variety, and that need contributed to the motivation for the establishment of Charity Organization Societies (COS). The various COS had a shared philosophy that people had a natural tendency to shirk duty and hard work and preferred the easy ("unchurchly") life (Iglehart and Becarra, 1996). So while the COS provided relief, that relief was limited to the "worthy" poor. The poor (even the "worthy" poor) were believed to be poor by their own doing, and the COS were to provide not only monetary relief but also training so the poor could "help themselves."

While charitable, the COS also were agents of social control. They hired private investigators to assure that the poor were worthy and often had the police jail those they saw as loiterers, vagrants, and beggars. The Charity Organization Societies played a major role in trying to "Americanize" the waves of immigrants that were arriving in the United States and in assimilating persons of color. The views of the COS members toward other cultures and races reflected the type of prejudices virtually all cultures held toward persons outside their own group (see Box 2.1).

BOX 2.1   Historical Prejudice

Discrimination, prejudicial beliefs and behavior, and an almost universal lack of cultural sensitivity were common in all cultures and expressed *toward* all cultures almost everywhere in the world at and before the turn of the century and until modern times. For example:

- Native American spiritual practices were the target of overzealous Christian missionaries.
- Native Americans were seen as childlike, ignorant, and shiftless.
- 1882: "Italians are truly foreign to us. We do not speak a common language, our standards have no meaning to them" (COS worker).
- Italians were believed to have a greater hereditary vulnerability for tuberculosis because of its high frequency in Little Italy in New York City, even though they were healthy when they arrived in the United States.
- 1860s: In eastern cities, signs saying "no Irish need apply" were common in help-wanted ads.
- African Americans were segregated in both North and South.
- In the 1920s in Tulsa, Oklahoma, four thousand African Americans were made to carry passports.
- Catholics were denigrated by Protestants with name-calling like "fish eaters." His Catholic religion was a campaign issue in 1960 when John F. Kennedy ran for president of the United States.
- Into the middle of the 20th century, Jews were not allowed in many membership organizations (fraternal lodges and country clubs). They were said to be money-hungry and untrustworthy.
- In 1908, the medical director of the U.S. Navy described Jews as congenitally prone to "mental and physical degradation," leading them to become "beggars, tramps, burglars, and other perverts who make life burdensome and fill our prisons with criminals, our asylums with the insane."
- Harvard University had a quota system to limit enrollment of Jews.
- Polish immigrants were ridiculed as stupid through the vehicle of "Polack jokes."
- Persons of Asian heritage were believed to be cunning, untrustworthy, and lazy.
- The Chinese were thought to be "walking time bombs" of infection in 1900, and San Francisco's 35,000 Chinese were once quarantined for weeks based on this notion.

Another important development was the spread of settlement houses. In the United States, many new immigrants were arriving, and settlement houses were established to help people who were often poor and had difficulty fitting into American culture (Dumont, 1998). The role of a settlement house was twofold: (1) to be of help to the immediate neighborhood surrounding the house and (2) to change, as much as possible, the social conditions that made living in a slum a wretched and demeaning existence. Many early settlement workers hoped to build a bridge between the wealthy and poor citizens of major cities. Early settlement workers were often upper-class women who donated their time; later, some of those who came as immigrants became workers.

The first recorded settlement house was begun in New York City by Stanton Coit in 1866. Settlement house workers saw themselves as friends and neighbors of the disadvantaged. They were advocates for the poor and often organized self-help clubs in disadvantaged neighborhoods. Their efforts can be characterized as early social action programs.

One settlement house is well known: Hull House in Chicago, which opened in 1889. It is one of the sites where social work was born. Today, the Jane Addams School of Social Work at the University of Chicago is named after the founder of Hull House. By the 1920s, the settlement houses had become institutions that employed people trained in the new career of social casework. Settlement houses are not just a curiosity. Hull House still exists in Chicago today, with five centers and thirty satellite locations around the city. Across the United States, there are still 900 settlement houses in operation, one part of the social services safety net trying to fill in for gaps left by welfare reform (Lydersen, 1999).

Unfortunately, the standardization of charity work into social casework had certain undesirable results. Social casework began to emphasize individuals' contributions to their problems rather than the contributions of a negative environment to social problems. This emphasis on individual culpability was given impetus in the 1920s by the publication of a major text called *Social Diagnosis* by the highly regarded social worker Mary Richmond. The emphasis of social diagnosis was on individual problems and their individual remediation. This individual focus paralleled the fragmenting of the study of human behavior into the various schools of thought described in this chapter. Especially in the 1920s, social work in a sense "surrendered to Freud" and the psychoanalytic viewpoint (Trattner, 1986). An individual clinical model of social casework predominated through the 1960s and is still somewhat common.

The years since 1900 have again seen accelerating change. In the period from 1910 to the present, World War I, the Depression, and World War II resulted in tremendous economic, social, and psychological upheaval. As after the Civil War, it became apparent that social as well as strictly personal factors were important in the existence of human services problems.

A period of major significance began during the Great Depression of the 1930s. Franklin D. Roosevelt was elected president in 1932 and brought with him his experience of trying to deal with a depressed economy as governor of New York. During the Depression, one-third of the U.S. labor force was unemployed.

Roosevelt was committed to sweeping social change in an attempt to get the economy back on track and to deal with the human misery resulting from the Depression. He promised a "New Deal" for U.S. citizens.

During Roosevelt's four terms in office, many of today's social welfare entitlement programs were begun. One of the most important was the Social Security Act of 1935. It established ten different programs: old-age retirement; unemployment compensation; state public aid for the elderly, blind, and dependent children; maternal and child health services; services to crippled children; child welfare services; vocational rehabilitation services; and public health services. It was a truly sweeping piece of legislation that resulted in dramatic changes in how we deal with the disadvantaged.

Social Security legislation was further broadened under President Eisenhower in the 1950s, to include coverage of the self-employed, clergy, farm workers, and members of the armed forces. In addition, Eisenhower established the federal Department of Health, Education, and Welfare and signed the Civil Rights Act of 1957, which was the basis for the government's civil rights activities in the 1960s.

Today, human services are provided within a social welfare safety net that owes much to the Social Security Act of 1935. Although many vulnerable persons live with and are cared for by their families, they also usually depend upon a complicated mix of income and public services that are the end result of two centuries of human services development.

There are many steps to becoming a beneficiary of these human services: (1) a person or family must know of the services, (2) the individual must fit eligibility criteria for that specific service, (3) the service must be provided in the state where the individual lives, and (4) the person must actively seek out the service. One individual might need four or five services and qualify for only one or find that only one of the four or five services is available.

The major legislative and systems changes that occurred from President Roosevelt's time through the Eisenhower years helped to create a foundation for the human services programs to come. A new perspective was being developed about the rights of the disadvantaged and their entitlement to services. Social welfare began to emphasize community approaches and a growing concern with social action, advocacy, and social development reminiscent of the settlement workers' approach years before.

Antecedents of the Human Services Concept

Following the upheaval of global conflict in the 1940s, people in the United States began slowly to realize that all was not well with the traditional helping systems or social welfare services. Prisons were dramatically overcrowded, the crime rate was rising, mental hospital populations soared, and educational opportunities were unequally distributed. In spite of advances in social welfare policy, psychology, education, and social work, it seemed as if society was waging a losing

Public mental hospitals became so overcrowded in the 1930s that some observers called them the shame of the states.

battle. What was particularly striking about the battle was that the losers were usually members of the lower socioeconomic strata. It was most often members of this group who ended up on welfare; in the prisons, jails, and mental hospitals; and in the ranks of the educational dropouts. They had no money to purchase high-quality medical care, legal representation, or education. Several sociopsychological studies in the fifties and early sixties focused on some of these problems and drew them to the attention of professionals and the public (Goffman, 1961; Harrington, 1962; Myrdal, 1964; Redlich et al., 1953).

It was becoming obvious that, in most cases, those with lesser need were receiving the most services, while those with the greatest need were receiving almost nothing at all. Although many helping professionals were being trained and were entering the world of work, by and large they offered their services to those who could pay—the White middle and upper classes.

The mental health delivery system is a particularly good example of the situation during that era. Beginning in the late 1940s, state and federal governments implemented massive efforts to train psychiatrists, psychologists, social workers, and a host of other mental health professionals. (In fact, in a period of twenty-five years, more than $2 billion was spent by the federal government alone on mental health training.)

During this period, the great majority of these individuals were trained in public mental hospitals through the use of federal and state tax dollars. A small percentage of the patients in these institutions, those who were considered good teaching cases, received excellent services. However, the rest were consigned to poorly staffed, overcrowded back wards in abysmal conditions. Once finished with training, many professionals quickly deserted the mental institutions for the more lucrative field of private practice, where they offered their skills to the better educated middle and upper classes who could afford to pay well for their services.

While the exodus of professionals continued, the hospital populations soared even higher during the late 1950s, until many institutions had two or three times as many patients as their rated bed capacity. It was during this period that some experts began to question the usefulness of the traditional medical-oriented approaches to dealing with people who had severe problems of life adjustment. However, the introduction of new, more effective drugs in the middle to late fifties both reinforced the medical approach to human services problems and paved the way for a conceptual change in mental health services. The masking of symptoms that resulted from the use of new drugs was one of the major factors in the growth of the notion that many people who were in mental hospitals did not belong there and could exist in the community. Slowly but surely, the movement of patients from the hospitals to the communities began.

The ability to control the more exaggerated behaviors of some patients (hallucinations, delusions) had a positive effect on the attitudes of mental hospital staff members. New ideas and treatments began to be introduced in the hospitals, such as patient government, group psychotherapy, and vocational rehabilitation. The movement of patients to the community gained momentum partly as a result of the success of the new modalities but probably more because of a new attitude on the part of many of the staff—something could be done. The change in attitude of staff members from a custodial approach to an active effort to help patients was a landmark in the history of mental health services.

While changes were taking place in the mental health systems, similar events were occurring in the legal and correctional systems. There, too, recognition was growing that different standards were applied depending on race and socioeconomic class. White middle-class citizens tended not to be charged as frequently for crimes (even when they *had* committed them), tended to be found innocent more often, and tended to receive lighter sentences when found guilty. In the correctional system, prisoners were mostly African American, Latino, or White members of the lower socioeconomic classes.

Recognition of the discrimination inherent in the differential treatment of low-income or minority group offenders and White middle-class and upper-class offenders has led to a gradual change in the judicial and correctional systems.

Today there is much more sensitivity to the impact of social conditions on the like-lihood of criminal behavior. In addition, there is much more concern with the rights of the accused and the convicted, and programs have attempted to address the social causes of crime. Rehabilitation of offenders is more of a goal now, although the judicial and correctional systems are still haunted by the specter of retribution and punishment.

The changes occurring in the mental health and correctional systems, al-though based on problems within those systems, were reflective of changes in the culture at large. There was, from the 1940s to the 1970s, a broad change in attitude from the conservative to the liberal in political and social life.

A major expression of social liberalization can be seen in the civil rights move-ment that began with the events around Little Rock, Arkansas, in the 1950s. Although focused on the plight of Black children and their problems in obtaining an education equal to that of their White counterparts, the civil rights movement has precipitated wide-reaching changes in the educational system. Although still not entirely successful, desegregation progressed significantly during the inter-vening decades, and we have witnessed the growth of a number of compensatory mechanisms, such as Head Start programs and busing. Among the broader effects of the movement has been the expansion of the concept that high-quality educa-tion is a right of all citizens, not a privilege, and that *all* disadvantaged persons must be served by the educational system.

For individuals with an investment in the notion that all members of our society have an equal right to needed services, the sixties were an exciting time. There was a massive growth in programs in all areas for the disadvantaged: the Economic Opportunity Act, the model cities programs, urban renewal, aid to education, and great strides in racial desegregation. As these programs continued, we seemed on the way to what President Johnson called the Great Society.

One important approach for achieving the Great Society was the development of programs that created a new kind of worker. The Economic Opportunity Act of 1964, for example, resulted in the employment within one year of 25,000 parapro-fessionals in community action programs and 46,000 paraprofessionals in the Head Start program for disadvantaged preschoolers. The Office of Economic Op-portunity thus attacked the problems of the disadvantaged on two fronts: (1) it employed the disadvantaged, who would (2) help other disadvantaged people. This frontal attack on the problems of poverty was replicated in federal funding for similar programs in law enforcement and corrections, education, health, voca-tional rehabilitation, drug abuse programs, mental retardation services, and men-tal health. The programs have all been instrumental in the creation of a wide ac-ceptance of new careers in the helping services, and in the early development of human service training programs (though not called by that name).

Even though developmental events in the areas of human services (mental health, mental retardation, corrections, public welfare, education, and so on) have not been completely parallel, the similarity is great enough to use mental health as an example. The mental health system is particularly appropriate as an

President Lyndon Johnson signed the Civil Rights and Voting Act into law as a step toward a more liberal society.

example because the concept that an individual's problems in living are internal in nature (caused by psychological problems of the person) has been widely adopted by the fields of correction, education, public welfare, and mental retardation.

In the realms of mental illness and mental retardation, two similar social change processes began in the late 1950s and early 1960s. In the mental health field, a growing dissatisfaction with available services stimulated Congress to pass a resolution that established the Joint Commission on Mental Illness and Health. Even more significantly, President Kennedy appointed a cabinet-level committee to study the commission's recommendations, which were published in 1961. President Kennedy was personally concerned about the national state of services for people who were mentally retarded. His own sister Rosemary was disabled by the condition, and the Kennedy family was well aware of the lack of progressive services. In October 1961 President Kennedy issued a public statement on the need for a national plan for mental retardation services. He said, "We as a nation have for too long postponed an intensive search for the solutions to the problems of the mentally retarded. That failure should be corrected" (1961). Kennedy appointed the President's Panel on Mental Retardation, which issued its recommendations in 1962. They included a much reduced reliance on large institutional facilities, or state residential schools, as they were sometimes called;

increased community services; and, most significantly, a strong statement that society's special responsibilities to persons with mental retardation are to permit and, in fact, to foster the development of their maximum capacity and to bring them as close to normalcy and independence as possible (President's Panel, 1962). In February 1963, Kennedy's State of the Union address to Congress dealt with these issues of mental illness and mental retardation.

In effect, several of the problems of human services had obtained a national political priority. By the end of October 1963, Public Law 88-164, the Community Mental Retardation Facilities and Community Mental Health Centers Construction Act, had been signed by the president. This law provided national direction for the near revolutionary changes in mental health and mental retardation services and indirectly was a major impetus to the development of human services.

What is particularly striking about this period is that much of the pressure for change did not come from the established systems. Although there were a few groups in the traditional human services who were working in new directions, most of the impetus was coming from what has been called the *grassroots level.* It was during this period that much societal dissatisfaction found expression in events such as the radical student movement, the riots in Watts and Detroit, the Attica prison riot, the ecology movement, and the actions of people such as Cesar Chavez and the United Farm Workers Organizing Committee, Ralph Nader and the consumer movement, the gay liberation movement, and the Gray Panthers. While the broader society was embroiled in the turmoil of this period, a series of events in the mental health system reflected that turmoil and a raised level of consciousness. It also reflected dissatisfaction with the mental health system itself. Events such as these were critical to the development of the human services concept.

Even though the concept that the community rather than an institutional setting is the appropriate place for intervention predated the report of the congressional joint commission, the enactment of Public Law 88-164 provided a major impetus for the changes of the sixties. It provided the sanction for moving patients from the institutional setting back to the community and for developing resources to support those patients once they had been moved. A major accomplishment of the federal legislation was the funding of about 600 comprehensive community mental health centers around the country. However, even in areas where these centers were not funded, local groups created county or city mental health centers that in many cases were supported by a local tax base.

The principal functions of the mental health centers as outlined in the joint commission's report were "(1) to provide treatment by a basic mental health team . . . for persons with acute mental illness, (2) to care for incompletely recovered mental patients either short of admission to a hospital or following discharge from the hospital, and (3) to provide a headquarters base for mental health consultants working with mental health counselors" (Joint Commission on Mental Illness and Health, 1961). In that early period, federally funded community mental health centers were required to have at least five essential services: (1) inpatient, (2) outpatient, (3) emergency services, (4) pre- and posthospital care, and (5) education and mental health consultation. The comprehensive mental health center was, in effect, proposed as a replacement for the large public mental hospital that had been the cornerstone of our mental health delivery system for 150 years. It was the beginning of a process of moving hundreds of thousands of people with mental illness out of mental hospitals and into the community.

A particularly important aspect of the community mental health center movement for human services has been its emphasis on serving the neediest. Not only were most of the public mental hospital patients who were being moved into the community originally from the ranks of the lower socioeconomic classes but also the priority for services in the new community mental health centers was focused on those same socioeconomic groups. It had become clear from a number of studies that the greatest *need* for services existed in the urban ghetto and among the rural poor (Hollingshead and Redlich, 1965; Srole et al., 1978). However, once traditional services began to be offered to the poor, it became apparent that these services (the verbal "talking cure") were frequently not appropriate. The poor were not interested in *talking about* their problems; they wanted to *do* something about them, and frequently that meant dealing with problems of physical health, living accommodations, food, clothing, police, and money.

The traditional professionals, usually White and from the middle class, were ill equipped to deal with such issues because of their critical insensitivity to the problems and life-styles of the client population. For these reasons and for the reasons of economy (lower salaries) and staffing needs, the community mental health centers and other public services agencies began to employ indigenous workers, paraprofessionals, case aides, or community mental health workers (Albee, 1961). By 1968, in community mental health centers alone, 10,000 such people were employed (Sobey, 1970). These early paraprofessionals were the forerunners of today's entry-level professional human service workers.

The first steps toward recognition of this level of workers (individuals with less than a master's degree) occurred, of course, in the early programs in which they demonstrated their effectiveness (Gordon, 1965; Rioch et al., 1963). Even though resistance to their use did (and does) exist (Rioch, 1966), a steady progression has occurred. In 1964, an associate-level degree program was begun at Purdue University to train mental health workers. By 1975, there were almost 1,000 training programs in the various subfields of human services (New Human Services Institute, 1975). From the late 1960s to the mid-1970s, major steps were taken in the mental health field by a National Institute of Mental Health (NIMH) subdivision, the Paraprofessional Manpower Development Branch. This agency funded numerous service-training programs whose goal was to develop service systems that use paraprofessional workers in innovative ways.

During the early 1970s, the agency began to focus on having an impact on large systems such as state mental health programs by encouraging the development of large-scale career ladders for generalist mental health workers. A number of states, including Illinois, Alabama, South Carolina, Massachusetts, Florida, Texas, Virginia, and Georgia, developed such systems, either through the efforts of this NIMH branch or on their own. The years to follow would see the proliferation of a wide spectrum of jobs with a variety of titles that would be available for entry-level and professional human service workers.

Such strides were made that human service workers developed several national organizations that were similar to the organizations of the traditional human service professionals. Two such groups were the National Organization of Human Service Workers and the National Association of Human Service Technology. These two groups have since gone out of existence, but their role has been supplanted and expanded by two other healthy organizations. The current active human services organizations are the National Organization for Human Service Education (NOHSE) and the Council for Standards in Human Service Education (CSHSE). Founded in 1975, NOHSE is a membership association of human services educators, students, and workers made up of both national and regional groups. NOHSE sponsors regional meetings, a human services newsletter *(The Link)*, and a journal *(Human Service Education)* focused on human services. Together, NOHSE and CSHSE have for a number of years cosponsored an annual national conference on issues in human services.[1] CSHSE was established in 1979 to provide direction to education and training programs in human services by identifying criteria for curricula, field instruction, faculty, student admission and advisement, and necessary resources. Its board's membership consists of regionally elected representatives of member educational programs. Council membership is open to any interested human services program. The council provides its members with a formal program approval process for human services education programs. The development of these two formal organizations is of major significance in the establishment of the human services approach as a viable field of study for the helping professions.

Although this brief description of the events of the last forty years has primarily used the example of the mental health system, similar events have occurred in other subfields of human services. These events have been described by Pearl and Riessman (1965) and Riessman and Popper (1968) in the antipoverty programs, by Bowman and Klopf (1968) in the educational system, by Blum (1966) in the social services, and by Wicks (1974) in corrections.

To sum up, since the late 1950s and early 1960s a variety of circumstances—some planned, others unplanned—have come together to generate a field called *human services.* Even though a list of the circumstances might differ depending on one's orientation, most of the following events probably would be included:

1. A dissatisfaction with the effectiveness of the traditional service systems of the 1950s
2. A growing sociopolitical awareness
3. The stimulus of federal funding for "people programs" during the Kennedy and Johnson administrations
4. A growing awareness of the relative inappropriateness of traditional helping technologies for the lower socioeconomic levels of society (and frequently for other levels as well)
5. A growing awareness of the need for new personnel resources
6. The development of early sociopsychological intervention strategies
7. The creation of formal human services organizations

TABLE 2.1   Historical Highlights and Their Relationship to
the Development of Human Services

Highlight	Relationship to Human Services
Trephining	First known attempts to change behavior of people who had difficulty belonging to the mainstream of their culture.
Code of Hammurabi	First written code of conduct supporting charitable acts, about 1750 B.C.
Henrican Poor Laws/Elizabethan Poor Laws	Mark the greater involvement of civil authorities in social services, A.D. 1536 and 1601.
New York Association for Improving Conditions of the Poor	Early organized private charity, 1843.
Dorothea Dix	Early reformer, instrumental in establishing public mental hospitals.
Hull House	Settlement house in Chicago, 1889, site of the birth of social advocacy social work.
Social Security Act of 1935	Established foundation of most of today's social welfare entitlements.
Civil Rights Movement	Expression of social liberalization of U.S. society.
John F. Kennedy's 1963 State of the Union Address	President "declares war" on mental illness, gives human services a national political priority.
The "Great Society"	President Lyndon Johnson supports numerous programs that jump-start the use of paraprofessionals in social services.
NOHSE/CSHSE	Two national organizations for the support of human services as a profession are founded in the 1970s.

Summary

1. The beliefs that a society or culture holds at any period of time have a major impact on how the society or culture perceives the needs of its members. Societal responses to disadvantaged people are determined by the same "truths."

2. As social organizations became more complex, codes of behavior were established, such as the Code of Hammurabi and the ethical writings in Hebraic law. The codes were mainly punitive but did establish charity or helping acts as important social behavior.

3. The early history of so-called helping services had many dark elements. Some of the "help" offered seems from today's perspective to be more like punishment.

4. Social welfare has become the province of civil government during the past hundred years. It began as an organized charity movement dealing primarily with the "worthy poor," moved into a social action phase with the settlement house, and switched to focusing on social diagnosis and individual treatment. More recently, social welfare has moved again toward social advocacy and social development. To some extent, it integrates the knowledge and techniques developed by the various behavioral science approaches.

5. A major impetus to the growth of the field was legislation in the 1960s, particularly that which resulted from a study commissioned by the Kennedy administration. Adequate and equal services became a national political issue after Kennedy's message to Congress in 1963. Since that time, there has been a major growth in the availability of human services to the needy.

6. The need for additional people to deliver relevant services to the needy led to the use of nonprofessionals in many fields. Between 1964 and 1975, almost 1,000 college programs were developed to train human service workers.

7. The existence of two national organizations, the National Organization for Human Service Education (NOHSE) and the Council for Standards in Human Service Education (CSHSE) supports human services as a maturing profession.

Discussion Questions

1. In what way is the current spirit of the times influencing how we conceptualize human behavior?

2. In what way does the human services approach reflect broad-ranging changes in society?

3. Why could one consider human services a grassroots movement?

4. An important aspect of human services is serving disadvantaged populations. Why?

Learning Experiences

1. Survey your friends.
   - How many of them believe in astrology? Why?
   - How many of them believe in demonic possession? Why?
   - How many of them have taken tranquilizers? Why?

2. Visit a local museum to get a feeling for the historical periods represented.

Endnote

1. National Organization for Human Service Education, National College of Education (Executive Office: Building Six, 2840 Sheridan Road, Evanson, IL 60201).

Recommended Readings

Grob, G. (1994). *The mad among us: A history of the care of America's mentally ill.* New York: Free Press.

Landon, J. W. (1986). *The development of social welfare.* New York: Human Sciences Press.

Macht, J. (1999). Human services: History and recent influences. In H.S. Harris and D. C. Maloney (Eds.), *Human services: Contemporary issues and trends* (2nd ed.). Boston: Allyn and Bacon.

Scheerenberger, R. C. (1983). *A history of mental retardation.* Baltimore: Paul H. Brooks.

Trattner, W. I. (1986). *From poor law to welfare state: A history of social welfare in America* (3rd ed.). New York: Free Press.

3

Human Service Workers
Agents of Change

- Can human service workers be considered professionals?
- What are the thirteen basic role functions of human service workers?
- Why are human service workers described as generalists?
- What are some real-life examples of the functions of human service workers?
- What impact does cultural diversity have on human services?
- Is there evidence to support the competence of human service workers?
- Do human service workers need to be credentialed?

In Chapter 1, human service workers were described as characterized by a dynamically evolving generic human services viewpoint, by a multidisciplinary (or interdisciplinary) focus, by a concern for the whole person, and by an approach that involves being a generalist change agent. That description leaves many questions unanswered. Are human service workers professionals? What do they really do on a daily basis? Can human service workers be as effective as traditional professionals? Do human service workers need special credentials?

Human Services, a New Profession

With growing acceptance of the evidence that one does not have to be a highly credentialed member of a traditional professional discipline to provide competent helping services, there has been a great deal of concern given to developing expanded roles for human service workers. Before examining these roles, however, it is important to consider briefly the professional–nonprofessional issue. It has been the prevailing attitude that professionals are the most qualified service deliverers and that the higher the educational degree and the longer the educational process, the better. For example, the psychoanalyst (ten years of specialty training) is viewed from this perspective as being better than the psychologist (six to seven years of university training), and the psychologist is better than the social worker (six years of university training). Psychologists, of course, would not agree that psychoanalysts are better than they, and social workers would not agree that psychologists are better than social workers! All would probably agree that each has a different focus and a contribution to make.

Sometimes the terms *nonprofessional* and *paraprofessional* are used to denote people without bachelor's or master's degrees, who are presumed to have less ability or expertise than the traditional professionals. However, although it is perhaps not extreme to require ten years of training to pursue the complex practice of psychoanalysis, to place the same expectations on all practitioners of helping services is absurd (Vidaver, 1973). In fact, relating professionalism to academic credentials alone (which is what happens in most instances) is a distortion of the true meaning of *professional*. Bay and Bay (1973) think that the usual concept of professionalism is eroding rationality in health care. They quote sociologist Philip Slater (1970) as asserting that "the principle behind every professional organization is (a) to restrict membership, and (b) to provide minimum service at maximum cost." These two goals are, of course, totally unacceptable from a human services perspective.

Unfortunately, since Bay and Bay and Slater presented their positions, many professionals continue to fight battles over turf issues. Psychologists are seeking medication prescription privileges in an ongoing contest with psychiatrists, both psychologists and social workers are seeking hospital admission privileges, and nurses wish to expand their right to practice health care independent of physicians. All these groups, in addition, seek to limit *others* from expanding their roles.

The true professional ethic, however, should relate to how people behave in their work and how well they do it, as much as to their credentials or training. *Profession* is, in fact, defined as an occupation or vocation requiring training in the liberal arts or sciences and advanced study in a specialized field, *or* as the body of qualified persons of one specific occupation or field. Significantly, a widely accepted definition of *professionalism* is the condition of having great skill or experience in a particular field or activity. Thus, it is rational to consider the competent human service worker a true professional.

Human service workers by and large do consider themselves professionals. Instructors in human services education programs in colleges and universities view their graduates as entry-level professionals, the term *paraprofessional* having outrun its usefulness (Kronick, 1987). However, the issue is not one of self-perception but of how others view us. Feringer and Jacobs (1987) point out two significant problems facing human services in the process of professionalization.

1. There is insufficient recognition by the public for human services as a profession. For example, our degrees are not sufficient and necessary conditions

for employment. Furthermore, the public does not differentiate us from similar and other related classes of workers.
2. There continues to be fragmentation in human services education. While providing a great deal of freedom for responding to local needs, we are limited in our ability to create coherent progressions of learning and articulation agreements between levels of curricula.

Will these problems be resolved, and will human service workers achieve recognized status as professionals? It seems very likely because substantial progress has already been made. We can appreciate the progress that has been made by comparing the development of the field of human services with the development of social work as a recognized profession.

Social work, like human services, traces its roots to humanitarian or charitable activities throughout history. The formal beginning of the profession of social work, however, is often traced to the establishment in 1898 of a summer school of philanthropy by Mary Richards, the director of the New York Charity Organization Society (Landon, 1986). This school later became known as the New York School of Social Work. A comparable event in human services was the establishment of the Purdue University two-year program in mental health technology in 1966. In the ten years following 1898, many new schools of social work were established around the country. In the ten years following 1966, hundreds of human service worker programs were established in community colleges, four-year colleges, and universities.

The next major step in the professionalization of social work was the establishment of a professional organization in 1918, and several others in the years that followed, all of which finally joined together in 1955 in a national organization that had local and regional chapters. The existence of a national professional organization allowed social workers to establish criteria for professionalism in social work and provided advocacy for the profession itself. The development of a national membership organization was preceded by the establishment (in 1946) of a national Council on Social Work Education, whose purposes were to set standards, review and accredit programs and procedures, and distribute materials related to social work education.

Do these developments in social work have a parallel in human services? They do to some extent. During the past twenty-five years, a number of national organizations of human service workers have formed, but for a variety of reasons most did not survive. One, the National Organization for Human Service Education (NOHSE), is, however, strong and healthy, with a number of regional and local chapters. Unfortunately, it has a membership of only about six hundred people, whose primary focus is on education of human service workers. A second organization, the Council for Standards in Human Service Education, could be compared to the Council on Social Work Education in 1946. What has not developed in the field of human services is a stable, viable, national organization of individual human service workers. It may be coming: The National Organization for Human Service Education does accept as members human service workers employed in field settings. Perhaps if that membership keeps growing, we will see a functional national organization of human service *workers* splitting off from NOHSE some time in the years to come.

Human services is a young field, only about thirty-five years old. It took social work, psychology, and nursing each about fifty to sixty years to become full-fledged, recognized professions. From that perspective, the future of profession-alization in human services may be very bright. The human service worker may soon be recognized by all traditional professionals, the lay public, and every social systems agency as a professional who has recognized human services credentials.

Role Functions of the Human Service Worker

As the use of people we now call human service workers has expanded, there has been increased concern with determining realistic and legitimate role structures for them and reasonable models for interaction between human service workers and the established professionals. Suggestions have ranged from proposals that human service workers be assistants to professionals, doing menial tasks, to proposals that they do everything the established professionals do.

Concern over this issue led a consortium of community colleges in fourteen Southeastern states called the Southern Regional Education Board (SREB) to try to develop a rational model of appropriate roles and functions for such workers. The results have broad applicability to human services in general. Over a period of several years, the project identified thirteen functional roles and four levels of workers who could or would perform human services (SREB, 1969). The project attempted to identify the needs of the clients, their families, and communities and then proposed activities or functions to meet those needs. The proposal included the following categories:

1. *Outreach worker*—reaches out to detect people with problems, to refer them to appropriate services, and to follow them up to make sure they continue to their maximum rehabilitation. (For example, an outreach worker may work with senior citizen centers. The worker would become aware of the seniors' needs, identify persons who need assistance, and refer them to appropriate services.)
2. *Broker*—helps people get to existing services and helps the service relate more easily to clients. (This role involves making contacts with the relevant agencies that offer service and helping the client obtain the most appropriate services.)
3. *Advocate*—pleads and fights for services, policies, rules, regulations, and laws for the client's benefit. (Advocacy may involve individuals or groups. The advocate generally can exert more influence on the powers that be than disadvantaged groups or individuals. The changes in services, policies, laws, and rules that advocacy can achieve may have a positive impact on large numbers of people in need [Sosin and Caulum, 1983].)

4. *Evaluator*—assesses client or community needs and problems, whether medical, psychiatric, social, or educational. Formulates plans. (This role is important in assessing the effectiveness of services delivered to individual clients but is also applied to the evaluation of whole programs and agencies.)

5. *Teacher–educator*—performs a range of instructional activities from simple coaching and informing to teaching highly technical content directed to individuals and groups.

6. *Behavior changer*—carries out a range of activities planned primarily to change behavior, ranging from coaching and counseling to casework, psychotherapy, and behavior therapy.

7. *Mobilizer*—helps get new resources for clients or communities. (*Mobilization* means becoming an initiator of new resources. It often involves bringing agencies or groups of service providers or citizens together to form networks that can support one another, share information, and advocate for change [Grossinger, 1985; Sarason et al., 1977].)

8. *Consultant*—works with other professions and agencies regarding their handling of problems, needs, and programs.

9. *Community planner*—works with community boards, committees, and so on to ensure that community developments enhance self- and social actualization or at least minimize emotional stress and strains on people.

10. *Caregiver*—provides services for people who need ongoing support of some kind (e.g., financial assistance, day care, social support, twenty-four-hour care).

11. *Data manager*—performs all aspects of data handling, gathering, tabulating, analyzing, synthesizing, program evaluation, and planning.

12. *Administrator*—carries out activities that are primarily agency- or institution-oriented (budgeting, purchasing, personnel activities). (This role generally develops after a person has had substantial experience working with clients. The transition from direct care work often requires additional training [White, 1981].)

13. *Assistant to specialist*—acts as assistant to specialists (e.g., psychiatrist, psychologist, nurse), relieving them of burdensome tasks. The types of tasks include administering psychological tests, taking blood pressures, escorting clients to agencies, and other duties that are viewed as an ineffective utilization of a specialist's time.[1]

In addition to identifying specialist functions, SREB specified the following four levels of competence at which these functions could be carried out:

- *Level I: Entry Level*—persons with a few weeks to a few months of in-service instruction but with little experience.
- *Level II: Apprentice Level*—persons with substantial formal training or experience; equivalent to the associate of arts degree.
- *Level III: Journeyman*—substantial formal training or experience functioning at the baccalaureate degree level.
- *Level IV: Master or Professional Level*—highly competent, equivalent of a master's degree or doctorate.[2]

These broad guidelines have been well accepted by many in the human services, and further work has refined them. For example, in one major study, 358 tasks of human service workers were identified (Austin, 1975, 1978). The study identified common tasks that cut across the various subspecialties of the Florida Department of Health and Rehabilitative Services, an umbrella agency, and provided empirical support for the broad categorizations of SREB.

The activities that human service workers engage in have been further detailed by the SREB (1979). Project staff members from that organization combined several task lists. The lists had been developed by projects around the country using job analyses of functioning human service workers. The projects included data from Texas, Illinois, Florida, North Carolina, and the U.S. Navy. Substantial work on these task lists resulted in the selection of 141 tasks that were organized into a survey administered to more than 200 human service workers across the country. The data indicated that human services tasks cluster around four main areas: (1) linkage/advocacy, (2) treatment/planning, (3) administration/management, and (4) therapeutic environment control.

The thirteen functional roles SREB had identified earlier (SREB, 1969) can be fitted into this more recent classification system.

Linkage/Advocacy

1. Outreach worker
2. Broker
3. Advocate
7. Mobilizer

Treatment/Planning

6. Behavior changer
10. Caregiver
13. Assistant to specialist

Administration/Management

4. Evaluator
8. Consultant
9. Community planner
11. Data manager
12. Administrator

Therapeutic Environment Control

5. Teacher–educator

With the exception of therapeutic environment control, the earlier SREB descriptions define the new clusters accurately. Therapeutic environment control involves more than just teaching. It involves activities such as teaching self-help and living skills and also involves structuring new environments, maintenance of stable behavior in old environments, and provisions for disruptive behavior.

Why is there so much emphasis on identifying tasks in human services? Human services is a broad field, new on the helping scene, so practitioners are still struggling with its identity. We need to know what human service workers do specifically, if for no other reason than to determine how to train, educate, and retrain individuals to work in this area.

Although definitions of the human service worker may vary, all share one characteristic. In effect, what is being described by these projects is a *generalist worker*, a concept that was touched upon by the Southern Regional Education Board (1973, 1978). The SREB describes five characteristics of the generalist that are applicable to human service workers.

1. The generalist works with a limited number of clients or families (in consultation with other professionals) to provide across-the-board services as needed by the clients and their families.
2. The generalist is able to work in a variety of agencies and organizations that provide human services.
3. The generalist is able to work cooperatively with all the existing professions in the field rather than affiliating with any one of the existing professions.
4. The generalist is familiar with a number of therapeutic services and techniques.
5. The generalist is a human service professional who is expected to continue to learn and grow.

These projects have made excellent beginnings in the identification and definition of human service worker roles and functions. There appears to be increasing agreement between such groups, at least on the broad outlines. The field seems to be moving toward identifying a core group of functions that will be the focus of most human service workers in every subspecialty; the core functions will embody the attributes of the generic human services field.

Human Service Workers as Agents of Change: Do They Help or Heal?

For almost two hundred years, there has been an increasing emphasis on the notion that *deviant* or problem behavior is the result of a disease process in either the physical or the psychological realm. In fact, many consider disruptions in psychological processes to be a function of an underlying physical disorder. The implications of such an approach are numerous. If problem behavior is a function of a physical disease, such behavior should be treated, the deliverers of service should be medical personnel, services should be delivered in medical settings (hospitals), and the goal should be cure. Not only should the behavior (symptoms) be changed but also treatment should continue until the underlying physical process is modified to be within normal limits. Patients should be *healed.* They will no longer commit crimes, be mentally ill, be mentally retarded, or sexually molest children; rather, they will obey laws, be satisfied, work, learn, and so forth.

The human services model does not totally reject this medical model. There are obvious values in many of its treatments, and there *are* behavior disorders that result from underlying physical causes. However, in a very real sense, human services expands the range of effective interventions, focusing particularly on types of interventions that have been relatively neglected because of what might be considered an overemphasis on the medical approach to psychological and behavior problems. Human services focuses on *helping* rather than *healing*.

The overall objective of the helping model is either to maintain and support the consumers in their own communities or to create new communities for individuals who have become so unlinked from the mainstream that they have no identifiable community.

Individuals who need assistance generally have a multitude of problems: medical, psychological, behavioral, educational, social, and environmental. A human service worker must act as a psychosocial helper to have an adequate impact on the client's problem network. The worker must deal with clients' feelings in a psychotherapeutic manner but also link the clients with the appropriate services and perhaps even change their life spaces. A client may need medication, a new job or public financial assistance, a place to live, a structured shelter-care setting, introduction to a peer support system, vocational training, education, or hospitalization.

Of major importance for human services is the ability to identify clients' needs and problems and then to provide the resources to meet the needs and solve the problems personally, by using existing institutions or by developing new institutions. Human service workers are crisis managers. They know who the current service providers are: physicians, mental health professionals, ministers, bartenders, hairdressers, lawyers, police officers, parole officers, grandparents, college students, and so forth. They use peer therapists such as Alcoholics Anonymous, ex-offenders, ex-addicts, and others. They set up entirely new systems, such as lodging programs for migrant workers or homeless people. Human service workers also help people help themselves. Rather than always doing *for* clients, they enable clients to do for themselves (Pearlman and Edwards, 1982). Once clients can become their own advocates, they develop the types of empowerment that the nondisadvantaged have (Rose and Black, 1985). To the degree that this can be accomplished, human services can have a major impact on social problems (Pinderhughes, 1983).

Obviously, any individual human service worker cannot be all things to all people. The preceding paragraphs, however, should give insight into the workers' range of activities. The substantive aspects of the field span this range of strategies and allow a wide variability in the actual roles human service workers perform.

Human Service Workers: What They Really Do

People new to the field frequently ask, "But what do human service workers *do?*" As has been pointed out, they do many things. Human service workers are employed in schools for the retarded, prisons, special education programs, primary grade schools, mental hospitals, mental health centers, foster care and adoption agencies, courts, preschool day care centers, public welfare agencies, crisis counseling centers, rape clinics, and hotline services. They are given a variety of titles: outreach worker, family specialist, behavior technician, mental health worker, human service worker, income maintenance worker, counselor, caseworker, social services worker, youth development specialist, community service worker, social welfare assistant, community development worker, rural development assistant, nutrition aide, and health education assistant (Brawley, 1982, 1986).

To get a feeling for what human service workers *do,* however, takes more than just listing where they work or what they are called. The examples that follow will provide more concrete details on how some human service workers spend their time.

Barb

■■ Barb is around forty-five years old and is the director of a cooperative nursery school. Although she hasn't finished her associate of arts degree, she keeps working at it and plans to graduate as a child care worker someday. Those who know her know that in terms of competence she doesn't really need that piece of paper. Barb is simply very good at working with children and their parents, not only because she has the natural ability for it but also because she's done a lot of learning on her own.

Her day is fairly busy. Early in the morning, she sets up materials for the kids to use that day, plans activities with the four mothers who will help her with the twenty children, and assigns the mothers to specific tasks. As the children arrive, Barb greets them and gets them involved in an activity until the morning program starts. Unlike some nursery schools, this is a low-pressure program that is very flexible in terms of demands.

Barb feels that the most important part of the program is balancing between helping the children develop their creativity and sense of who they are and the requirements that people place on children to be nice and to share and cooperate. Each day, says Barb, has at least one crisis. "Most of these crises center around anger," says Barb, "or around hurt feelings. It's really important to help the children express their feelings fully, but in such a way that they don't really hurt others. It's important for kids to learn that they can be angry without hitting, and that they're still worthwhile even when they do make a mistake. That's the big thing, letting them know that they're all worthwhile."

After cleaning up the rooms, Barb ends her day by planning special events, ordering supplies, and planning parent–staff meetings.

Art

■■ Art is a twenty-three-year-old human service worker who works in a gas station. However, this gas station is unlike most others: it's leased and operated by a Midwestern state hospital. Although it provides all the regular services to its customers, its main purpose is to train patients from the state hospital for employment after they are discharged.

So while Art pumps gas, changes oil, and does all the other things a regular gas station attendant does, he also trains his clients to do those same things, and as he says,

"That's the most important part, the other stuff is just a means to an end. I really feel good about it when one of these guys gets a job as a pump jockey in one of the other stations in town." Art is a one-on-one teacher and trainer; in addition, he spends at least one day a week formally advocating for his clients. He goes to all the surrounding gas stations trying to persuade the managers to hire clients he has trained. Sometimes he's successful and sometimes not, but as his relationship grows with the area service station managers, more of Art's clients are getting jobs.

"What's important about this," says Art, "is that if these folks have jobs when they get discharged, they're less likely to have problems again. It boosts their self-concept to know they can work like anybody else, and they have less time on their hands to worry about their problems. Besides, if they're working, they won't have as much time to do something screwy."

Phil

■■ Phil is twenty-six years old and is a human service worker in a juvenile correctional facility. His main job is to counsel kids who have gotten into trouble with the police. The counseling is usually on a one-to-one basis, and Phil is mainly interested in developing a trust relationship with his clients. He explores why they got into trouble, what happened afterward, how they feel about it, how things are going in their relationships with the other boys, and what they'll do when they get out.

"The important thing is that they know I'm on their side—that they can trust me," says Phil. "I really care about what happens to them. Brother! You ought to see some of the crap these guys have had to put up with. It's unbelievable. A lot of my time is spent talking with my case load, but a lot of it is being involved with their day-to-day activities. We play ball together, eat together, go on trips together. I enjoy it. But mostly we talk. The one thing I don't like is the paperwork—there's too much of it. This form to fill out, that form to fill out. It's a pain in the butt."

Trish

■■ Trish is twenty-seven years old. After obtaining a master's degree in human services, she began working in a rape counseling center. Her main role is counseling women who have been raped, in terms of their feelings about the rape and about the reactions to them from others. Most of her time is spent in one-to-one counseling, but she also sees married couples, runs a group, and does community education.

"Women who have been raped need a lot of help to get over it. They bury a lot of their feelings," says Trish, "and they need to get them out on the table, look at them, deal with them, and then get on with life. Mainly, I help them get those feelings out and work them through. They feel a lot better after being able to talk about it. Some of the problems are really severe before they come in. They may be afraid to leave their home, they may feel ashamed when they go to work, and often there are problems with their husbands if they're married. It's really a kind of crisis counseling that I do. Besides that, of course, I'm working with the police department in terms of how they treat rape victims. It's been an educational experience *both* for the police and for me. Now when there's a rape case, we get called right away, and I or one of the other counselors goes over right away to act as a friend for the victim. It makes a big difference."

Trish is now faced with a major decision. She has been offered the recently vacated position of executive director of the counseling center. She would like the promotion and the new challenge but is worried that she will miss the direct contact with clients that her current role involves.

Dorrie

■■ Dorrie is a twenty-nine-year-old human service worker in a state hospital for the mentally ill. She has an A.A. degree from a human services program, which she obtained by going to evening classes while working full-time. Dorrie is a hard worker on the day shift. She does a variety of things, including serving food to the patients at mealtime, maintaining a case load, and doing treatment.

Says Dorrie, "A lot of the things that I do are routine but important, like filling out forms, but what I really like is working directly with the patients. They're really interesting what with all the strange things they do. Of course, most of the time they're not that different from anybody else.

"I do a lot of activity work, trips, crafts, games, and cards, but I guess the thing I like the best is doing the behavioral treatment programs. I develop them myself, with the help of the unit psychologist, and then do them. Since I really like it, I've taken a lot of training in it, so I know what I'm doing. The way it works is that I identify a problem behavior that needs to change, like yelling, and then work out a reinforcement program that will substitute a more acceptable behavior, like conversation in a normal tone. Then we reward the acceptable behavior when it occurs with goodies like candy or social reinforcement like attention, and punish the unacceptable behavior by ignoring it or withholding reinforcement.

"The other really important thing I do is that I have a case load of six patients. I'm responsible for knowing everything there is to know about those six people, including what we know about their past life, family, problems, current behavior, treatment plan, and everything else. Where that's really important is in the weekly team meetings where we review all the cases and make decisions about passes, treatment plans, and discharges."

Lynn

■■ Lynn is fifty years old and has been a human service worker since the late 1960s. She began her career as a psychiatric aide at a mental hospital after graduating from high school, worked for several years, and then went to college full-time to obtain a degree in English literature. After graduation from college, she returned to the mental hospital to work as a bachelor's level mental health worker, becoming a ward manager after several years.

Since that time, she has received numerous promotions for her competence and on her own has obtained formal training as an administrator. She now is the director of a forty-bed residential program for developmentally disabled (mentally retarded) clients. She currently has almost no client contact, focusing mainly on administrative matters.

"My main function is administrative and supervisory," says Lynn. "I'm a member of the executive committee of our facility, and so am involved in a great deal of decision making regarding the total facility. I'm involved in budget development, personnel issues, physical plant concerns, and all the other problems inherent in running a large facility. In terms of the supervisory and programmatic issues, I supervise a staff of almost forty, and I'm involved with such issues as hiring, direct supervision, disciplinary actions, and sometimes firing.

"A major responsibility that I have, of course, is for the smooth functioning of the habilitation program for our residents. I don't do a lot of direct work with residents, though, and most of my time is spent in meetings with staff or other administrators."

Jorge

■ ■ Jorge is twenty-eight years old, a graduate from an A.A.–degree human services program who works in a Latino community referral center. His main role is to provide assistance to members of the Latino community who are having difficulty.

Jorge says, "I do *everything*, or at least it seems like it! People come in with all sorts of problems; some speak no English, and they all need assistance of some kind. My main job is to link them with the services they need, and sometimes I follow through as an interpreter. To do my job, I have to know all the resources that are available, and that covers the well-child clinic, legal aid, public welfare, employment opportunities, the mental health clinic, and the state hospital. Although some of the people who come to our center are really messed up, most just do need a little support and a lot of information.

"Most of my time is spent in information counseling and hooking people up to the proper resources so that they can deal with their problems. It's really rewarding when we do follow-up and find out that folks are doing okay. Right now I've got a special community action project going that I really enjoy. It means a little extra time, but it gives me the opportunity to get around the city and let people know what we're doing. It seems to be working too, since we've had people coming in who said they've heard about us that way."

These examples begin to provide a sense of the types of jobs human service workers hold and the range of activities they engage in. It is clear from these examples that human service workers encounter a broad range of clients whom they assist in a variety of ways. The seven individuals who have been described perform, in one way or another, most of the activities that have been identified in studies such as those done by the Southern Regional Education Board. The National Organization for Human Service Education (NOHSE) and the Council for Standards in Human Service Education (CSHSE) have offered a generic job description for a human services worker that identifies six major areas of knowledge, skills, and attitudes that appear to be required by all human service workers (Harris and Maloney, 1999; NOHSE, 1996). The job description includes:

1. Understanding of the nature of human systems: individual, group, organization, community, and society, and their major interactions. All workers will have preparation that helps them to understand human development, group dynamics, organizational structure, how communities are organized, how national policy is set, and how social systems interact in producing human problems.

2. Understanding of the conditions that promote or limit optimal functioning and the classes of deviations from desired functioning in the major human systems. Workers will have understanding of the major models of causation that are concerned both with the promotion of healthy functioning and with

treatment and rehabilitation. This includes medically oriented, socially oriented, psychologically behavioral-oriented, and educationally oriented models.

3. Skill in identifying and selecting interventions that promote growth and goal attainment. The worker will be able to conduct a competent problem analysis and to select those strategies, services, or interventions that are appropriate to helping clients attain a desired outcome. Interventions may include assistance, referral, advocacy, or direct counseling.

4. Skill in planning, implementing, and evaluating interventions. The worker will be able to design a plan of action for an identified problem and implement the plan in a systematic way. This requires an understanding of problems analysis, decision analysis, and design of work plans. This generic skill can be used with all social systems and adapted for use with individual clients or organizations. Skill in evaluating the interventions is essential.

5. Consistent behavior in selecting interventions that are congruent with the values of one's self, clients, the employing organization, and the human service profession. This cluster requires awareness of one's own value orientation, an understanding of organizational values as expressed in the mandate or goal statement of the organization, human service ethics, and an appreciation of the client's values, lifestyle, and goals.

6. Process skills that are required to plan and implement services. This cluster is based on the assumption that workers use themselves as the main tool for responding to service needs. Workers must be skillful in verbal and oral communication, interpersonal relationships, and other related personal skills, such as self-discipline and time management. It requires that workers be interested in and motivated to conduct the role that they have agreed to fulfill and to apply themselves to all aspects of the work that the role requires.

One concept is common to all the role descriptions or job descriptions offered in this chapter and common to the individual example of human service workers provided. The concept is that human service workers are agents of change. Wherever human service workers are employed, whatever they do, they seem to be commonly engaged in attempts to generate change: change in their clients' behavior, change in the behavior of others toward their clients, or change in larger social systems, such as agencies, communities, or other major sociopolitical systems (Perls, 1979).

Human Service Workers in a Multicultural Society

Changing immigration patterns in the United States have ensured that human service workers will inevitably encounter and work with persons of distinctly different backgrounds and cultures. We are a pluralistic society composed of a variety of peoples of many racial, ethnic, and cultural backgrounds: Black, Hispanic, European, Asian, Middle Eastern, and many others. Each of us views others based on preconceptions that we have developed in our own subculture about the culture

TABLE 3.1   Contrasting Cultural Values

As with all generalizations, within any culture, there are many exceptions.

European American	Other Ethnocultures
Independence	Interdependence
Mastery of nature	Harmony with nature
Personal control	Fate
Doing	Being
Time bound	Interaction bound
Human equality	Rank and status
Individualism	Family and group welfare
Freedom for self	Inner discipline
Youth focus	Elder focus
Self-sufficiency	Birthright inheritance
Competition	Cooperation
Future oriented	Present oriented
Informality	Formality
Lack of conformity	Conformity
Materialism	Spiritualism

of others, and typically we overgeneralize the simplistic cultural stereotypes we may have learned during childhood and adolescence to the persons from other cultures we encounter as adults.

In the United States, the traditional cultural majority consisted of European Americans, with other cultural and racial groups in the minority, either in numbers, or power, or both. The cultural makeup of the helping professions has mirrored this split, and the helping services have usually been designed to provide services for persons who conform to European American cultural values, beliefs, and practices. However, some of the common values of the growing non-European American population depart significantly from European American cultural values (see Table 3.1). Remember, however, that there are important differences between many of the non-European American groups also.

Cultures are more complex than we may first believe, and they defy easy generalization. For example, consider the term *Hispanic*. In the year 2000, Hispanics in the United States are expected to number above 30 million. To provide effective human services to Hispanics, human services agencies and workers must understand the diversity of the cultural groups that fall within the term *Hispanic* (Santiago, 1993). Hispanics are sometimes categorized into Puerto Ricans, Mexican Americans, Cuban Americans, Central or South Americans, and others, but even these distinctions do not capture the full richness and diversity within the subcultures represented by the term *Hispanic.* For example, among Mexican Americans, there are major differences between those who are born to families who have lived in the United States for many generations and those who are recent immigrants from Mexico.

Much the same kind of diversity can be identified for almost all groups. For example, Blacks: Is the person from an inner city, the rural deep South, the West Indies, an affluent suburb, or Nigeria? Baptist, Catholic, or Muslim? Asians: Is the person Chinese, Korean, Japanese, Thai, or Cambodian? Caucasian: a city dweller, rural, Mormon, Amish, Orthodox Jew, recent Russian immigrant? The diversity of races, religions, and cultures in the United States make cross-cultural issues especially important for human service workers.

A major issue that human service workers face is the need to understand the impact of a culture on the behavior of its members. Human service workers must develop an ability to work with and have respect for persons from distinctly different cultural backgrounds.

Many cultural differences are quite subtle. Some, however, may have a profound impact on behavior, and a lack of cultural sensitivity may lead the human service worker to misperceive the significance of behaviors. Consider, for example, the following:

> *Native American children are often mistakenly thought to be abused because they have "mongolian spots," which appear on many children of color and can look like bruises.*
>
> *In some Hispanic cultures, the family conducts a ceremony in which adults kiss an infant male child's genitals. In another culture, adults surgically remove a portion of the male infant's genital skin. In some Pacific Island cultures, crying infants are quieted by gentle rubbing of their genitals. All these practices would be considered abusive by the laws of most states.*
>
> *In a Appalachian community religious service, a man convulses, falls to the ground, speaks in an incomprehensible language, and then rises. He sees what he calls "demons" hovering over a bystander. He then engages in an argument with the demons and sees them flee. Outside his religious community, the same behavior would be likely to lead to psychiatric hospitalization.*

The culturally unsophisticated human service worker may perceive these behaviors as manifestations of severe problems. In fact, the examples describe culturally sanctioned acts or experiences.

To work effectively with individuals and groups of varied cultures, human service workers must develop cross-cultural sensitivity and a multicultural perspective (Sue, 1992). We must become aware of the prejudices and stereotypes we may hold toward other cultural groups and begin to work toward correcting our biases (McClam and Woodside, 1994). Human services delivery systems are most often funded, organized, and controlled by a government that reflects the biases of the power base, the European American culture. Within that culture, there is unfortunately racism, sexism, ageism, and heterosexism operating more or less subtly (Petrie, 1999), and there has often been much dissatisfaction about the effect of these values in social service systems. The recognition of the insidious effects of unicultural values and prejudices has led to interest in a multicultural approach to human relations. This approach is seen to hold promise for replacing or at least diminishing rifts between Whites and people of color, between established citizens and new immigrants, and between American ethnic communities and Third World cultures (Gould, 1995). However, like all new notions, multiculturalism may be taken to an extreme (Fowers and Richardson, 1996). Sometimes, its proponents take a position that, in effect, posits that European American culture is bad by definition and that non-European American cultures are universally good. Such thinking and assertions are of little use in our attempts to help others.

What multiculturalism or cultural sensitivity can effectively offer us is a model of cultural competency or ethnic sensitivity that can help human service workers of all races and ethnic backgrounds to function more effectively (Pierce and Pierce, 1996). The culturally competent human service worker or human service agency must (1) value diversity, (2) have the capacity for cultural self-assessment, (3) become conscious of the dynamics inherent when cultures interact, (4) institutionalize opportunities for building and developing cultural knowledge, and (5) adapt strategies that guarantee policies and programs that will be culturally enriching.

1. *Valuing diversity.* The human service worker is strengthened who is aware and accepting that the clients served often are from different backgrounds and cultures (see Table 3.2). While sharing basic common needs, people of various cultures go about meeting and prioritizing those needs in very different ways. Accepting that each culture finds some behaviors, interactions, or values more important or desirable than others can help the human service worker interact more successfully with differing cultures. Valuing diversity, however, does not mean one must embrace every facet of another culture.

2. *Cultural self-assessment.* Human service workers must be aware of their own cultures and how that impacts their views of other cultures. This process begins with an exploration of an individual's own heritage, encounters, and experiences. One route is to collect oral histories from older family members. Topics such as country of origin; era of immigration, relocation, or colonization; and language(s) spoken help to define a cultural frame of reference. A next step is to examine the beliefs, values, behaviors, and customs connected with that cultural heritage. Examination of our own cultural values, beliefs, and preconceptions allows for in-depth examination of the issues that impact specific communities being served and methods for identifying barriers, resources, and strategies for creating more inclusive, culturally relevant, and responsive human services.

3. *Dynamics of difference.* The human service worker must be sensitive to the dynamics of relationships between individuals of differing cultural backgrounds. Often one individual belongs to a more politically powerful or majority culture, and the person from the minority or less powerful culture may behave in ways that reflect tension or frustration, which may make the person from the majority culture uncomfortable. Both may misjudge the other's actions based on past prejudices or beliefs. Both bring culturally prescribed patterns of communication, etiquette, and problem solving. Each may bring stereotypes about the other into the rela-

TABLE 3.2   Leading Source of Origin and Destination of Immigrants in 1998

Top 10 Countries of Origin	
1. Mexico	131,575
2. China	36,844
3. India	36,482
4. Philippines	34,466
5. Dominican Republic	20,387
6. Vietnam	17,649
7. Cuba	17,375
8. Jamaica	15,146
9. El Salvador	14,590
10. South Korea	14,268
Total for top 10	660,477
Top 10 Destination Cities	
1. New York	59,585
2. Los Angeles area	30,355
3. Chicago	28,853
4. Miami	24,034
5. Washington, DC	15,091
6. San Francisco	14,540
7. Oakland	13,437
8. Houston	13,183
9. Boston area	12,725
10. San Jose, CA	12,656

Source: Immigration and Naturalization Service.

tionship. The dynamics are a two-way process, but here the helper has a greater responsibility to nurture the relationship and break through the cultural barriers.

4. *Development of cultural knowledge.* All elements of the service system must actively gain knowledge about the diverse cultures it serves. The human service worker must understand the culturally different clients' values, beliefs, and expectations about health, family, and community and must be able to communicate effectively. The supervisor must know how to provide supervision to culturally diverse staff *about* culturally diverse clients. The administrator must understand the culturally diverse populations that the agency serves in order to be able to plan and implement culturally sensitive services that will be effective.

5. *Adaptation to diversity.* The human service worker who understands other cultures and accepts the value of other's cultural practices can adapt his or her helping approach to generate a better fit between the needs of the other culture and the services that are available.

Cultural competence may be present in individuals or agencies on a continuum from none to much. Becoming culturally competent is a developmental process with a person or system at any point falling somewhere on that continuum (Cross and Bazron, 1996). A continuum to assess cultural competence can consist of six anchor points.

1. *Cultural destructiveness:* The most negative end of the continuum consists of attitudes, values, policies, and actions that are destructive to a culture and to persons within it. Perhaps one of the most egregious example is the early policies of the Bureau of Indian Affairs and various social services it set up to "help" Native Americans by boarding out children in schools far from their families and tribes and forbidding the children to use their native language at *any* time. Less obvious are many examples in recent times of "services" that demean important aspects of one or another culture.

2. *Cultural incapacity:* At this point on the continuum, there is no intention to be destructive, but there are biases, belief in the superiority of the dominant culture, and a paternal posture toward "lesser" cultures (or races). There may be discriminatory hiring practices, and subtle messages to minorities that they are not valued. Just three or four decades ago, this point was where many social service agencies were.

3. *Cultural blindness:* The midpoint of the continuum is characterized by an expressed position of being unbiased. There is a belief that color and culture make no difference. We are all the same. There is a belief that helping approaches that work with the dominant culture and are traditionally used should work with persons of any culture. It is a well-intentioned liberal philosophy, but usually it results in services that are so ethnocentric to the majority culture that they are useless for all but the most culturally assimilated person of color or cultural minority.

4. *Cultural precompetence:* Culturally precompetent agencies or workers realize their weaknesses in serving minorities and make attempts to improve services. Precompetent agencies hire minority staff, begin training workers in cultural sensitivity, and do needs assessments of minority communities. Culturally precompetent workers have recognized their lack of knowledge about the culture of the client(s) they work with, seek out information, attend training classes in cultural sensitivity, and struggle to keep from prejudging their clients' behaviors.

5. *Cultural competence:* Cultural competence is characterized by acceptance and respect for differences, continuing self-assessment regarding cultural differences, expansion of cultural knowledge and resources, and adaptation of service models to better serve minority clients. Such agencies actively seek advice and consultation from the leaders of the minority community.

6. *Advanced cultural competence:* At this positive end of the continuum, the culture is held in much esteem, with continuing attempts to add to the knowledge base about it. The agency or worker seeks to develop new helping approaches based on relevant aspects of the culture and advocates for cultural competence throughout the system and for improved relations between cultures throughout society.

The growing emphasis on multiculturalism, cultural competence, and cultural sensitivity has resulted in a proliferation of college classes, in-service sessions, and

TABLE 3.3   How Much Cultural Diversity?

In 1998, almost 1,000,000 legal immigrants entered the United States. Here's how diverse the cultures were for immigrants in three major cities, showing the percentage (rounded to the nearest 0.5%) arriving in the city.

City	Country of Origin	Percentage of Immigrants
Manhattan	Dominican Republic	41
	China	17
	Philippines	3.5
	Ireland	2.5
	Ecuador	2
Chicago	Mexico	19
	China	6
	Philippines	5
	India	3.5
	Poland	3.2
Los Angeles	Mexico	18.5
	El Salvador	17
	Guatemala	8.5
	Armenia	7
	Philippines	7

Source: Immigration and Naturalization Service.

special conferences that have the intent of training human service professionals about other cultures. No one can learn all about another culture in a few training experiences. Cultural competence or sensitivity does not mean knowing everything about every culture or knowing just a bit about every culture. It is more appropriately a respect for differences, eagerness to learn about others, and an openness to the view that there are many right ways of behaving in the world (and some wrong ways). Culture is not the simple artifacts or materials owned by a people, not a laundry list of behaviors, values, and facts, not the stereotypic images of groups depicted in the media, and not the romanticized image of a people often seen in folk music and folklore. Cultural competence or sensitivity recognizes that individuals are individuals; they cannot be categorized into totally discrete groups because much within-group variability exists.

For the human service worker, cultural sensitivity is an important aspect of being a change agent. Some human service workers work exclusively within their own cultural group. The vast majority, however, need to be able to work with multiple diverse cultures, particularly in cities such as Los Angeles, New York, Chicago, and Miami. In Los Angeles, for example, a human service worker may find that a client case load includes not only European Americans, African Americans, and Hispanics, but also Pacific Islander, Korean, Chinese, Thai, and Vietnamese clients (see Table 3.3). Most people who attempt to be culturally sensitive can come to fully understand at most three or four other cultures in a lifetime. (Rodriguez, 1996). The human worker who deals with clients from many cultures is thus continually working to understand other cultures.

Competence and Credentialing

Are human service workers competent? *Competence* is the overall ability to function satisfactorily in a given role or job. It involves having many competencies—skills or characteristics necessary for carrying out a discrete portion of a job that can be operationally defined and assessed. The question of competence of human service workers can be looked at from several perspectives. We can assess an individual worker in regard to specific skills, or we can assess workers as a group in reference to other professional groups. Although individual skills are important, the most important issue at this point is the overall competence of human service workers as a group. Do they do as well as the professional disciplines in providing human services? The answer is a qualified but resounding yes.

Human service workers do not do some things as well as trained professionals from other specialty disciplines. For example, human service workers are not as good as physicians at diagnosing and prescribing treatment for medical problems. They are not as good at giving and interpreting psychological tests as psychologists. However, human service workers do seem to be equally as good at those activities that both they and the disciplinary professionals are trained for and do.

The fact that human service workers can provide helping services that are as effective as the same services given by disciplinary professionals has been documented consistently for more than thirty years. In the early 1960s, however, the issue had not yet been resolved. Many professionals in the helping services believed that individuals with no graduate training could not provide services as well as the services that M.S.W. social workers, Ph.D. psychologists, and M.D. physicians could provide. Undoubtedly, some still feel that way.

Gartner (1979) and Durlak (1979) surveyed a number of evaluation programs that assessed the effectiveness of human service workers. Of the hundreds of studies surveyed, almost all showed that human service workers were as effective as or more effective than traditional professionals. A few studies can be used as examples. One of the earliest studies of human services counseling was completed in the mid-1960s. Truax (1969) compared nonprofessionals who had 100 hours of training in counseling to clinical psychology graduate students and to experienced therapists. An evaluation of the three groups' effectiveness with 150 people hospitalized for chronic schizophrenia demonstrated that the nonprofessionals provided counseling that was only slightly less effective than that provided by the professionals and was considerably above the counseling provided by graduate students. In a client population of people addicted to drugs, a more recent study found that ex-addict nonprofessionals and non–ex-addict nonprofessionals were as effective in therapeutic counseling as traditional professional counselors (Aiken et al., 1984). Many other studies have found strikingly similar results.

Brown (1974) suggests that nonprofessionals are effective counselors partly because they are selected on the basis of personal characteristics that are important for effective helping rather than on characteristics important for success in graduate school. Success in graduate school requires drive, single-mindedness, and a focus on abstract concepts. Human service workers may have these qualities; they also have "a capacity for empathy, warmth, sensitivity in interpersonal rela-

Cultural diversity calls for cross-cultural sensitivity on the part of human service workers.

tions, high self-confidence and self-regard, and the ability to accept people with values different from their own" (Brown, 1974).

The effectiveness of human service entry-level professionals as classroom educators has been amply demonstrated. Kaplan (1977) reported on a major evaluation study of nearly 20,000 human service entry-level professionals working in classrooms in 132 school systems in 48 states from 1969 to 1976. Children who had been assigned to classrooms with human service workers did better on standard reading and math tests after their experience than students in classes where human service workers were not used. Another study (Costa, 1975) demonstrated that human service workers who later qualified for teaching licenses (by obtaining further education) had more positive attitudes toward children and received better performance ratings than teachers who had not been human service workers. In addition, their classes performed better than the classes of traditional teachers.

The demonstrated effectiveness of human service workers in a variety of settings has helped broaden their acceptance as competent new professionals. In fact, the demonstrated competence of nontraditionally trained human service workers has contributed to a belief that such workers should no longer be referred to as *nonprofessionals, subprofessionals,* or even *paraprofessionals.* Of these three terms, *paraprofessional* is perhaps the least offensive (Perls, 1978), although it is still subject to some criticism. A much preferred term that is now coming into use is *entry-level professional.* It appears likely that the terms *nonprofessional, subprofessional,* and *paraprofessional* will be used less once some form of credentialing becomes standard for human service workers.

Credentialing

Are credentials really necessary? If human service workers are to be formally recognized as functional, competent professionals in their own right, a credentialing or certification process is probably necessary (Petrie, 1984). The traditional professions are credentialed by their graduate education (and academic degrees), by state government licensing exams, and by membership in certifying organizations. There may ultimately be similar advanced graduate programs in the generic field of human services. There already are, of course, hundreds of A.A. and B.A. degree programs and a few master's-level programs in interdisciplinary human services (Clubok, 1984). In a number of states, new legislation is establishing a licensure status for bachelor's and master's degree–level counselors to be available for human service degree graduates. In Illinois, for example, at the B.A. level one can become a Licensed Professional Counselor and at the master's level, a Licensed Clinical Professional Counselor.

There are currently two organizations exploring or working on the issue of credentialing processes for human service entry-level professionals: the National Organization for Human Service Education and the Council for Standards in Human Service Education. Both have been mentioned previously in other contexts.

The National Organization for Human Service Education (NOHSE) was founded in 1975 in response to a need perceived by professional care providers and legislators for improved methods of human services delivery. With the support of the National Institutes of Mental Health and the Southern Regional Education Board, NOHSE focused its energies on developing and strengthening human services education programs at the associate, bachelor's, master's, and doctoral levels.

The current purposes of the organization are (1) to provide a medium for cooperation and communication among human services organizations and individual practitioners; (2) to foster excellence in teaching, research, and curriculum development for improving the education of human service delivery personnel; (3) to encourage, support, and assist the development of local, state, and national organizations of human services; and (4) to sponsor conferences, institutes, and symposia that foster creative approaches to meeting human services needs.

Members of NOHSE are drawn from diverse educational and professional backgrounds that include corrections, mental health, child care, social services, human resource management, gerontology, developmental disabilities, addictions, recreation, and education. Membership is open to human services educators, students, field work supervisors, direct care professionals, and administrators. Five regional organizations are affiliated with NOHSE: the New England Organization of Human Service Education, Mid-Atlantic Consortium for Human Services, Southern Organization for Human Services, Midwest Organization for Human

Service Education, and Northwest Organization for Human Service Education. It is closely allied with the Council for Standards in Human Service Education.

The Council for Standards in Human Service Education was established in 1979 to give focus and direction to education and training in mental health and human services throughout the country. The council exists to help human service educators and college administrators who are interested in achieving maximum educational effectiveness and to give formal recognition and approval to programs whose excellence warrants public and professional confidence. Although the council's major aim is to assist educational institutions in improving the quality and relevance of their mental health and human services training programs, it is expected that employers, public and voluntary agencies, faculty, and students will seek the council's help in identifying high-quality training programs.

The council's approval process is designed to assist programs in self-study, evaluation, and continual improvement and to produce new, creative approaches to the preparation of human service practitioners at the undergraduate level. Validated national standards serve as the base for guiding and reviewing programs; council approval attests to a program's compliance with these standards.

In addition to maintaining training program standards and assessing applicant programs against these criteria, the council provides information and technical assistance to help programs make necessary modifications or improvements. It advises and informs education boards, program directors, and college administrators. The council maintains a network of resource persons, including educators, administrators, and evaluators, and cooperates in sponsoring regional technical assistance workshops.

The National Organization for Human Service Education and the Council for Standards in Human Service Education agreed to jointly sponsor a group to examine the issues inherent in certification of human service workers (Macht, 1986). Work on the issue of credentialing continues through CSHSE and NOHSE (Giovanni, 1999). Although standards are not yet available, it seems likely that certification or credentialing is on the horizon for human service workers. Its exact form remains to be seen.

Summary

1. Human services is a new field and has not yet attained recognition as a full-fledged profession. But there are signs that such recognition is growing.

2. The need to specify the activities of the human services field has led to a number of studies that have attempted to identify the functional tasks and roles of human service workers. One study identified thirteen functional roles that can be organized as follows:

   Linkage/Advocacy
   - Outreach worker
   - Broker
   - Advocate
   - Mobilizer

Treatment/Planning
- Behavior changer
- Caregiver
- Assistant to specialist

Administration/Management
- Evaluator
- Data manager
- Administrator
- Consultant
- Community planner

Therapeutic Environment Control
- Teacher–educator

3. Human services focuses on the relatively neglected aspects of human problems and their effects on clients' existence. The human service worker must be a psychosocial helper dealing with the complete person—his or her internal environment and external environment.

4. Human services agencies focus on clients' psychological well-being but also are concerned with the clients' physical well-being, financial resources, and social relationships. Workers in this field are concerned with how these factors can be altered to help clients enter or reenter the mainstream of functional adjustment.

5. It is often difficult to translate general descriptions of the roles of the human service worker into concrete notions of what human service workers really do. Seven examples have been given of actual human service workers.

6. To work effectively with clients from other cultures, the human service worker must be aware of his or her own cultural attitudes and beliefs and must develop a broad understanding of other cultures and respect for persons from those cultures.

7. Cultural competence includes valuing diversity, self-assessment, understanding the dynamics of difference, gaining cultural knowledge, and adapting to diversity.

8. The presence or absence of cultural competence can fall on a continuum from destructiveness, through blindness, to advanced competence, in which one holds the other culture in esteem and advocates for improved relations.

9. Evaluative research has clearly demonstrated that human service workers are as effective as traditionally trained professionals in providing a range of generic helping services.

10. Full official acceptance of human service workers as entry-level professionals rather than as nonprofessionals or paraprofessionals may not occur until some formal process of credentialing is developed. A number of national organizations are trying to develop a credentialing process.

11. Many people in the field, including many traditionally trained professionals, accept human service workers as professionals in the true sense of the term: qualified members of a specific field who are very experienced and skilled and who function competently.

Discussion Questions

1. Why can we consider human services to be a profession?
2. What might be the advantages of the generalist approach? The specialist approach?
3. Should human service workers focus on helping or healing?
4. Is a lack of cultural sensitivity natural in all people?

Learning Experiences

1. What was your first awareness of skin color as an ethnic factor? Visualize and vividly recall the event. Exchange experiences with a classmate.
2. Interview several community human service workers to find out which of the SREB functional roles they perform. What additional things do they do?
3. Start thinking about which of these roles *you* would like to fill.
4. See how many distinct human services jobs you can identify in your community.
5. What happens when someone expects a particular behavior but encounters something different when interacting with people from another culture.
   a. Pinpoint an occasion when you have felt different or have noticed something different when interacting with a person from another culture.
   b. Detail the situation.
   c. List the behaviors of the other person.
   d. List how you behaved.
   e. Describe your feelings on that occasion.
   f. List the behaviors that you expect from people in your culture in the same situation.
   g. Reflect on the underlying value in your culture that makes your people behave the way you expect in this situation.

Endnotes

1. *Roles and functions for different levels of mental health workers.* Atlanta: Southern Regional Education Board, 1969, pp. 29–30. Reprinted by permission of Southern Regional Education Board, Atlanta, Georgia.

2. *Roles and functions for different levels of mental health workers.* Atlanta: Southern Regional Education Board, 1969, p. 34. Reprinted by permission of Southern Regional Education Board, Atlanta, Georgia.

Recommended Readings

Iglehart, A. P., & Becerra, R. M. (1996). *Social services and the ethnic community.* Boston: Allyn and Bacon.

Russo, J. R. (1980). *Serving and surviving as a human service worker.* Monterey, CA: Brooks/Cole.

Simons, R., & Aigner, S. (1985). *Practice principles: A problem solving approach to social work.* New York: Macmillan.

Vacc, N. A., DeVaney, S. B., & Wittmer, J. (Eds.). (1995). *Experiencing and counseling multicultural and diverse populations* (3rd ed.). Bristol, PA: Accelerated Development.

4

Human Services

Identifying Problems and Causes

- What types of problems should human services target?
- What is meant by *problem behavior* or *deviance?*
- How is problem behavior defined from an intrapersonal perspective or as a result of an individual's psychological maladaptation?
- How is problem behavior defined from an environmental or extrapersonal perspective?
- What are the major viewpoints about the causes of problem behavior?

In its broadest sense, the term *human services* can be viewed as encompassing all helping services that are aimed at dealing with every human problem. As young as the field of human services is, some published material suggests that *all* of humanity's problems are the province of the human service worker. The range of issues addressed in the literature has included physical health, crime, education, poverty, homelessness, aging, drug abuse, severe mental disorder, mental retardation, depression, loneliness, and shyness, among many others. A comprehensive list could go on for many pages.

Should we define human services so broadly that the field includes every problem that people have? To do so does not appear either useful or functional. We live in a world of limited resources, and it seems important to focus on a more limited set of issues in order to maximize our impact. One possible way of defining the focus of the new field of human services is in terms of problem severity. The more severe the problem and the greater the risk to the individual, the more likely that the problem falls into the human services sector.

Human services should deal with problems of psychological or social *survival* rather than problems of satisfaction. The client is generally not the middle-class educated person who is experiencing problems of dissatisfaction and unhappiness. Rather, clients have such massive problems of survival that if they reach the level of adjustment of having only problems of dissatisfaction or loneliness, we feel we have helped them join the mainstream.

Problems of survival are problems that threaten clients' psychological, social, or economic existence and, in some cases, may threaten the continued existence of their lives or the lives of others. The target groups of human services include those people who:

1. Can't maintain contact with reality. They hallucinate (see and hear things that aren't really there), have unrealistic suspicions and fears about others, or withdraw from human contact.
2. Violate important cultural norms. They may, for example, abandon spouses, abuse their children, abuse drugs, or go into the streets naked.
3. Violate major laws or repeatedly violate minor laws. They may steal, embezzle, shoplift, drive while intoxicated, make obscene or threatening phone calls, or stalk acquaintances or public figures.
4. Are self-destructive. They are suicidal, mutilate their bodies, stop eating or eat and then make themselves vomit, or engage in high-risk sexual behaviors.
5. Are destructive of others. They may kill, assault, or rape.
6. Can't maintain their own welfare. They don't protect their physical health, are infirm, live in the streets, are social isolates, or are senile or demented.
7. Experience chronic poverty. They may live on public aid, be unemployable or uneducated, or seem unmotivated.

Although some target groups may be defined by behaviors that are not acceptable in the broader society, some may be defined as needing intervention simply by facts of their existence over which they have little control. For example, they may be young children or elderly, they may be members of a persecuted racial or religious minority, they may be poor, they may be homeless, they may be laid off from work, or they may be disabled. These groups may receive a special societal response because we think they are more at risk than other groups. When individuals in these target groups also manifest problem behaviors, society may have a traditional response: commitment to a mental hospital, enrollment on public welfare, placement in a foster home or nursing home, prison, job training, or remedial education. In effect, society defines such cases as problems to which societal responses are imperative.

In other times or in other places, people with problems of psychological or social survival have not been seen as requiring help. A homeless child in the streets of Bombay, India, or Rio de Janeiro, Brazil, is an all too common occurrence, and there are few formal helping services for such children. In the United States, however, a major effort is made to provide social services for such children.

We have deemed child homelessness as unacceptable in our culture (Bassuk and Rubin, 1987). Lest we feel too smug, however, we should be aware that the recognition or definition of a problem does not necessarily result in adequate handling of the problem in our society. Although we provide services for young homeless children in this country, adolescent children who are homeless (that is, the 1.2 million teenage runaways in the United States) have few helping services available to them (Hersch, 1988). Defining a condition or behavior as a problem is only one step in a lengthy process of conceptualization that may lead to a formal societal response. It is, of course, a very important step.

Identifying Problems

Perspectives for identifying whether a behavior is a problem requiring a helping response may differ, depending on the yardstick against which the behavior is measured. We may use a yardstick that is based on internal aspects of the person, which we can call an *intra* (within) personal perspective, or we may use standards outside the person to define a behavior as a problem. We call that an *extra* (outside) personal perspective. In each approach, there are several differing "sets" of standards to which we can compare a particular behavior.

Intrapersonal
1. Use of biological norms
2. Comparison with an optimal psychological state
3. Assessment of personal discomfort

Extrapersonal
1. Comparison with statistical norms
2. Comparison with cultural and societal standards of behavior

The Intrapersonal Perspective

Biological Norms
Among those who propose that deviant or problematic behavior is a disease, the concept of biological norms is extremely important. Basically, the approach assumes that deviance is a function of biological structural formations or their functions. Adherents to this approach would not necessarily say that a *particular* abnormal behavior is related to one specific function or structure (although that remains a possibility) but rather that the usual biological system defines a potential *range* of normal behaviors. Bateson (1987), for example, discusses how the emerging abilities of a child might result from an interplay between the child's genes and existing environmental conditions. Obviously, the biological perspective involves the consideration of genetic abnormality as a possible underlying

biological factor in the structure or function of a person's brain, with a corresponding impact on behavior (Andreasen, 1984).

Although much investigation has been done recently on the structure and function of the brain, it seems unlikely that in the near future a useful biological definition of normal or abnormal behavior will be developed. The biological approach has at least two major weaknesses: (1) it is too reductionistic; it reduces the mental and behavioral to physical issues without considering other factors such as environment; and (2) it does not adequately take into account the vast individual differences in the range of structure and function among normal persons (Offer and Sabshin, 1991).

The Optimal Psychological State

A common concept in the helping professions is that there is some ideal psychological state that is or should be normal (Sabshin, 1989). This psychological ideal includes concepts of adequacy, maturity, actualization, and productivity. An individual who does not match this ideal, by definition, has a problem. The various descriptions of the ideal psychological state vary from theorist to theorist, but most have a number of common elements. One of the most popular is that of Abraham Maslow.

Maslow proposes that the differences between normal and abnormal persons are differences in degree only and that normality relates to cultural adaptation. He lists ten criteria or signs of normal psychological functioning (Maslow and Mittelman, 1951):

1. Adequate feeling of security
2. Adequate spontaneity and emotionality
3. Efficient contact with reality
4. Adequate bodily desires and the ability to gratify them
5. Adequate self-knowledge
6. Integration and consistency of personality
7. Adequate life goals
8. Ability to learn from experience
9. Ability to satisfy the requirements of the group
10. Adequate emancipation from the group or culture

The major criticisms that can be leveled against such definitions of normality are that they are based on value judgments of the theorists and especially that they are unrealistic. How many of us meet all ten criteria of Maslow or those of the other theorists who have developed similarly comprehensive definitions of good psychological functioning?

Personal Discomfort

Many individuals define or identify *themselves* as problematic. Usually, this identification relates to a subjective sense of personal discomfort. Very often, such individuals perceive themselves as falling short of some idealized state similar to that described previously. Of course, if one does not achieve an idealized level of functioning but does not *care,* one is unlikely to be discomforted by that fact. However, when people feel they should be happier, less depressed, calmer, or more (or less) independent, their subjective distress may become great enough to result in a self-perception of being abnormal, or different from most other people. This subjective evaluation may lead them to present themselves to a human service worker for help, and the label of abnormality may become formalized.

This self-definition of abnormality rests on a belief that one's feelings, thoughts, or behaviors are not right and involves personal value judgments. The casual observer may not label these individuals as abnormal and would probably do so only after extended discussions with them. In more extreme examples, the personal discomfort may be manifested in outward behavior. The individual who subjectively experiences depression may, for example, begin having difficulty concentrating at work or doing the housekeeping or may burst into tears when talking to friends or acquaintances.

However, some individuals manifest troublesome behavior that disturbs *others* more than it disturbs them. The concept of personal discomfort does not fit such persons. For example, juvenile gang members are often quite satisfied with their behavior. The victims of their aggression or criminal behaviors are the ones who identify them as needing to be changed. Thus, the gang members' problem is defined from an extrapersonal perspective.

The Extrapersonal Perspective

Statistical Norms
In the statistical approach to the definition of problems, normality is what is average; deviance is behavior that falls outside of what is considered usual. To use this approach, one must make the assumption that the behavior being considered is distributed on the normal, or bell-shaped, curve (Figure 4.1). Most biological and many psychological or social traits appear to be distributed in such a manner in the general population (e.g., height, weight, intelligence, and economic level). To use the example of intelligence, *normal* is considered to be the central section of the IQ curve (an IQ of 85 to 115). At both ends of the curve are the abnormal or deviant scores, mental deficiency (IQ of 69 or less) and the very superior (IQ of 130 and above) (Wechsler, 1958). Several problems exist with the use of statistical norms in the definition of deviant, abnormal, or problematic behavior. Because the approach is based on the incidence of behavior within a population, any frequent behavior is considered normal. However, that would make poverty normal in many Third World countries, even though it is obviously a problem. A second difficulty is that cutoff points are drawn arbitrarily, and people falling on either side of the line are thought of differently. For example, a person with an IQ of 69 would qualify as mentally retarded with eligibility for funding for special programs, while a person with an IQ of 75 would not, even though there might be little real difference in their functioning. Finally, there is some question as to whether many behaviors actually are normally distributed in this statistical sense.

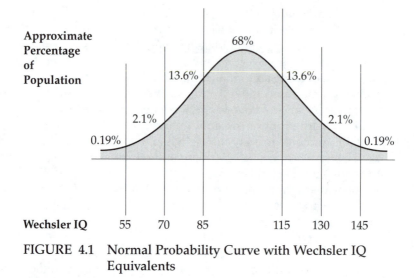

FIGURE 4.1   Normal Probability Curve with Wechsler IQ
Equivalents

Cultural/Societal Norms

Norms are standards of behavior that are maintained by individuals and groups. The norms held by individuals are usually determined by the referent groups to which they belong and by which they are accepted. Each individual belongs to many referent groups: family, friends, gangs, clubs, profession, race, sex, age, culture, country, and so forth. From the cultural/societal perspective, normality is behavior that fits in with these normative standards of the culture or society. *Deviance* is behavior that varies so much from the norms of a group that, if it became known by others, it could be used as a legitimate basis for negative sanctions in informal social interaction or by official agencies of the society (Wood, 1974).

> *A community youth program minister is discovered to be having sexual encounters with some of the preadolescent boys from his youth group. Upon this discovery, members of the community shun him (an informal sanction). The church suspends him (formal sanction), and he is arrested, charged, tried, and convicted of child molestation. After serving a brief sentence, he is placed on parole, but ordered by the court to have treatment for pedophilia (formal sanction, human service involvement).*

In this example, the norm was also codified as a law, and thus the formal sanction was punishment, which included court-ordered human services. The informal sanction was that community members shunned him. If the behavior had not been illegal—say, for example, it was a display of public drunkenness, he would have been breaking a residual rule, and if community members shunned him, that would have been an informal sanction. *Residual rule breaking* is a term that describes deviance that is not formally proscribed but that does violate social norms (Scheff, 1984). Examples include alcoholism, many of the behaviors exhibited by persons who have a mental illness, avoidance of employment by able-bodied people, extreme social isolation, and devil worship. Scheff (1984) suggests that there is a lot of residual rule breaking, that it has diverse causes, and that much residual rule breaking is of no social significance and is therefore ignored. Occasionally, however, others invoke socially shared ideas of, for example, mental disorder as the explanation for the residual rule breaking and so label the person who is deviating. The person may, because of being vulnerable or suggestible, accept the label, make it a part of his or her self-image, conform to it, and be rewarded for conformity. The person actually starts to conform to the socially shared idea of *mental illness behaviors* and thus is defined as mentally ill in his or her own view and the view of others.

In other cases, behavior that is *syntonic* (acceptable and valued) to a small culture (perhaps a delinquent gang) may violate the norms of the main culture. For example, the use and sale of illegal drugs such as cocaine constitutes a violation of our cultural norms. However, within the subculture of those who abuse or distribute illegal drugs, drug use and trafficking are accepted behavior. This type of subculturally promoted behavior to a great extent explains the performance of many criminal acts and the failure of correctional systems to be effective at changing convicted felons' behaviors.

The structure of society (its norms) determines its culture, and culture determines the thought processes of individuals (Eaton, 1986). Based on this approach, then, an individual who is deviant does not abide by the norms of society, and one who abides by the norms of society is not deviant but normal. Criticisms of this approach to the definition of deviance include the concern that a society's *norms* may in themselves be deviant or unacceptable. For example, the persecution and genocide of Jews in Nazi Germany became a norm of that society, yet most of us would not accept such behavior as normal. In that particular culture, the person who did *not* relate to Jews in a prejudicial manner was deviant and obviously (from that perspective) needed to be helped to overcome his or her problems. To those of us outside of that short-lived culture, the idea is repugnant. How could such behavior occur? The power of shared beliefs that are embedded in culture are immense. During the 1990s, the war in the Balkans between Christian Serbs and Muslims that included the wholesale genocide of Muslim civilians once again demonstrates that humans may engage in very deviant behaviors if those behaviors are supported by a referent group. Another culture whose norms seem unacceptable to most of us is that of some Middle Eastern Muslim extremists. In those groups of terrorists, suicidal attacks on others, in which the attacker has no chance to survive, are accepted, even encouraged, by the referent group. It becomes obvious that in defining deviant behavior, the definer's values must be taken into consideration, as must the values of the culture to which he or she belongs. To a very real extent, we are culture bound.

Theoretical Causes of Problem Behavior

Some would argue that one must know the cause of problem behavior to deal with it effectively. Others would say that cause is not important; rather, what one must understand is how to change behavior regardless of its causality. Although, in many cases, one can alter the behavior of individuals and groups without knowing cause-and-effect relationships, it seems important for human service workers to have some sense of possible causal systems if for no other reason than to provide a perspective from which to view one's world.

Four major current approaches exist in the conceptualization of causes of problem behavior or deviance. The first three approaches fall within the intra-personal perspective: (1) the organic, (2) the psychodynamic, and (3) the psycho-logical, including Rogerian theory and learning theory. The fourth approach, falling within the extrapersonal perspective, is the cultural/societal conception of causality. Each approach has adherents who rigidly reject the others, but most helping professionals would acknowledge that the evidence supporting any one approach over the others is not overwhelming. The specific causes of the various human services problems remain open to investigation. It remains to be seen whether any one approach will prove superior over the others in a functional sense or whether causality is some function of all four issues acting in an inter-relationship.

The Intrapersonal Perspective

Organic Causality

The organic approach proposes that a person's behavior, particularly deviant or abnormal behavior, is a function of physical causes, such as genetic makeup, brain chemistry, infection, toxins, or brain trauma (tumors, a blow to the head). The abnormal individual is as sick as a person who has cancer, pneumonia, or heart disease, and it is considered likely that a medical treatment can be found that will cure or arrest the disease process. A great deal of research is under way in this model, and impressive evidence indicates a biological component in at least the more severe disorders (Eysenck and Eysenck, 1985; Gottesman, 1990).

How can a physiological disorder influence behavior and create a human ser-vices problem? It is estimated that by the year 2000 about 4 million Americans over the age of sixty-five will have a disorder called senile dementia, Alzheimer's type, or *Alzheimer's disease* (Shodell, 1984). In this disorder, for an unknown rea-son, there are degenerative changes in brain fibers. When a victim of this disease is autopsied, there is a plainly visible shrinkage of parts of the brain. The person has clearly suffered from an organic disease process. However, during the victim's later years, the symptoms of the problem are mainly behavioral. A person with this disorder suffers from memory problems, emotional irritability, difficulty in concentration, neglect of personal hygiene, poor judgment, general intellectual decline, outbursts of anger and suspicion, and inability to complete routine house-hold tasks. More than 50 percent of nursing home residents have this disease or similar disorders in addition to any physical impairments they may have due to other ill health or aging (Niccum, 1999). The following illustrates the gradual onset and progressive decline that is the result of an organically caused disorder leading to a variety of human services needs.

Joan

■■ Joan lived a normal life as a wife, homemaker, and mother until her late fifties. Her husband and two daughters described her as a friendly, warm, and quiet woman. At the age of fifty-eight, she seemed to become depressed, apathetic, and forgetful. A particularly disturbing behavior consisted of wandering away from home and entering nearby houses unannounced and uninvited. Her husband and daughters took her to a local hospital for evaluation; she was diagnosed as having an anxious depression and released. Joan's confusion and disorientation became worse during the next few months. Her housework and personal hygiene suffered, and she had to be constantly supervised. A readmission to the medical hospital and extensive tests revealed mild diffuse atrophy of the brain, and she was finally diagnosed as having senile Alzheimer's disease.

Her continued deterioration required that Joan be placed in a state mental hospital. The next four years were marked by increasing immediate and long-term memory deficits, confusion, disorientation, and emotional outbursts. Her judgment suffered, she began to take others' possessions for her own, she constantly paced or slept in a ward chair, and her rambling speech became incomprehensible. She could (or would) no longer dress herself or bathe.

As two more years passed, Joan became incontinent and no longer fed herself. When fed by others, she would spit out the food. Lack of nourishment led to a physical decline, and she was fed through a tube. Joan's motor coordination became poor, her movements were slow, and her vocalization consisted of unintelligible crying noises.

Joan was finally placed in a custodial nursing home. She cannot stand unsupported, is totally nonverbal, and has a vacant, wide-eyed expression. She continues to be tube-fed, and her basic needs are cared for. Joan is now sixty-nine years old; she has declined for ten years.

The emotional and behavioral problems of senile dementia, Alzheimer's type, appear to be directly due to an organic cause, yet there is no effective organic treatment. Most people with this disorder spend their declining years in nursing homes and require primarily a human services approach to treatment until care must be mainly physical.

Organic explanations may also be advanced for more common behaviors. For example, some individuals do well in school; others do not. Some experts believe the critical factor in school performance is intelligence and that intellectual potential is the most important factor in one's intellectual ability (Herrnstein and Murray, 1994). Others strongly dispute the position that intelligence or intellectual potential—and thus school performance—is the result primarily of genetic influence (Bouchard and Dorfman, 1995). They take a strong position that environmental factors are most important. It is an ongoing controversy that will not be soon resolved. Another common problem for which an organic explanation is proposed is severe depression. Some researchers have identified a possible genetic fault that may contribute to the severe depression seen in some of the 13 million depressed Americans (Nadi, Nurnberger, and Gershon, 1984; Klein and Wender, 1993). These preliminary findings have raised the hope that potential severe depression sufferers could be identified and treated before the depression begins.

There is no question that a number of severe behavior disorders have organic causes; however, in terms of incidence in our society, they are relatively rare. We do see individuals who are dangerously violent because of brain tumors, old people with strange behavior because of cerebral arteriosclerosis, and the like. In addition, we know that certain drugs modify the behavior by affecting brain chemistry. We cannot deny the importance of organic factors; however, at the same time, the evidence indicates that organic factors alone are not sufficient to explain all problem behavior.

Psychodynamic Causality

The Freudian psychodynamic approach is a major alternative to the organic concept of causality. It is similar to the organic approach in that persons who have problems in living or who behave deviantly are seen as sick. They behave as they do because of unconscious motivation and are prisoners of early formative experiences. Sigmund Freud considered human beings to be motivated unconsciously by the desire for pleasure and the avoidance of pain. Unconscious demands and reality are usually in conflict, and, to cope, a person's thinking operates on primary and secondary levels. Primary process thinking is primitive, operating on the pleasure principle, and it embodies the base instincts and needs of the id. Secondary process thinking consists of the reality forces that inhibit and constrain the base drives.

Freud proposed three components of personality: id, ego, and superego (Figure 4.2). The *id* is the pleasure-oriented source of psychic energy, totally unconscious. It consists of the instincts, drives, and libido or sexual energy of the personality. The *ego* serves as the mediator between inner drives and outer reality. Its functions include perception, memory, judgment, conscious thought, and action. A strong ego deals with the dangerous id impulses and threats from the external environment. A major function of the ego is *reality testing,* or separating fact from fantasy. If this function is impaired, primary process thinking can break through unmediated by the ego, and the individual may behave in a *psychotic* manner. The *superego* is a function of the personality that introjects or internalizes the parental and societal moral teachings. If effectively internalized, it becomes the personality's "police officer" or conscience and is self-critical and prohibitive, controlling sexual and aggressive impulses.

A major emphasis of psychodynamics is on the development of personality through psychosexual stages. At birth, the child has libido or sexual energy, the discharge of which is pleasurable and the blocking of which causes tension. The discharge of this energy focuses on different erogenous zones—oral, anal, phallic, and genital—during various developmental periods. The *oral stage* consists of the first several years of life when the mouth is the primary area of gratification. The *anal stage* occurs around the third and fourth years of life, when the retention

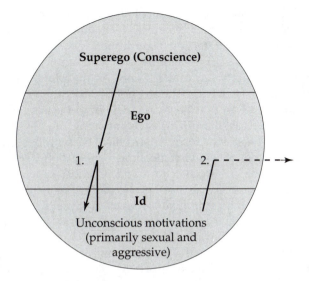

1. Some unconscious impulses are totally unacceptable. The superego blocks their expression and pushes them back into the unconscious.

2. Unconscious impulses that are not totally unacceptable can be expressed after they are modified by the ego. The ego thus acts as a mediator between instinctual drives and the environment.

FIGURE 4.2　Functions of the Id, Ego, and Superego

or expulsion of feces is the focus of concern, attention, and pleasure. During the *phallic stage,* the genital area becomes sensitized, and the child and parents must deal with the Oedipus (or Electra) complex, when the child becomes emotionally attached to the parent of the opposite sex and hostile toward the parent of the same sex. Depending on how this attachment and hostility are resolved, the child's adult sexual relationship will be normal or abnormal. The phallic stage is followed by a period of latency, a nonsexual stage of development that is a result of repression. The *genital stage* occurs during adolescence, when a person's libido becomes channeled into love of others rather than love of self.

According to Freud, everyone goes through the stages of development and has to resolve conflicts at each level. Individuals who have problems in living have failed to complete the task successfully because of either excessive frustration or overgratification at particular stages. If the conflicts are not resolved, fixation may occur, and the adult, under stress, will regress to the unresolved conflict, displaying symptoms of that stage of behavior.

This perspective on human behavior may be clearer if we consider an example. Human service workers often must deal with individuals who have become dependent on a chemical substance, such as alcohol. The psychoanalytic conception of alcoholism asserts that alcoholics are fixated at the oral stage of development. During those first few years of life, the individual who later becomes an alcoholic was either frustrated or overgratified by the parents. Because the mouth is the primary area of gratification during the oral stage, this frustration or overgratification results in an oral fixation. As an adult, the individual finds a sense of relief in oral behavior. The alcoholic is thus an individual who in the face of stress regresses to an oral behavior (drinking) because it reduces anxiety, just as the bottle or breast did during early infancy.

Psychoanalytic formulations have been proposed as the causal factor of virtually all types of behavior: alcoholism, sexual offenses, crime in general, depression and suicide, irrational actions and psychosis, and a host of other behaviors ranging from the everyday normal slip of the tongue to the extremely disturbed. However, there is no empirical evidence that supports any of the specific concepts of psychoanalytic theory such as the specific stages of development, fixation due to sexual frustrations, and the three structural components of personality (id, ego, and superego) and the mechanisms of their functioning that Sigmund Freud theorized about (Kihlstrom, 1999). There is, on the other hand, some empirical support for the existence of the unconscious "mind," and for the action of some kind of unconscious processes on our behavior (see Bornstein and Masling, 1998). Given this lack of evidence in support of psychoanalytic theory, why include it in a human services textbook? The reason is, of course, that many human service professionals, especially those trained a quarter century or more ago, still believe that the theory has merit. New human service workers need to have a basic understanding of this approach in order to work with those who still adopt it as their framework.

Psychological Causality

Although the psychodynamic concepts are a subgroup of psychological theory, they have been treated separately because of their strong association with the organic model. The two major approaches of psychological causality that are dealt with here are the self theory of Carl Rogers and learning theory.

Client-Centered Self-Concept Theory.   Rogerian theory views humans from a basically positive perspective. It proposes that the newborn infant or young child has organismic wisdom. Young infants know what is good for them; their behaviors, feelings, and thoughts are working together or congruent. As the child develops, society, in the person of the parents or caretakers, begins to put conditions on the child's worth. The child strives for self-actualization, but the conditions of worth ("If you get angry, you're not lovable," for example) may generate a defeating self-concept.

In essence, Rogers proposes that behavior is a function of how one sees one's self. The self-concept develops out of interaction with the environment in the process of self-actualization, the basic motive of existence. In this process, the self may introject the values of others or perceive those values in a distorted fashion. Because the self strives for consistency, experiences that are not consistent with the self-structure are perceived as threats. When the mind blocks awareness of significant sensory and visceral experiences, they are not symbolized and integrated into the self; hence, psychological tension occurs and may lead to maladjustment. The more such experiences occur, the more rigidly the self-structure is organized as a defense against the threat and the greater the loss of contact with reality. The person becomes more and more maladjusted in a vicious spiral.

As people grow into adulthood, they have many experiences that are incorporated into their self-concepts. If, for example, individuals have a number of failure experiences while growing up, they may develop a self-perception of inadequacy. We all fail sometimes, of course, but when these failures become very important because of the values of others (such as parents), they can color our overall valuation of ourselves. If parents focus on their children's failures, those children as adults may have such a strong self-image of failure that they will not even see their own successes. A self-image of inadequacy may lead to behavior that is inadequate or to the avoidance of even attempts to try things at which the person might fail. The individual does not try very hard to succeed because he or she knows that failure will result. The less the individual tries to succeed, the more failures occur, and the self-image of inadequacy is confirmed. The individual becomes inadequate as time passes because of the self-image.

Many of the critics of psychodynamics have included self theories in their criticisms (Eysenck, 1966; Rimland, 1969; Wood, 1974). The major criticism of the self theory of causality (and also of psychodynamic causality) is that there is little hard evidence that such theories have a functional relationship with behavior.

Learning Theory.   The second major psychological type of approach to behavior is that of the learning theorists. In essence, this view maintains that problem behavior is learned through the normal learning process and is simply an exaggeration of normal behavior. Behavior is seen as a response to external and internal stimulation. However, a number of theorists insist that more is involved with behavior than simple stimulus–response (S–R) relationships.

Eysenck makes a strong case for a biological predisposition toward the learning of a range of maladaptive responses. Both Eysenck and Yates (1970) emphasize that major disturbances (such as psychoses) have a perceptual–neurological component that interferes with data processing but that learning and motivation figure into treatment. It is commonly accepted that many of the so-called symptoms of major disturbances *are* the result of learning. The implication of this position is, of course, that although behavioral therapy cannot cure the psychotic condition or predisposition, it can modify many or most of the deviant behaviors manifested by persons with such predispositions. Not all behaviorists would agree with this position, however, and many would take the position that extremely deviant behaviors, such as the psychoses, are a function purely of stimulus–response reinforcement learning or operant conditioning.

Current-day theorists and practitioners have expanded the scope of behavioral explanations of problem behavior to include *cognitive* factors such as thoughts, talking to oneself, mental images, self-evaluation, feelings, memories, and beliefs. They have developed a cognitive learning approach. Cognitive learning theorists believe that simple stimulus–response learning is important but that to explain fully why certain behavior occurs requires taking into account a person's inner experiences or cognitions.

Variables seen as important include (1) encoding, or how people selectively attend to specific aspects of their environments; (2) expectancies, or what outcomes people expect, in terms of both what their behavior can achieve and what they expect to be the results of events in their environment; (3) the values that people attach to outcomes; and (4) the goals and standards that people set for themselves.

The increasing emphasis on the cognitive factors in learned behavior has resulted in a more comprehensive view of behavior on the part of many learning theorists. Bandura (1978, 1982), for example, sees behavior as due to a process of *reciprocal determinism.* Specific acts or ways of behaving that have been learned through reinforcement are influenced by the environment and cognitions, behaviors act on the environment and also influence cognition, and cognitions affect how people perceive the environment and how they behave (see Figure 4.3). Under certain circumstances, one factor may clearly dominate the others, but usually cognitions, strengths of learned behaviors, and environment are all factors that must be considered to understand why people behave in particular ways.

The major criticisms of the learning or behaviorist approach to understanding behavior follow:

1. Except for the cognitive approach, it is too simplistic, in that it usually ignores the problem of a person's experiences, of who and what the person is; that is, the behaviorist treats the mind as a mysterious black box.
2. It assumes that a particular behavior change is accomplished by applying a certain behavior principle because the original behavior was learned through a similar principle. It is unwarranted to assume that a behavioral principle is responsible for developing a particular abnormal behavior simply because the later application of the principle can change the behavior.
3. Some critics claim that only symptoms are dealt with, not the true underlying cause, and symptom substitution will result.

On the other side of the issue, however, is a massive amount of evidence that indicates that therapy based on this theory of causality is demonstrably effective in dealing with an extremely wide range of behaviors: enuresis, stuttering, phobias, obsessions, compulsions, delinquency, psychopathy, criminality, sexual disorders, alcoholism, drug addiction, retardation, mutism, delusions, hallucinations, regression, suicide threats, incontinence, violence, and disturbances of children. Also, this approach can be used in a wide variety of settings: schools, mental hospitals, mental health centers, general hospitals, and the home. In Chapter 7 we'll see some of the ways in which human service workers make use of the behavioral approach.

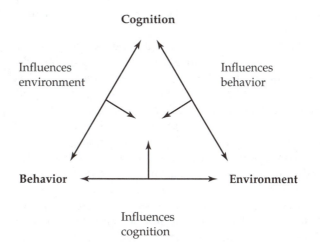

FIGURE 4.3   Reciprocal Determinism

The Extrapersonal Perspective

Cultural/Societal Causality

This approach suggests that maladaptive behaviors are an aspect of achieved or granted social or cultural roles. The approach is similar to learning theory but differs in that it emphasizes the consideration of role structure rather than principles of learning. Sarbin (1968) identified three critical dimensions of social identity (role functioning that answers the question, Who am I?): (1) the status dimension, (2) the value dimension, and (3) the involvement dimension.

Granted roles (age, sex, kinship, and so on) carry relatively neutral status; achieved roles can carry low or high status. The value continuum is different for the performance or nonperformance of roles at different points of the status dimension. Nonperformance of achieved roles (baseball player, musician) tends to be neutrally valued; proper performance of achieved roles is positively valued. For example, if one is unable to play a musical instrument (the achieved role of musician), little issue is generally made of it (unless, of course, one is trying to be a professional musician). However, if one can play a musical instrument well, status is gained. Nonperformance of ascribed or granted roles (e.g., husband, female, child) is given a strongly negative value; proper performance is neutral. Poor performance of roles that are ascribed or granted generally results in formal or informal social sanctions. An irresponsible or abusing husband, a homosexual, or a disobedient, disrespectful child is viewed as violating the norms of our culture and faces negative sanctions from others. Then again, acceptable behavior in these granted roles is simply expected, and when it occurs, no special consequences follow. The involvement dimension is determined in two ways: (1) the amount of time a person devotes to a particular role enactment and (2) the degree of organismic energy expended. Involvement in achieved roles is usually variable, depending on time and place; involvement in ascribed roles is usually high and consistent.

Most deviant roles (delinquent, crazy person, crook, retardate, street person, bum) are ascribed; that is, a person is assigned that role by society. Certain behaviors are seen by observers (members of society) as characteristics of the deviant role. When a person exhibits some of these role characteristics, the person often is perceived as belonging to the class of people given that role label. The unemployed man who is unkempt and is found sleeping in a building doorway or train station may be assigned to the class of vagrants or bums. Such a man may then confirm the role label by thinking of himself in those terms. When people act toward him as if he *is* a vagrant or bum, he begins to self-identify in that role and may become locked into behaving even more like his conception of how a vagrant is expected to act. Thus, he is subtly pushed toward taking on the ascribed role (Eaton, 1986). The social conditions that led to the development of the deviant role hinder the individual in using techniques that would help him break out of the deviant role behavior.

Cultural Variation in Role Performance

Social role performance and role expectations vary from culture to culture, and this may at times lead people from culture A to judge behaviors of a person from culture B as being problematic and in need of intervention.

■■ A human service worker in San Francisco was running a support group for military wives whose husbands were stationed out of the country. In this women's group, she found one member to be extremely passive, reticent about openly discussing any personal issues or offering any opinions, and never able to discuss her relationship with her husband. The group member would sit with downcast eyes, often sitting through several sessions without saying a word. The human service worker was considering a psychiatric referral in fear that the woman was depressed and pathologically passive and withdrawn.

During consultation with her supervisor, the human service worker was reminded that the woman was a Kurdish Muslim married to a U.S. Army corporal. The passivity and avoidance of self-disclosure and sharing about her relationship with her husband, who was stationed now in Germany, were culturally acceptable (valued) behavior in the Kurd culture. Simply coming and staying in the group would be quite an achievement for this woman for some time to come. The first-generation immigrant Vietnamese American human service worker, who had come to the United States at age eight, had found herself more acculturated to the European American culture than she expected!

Critical to this definition of causality is the concept that social conditions lead to maladaptive roles. Certainly, adverse social conditions can lead to problematic behavior or lifestyles. We can, for example, consider life in the urban inner-city. It is not surprising that lifelong ghetto dwellers do not conform to middle-class expectations of behavior. As children, their predominant role models are often adults who may be unemployed, who may use drugs, and who often receive some form of

Other cultures may have very different healing and helping rituals that are specific to cultural determinants of behavior.

social welfare. Minor and major illegal activities are common. Schools are agencies of social control rather than institutions of education. With so many problematic role models, what is really surprising is that so many people can surmount their role training and become part of the mainstream.

Another example of problematic roles is in the area of criminality. This approach suggests that the *role* of criminal is a product of society. Social conditions are the stimulus for a response labeled "criminal." Once the person is so labeled, the individual enters into a role structure supported (often inadvertently) by the behavior of others, such as police, corrections workers, parole officers, judges, lawyers, cellmates, and the general populace. Given this situation, deviant roles would be very difficult to change unless the individual relocated to a setting that did not support the deviancy and would lead to the development of techniques for dealing with the psychological strain resulting from a life of denigration.

Although a number of other concepts fit under the cultural/societal approach to deviance, the notion that problem behavior is a function of cultural or societal organization is common to all of them. What is different about this approach is that it minimizes examining the individual and emphasizes examining the societal or cultural environment. If the root problems of a culture or society can be eliminated, it proposes, there should be a decrease in the individual deviance seen in the members of the culture or society.

There are two major concerns about this approach: (1) it does not seem to be easily utilized for explaining extreme deviance of individuals, and (2) it seems to accept the norms of the parent culture as the appropriate standard for assessment of deviance, when some would argue that a wider frame of reference is necessary. Although significant problems exist for the use of this approach as a causal theory, an abundance of evidence indicates that cultural and societal factors are highly important in the development of problem behavior (Grier and Cobbs, 1968; Krassner, 1986; Scheff, 1984; Srole et al., 1978; Zimbardo, 1970).

An Ecological Synthesis: The Life Matrix

Human behavior, both functional and dysfunctional, is clearly the result of *something*; it has meaning, purpose, and goals. The preceding surveys of approaches to defining behavior and of concepts of causality demonstrate that no one concept is superior as the *prime* explanation of problem behavior. Human services is built on a pluralistic theory base (Fullerton, 1999), which allows more flexibility to deal with diverse personal and social issues. Yet, human service workers would benefit from a broad conceptual framework that can be used to organize their thinking about human behaviors. A major facet of such a broad conceptual framework is the concept of multifactored causality.

For the human service worker, it seems most functional to think of specific human behaviors as the functions of networks of issues. Behavior is the function of the life matrix in which people exist (Figure 4.4), a combination of physical, psychological, and environmental issues. The life matrix would include people's organic makeup, psychodynamic character, self-concept, learning, the cultural or societal complex in which they live, their physical environment, and any particular stress events they experience.

Any individual's behavior at a particular time may be a predominant function of one of the factors (for example, a high-stress event or a brain tumor). However, in most cases, behaviors are a function of the total matrix of internal and external forces operating on the individual. That matrix represents an ecological approach to synthesis of the many factors influencing human behavior. Two basic assumptions underlie the ecological approach: (1) that organisms are interdependent with the environment and (2) that interaction patterns are dynamic, adaptive, and reciprocal (Fullerton, 1999).

The ecological paradigm (model) stimulates us to look beyond simple explanations for behavior and to explore what interactions may be occurring between variables that result in specific behaviors or social conditions. We are challenged to identify the interactions among individuals, culture, and environment in order to enhance our understanding of human behavior and social processes (Edell, 1999) and to improve human service strategies for prevention and treatment (Heckman, 1999).

Whether specific human service problems are *primarily* a result of biological, psychological, or social factors may be important in terms of determining a rapid route for dealing with the problem. However, the ecological approach helps us

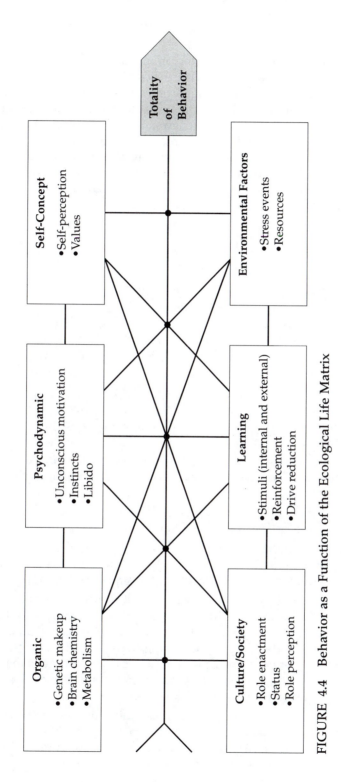

FIGURE 4.4 Behavior as a Function of the Ecological Life Matrix

understand how to go beyond this immediate response and more comprehensively deal with major human service social policy issues.

In the chapters to come, I survey the techniques most commonly used with persons who have difficulty in society: the kinds of clients most likely to relate to a human services system. Even though some of the strategies based on the concepts of causality introduced in this chapter would be used only by a specialist (for example, a physician or psychologist), human service workers must be familiar with these techniques in order to know both their usefulness and their limitations. With this familiarity, they gain the expertise needed to make rational referrals and recommendations.

Summary

1. Human services is concerned with problems of psychological or social survival rather than problems of satisfaction.

2. Problem behavior or deviance can be defined from several different perspectives. Intrapersonal perspectives focus on inner or personal aspects of the individual, including (a) biological norms, (b) comparison to an optimal psychological state, and (c) assessment of personal discomfort.

3. From an extrapersonal perspective, the definition of problem behavior or deviance focuses on environmental or social factors. The definition is based on (a) comparison to a statistical norm or (b) comparison to cultural/societal standards of behavior.

4. Four major approaches exist in the conceptualization of causes of human behavior: (a) organic, (b) psychodynamic, (c) psychological, and (d) cultural/societal.

5. The organic approach focuses on physiological causes of human behavior. It has been criticized for being too limited.

6. The psychodramatic approach, as illustrated by Freudian theory, focuses on unconscious motivation and early childhood psychosexual development. Psychoanalytic theories are difficult to support scientifically.

7. Psychological theories of causality are illustrated by client-centered self theory and learning theory. This theory emphasizes the development of the self-concept and its importance in determining behavior. Like psychoanalytic theory, it is difficult to support using scientific methodology. Learning theory suggests that problem behaviors are learned according to the same principles that govern the learning of all other behaviors. This model has been criticized as too simplistic to explain complex behavior.

8. The extrapersonal perspective of causality focuses on the impact of culture and society. It is concerned with external factors in the development of human services problems. There are several concerns about this approach, including the following: (a) it does not seem very useful for explaining individual cases

of extreme problem behavior, and (b) some cultures or societies may have norms that promote problem behavior in a wide segment of the population.

9. Human behavior can best be viewed from an integrated perspective. Behavior results from a dynamic ecological interaction of organic or biologic factors, psychodynamic character, self-concept, learned behavior, and socioculturally influenced roles. An ecological synthesis of these factors results in a broader and deeper understanding of human service problems both of individuals and in society.

Discussion Questions

1. What problems should be the primary concern of human service workers?
2. How would you define normality?
3. Do human service workers need to understand the theory of ecological synthesis?

Learning Experiences

1. Using each of the most common approaches to defining abnormality (biological norms, optimum psychological state, personal discomfort, statistical norms, and cultural/societal norms), try to identify a personal behavior that you or an acquaintance exhibits that each of these approaches would define as abnormal (one behavior for each approach).
2. As in Learning Experience 1, use the approaches to identify behaviors described in your community newspaper.
3. Think about your own ecological life matrix and try to describe it in writing as fully as you can.

Recommended Readings

Fullerton, S. (1999). Theories as tools and resources for helping. In H. S. Harris and D. C. Maloney (Eds.), *Human services: Contemporary issues and trends* (2nd ed.). Boston: Allyn and Bacon.

Hess, R. E. (1987). *The ecology of prevention: Illustrating mental health consultation.* New York: Haworth Press.

Scheff, T. (1984). *Being mentally ill: A sociological theory* (2nd ed.). Chicago: Aldine.

5

Human Services Boundaries

Special Populations, Special Systems

- What special populations and service systems fall within the boundaries of human services?
- Why are children particularly at risk for the development of problems?
- Why are older people at risk for the development of problems?
- How serious a problem is drug abuse?
- What types of human services programs are available for people who are mentally retarded?
- What service systems are available for people with mental health problems?
- What are the goals of the correctional system in dealing with criminal offenders?
- How does poverty relate to human services problems?

Human service workers are involved in providing many forms of assistance to a broad range of people. Individuals receiving human services fall into many categories and have many different problems. Some groups of people have been identified as needing services because we believe that some special degree of vulnerability puts them at risk for developing problems. Examples of these types of groups include children, older adults, and poor people. Others receive services because our society has traditionally perceived them as requiring a formalized response and has created systems for the provision of those services. Examples here include people who abuse chemical substances, people who are mentally retarded, people who have severe mental disorders, and lawbreakers.

Through the first half of this century, many of the helping systems had primarily an exclusionary focus. Disadvantaged people or people with severe problems often were excluded from community life. The organized formal responses of society toward people with human services problems frequently consisted of institutionalization. Children without parents were placed in foundling homes or orphanages. Juveniles in trouble with the law were routinely placed in youth detention facilities. People who were mentally ill were kept in mental hospitals in remote rural areas, far from their relatives' communities. Mentally retarded persons were put in residential schools far from their homes.

Institutionalization was the social response even to some medical illnesses. For example, before an effective treatment was developed for tuberculosis, people with this disease were sequestered in residential sanatoriums operated by state or county governments. The disease was considered too contagious to be treated in community hospitals; thus, willing or not, those afflicted were segregated from friends and family for long periods while the disease was active.

In the past thirty-five to forty years, there has been a distinct change in attitude about the value of excluding people from their communities because of behavioral, emotional, social, or economic problems. Workers in the helping professions have begun to realize that excluding a person from the community in order to provide services has many negative effects. In this context, *community* does not simply refer to a geographical place of residence but also refers to a social support network of loved ones, relatives, friends, coworkers, and employers who care about and can provide support for an individual. Recognition of the negative effects of exclusion from supportive social networks has led to the development of a strong emphasis on community-oriented helping programs. The boundaries of human services are inclusionary rather than exclusionary, integrative rather than segregative.

The boundaries of human services have been drawn very broadly and include a great variety of helping programs. The diversity of populations and programs that fall into the boundaries of human services allows the human service worker to focus on any one of a number of specialty areas for long-range career planning.

Some of the areas of special focus in human services revolve around special populations, and others center on the formal systems that have been developed to provide services to people with certain kinds of problems. This chapter introduces some of the special populations and special systems that fall into the boundaries of human services.

Problems and Services for Children and Adolescents

Human service workers see children and adolescents as particularly at risk for the development of problems. Children lack many of the coping skills that are developed by adults and thus are more sensitive to the negative effects of events such as family disruptions, physical illness, and the stresses of school and poverty. Children undergo a process of change and development from birth to adulthood, during which they learn many behaviors and skills, develop a self-concept, and create a style of life that may be adaptive or may result in problems in adulthood. The process of development is neither simple nor easy.

The difficulties of human development are illustrated by estimates of the number of children who have significant psychological problems. In the United States today, perhaps 6 to 7 million children between the ages of five and nineteen have emotional problems that interfere with their learning in school and require human services interventions. For some children and adolescents, these emotional problems are so distressing that they feel there is little point in continuing to live. About 6,000 children or adolescents (usually the latter) kill themselves each year in the United States, and every twelve months as many as 2 million unsuccessfully attempt suicide (Grimes, 1986). The suicide rate for children and adolescents, and adolescents in particular, rose sharply for the decades from the 1950s to the 1990s. Reported rates for adolescents and young adults nearly tripled during those decades, and for young people fifteen to twenty-four years old, suicide is the third leading cause of death (U.S. Public Health Service, 1999). The suicide rate in the 1990s was about 1.5 suicides per 100,000 children aged ten to fourteen, and eleven per 100,000 adolescents aged fifteen to nineteen, according to the Bureau of the Census (Styron, 1994). Most typically, the risk of suicide is increased for children or teens who are depressed and have a sense of personal inadequacy, are socially isolated, under stress, or use drugs (Henry, 1996).

Another growing and often unrecognized and unaddressed problem is teen-age runaways. There may be as many as 1.2 million adolescents who have run away from home and live a hand-to-mouth existence on the streets of major cities. Most are not boldly seeking adventure and challenge but are members of dysfunctional families who are fleeing from stressful environments (De Angelis, 1994). They are not modern-day hippies who choose to hit the road for the glamour of it. There is little of that. Only about half of the runaways have any realistic prospect of ever returning home to live. Of the remainder, about 300,000 are hard-core homeless. Thirty-six percent of all runaways are fleeing physical and sexual abuse; 44 percent are running away from other severe long-term crises such as drug-abusing or alcoholic parents or stepfamily crises; and 20 percent are attempting to escape short-term crises such as divorce, sickness, death, or school problems. Approximately 70 percent of the runaways who come to emergency shelters have been severely physically abused or sexually molested. Many of the children are "throwaways," kicked out because family resources are inadequate, because a parent cannot accept a son or daughter who is gay, or perhaps just because a parent "can't handle" the adolescent (Hersch, 1988).

Homelessness of children is also a growing problem. Mothers with children are the fastest growing portion of homeless persons. When combined with youth who have run away or been thrown out of their homes, the total population of homeless children and adolescents in the United States is approximately 1.5 million. It is estimated that worldwide over 100 million children and adolescents are homeless (Kazdin, 1992). The consequences of homelessness are many. There are physical consequences such as chronic disease and poor nutrition and hygiene, higher rates of emotional and behavioral problems, academic and developmental impairment, increased incidence of drug and alcohol abuse, and an increased risk of HIV infection and subsequent AIDS because of increased sexual activity and intravenous drug use.

Equally important, though less dramatic, are the millions of children who spend their childhoods in the squalor of disadvantaged urban or rural environments. Almost one in three of these children will have significant emotional or behavioral problems. They lack proper food, clothing, education, and physical health care. Without human services assistance, a disproportionate number of these children will do poorly in school, be unemployed (and perhaps unemployable) as adults, end up in prison, abuse drugs or alcohol, and experience other life problems at a higher frequency than children who have had the good fortune to be raised in more positive settings.

The increased risk of disturbed functioning faced by children and adolescents from all levels of society has led to the development of many human services programs that focus on enhancing young people's developmental environments. Human service workers in such programs may do many different things, depending on the particular focus of the program, as illustrated in the following examples.

1. *Well-child clinics.* Physical well-being is a critical factor in childhood. In well-child clinics, the focus is on preventive health care for infants and children and on training mothers to provide adequate physical and emotional care for their children. In many well-child clinics, as in other human services settings, human service workers (child care workers) are an important element in the teaching of child management and functioning as family change agents (Dangel and Polster, 1988; Garland, 1987). As Wise (1968) describes the role:

> *The Human Service health worker . . . has incorporated into her role some of the functions of the public health nurse, the lawyer, the social worker, the physician, and the health educator. . . . The worker's base is the health center, but much of her time is involved in making home visits in the community. . . . She is assigned from 40 to 60 families. . . . Daily activities . . . include a variety of health education, patient care, and social advocacy activities. She instructs the new mother how to bathe and feed the baby, and is alert to household hazards such as fire traps and broken paint on walls. In her training, strong emphasis is placed on patient education, case finding, the preventive aspects of medical care, and the emotional factors influencing illness.*

2. *Education.* Socially, emotionally, and physically deprived children often have serious difficulties in educational settings. Large numbers of human service workers provide a variety of remedial experiences to preschool and primary school children who need special help. Major federally funded programs for early intervention such as Head Start and day care programs have provided such services to millions of disadvantaged children (Zigler, 1985). During any year, Head Start provides medical, dental, nutritional, social, educational, and mental health

BOX 5.1   Cultural Diversity in the Workplace

At Hull House Uptown in Chicago, the Head Start program serves 102 families that speak ten different languages. The culturally diverse staff subscribes to a multicultural philosophy that values understanding, respect, and responsiveness to all cultures but especially toward the cultures of the enrolled children and their families. It is not an easy road to walk down, however.

Some families viewed the Mexican celebration of the Day of the Dead as "devil worship."

Some Christian families rejected the opportunity to attend the African American Kwanzaa celebration because it is not Christian. Some Africans rejected it because it is not African.

There are successes, however. There was broad participation in the Mexican American reenactment of the Christmas story called Posada.

The program director, a European-American Jew, and her staff struggle with cultural issues every day. It takes a great deal of courage, risk taking, and communication to foster cultural sensitivity.

services to 750,000 low-income children aged five and younger and to their families (Murray, 1995) (see Box 5.1). Early childhood education has expanded substantially in the past few decades. In the 1970s, only about 15 percent of three- to four-year-old children attended some type of preschool setting. In 1996, more than half (53 percent) of this age group attended formal preschool programs like Headstart, day care centers, or prekindergarten programs (Forum on Child and Family Statistics, 1997).

Human service workers in educational settings are often called teacher or classroom aides. Working alongside the classroom teacher, they provide individualized instruction and activities for needy students. They often work with the students with the most difficult problems. Human service workers in the school system also engage in counseling programs for students in some settings, do outreach work with truant children, run adult education programs, and do many nonteaching tasks that would otherwise be done by regular teachers. Formal jobs for human service workers have increased dramatically in school systems. In 1968, there were about 35,000 paid human service workers employed by school districts and more than 45,000 in Head Start programs (Gartner, 1971). By the end of the 1970s, those figures increased tenfold; they remained at that level in the early 1980s (Zigler, 1985).

Although there were some reductions in education employment in the mid-to-late 1980s due to federal and state funding cutbacks, the future of human services employment in education looks positive as we enter a new century. There is undoubtedly going to be continued diversification in staffing patterns in school systems, with human service workers able to take a lead in providing services aimed at maximizing inclusion of all children in the public school system (Parlin and Grew, 1999).

3. *Protective services.* State governments fund programs that specialize in detection of problems and provision of services for children in families in which the emotional and physical well-being of the child is at risk. In Illinois, for example, this social service system is called the Department of Children and Family Services (DCFS). A major problem that these agencies confront is child abuse, ranging from home environments in which the basic physical needs of children are neglected (lack of nutritious food, heat, and clothing) to those in which children are psychologically abused, those in which children are sexually abused, and those in which children are repeatedly severely physically injured by parents or other caretakers (Walker, Bonner, and Kaufman, 1987).

The incidence of child abuse and neglect is staggering, and the reported cases have increased astoundingly in recent years. It is not clear if the increase is due to a rise in actual abuse and neglect over the years or to improved case findings and reporting by state agencies. However, the number of reported cases has risen by one estimate from 670,000 in 1976 to about three million in 1995, of which almost one million are confirmed cases of abuse. Of these near–one million cases, 54 percent are due to neglect, 25 percent are due to physical abuse, and 11 percent are due to sexual abuse (Emery and Laumann-Billings, 1998).

Each year about 500,000 children are removed from their families and placed in other care settings to protect them from abuse. For the other children, the problem is dealt with through family prevention programs (parental training) and caseworker home visitation. Although the majority of the reported cases involve neglect rather than physical abuse, in 1993 at least 1,300 children died from abuse by their parents and tens of thousands were seriously injured. The unreported incidence of abuse is even more astounding. Several well-regarded surveys have estimated that 14 percent of youth were subjected to physical abuse and another 15 percent were subjected to sexual abuse before the age of eighteen (Kazdin, 1992). That would mean that about 9 million youths in the United States are subject to these problems.

Protective service agencies have a dual role: preventing child abuse and providing services to maintain families. Family preservation has been the foundation of the child welfare system since a 1909 White House conference on the care of dependent children. This dual role can cause conflict for protective service caseworkers who must sometimes be both helper and police officer. They provide assistance and counseling to parents who are having difficulties but, when a child is endangered, the caseworker's first responsibility is to protect the child (Edell Lopez, 1999). In extreme cases, they may remove endangered or neglected children from the custody of parents. In such situations, the children are placed in foster homes, families who either volunteer or are paid to take in neglected children and provide them with a physically safe and emotionally secure environment, with the support of case management services from a human services agency (Zlotnick, Kronstadt, and Klee, 1999). Such placements are usually temporary while the child's legal parents receive counseling or other services that will help them be fit parents. Group homes are another kind of temporary placement. A group home is generally operated as a formal agency with a human service staff

---

BOX 5.2   Types of Out-of-Home Placement

Orphanage: Private and public institutions for children whose parents died or abandoned them. The word has fallen into disuse for children's homes, which are now known as *group homes* or *residential treatment centers.*

Kinship care: The placement of children with relatives other than their parents.

Foster care: The placement of children with individual families to whom they are not related. The foster care families get special training.

Group homes: Individual, private homes in neighborhoods where usually five to eight children live in a family-like atmosphere with houseparents hired by a public or private agency.

Residential treatment centers: Larger facilities that care for dozens of children, often in cottages or hospital-like facilities.

---

that cares for children in a group setting. The staff of a group home requires special training and preparation for dealing with needy children in such a setting (Maier, 1987). Foster home parents are sometimes formal human service workers; when they are not, they receive at least some formal training.

In the mid-1990s, the issue of out-of-home placement received brief but intense attention when the speaker of the U.S. House of Representatives proposed that we should return to the use of orphanages for the children of single mothers on welfare. Orphanages have fallen out of favor due to some evidence from a number of studies that long-term institutional care had negative emotional, cognitive, and behavioral consequences for children (Andreasen, 1998). However, well-staffed, well-run orphanages might do as well as current approaches. At any rate, after the brief controversy, the idea of a systematic return to orphanages for that purpose quietly faded. However, the need for out-of-home placement remains for almost 500,000 U.S. children and adolescents (Shealy, 1995). It is a need that is real and likely to remain so, but removal of children can often be prevented, may or may not represent an improvement on the home of origin, and should occur only when there is justification and skillful intervention (see Box 5.2).

The type of intervention that may be required when a parent or caretaker lacks appropriate parenting skills is illustrated in the case of Amanda. In this example, a human service worker provides a variety of services aimed at improving the parenting and caretaking skills of a mother to deal with the early identification of child abuse.

Amanda

■■ Amanda, at the age of 28, had her second child just after the child's father had left the family. Two years later, Amanda was still struggling. With two children, no work, and public assistance, her life looked anything but beautiful. Amanda came to the attention of protective services (PS) when Johnny, age 8, her first child, was discovered to be covered with bruises on his buttocks and the backs of his legs. Johnny's condition was reported to Protective Services by his school, as mandated by state law.

A PS caseworker investigated and concluded that Johnny was in no immediate significant danger, but determined that Amanda did need parenting services to be able to manage her children without resorting to abusive physical punishment. She also was enrolled in a support group of other single mothers to help her deal with her personal frustrations. In the next two years, no more instances of abuse occurred, and Amanda was feeling much more positive about her situation.

This example of the human services problems of childhood and the types of services provided only scratches the surface of the many problems and services that exist for this particular population. Childhood is not the idyllic period we often think it is. Programs for children are thought to be very important because adequate services for a troubled child may allow that child to develop into a healthy, functional adult.

Domestic Abuse Services

It is estimated that one of every 185 women is a victim of domestic abuse every year, a total of 570,000 cases each year (Edmonds and Cauchon, 1994). They are mostly young and mostly, though not exclusively, poor. There are no publicly mandated and operated protection services for adult women like those for children. Women who experience spousal abuse rely mostly on the police and courts for protection, just as does any other citizen.

Three decades ago, police either didn't respond to spouse abuse calls or said there was nothing they could do. This lack of interest was partly an issue of women who withdrew their complaints or were not willing to make a complaint because of fear of what their partner would do to them afterward, and partly due to a male-dominated police force's attitudes toward women's complaints. Today, family violence calls account for about 25 percent of police patrol activity, but only about one-sixth of women who are abused report it to police.

In 1972, the first refuge for battered women opened in Britain, and soon shelters or refuges were opened in most European countries, the United States, Canada, and Australia (Munoz-Kantha, 1999). Shelter workers soon found that they had to plan for the needs of children also because most women fleeing their husbands brought children with them.

The reason for spousal abuse are not simple.

1. The abusing male is often using alcohol.
2. Sex-role stereotypes influence men to be controlling and women to be helpless.
3. Abusing men often saw their fathers abuse their mothers.
4. Physical violence sometimes counters men's low self-esteem. It helps them feel in control and powerful.
5. Abusers tend to be poor and thus perhaps frustrated and angry, more likely to lash out.

Why doesn't she just leave him? A common view held for many years was that, if a woman didn't leave her husband, then the abuse couldn't be all that bad. More recently, the battered woman syndrome, which often develops in cases of spousal abuse, has been well established (Walker, 1984). In the syndrome, a woman moves in a repetitive cycle through a series of stages. In the first stage, the man is angry, breaks *things,* and then deeply apologizes. She pacifies him in hopes of preventing another outburst. In the second stage, the man explodes over some event and attacks the woman with physical violence. The third stage consists of a "honeymoon." The man is apologetic, loving, gentle, and seeking forgiveness. He buys her flowers, promises it will never happen again, and becomes a caring, nurturing provider. The wife is drawn back into the relationship. Unfortunately, the cycle starts again, each time ending with false hopes. Breaking this cycle is very difficult for a woman to do if she is economically dependent or fearful for her life. Each year, several thousands of U.S. women lose their lives to battering husbands (Munoz-Kantha, 1999).

Human service workers can help break this cycle of violence through providing counseling, support groups, and outreach service. Battered women also often need legal services, shelter, and protection. Generally, a battered woman has a very hard time getting away from an abusing husband unless she can come to feel empowered to change and be independent.

Problems and Services for the Elderly

Older adults account for about 13 percent of the population of the United States, which means that more than 35 million people are at least sixty-five years old (Niccum, 1999). By the year 2030, about 20 percent of the U.S. population are likely to be in this age range.

Many factors come together to make the aged a group at risk for human services problems. Many older adults live a life of loss: loss of physical stamina, loss of health, loss of friends, loss of loved ones through death, and loss of income (one third of older Americans live at or below the poverty level) (Krause, 1987). Their roles in life change. They are no longer breadwinners, and their children are now independent adults. Rather than taking care of others, they often need to be taken care of. In our culture, old age carries a stigma of fading worth. The physical and psychological losses of old age take a heavy emotional toll. Many older Americans are lonely, depressed, and frightened. Some have serious problems of mental deterioration leading to confusion, memory loss, and odd behavior (Gallo and Lebowitz, 1999). Others, even those whose minds are clear, have multiple physical problems (see Table 5.1).

As our population ages, the proportion of older people increases, and advancing medical science assures that a higher proportion live to advanced age, increasing the risk for a disorder of the brain called *Alzheimer's disease* (Cummings and Jeote, 1999). Its victims suffer impairments of memory and other intellectual abilities that leave them confused, disoriented, and incapable of communicating normally. They show personality changes, various emotional reactions to their illness, and behavioral symptoms such as a tendency to wander. Over time, they experience increasing difficulty in carrying out even simple activities

TABLE 5.1   Health Status of the Elderly

Condition	Elderly Population with Condition (percent)
Visual impairment	9
Diabetes	11
Cataracts	17
Hearing impairment	32
Heart disease	32
Hypertension	36
Arthritis	48

Source: Data from U.S. Census Bureau, 1990.

of daily life, may lose bladder and bowel control, and ultimately become totally dependent on others to provide for their personal needs and safety. The peculiar tragedy of Alzheimer's disease and other related dementias is that they dissolve the mind and steal the humanity of the victim, leaving a body from which the person has largely been removed. Simultaneously, these disorders devastate the lives of spouses and other family members, who must endure this deterioration of their loved ones and the loss of the people and relationships that is implied and typically shoulder heavy burdens of care over a prolonged period.

The tragedy of Alzheimer's disease and related dementias is one of growing proportions, with potentially catastrophic public health consequences. Projections based on a recent study suggest that by the year 2040 the number of cases of Alzheimer's disease may exceed 6 million. The human and economic consequences are incalculable, particularly as we live longer. Indeed, the over-eighty-five population, the fastest growing age group, whose numbers will increase fivefold in the next fifty years, is particularly at risk for Alzheimer's. The prevalence of Alzheimer's-type disorders in that population approaches 25 percent (Advisory Panel on Alzheimer's Disease, 1991).

A particularly distressing issue that is becoming more common as the number of older people increases, is *elder abuse and neglect.* Conservative estimates are that 2.5 million incidents of elder abuse occur in U.S. domestic settings each year (Niccum, 1999). Only within the past decade have most states (forty-two) had mandatory elder abuse reporting laws. Most elder abuse is committed by spouses (60 percent) and adult children (20 percent), and the remainder by a mix of siblings, grandchildren, and boarders. The abuse is due to many factors, including the frustrations of caregivers, and some is purposeful (for example, taking control of an elder's estate or financial resources and using it for personal gain). Some signs of elder abuse are visible and easy to identify: cuts, bruises, broken bones, dehydration, and weight loss. Other indicators—home or bed confinement, fear, withdrawal, confusion, disorientation, and financial exploitation—are harder to detect.

Although physical abuse is most known and visible, the most common type of abuse is financial exploitation that occurs when family members take control of an elderly person's finances. Before others become aware of it, financial resources are drained, bills have mounted, and houses are repossessed. In extreme cases, there is no money left for food, clothing, or medication.

Grandmother

■■ When Alice left her home early last year and arrived at the Indiana home of her eighty-six-year-old grandmother, she was appalled to discover her lying in a bed soaked with urine.

That wasn't the worst of it. Grandmother, who has severe diabetes, chronic bronchitis, and emphysema, was unusually frail and thin and had numerous bruises on her arms and a bedsore on her bottom.

In a matter of hours, Alice's worst fears were confirmed. She learned her grandmother had been physically and emotionally abused by Alice's aunt and cousin. They had physically neglected her, hit her arms to "punish" her for complaining or wailing, and had squandered her savings on a new car for each of them. When questioned as to why they did it, Alice's aunt replied that her mother "never did me any favors" and seemed to feel that she and her son deserved the cars for "taking care of" her mother. Alice arranged for her grandmother to be placed in a local nursing home with a good reputation.

Growing recognition of and sensitivity to the plight of older adults has led to the development of community human services programs for this population. These programs, often called *senior citizen centers,* provide social, nutritional, and health programs for their participants. Human service workers in such programs often engage in outreach activities to encourage seniors to come to the center or may regularly call on homebound clients. Human service workers in these programs can be a first line of intervention in potential or actual elder abuse situations.

Many older Americans are physically or psychologically unable to continue to live independently. In the United States, these individuals often find themselves spending their remaining years in nursing homes. In 1995, there were 1.6 million residents in nursing homes who were age 65 or older. By the year 2020, it is estimated that this number will be 2.6 million. More elders are in nursing homes than probably really need to be there because of lack of community services that can keep the elderly in their own homes or in small group homes. During the next thirty years, more opportunities for human service work with the elderly in the community and in nursing homes are likely. Unfortunately, today, the quality of care in many of these homes is poor, although some are very good. However good the care may be, they are still institutions. A major problem in these settings is the lack of social involvement and the routine days that the elderly must confront (Gutheil, 1985). Some homes have begun to make major strides in creating a more psychosocially positive atmosphere.

Drug Abuse: The Problem and Human Services

Many chemical substances have significant effects on human behavior, thinking processes, and emotions. Some of these substances have long histories of social use and abuse. A few of the more important substances are listed in Table 5.2, along with their immediate effects and the symptoms of overdose. When an individual uses these types of drugs frequently, a physical or psychological dependence may develop. The individual becomes a drug abuser. The person must take the drug either to avoid painful or unpleasant physical withdrawal symptoms or to avoid unpleasant psychological experiences.

World War II was a major turning point in the incidence of drug use. Individuals born before and after World War II differ dramatically in the range and diversity of their drug use. For example, only two drugs, cigarettes and alcohol, were used by more than 6 percent of individuals born between 1919 and 1940, by the time they had reached thirty-five years of age (after that age, there was very little initiation of drug use). By comparison, ten drugs were used by more than 6 percent of the 1951–1955 birth cohort by the time they reached age

TABLE 5.2   Some Commonly Abused Substances and Their Effects

Drug	Effect	Overdose Effects
Alcohol	1. Initial sense of stimulation 2. Loss of judgment 3. Poor coordination 4. Loss of peripheral vision	1. Disorientation 2. Depressed breathing 3. Coma 4. Possible death
Heroin	1. Euphoria 2. Floating feeling 3. Drowsiness 4. Constricted pupils	1. Coma 2. Convulsions 3. Depressed breathing 4. Possible death
Tranquilizers	1. Sense of relaxation 2. Drowsiness 3. Slowed reflexes 4. Impaired sensation	1. Stupor 2. Coma 3. Death
Marijuana	1. Mild euphoria 2. Relaxed inhibitions 3. Large doses lead to hallucinations and impaired sensation	1. Disorientation 2. Agitation 3. Severe hallucinations 4. Paranoid suspicions
Cocaine	1. Intense euphoria 2. Increased energy 3. Heightened alertness 4. Labile emotions	1. Anxiety 2. Confusion 3. Cocaine psychosis 4. Violence

	*Number of Persons with Drug Problem or Illegally Using**
Alcohol	18 million problem drinkers
Heroin	300,000–600,000 addicts
Tranquilizers	300,000 addicts
Marijuana	22 million users
Cocaine	5.8 million users

Source: National Clearinghouse for Drug Abuse Information, 5600 Fishers Lane, Rockville, MD.

thirty-five. Between the early 1960s and mid-1970s, there were increases in the rates of initiation of all drugs except cigarettes. From the mid-1970s to the early 1990s, trends in rates of initiation were more complex, depending on the particular drug and the age group. For example, rates of first use of alcohol, inhalants, and analgesics increased, but the increases in alcohol and inhalant initiation were largely restricted to youth aged twelve to seventeen (SAMHSA, 1996).

The most abused drug is alcohol. About 18 million Americans are problem drinkers; that is, alcohol use causes them significant problems in living. Unfortunately, the large majority of problem drinkers do not recognize their problems with alcohol abuse and do not seek treatment. Since the late 1970s, though, the numbers of people in treatment and the number of treatment programs have increased substantially. The number of alcoholism and other drug treatment programs increased from 465 in 1978 to 829 in 1984, an increase of 78 percent. On any one day, about 210,000 people with alcoholism and 90,000 people who abuse other drugs are in treatment. A national survey in 1997 found that during a year's time about 3 million people receive treatment for alcohol abuse, and another 2 million receive treatment for the abuse of illegal drugs (Office of Applied Studies, 1999).

In recent decades, cocaine abuse has soared dramatically. It is estimated that 5 million U.S. citizens use cocaine regularly, and 1 million are significantly dependent on it. For many years, it was believed that cocaine use did not cause a physical dependence like alcohol and heroin, but experts today have determined that cocaine is, in fact, physically addictive (Franklin, 1990). In the mid-1980s, a new form of cocaine called *crack* became common on the streets. This crystallized form of the white cocaine powder sells relatively cheaply and introduced cocaine addiction to poorer people. Cocaine in its powdered form is quite expensive and had been a drug more common to the well-to-do. Crack cocaine rapidly produces an intense high that is relatively short term, and this, combined with its low price, results in a drug that is ranked as more addictive than heroin. Heroin abuse is a serious problem for about 300,000 Americans (some estimates say 600,000). The incidence of abuse of marijuana is estimated at 1.5 million *new* users each year and a total of 22 million in a year (Office of Applied Studies, 1999).

Drug abuse, a serious problem in its own right, is associated with many other problems. For example, alcohol abuse by pregnant women may lead to fetal alcohol syndrome in their children, with possible physical birth defects and mental retardation. In recent years, the increase in crack cocaine addiction among pregnant women has resulted in the births of many thousands of infants who are addicted at birth and must experience drug withdrawal immediately after birth. These children have been noted to be in generally poor physical health and to have a variety of behavioral deficits (Chasnoff and Schnoll, 1987). Infants born to addicted mothers are a new population that will need more human services in the years to come.

The incidence of abuse of drugs is particularly high among the urban disadvantaged, although drug abuse has become much more common throughout all strata of society. With the exception of alcohol, the social use of most drugs is illegal, and thus drug abusers frequently have problems with criminal convic-

Use of illegal drugs, such as smoking crack cocaine, complicates all other human service problems as well as being a serious problem in its own right.

tions. Contrary to popular belief, however, drug users do not necessarily engage in acts of criminal violence because they are high on drugs. Addicts (especially heroin and crack-cocaine addicts) do have a higher rate of criminal behavior than nonaddicts, primarily because of their efforts to obtain money to buy the illegal drugs. It is difficult to support the many hundreds of dollars a day cost of an illegal drug addiction through legal means.

Chronic drug abuse has a variety of negative consequences, depending on the particular substance used. Most addicts experience serious deterioration in personal relationships, problems in maintaining job functioning, and related health problems. Some drugs (alcohol, for example) damage brain tissue and lead to significant mental deterioration, as illustrated in the following case.

■ ■ Mr. Wells is a fifty-five-year-old man who has been a chronic alcoholic for at least fourteen years. He has recently stopped drinking and experienced withdrawal symptoms. As he began to recover from the withdrawal symptoms, Mr. Wells displayed signs of significant brain damage from the long-term effects of alcohol abuse. His memory for recent events is extremely poor, and he fills the gaps with fabrications that he believes are the truth. He is disoriented in relation to time and does not know what year it is. When asked to subtract 7 from 100 successively (93, 86, 79, and so on) his responses were 93, 89, 72. . . . His intellectual impairment and faulty memory present a serious impediment to his return to employment.

The serious, sometimes life-threatening effects of drug abuse are considered a major social problem in the United States, and a large number of human service workers are employed in agencies that treat substance abusers. Workers in these types of programs perform many functions: counseling, group problem solving, family counseling, outreach, community education, employment linkage, referral to other services, and administration.

Three major types of services are available for substance abusers: methadone maintenance programs for heroin abusers and self-help programs and therapeutic community programs for abusers of all types.

Heroin abuse is often treated in methadone maintenance programs. Methadone is a drug that substitutes for heroin. It does not produce the psychological effects of heroin but prevents the physiological symptoms of withdrawal. The focus of these programs is on the maintenance of individuals on methadone so that they will not need to use heroin. Ideally, while in such a maintenance program, the individual is provided with other rehabilitation services. When such rehabilitation services are provided, methadone maintenance can be fairly effective in reducing heroin use and criminal behavior (Thombs, 1999).

Although self-help groups are available for addicts of all types (McAuliffe and Ch'ien, 1986), the best example of an addicts' self-help group is Alcoholics Anonymous (AA). Today, there are more than 87,000 AA groups with 1.7 million members in 150 countries (Maisto, 1995). Basically, AA is a self-help organization that focuses on helping members (1) admit they have a drinking problem, (2) make amends for the problems they have caused, and (3) commit themselves to a "higher power" (which some choose to call God). It has abstinence as a goal, and members try "one day at a time" to accept that they can never drink again. Members stand ready to provide support to those in crisis and to help each other avoid the bottle and learn to live by new rules. The approach is reported to be more successful than traditional professional approaches, and tens of thousands of people have been helped by this organization. However, the structure of AA, with its lack of membership lists and case history files, prevents accurate evaluation of its effectiveness. Its effectiveness must be taken on faith, an important ingredient in its overall approach.

Therapeutic communities are oriented around drug-free treatment of addicts in residential programs. The therapeutic community philosophy is that treatment should be aimed at modifying negative patterns of behavior, thinking, and feeling that lead people to use drugs, and that treatment should encourage responsible, drug-free lifestyles (DeLeon and Ziegenfuss, 1986). Participation, which is voluntary, includes confrontation of "addict behavior" in group settings. The confrontation is often brutal (perhaps necessarily so) and demands a change of lifestyle. This approach has been relatively successful with addicts who stay with the programs. However, dropout rates for these types of programs appear high (DeLeon and Schwartz, 1986). A major evaluation of therapeutic communities and methadone maintenance programs (Bale et al., 1980) found that participants who had been in therapeutic communities or who were continuing in methadone maintenance longer than seven weeks were more likely to be working or attending school and less likely to be in jail, using heroin, or convicted of a serious crime than those who had only been detoxified. However, Bale et al. found that therapeutic communities had a dropout rate of 61 percent and methadone programs had a dropout rate of 69 percent. Only 18 percent of the patients assigned to the therapeutic communities actually entered treatment, and only 30 percent of those assigned to the methadone program actually entered treatment. Of the total addict populations surveyed, only 10.3 percent entered and stayed in treatment for the recommended length of time. The data clearly suggest that, although these two treatments are somewhat successful, the large majority of addicts either will not or cannot take advantage of them. Until some way is found to maintain addicts in treatment, the dropout rates of over 90 percent in some programs will prevent real impact on the addiction problem through these types of approaches.

The challenge for human services is to find effective approaches for dealing with addictions of all types and to integrate approaches such as Alcoholics Anonymous and therapeutic communities into the wider human services network. Approximately 950,000 persons per day undergo substance abuse treatment. Eighty-seven percent of them were enrolled in outpatient rehabilitation, and 13 percent were in residential treatment (Novak, 1996). Human service workers respond to the need for substance abuse services in three ways: education, prevention, and treatment. The goal is to encourage, assist, and enhance the recovery process with the specific skills, knowledge, humanity, and genuine caring that is characteristic of human service workers, regardless whether they have a specialty certificate in alcoholism and substance abuse treatment (Duclos and Gfroerer, 1999).

Services for Mentally Retarded People

There may be as many as 3 million mentally retarded citizens in the United States (Braddock, 1997). Roughly 1 million children with mental retardation are served in public schools under the requirements of Public Law 94-142, the Education of the Handicapped Act of 1975 (Schroeder, Schroeder, and Landesman, 1987).

Although the majority of mentally retarded individuals live at home or fairly independently in community settings, some are so disabled, either by their level of intellectual retardation or by associated behavior problems and skills deficits, that they require twenty-four–hour residential care. Of this group, about 53,000 were residents of state institutions in 1998 (Braddock and Hemp, 1999).

Four levels of mental retardation are commonly described: mild, moderate, severe, and profound. The majority of mentally retarded individuals fall into the higher intellectual levels of moderate and mild. Those with moderate retardation may require some supervision and assistance but can usually live outside institutions. Depending on their functional difficulties, they may be able to live alone or may need a more structured group home setting. The mildly retarded often can live independently and work at unskilled jobs. Those who are severely or profoundly retarded usually require constant care and supervision, as illustrated in the following example.

■■ Alberta is severely retarded. The highest score she has ever attained is an IQ of 27 on the Stanford-Binet intelligence scale. Now forty-seven years old, she has been a resident of a state school for the retarded since the age of eleven. She was institutionalized when her mother became ill and could no longer care for her at home. Her mother died when Alberta was twelve, and she has not seen her father since he remarried when she was thirteen.

Alberta was born with a disorder called phenylketonuria. This defect of recessive genes results in mental retardation unless the child is provided with a special diet from birth onwards. The disorder was first identified in 1934, but by the time it was widely known, it was too late to treat Alberta. Intensive training since childhood has enabled Alberta to talk in simple sentences and to make her wants known. Continuing supervision ensures that Alberta washes and bathes regularly and, with some help, dresses herself. She enjoys watching television, particularly action-filled cartoons. Alberta has tried doing simple tasks in the school's workshop, but she cannot attend to a single task long enough to be productive. A major current problem for Alberta is that she is self-mutilative. She hits herself in the head rapidly with her closed fist and picks and scratches at her arms and legs. She may go months at a time with open sores from the picking and scratching.

The following features of Alberta's case are typical of a severely retarded individual:

1. There is clearly impaired development in infancy or early childhood.
2. Usually a genetic or other obvious organic cause, such as physical injury, infection, or metabolic disorder, is found.
3. Usually these individuals can profit only from lengthy training in self-care skills and habit training.
4. Parents have major difficulty managing the individual in the home and usually must place the child in an organized institutional setting where almost constant supervision is available.
5. Social adaption skills are minimal even in adulthood, and major behavior problems may occur.

The incidence of severe and profound retardation is equivalent across all socioeconomic levels. But, as in many human services problems, the problem of mental retardation at the mild and moderate levels occurs with greater frequency among the socioeconomically disadvantaged. The greater incidence of mild and moderate retardation in the lower socioeconomic levels supports the idea that although some retardation is due to organic causes, much of the mental retardation in our society is due to cultural–familial causes. That is, it is due to a combination of sociocultural deprivation and genetic predisposition.

The mentally retarded citizen faces more problems than learning and functioning at a lowered intellectual level. At the levels of severe and profound retardation, there are often physical disabilities and deformities associated with the retardation. At all levels of retardation, these individuals must face a lifelong public stigma that influences how they are viewed by both professionals and

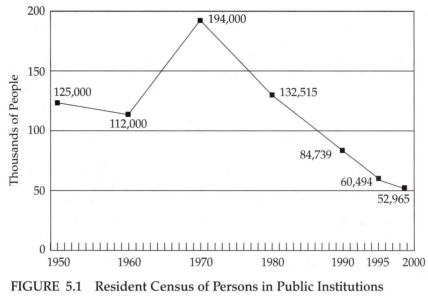

FIGURE 5.1   Resident Census of Persons in Public Institutions
for the Mentally Retarded

laypeople (Castles, 1996). They encounter problems in school, family, and employment. They have difficulty avoiding dependence and have impaired coping skills. People who are mentally retarded often experience crises when facing developmental milestones that normal people handle with much less difficulty, such as starting school or the birth of a sibling. The mentally retarded person experiences anxiety, depression, and a sense of loss, brought on by incomplete mastery of these milestones and the unmet need to develop greater independence and autonomy (Gilson and Levitas, 1987).

Program delivery systems for mentally retarded people have changed dramatically in the past few decades, illustrating the movement toward community-based programs in human services and away from institutions. The number of residents in state-operated "schools" for the retarded has decreased from 139,000 in 1980 to 52,965 in 1998 (Braddock, 1997; Braddock and Hemp, 1999). As recently as 1967, there were almost 200,000 persons residing in 165 such large institutions (see Figure 5.1). The decline in census has allowed the closure of 130 of 348 state residential institutions for the mentally retarded across the country. Some states, through the aggressive funding and use of a range of community programs, have completely done away with state-operated residential institutions for the population (Rhode Island, the District of Columbia, Vermont, New Mexico, New Hampshire, and West Virginia).

Where have they gone? The people who in the past were served for long periods in these residential settings, often far from home, now live and receive services in the community. They live in group homes of sixteen or fewer (usually much smaller) (NARF, 1983), in supervised apartments, and in supported living arrangements. To illustrate the magnitude of this change, the total number of individuals served in U.S. community residential settings grew from under 5,000 in 1960 to over 181,000 in 1994 (Prouty and Lakin, 1995). The number of U.S. out-of-home long-term care community settings (excluding foster homes) grew from 336 in 1960 to 48,245 settings in 1994, and there were an additional 16,464 foster home settings in 1994 (Braddock, 1997). Yet, waiting lists of mentally retarded persons for community settings remain around 60,000, and about 34,000 such individuals were still inappropriately residing in nursing homes in 1996 (Braddock, 1997; Braddock et al., 1995).

Life in group homes for the mentally retarded is believed to be a positive experience because it provides a more normal environment than an institutional setting (Blake, 1985–86). Unfortunately, there continues to be some prejudice against group homes from communities that find out that such a home is to be opened. Because more group homes are needed, one of the areas of focus for human service workers in the field of mental retardation will be to develop strategies for obtaining community support for opening additional group homes (Hogan, 1986).

The development of community group homes has been paralleled by the development of other types of community services. One provides employment training and productive paid work for mentally retarded adults. Many retarded adults have the potential to be self-supporting or to contribute to their support, but for many years this potential was unrealized. However, there has been dramatic growth in sheltered workshops in which people who are retarded can be trained to engage in productive work for pay. Between 1972 and 1979, the number of these workshops expanded 600 percent. They now provide training and employment for 100,000. A step beyond the sheltered workshop is "supported employment." In this program, individuals who are mentally retarded are assisted in working in competitive employment settings alongside nonclient employees. Clients receive special training, job coaching, and counseling but are expected to perform competitively. From 1988 to 1996, those in the United States receiving this service increased from about 14,000 to almost 90,000 (Braddock et al., 1995; Mental Health News Alert, 1998). Programs like this allow people to obtain meaningful employment, experience real community inclusion, socialization, and the self-esteem that comes with real work (Braddock, 1997). However, supported employment programs have not yet been effectively provided for persons with severe mental retardation, and additional effort is needed in this area.

In addition to new structured community living settings and employment, virtually every state offers "family support" programs. These programs typically consist of fiscal support for families and the person with retardation to help keep the person living in the family setting. The financial support is usually available even to middle-class families. Besides the fiscal subsidy, there are usually counseling and other in-home support programs available. Both family members and persons who are intellectually retarded may need counseling and psychotherapy in order to deal with the perceived losses. It has become clearer that people with mental retardation are at greater risk for a variety of emotional disorders. Those who do develop a "dual disorder" (such as mental retardation and depression) present special challenges to human service workers (Reiss, 1994; Gaus, Steil, and Carberry, 1999).

Mental Health Problems and Service Systems

Many of the problems that human service workers deal with have traditionally been seen as mental health problems. Some observers have described the mental health service system as the octopus of human services, with tentacles everywhere.

When behavioral problems are defined as having organic or intrapsychic causes, the mental health system is usually the provider of services. These services may be provided by traditional professionals such as psychiatrists, psychologists, or social workers in private practice or in publicly funded systems. The public systems include county, state, and federal mental hospitals and comprehensive community mental health centers. Mental hospitals provide services to individuals with behavioral disorders. They have a special responsibility to provide care and security for people who are dangerous to themselves or others as a result of psychological dysfunction. Comprehensive community mental health centers often provide short-term inpatient care, but most of their services are on an outpatient basis. These centers offer many services that are helpful to people who have not been traditionally seen as having mental disorders. They offer crisis counseling, marital therapy, family therapy and consultation, and education services.

As in other human services subsystems, emphasis on community-based services has grown in the mental health sector. The population in mental institutions dropped from almost 600,000 in 1955 to under 70,000 in 1999 (NASMHPD, 1999), and over fifty-four state hospitals have been closed since 1970, with over forty of these closures occurring since 1990 (McGrew, Wright, and Pescosolido, 1999). Many who might have spent most of their lives in mental hospitals live in sheltered settings in the community and receive services from a variety of community-based programs, in addition to mental health centers. Yet almost 300,000 mentally ill persons are estimated to be living in nursing homes, settings that are considered inappropriate due to their level of restrictiveness (Braddock, 1992); the majority could be living in more normalizing settings, if such settings were developed in the community.

A significant problem for the provision of community services for those who are labeled mentally ill has to do with the stigma attached to mental illness. While seven of ten Americans have come to believe that mental illness is on the rise (with one of three people knowing an acquaintance or family member who has been treated for it), much misinformation is common. Chronic mental illness is among the most stigmatizing of disabling conditions, and that stigma has discouraged relatives of mentally ill persons, and mentally ill persons themselves, from creating effective advocacy organizations. Lack of consumer advocacy has prevented the expansion of resources for community mental health services. The problem exists in spite of the efforts of persons such as Rosalynn Carter, wife of past president Jimmy Carter, and Tipper Gore, wife of Vice President Al Gore, to make improved community mental health services a national priority. The proposed development of community residential treatment programs often runs into the NIMBY ("not in my back yard") phenomenon. Many people think the development of community programs is a good idea until one is proposed for their neighborhood. They then fight to keep it out because they fear what it might do to their property values, and the supposed dangers for their children of having the mentally ill near their homes (Program on Chronic Mental Illness, 1990).

Unfortunately, the push to deinstitutionalize persons who in the past would have been kept in mental hospitals has created a new human services problem. The need for community services has far outstripped the available resources. Many mentally disturbed individuals have become homeless street people, particularly in large cities. There are as many as 1.5 to 2 million homeless people in the United States, and of these, up to 50 percent may have severe, persistent mental disorders, or drug and alcohol abuse (Phelan and Link, 1999). Many of the seriously mentally ill are also locked away in jails and prisons. They are often charged with minor crimes simply to get them off the street. For example, one individual in Illinois was arrested and charged with stealing a $1.88 item from a store and to date has spent over six months in a moderate security setting because he is not fit to stand trial due to his mental illness. It is estimated that between 35,000 and 150,000 jail and prison inmates are seriously mentally ill (Torrey, 1989). Few receive appropriate treatment for their mental illness. Many simply move between jail and the streets, where they become homeless again, and back to jail when their behavior comes in conflict with the law. The recognition of the plight of the homeless mentally ill, and of homeless people in general, will, it is hoped, lead to the development of more human services programs for these individuals.

Although deinstitutionalization has worked in the sense of increasing the freedom of ex–mental patients and new homeless mentally ill people, we must now help these people deal with the risks of freedom. There is more to a successful community support system than a collection of programs. In each system, planners and clinicians must analyze the total system design in terms of ease of engagement and continuity of services (Minkoff, 1987). The increased funding will do little good if the homeless mentally ill do not have easy access to it or interest in using or motivation to use the services.

Correctional Systems

Crime is a major social problem in the United States. Until recently, each year saw significant increases in reported crimes. By mid 1998, 1.8 million people were inmates in federal or state prisons or local jails, and another 3.7 million people were on parole or probation (Bureau of Justice Statistics, 1999). Prisons generally hold individuals convicted of a crime and sentenced to terms of one year or more, while jails usually hold people waiting for trial, or people who have been convicted and sentenced to a term of one year or less.

In the recent past, the most rapidly growing segment of the correctional population has been women. The population of women in jails and prisons has tripled in the 1980s, in 1989 alone rose 22 percent, and in the 1990s doubled again (Haney and Zimbardo, 1998). This increase in the female correctional population is due mainly to arrest and conviction for drug-related offenses. Women in jail and prison have special problems, including the fact that 80 percent of them are mothers, and, of those, 85 percent have custody of their children. Female prisoners share some similar problems, such as histories of drug abuse and poor education, but also have a high incidence of histories of physical or sexual abuse, including rape (Fulla, 1998). Today's jails and prisons are ill equipped to deal with the problems of female inmates. The dramatic increase in population has placed a severe strain on correctional facilities oriented toward dealing with male inmates.

The worker in the field of corrections may focus on crime prevention, rehabilitation of offenders, or both. Prevention often involves working with juvenile offenders to get them off the route to becoming adult criminals. It may also involve more indirect efforts, such as working with street gangs to redirect their activities into legal, community-supportive behaviors. Even more indirect are attempts to modify the social ills, such as poverty, that increase the likelihood of criminal activity.

Rehabilitation of offenders can occur through a number of systems. Human service workers in probation and parole systems deal with people who are under the supervision of the court after committing a crime. In probation, the convicted person is not imprisoned but placed under the supervision of a worker whose duty is to counsel, broker services, and supervise the individual's behavior in the community. Probation can, in the event of a lack of success, require that the individual be returned to court for sentencing to imprisonment. Parole is a similar process that occurs after an individual has spent some part of the court sentence in prison. The person is given an early but supervised release that has the goals of reintegration into the community and future compliance with the law. The parolee is under the guidance of a parole officer (a human service worker) who provides counseling and referral to necessary services. Parole failure also can lead to reimprisonment while the individual serves out the sentence. Although progress has not been as widespread as in other areas, there has been a growing emphasis on community services in corrections.

Imprisonment has at least three goals: rehabilitation, punishment, and deterrence. Of these, only rehabilitation is a service provided for the offender; punishment and deterrence are services for society. Within most prisons, human services are relatively scarce. Prisons are oriented more toward containing criminals than toward rehabilitating them. The penitentiary has always been, in practice, a custodial institution. Custody is a part of the heritage of the prison, with or without an agenda of human services reform. This reflects the prison's ancient origins as a vehicle for exclusion and containment of society's rejects (Johnson, 1987). Thus, a custodial reality forms the backdrop for any rehabilitative services that are provided. Some services do exist, however: human service workers provide work-training programs, education, counseling, and recreational services, among others. Unfortunately, only a minority of correctional employees working in prisons have human services–oriented duties. During the past twenty years, there has been a clear movement away from a correctional rehabilitation focus and toward a containment and punishment focus (Haney and Zimbardo, 1998).

Poverty: A Common Denominator

In the mid 1990s there were just over 38 million people living below the poverty line in the United States. Over the next few years that number decreased to about 34 million by 1998, the lowest level since 1989 (Uchitelle, 1999). That decrease had much to do with an improving national economy and the availability of more employment, much of which was at the minimum wage. For the 12.7 percent of the population in 1998 below the poverty level, that meant that a single person had less than $8,240 in income, a two-person household had less than $11,064, and a family of four had less than $16,700 in income. While the overall decrease is good news, some segments of society continue to experience high rates of poverty: children have an 18.9 percent rate of poverty, Hispanics a 25.6 percent rate, and blacks a 26.1 percent rate.

In the early 1970s, there was much optimism that poverty could be nearly eradicated or at least reduced to the levels of other industrialized nations that have served their populace well. If one considers children, for example, the rate of child poverty in Canada is half the U.S. rate; in Britain, it's one-third; in France, one-fourth; and, in Germany, Holland, and Sweden, about one-tenth (Ewalt, 1995). By the end of the 1970s, the United States had reduced the number of children living in poverty to about 10 million, but, since then, the numbers have soared. In 1998, there were still 13.5 million children in poverty. The jump in the number of children in poverty is due to many factors, not the least of which is a major change in family structure. From 1960 to the 1990s, the number of children living in single-parent families has jumped from 10 percent to over 25 percent. Thirty-five years ago, only 5 percent of children were born out of wedlock; now, the rate is over 30 percent. Almost all of the children of single-parent families live with their mother, and it is difficult for a single mother to find work that pays enough to support a family when no or little child support is available from the father. However, while such changes have contributed to the rise in poverty, other countries faced similar problems but kept their rates lower. They have simply been more generous in their funding for social services.

Who are the poor? When one thinks about poor people, the usual image is a person who has no money and who either ekes out an existence by panhandling or lives on welfare. A fair percentage of moneyless people (often homeless street people) do not receive any welfare money. The nonworking poor who live exclusively on welfare comprise less than 4 million U.S. citizens.

About one of twenty U.S. residents lives near or below the poverty line. This is an increase of nearly 45 percent since 1980. The poor have become even poorer in the past two decades. These hyperpoor live in mostly single-parent female-headed families and are 61 percent White and 35 percent Black. Less than two of five receive welfare benefits. Even among the hyperpoor, 46 percent of the households have *some* earnings, yet still cannot get more income than one-third of the poverty level for a family of four (Whitman, 1990).

Another roughly 6 to 8 million Americans work full-time or part-time but still are unable to earn enough to break out of the ranks of the poor. These are the hidden poor, employed yet poverty-stricken. The hard-core inner-city poor make up only 7 percent of the nation's poor. Sixty percent of all able-bodied poor adults work and are evenly divided between urban and rural areas.

Poverty is clearly not confined to some stereotype of black and brown children in inner cities whose parents are simply lazy and want to live on welfare (Edelman, 1994). In reality, there are many more poor Whites than poor people of color, and more rural poor than urban poor. Poverty is a universal problem in the United States, with a profound impact on those who experience it. It doesn't take much experience at living in poverty to develop a sense of despair about improving one's life. For children, poverty is particularly damaging. It is highly associated with low birth weight of infants, injuries, accidents, poisoning, stunted growth, mental retardation, mental illness, and infant or childhood death (Black and Krishnakumar, 1998).

Homeless People

Over the past twenty years, homelessness has gained a great deal of popular attention. Prior to 1980, most Americans would have asserted that very few people were homeless and living in the streets. The last time homelessness was emphasized as a problem was during the Great Depression of the 1930s, when it was estimated that between 200,000 and 1.5 million people were homeless (Rossi, 1990). After that time, the number of homeless people declined drastically and in the 1950s consisted primarily of older men living in skid row areas of cities. It was predicted that homelessness would virtually disappear by the 1970s. However, since the 1980s, homelessness has risen dramatically, and as many as 1.5 to 2 million people are homeless at some point during the year in the United States (Phelan and Link, 1999). Among the reasons given for the increase in homelessness are loss of housing stocks to gentrification and the aging of the baby boom generation of 75.8 million people. That group has caused a swelling in the need for service in all areas, from overcrowded delivery rooms when they were being born, to crowded public schools, and now perhaps an increase in the homeless (Baum and Burnes, 1993).

When the new homeless people of the 1980s and 1990s are compared to those of the 1950s and 1960s, some important differences are found. Few of the old homeless people had to sleep in the streets, while today it is common. Today's homeless people include many more women and an increasing number of families with children. About half of the homeless people of the midcentury were employed at least intermittently. Of today's homeless people, only about 3 percent work steadily and 39 percent work intermittently. Few homeless people receive welfare payments because they lack a permanent address. Given these income levels, it is no mystery why homeless people are without shelter. Their incomes simply do not let them compete effectively in the housing market, even on the lowest end. The only way most homeless people can survive at all is to use shelters for a free place to sleep, food kitchens and soup lines for free meals, free community health clinics and emergency rooms for medical care, and the clothing

TABLE 5.3   Shelter Beds in Major Metropolitan Cities

Estimated Number of People in Temporary Shelters
on One Night in February, 1996

New York	44,794
Los Angeles	26,554
Philadelphia	14,123
Boston	13,483
Chicago	13,307
Washington	13,166
St. Louis	12,794
San Francisco	12,410
Pittsburgh	8,882
Denver	8,635

Source: Department of Housing and Urban Development.

distribution depots for something to put on their backs. That homeless people survive at all is a tribute to the many charitable organizations that provide these and other essential commodities and services, and local governments that provide a surprisingly large (yet inadequate) number of temporary shelter beds (see Table 5.3).

People who are homeless have high levels of disabilities, including physical illness—two thirds suffer from infectious illnesses other than AIDS, and have no medical insurance. Thirty-nine percent have signs of mental illness or alcoholism, and another 10 percent abuse other drugs. Serious childhood traumas have been experienced by many of the homeless, with 25 percent reporting child abuse, 33 percent having run away from home, and 21 percent having experienced homelessness as a child (Bernstein, 1999).

The homeless need human services of a variety of kinds, beginning with emergency housing. Housing alone, however, will not solve the problem.

■ ■ Jacqueline Williams, mother of fourteen children, appeared on *The Donahue Show* (a television talk show) and confronted the mayor of Washington, D.C., about the city's duty to provide individuals with adequate housing. In response to the program and its aftermath, the city placed the Williams family in a freshly renovated house. Just a year later, that same unit was deemed unfit for habitation by municipal inspectors. Plumbing fixtures, furniture, and kitchen cabinets had disappeared, waste of many kinds was deposited on the floor, and the younger children, who had been abused and neglected, were placed in foster care.

There are not enough details available to specifically identify why the situation went so wrong, but in general it's clear that Williams and her children needed much more in the way of services than a new house. Federal, state, and local governments will have to devote significant resources to this problem if this incidence of homelessness is to be rolled back to where it was twenty years ago.

The homeless need shelters; food programs; access to health care, substance abuse, and mental health treatment; case management; job training and linkage; education services for homeless children; housing; clothing; sanitation facilities; storage facilities; a mail drop; and other services (Long, 1999). Few places in the country provide all these services at a level sufficient to meet the need.

Not every human services client is poor, and being poor does not necessarily mean that a person requires services beyond financial assistance. However, human services problems are significantly more frequent among people who live in poverty. There is a greater incidence of problems for children, such as poor health, behavior disturbances, poor school functioning, parental abuse, and mental retardation. The elderly poor have more survival problems than middle- or upper-class aged who have pensions and caring, intact families. The poor are more likely to abuse chemical substances, such as alcohol, perhaps to escape from the harsh realities of poverty. Major psychiatric disorders are more frequently diagnosed among the poor, who are more likely to require hospitalization in public mental hospitals than are people from higher socioeconomic classes. Criminal convictions are more likely among the poor, and criminals most often prey upon poor people.

Poverty does not cause all the human services problems. It appears to cause some, and it certainly is a contributing or complicating factor in many. Some human services problems may lead to poverty for some individuals. It is a complicated relationship. However, whatever the relationship, poverty has a severe im-

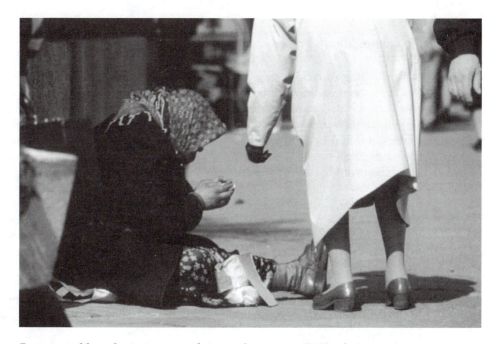

Poverty and homelessness are, unfortunately, not rare in North America.

pact on human functioning, and human service workers have to confront the problem of poverty in their clients. Its eradication is unlikely, and even if that could be accomplished, it would not solve most human services problems. However, programs that focus on the elimination of poverty for individuals or groups are within the boundaries of human services.

Many human services systems have been established with the goal of reducing poverty and its impact in the United States. These include portions of the Social Security Administration, aid to families with dependent children, state-funded public aid, and Medicare and Medicaid. Some types of social welfare programs focus on providing financial aid to poor people. Other human services programs provide assistance to people by educating or training them for paid employment and by finding them jobs. However, it is clear that we have a goodly distance to go before we successfully combat this problem.

Poverty can be multigenerational for some, but it is increasingly a condition that people may slide into when employment is lost, and many people move back out of poverty after falling into it. There is, in fact, much turnover in welfare rolls. However, the subgroup of people who have always been poor and whose parents were poor are particularly vulnerable to these destructive effects of poverty. One would think that, with all of our knowledge about the effects of poverty, we would have crafted a social policy that is similar to those in nations where poverty is less common. Unfortunately, we have not, and we will see what impact welfare reform has on this pernicious problem.

The Multiproblem Client

In the helping professions, we often talk about specific problems and the services that have been organized to deal with them: child abuse treatment, education, alcoholism, mental retardation, crime, delinquency, depression, suicide, and poverty.

We do that, perhaps, because it simplifies the issues and makes them easier to understand. But in another way it hampers our understanding if it oversimplifies the issues and leads to a fragmentation of service systems. The typical human services client rarely has only one problem. It is more likely that the individual has interlocking problems that must all be dealt with. For example, a typical client might be poor, depressed, unemployed, and abusing alcohol; be in an unstable marriage; have a mentally retarded child; and have another child in trouble with the law. Another client might be an ex-convict who is abusing his wife and having trouble in his job. A third might be poor, old, in ill health, and wandering the streets.

When more than one major problem occurs concurrently in an individual and occurs frequently, the condition is sometimes described as a dual diagnosis. Two of the most common such dual diagnoses are known by their acronyms, MICA or MISA and MIMR.

MICA or MISA refers to an individual who suffers both from a mental illness and also from chemical abuse (MICA) or substance abuse (MISA) as some prefer to call it. Combined mental illness and mental retardation is known as MIMR. The significance of dual diagnosis is that coexisting conditions can complicate providing treatment or helping services. The issue of assessing and planning for services for dual diagnoses is addressed in later chapters. The main point to be made here is that service systems are often organized along categorical lines, and a person with two major problems thus gets services from at least two different sources. For example, in many states, the mental health services system and the substance abuse service system are separate, with different funding sources and different providers. A person with a dual diagnosis of mental illness and substance abuse would have to go to two separate places and see two different professionals (at least). The treatments would not be coordinated and, in fact, might even be less effective because the professionals might be working at cross-purposes.

It is partly to deal with this problem that many states are trying to reorganize their categorical service systems into generic human service systems.

Summary

1. Over the past several decades, there has been a distinct change in the helping services from an exclusionary/segregating attitude to an inclusionary/integrating attitude. The negative effects of excluding people in need from supportive social networks are being combated by means of an increased emphasis on community-based human services.

2. Children are viewed by human service workers as particularly at risk. The types of services and service systems available for children and their families include well-child clinics, educational services, and state and community protective service agencies.

3. Older adults constitute a growing segment of the population that may reach 20 percent by the year 2030. The physical, social, and psychological losses experienced by many elderly people make them vulnerable to many problems; thus, they require extensive helping services.

4. Human services programs for those who abuse legal or illegal chemical substances must address the physical, social, and psychological problems associated with this phenomenon. The major types of services available for substance abusers include methadone programs, self-help programs like AA, and therapeutic community programs.

5. Community services for mentally retarded people have been growing at an astounding rate. These programs focus on maximizing the potential for self-support of mentally retarded citizens and have contributed to a decline in institutional populations.

6. The mental health system is another area in which deinstitutionalization and community services have become a major aspect of human services. Homeless mentally ill people present a problem because of a lack of sufficient

resources for community services. The provision of effective services for this group will require an even greater emphasis on community programs.

7. Crime is a major social problem, as illustrated by more than 1.8 million people held in jails and prisons. The goals of the correctional system are rehabilitation, punishment, and deterrence. Community human services programs in corrections focus on rehabilitation.

8. Poverty may be considered a common denominator for human services clients. Although not all clients are poor, those who are show a greater incidence of problems. Many human services systems address the problem of poverty directly, and all systems serve clients who are poverty-stricken.

9. The typical human services client has multiple problems that cut across systems of categorization. These needs determine the broad boundaries of human services.

Discussion Questions

1. Why is it important for human services to take a community-based approach?
2. Why are children identified as particularly at risk for human services problems?
3. Why are so many elderly people poor?
4. Why is alcohol the most abused drug?
5. What factors about life in the lower socioeconomic levels might contribute to the higher incidence of mild and moderate mental retardation at those levels?
6. Why does the correctional system emphasize punishment more than rehabilitation?
7. What do we mean by defining poverty as a common denominator in human services problems?

Learning Experiences

1. Attend a special education class at a local primary school.
2. Volunteer at a nursing home for the elderly.
3. Monitor your drug intake for one week. Do not forget that coffee, tea, and some soft drinks contain caffeine (a stimulant drug) and that cigarettes contain nicotine.
4. Find out if there are any community facilities for mentally retarded people in your locality. Visit one if you can.
5. Find out whether there are services for homeless street people in your community.
6. Visit your local city or county jail or find out the location and size of each of your state's prisons. Do they have any human services programs?

Recommended Readings

Castles, E. E. (1996). *We're people first: The social and emotional lives of individuals with mental retardation.* Westport, CT: Praeger.

DeVine, J. A., & Wright, J. N. (1993). *The greatest of evils: Urban poverty and the American underclass.* New York: Aldine de Gruyter.

Kozol, J. (1987). *Rachel and her children: Homeless families in America.* New York: Crown.

Meyer, L. H., Peck, C. A., & Brown, L. (Eds.). (1991). *Critical issues in the lives of people with severe disabilities.* Baltimore: Brooks.

Roberts, A. (Ed.). (1983). *Social work in juvenile and criminal justice settings.* Springfield, IL: Charles C. Thomas.

Vander Staay, S. (1992). *Street lives, an oral history of homeless Americans.* Philadelphia: New Society Publishers.

6

Medical/Psychiatric Approaches and the Person in Need

- Why is a basic understanding of the medical/psychiatric model important?
- How does HIV/AIDS illustrate the relationship between the medical/psychiatric model and human services?
- What are the primary assumptions of the medical/psychiatric model?
- What are some of the common treatment strategies of the medical/psychiatric model?

Medical and psychiatric problems are among the most frequent and costly problems of people in need. Well over $900 billion is spent on health care each year in the United States. Thus, it is not surprising that the medical/psychiatric model is one of the most common models for conceptualizing human problems and for dealing with people in need.

There are actually at least two medically oriented models. The strict medical approach deals with people who have problems related directly to physical health. When one has a health problem, such as appendicitis or a broken leg, one seeks help from physicians and other caregivers who specialize in this approach. The other approach, the psychiatric model, applies a medically oriented view to a wider spectrum of behavioral, emotional, or cognitive problems. Many professionals from social work, psychology, and other human services fields, in addition to physicians and nurses, function in accordance with medical/psychiatric assumptions.

Focusing for a moment on the strict medical approach, even acute or chronic medical disorders have human services implications. Physical illnesses (especially when they are severe or devastating) can result in psychological, social, and economic problems for the individual, that are usually not addressed by the purely medical specialists who treat the physical aspects of the disorder. The other problems associated with physical diseases often fall within the boundaries of the human services field and are dealt with by human service workers.

AIDS: Physical Disease—Human Services Issue

A modern-day disease that illustrates these issues is acquired immune deficiency syndrome, or HIV/AIDS, a viral disease affecting the immune system of the body. The immune system is our defense against diseases. If it is impaired, it allows otherwise controllable infections to invade the body and cause additional disease. At the current time, there is no effective cure for AIDS. It leads to death caused by massive infection such as pneumonia, by tuberculosis, or by diseases like cancer. (*HIV* refers to the human immunodeficiency virus that results in AIDS. A person who is HIV positive has the virus, but may not show symptoms of diseases seen in AIDS.)

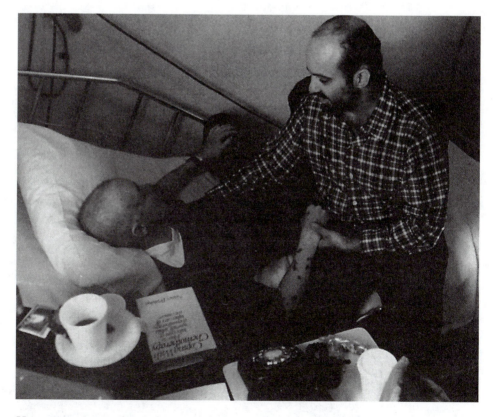

Human service workers who care for people who are terminally ill have a special dedication to helping others.

The first U.S. cases of HIV/AIDS were reported in 1981, although it is suspected that some cases had occurred elsewhere in the world during the middle to late 1970s. This disease, never seen before, took the medical establishment and the rest of the world by surprise. From 1981 to 1998, at least 1.5 million people in the U.S. became infected with HIV, 600,000 have been diagnosed with symptoms of AIDS, and more than 300,000 have died of it. In 1996 alone, 61,300 deaths were due to HIV/AIDS (Purvis, 1997). In the United States during the early years of the AIDS crisis, the disease appeared to affect primarily men who engaged in homosexual behavior and intravenous drug users, and most other people believed they were at low risk for the disease.

Many believed that cases of HIV/AIDS in heterosexuals were likely caused by some accident such as a contaminated blood transfusion during a surgical procedure. In the 1980s, there were many well-publicized cases of children and adults who developed AIDS in this manner, which led to serious concerns about the safety of the U.S. medical blood supply. After aggressive public health action, including mandatory testing for HIV for blood donors, the risk of receiving a transfusion of HIV-contaminated blood declined from 5,550 in 100,000 ten years ago to 1 in 500,000 by 1996 (Vigoda, 1996).

Today, while the groups at highest risk for infection in the United States continue to be those who engage in homosexual behavior or who are intravenous drug users, the fastest increase in *rate* of infection is among heterosexuals (through heterosexual contact), particularly adolescents (DiClemente, 1992). In 1994, 22 percent of people newly diagnosed with HIV/AIDS in the United States were infected as adolescents (CHIME, 1995). In some parts of the world, the *primary* mode of transmission of HIV/AIDS is heterosexual sexual contact (in sub-Saharan Africa, southern and southeastern Asia, and the Caribbean). In the worldwide context, the impact of HIV/AIDS in less than twenty years has been catastrophic. About 40 million people have become HIV-positive, and there have been 15 million deaths from AIDS through January of 2000 (Ho, 1999). In 1999 worldwide, there were more than 3 million new cases of HIV infection, and 70 to 75 percent of those new cases were transmitted by heterosexual behavior (Ho, 1999; Purvis, 1997).

Despite promising recent treatment breakthroughs, HIV/AIDS continues to be a major threat to world health (see Box 6.1). Several drug therapies now can slow the progress of the HIV virus and AIDS symptoms (for example, a drug known as AZT), and, in 1996, protease inhibitors, if given soon enough, were found to be capable of reducing the virus in the bloodstream to undetectable levels (Gorman, 1997), with some people showing remarkable improvement. However, not all people respond well to these drugs, and many people cannot afford the almost $20,000 per year that treatment with protease inhibitors costs. There still is no cure for HIV/AIDS, and none is really expected before 2025. The best hope is that a viral immunization can be developed that will slow the spread of the disorder (Ho, 1999).

The HIV/AIDS epidemic, although a medical crisis, has a direct bearing on human services. The disease spreads because of *behaviors* that result in the sharing of

BOX 6.1   HIV/AIDS in the Cross-Cultural Context

In the United States, it is not surprising that the focus of attention on AIDS is in regard to its impact within U.S. borders. However, from a worldwide perspective, the HIV/AIDS problem becomes immense. The numbers of people who lived with HIV/AIDS in 1998 and the numbers who died in 1996 are estimated as follows:

	Number Living with AIDS in 1998	Number Dying in 1996
North America	890,000	61,300
Latin America	1,400,000	70,900
Caribbean	330,000	14,500
Sub-Saharan Africa	22,500,000	783,700
North Africa and Middle East	210,000	10,800
Western Europe	500,000	21,000
Central and Eastern Europe and Central Asia	270,000	1,000
Southern and southeastern Asia	6,700,000	143,700
Eastern Asia and Pacific	560,000	1,200
Australia and New Zealand	12,000	1,000

bodily fluids, for example, homosexual intercourse, the use of HIV-contaminated needles by drug users, and heterosexual intercourse. Thus, to slow down the spread of AIDS, people must change their behaviors. Human service workers contribute in this area by providing prevention education for people at increased risk for HIV infection, such as homosexuals, and heterosexuals who have multiple sexual partners and intravenous drug users. Human service workers also provide services to clients who have AIDS, and, in today's world, every human service worker will almost certainly work closely with people who live with HIV and AIDS (McKinney, 1999). A variety of social and psychological problems develop when an individual has AIDS (Kalichman, 1998). Patients and their families and friends require human services support by human service counselors and volunteers. The types of services needed by persons with HIV/AIDS include:

- *Housing:* The stigma of AIDS and people's fear of becoming infected make it difficult for AIDS-infected people to find adequate affordable housing.
- *Income maintenance:* The loss of income from being unable to work and the costs of treatment are financially devastating.
- *Long-term and hospice care:* People with AIDS often have no one to care for them as they become more and more disabled.
- *Child care:* Mothers with AIDS or mothers of children with AIDS often need assistance in care for their children either when the mother is hospitalized or disabled or when the child is disabled at home.
- *Legal assistance:* Help will be needed at a minimum in preparing for financial matters after death.

- *Medical care:* As a debilitating, fatal disease, AIDS requires major medical interventions.
- *Counseling and mental health services:* People with AIDS need assistance in dealing with their debilitation and impending death. Some will develop AIDS dementia, an organic brain disorder caused by destruction of brain tissue and may need residential care for that problem.

As more individuals develop acute symptoms of AIDS, it becomes clearer that AIDS, like any other debilitating and fatal disease, has a significant impact on the psychological functioning of the affected person. The disease results in loss of both physical and mental capabilities, disfigurement, pain, chronic fatigue, and the likelihood of early death, and this is likely to result in a variety of psychological and behavioral consequences. Among the associated problems reported are anxiety attacks, depression, feelings of helplessness, irrational guilt, lowered self-esteem, social withdrawal, drug and alcohol abuse, cognitive impairment, and, for some, cognitive dementia resembling Alzheimer's disease. Human services agencies have had a comprehensive role to play in the AIDS crisis, beginning with encouraging clients to be tested for the AIDS virus if they are at risk or likely to be infected. Testing provides an opportunity for early preventive education and counseling and an opportunity to limit further spread of the disease (McKinney, 1999).

As the numbers of persons with AIDS have increased, more human service workers have found themselves working with people with AIDS (McKinney, 1999). Human service workers who come in contact with AIDS-infected clients have to deal with their own fears and anxieties about the risk of becoming infected themselves (Wallack, 1989). Even among physicians and nurses who could be expected to be well informed, about 25 percent of those surveyed feared that they would become infected. In fact, very few health care professionals have developed AIDS from treating AIDS-infected patients. Human service workers have to become better educated about this disease to understand the plight of AIDS-infected people, to help their clients who are at risk for AIDS or who have already been infected, and to understand their own feelings and fears about the risk of becoming infected and the relationship of those fears and feelings to the factual risks.

Facts About AIDS

1. There is no known risk of nonsexually related infection from casual contact.
2. Health workers who are exposed to AIDS patients' blood, stool, and other bodily fluids have not become infected unless they received a needle stick from a contaminated needle.
3. Risks of infection increase if
   a. You are homosexual and do not know if your partners are free of infection.
   b. You are heterosexual and you have multiple sexual partners whose history you do not know.

    c. You have even microscopic tears in the tissues of the penis, vagina, mouth, or rectum and engage in sexual behavior with a partner who is infected and contacts those areas.

    d. You frequent female or male prostitutes.

    e. You share intravenous drug needles with others.

4. Risks are minimized if

    a. You have had a monogamous sexual relationship for five years.

    b. A condom is used during intercourse.

    c. Intravenous injections are done *only* with sterile needles.

5. There is no risk

    a. In casual nonsexual social contact with an AIDS-infected person.

    b. In 499,999 blood transfusions of 500,000.

    c. In caring for a person who has AIDS.

    d. In having contact with one of the few children who have AIDS who are in school settings.

The Basics of the Medical/Psychiatric Model

In contrast to the medical approach, the psychiatric approach is likely to enter into human service work on a frequent basis. Many people in need of human services help have had and continue to have contact with traditional professionals or service systems that are oriented to the psychiatric approach. In the past thirty-five to forty years, a growing criticism of this approach has developed. In spite of this criticism, the model remains extremely widespread. In fact, even the language of some human services systems reflects the medical/psychiatric model; for example, problem behavior may be called *pathology,* may be grouped according to *symptoms,* may be classified in a process called *diagnosis,* and may be changed in a process called *therapy* (Maher, 1966).

The widespread acceptance of the psychiatric model makes it critical for human service workers to have a basic understanding of the model's assumptions, philosophy, concepts, and approaches to persons in need. Whatever the setting in which human service workers are employed—schools, prisons, mental retardation facilities, mental hospitals, neighborhood service centers, public aid departments, or community mental health centers—they encounter and work alongside persons who are strongly influenced by the medical/psychiatric model. The human service worker must be able to assess adequately the pros and cons of this particular approach to persons in need.

One of many specific examples of the involvement of the medical/psychiatric model approach in nonmedical settings occurred in my experience several years ago. In a large Midwestern city, a state employment office frequently had difficulty maintaining its clients in jobs. Many of the clients had difficulty dealing with job interviews, and, once placed, many were quickly fired or quit. The clients often responded to these events with emotional reactions such as anxiety, anger, sadness, and guilt. The frequent response of the employment counselor was to refer them to a local mental health clinic to straighten out their "problems." Once at the clinic, the clients were most often seen quickly by a physician whose prime response was to prescribe a tranquilizing drug so that they would not "get upset" on the job. In effect, a medical/psychiatric model approach became a primary tool of the employment counselor.

We have seen how both medical problems and a psychiatrically oriented approach impact the human service worker. Let's consider the *medical/psychiatric model* as a unified mind-set. The primary assumption of the medical/psychiatric model is, of course, that abnormal behavior is a function of a disease process; that is, people behave abnormally or deviantly because of some disturbance of their body that then affects their psychological processes and behavior. The physical disturbance is usually considered the result of one or more of the following problems: genetic inheritance, biochemical metabolism, or brain tissue damage. Although little hard evidence exists for the application of this model to the complete range of human behavior problems, many disorders have documentable physical causes and fit the disease model.

The best examples of disorders that fit the medical/psychiatric model are inherited disorders, such as Huntington's chorea and many forms of mental retardation, and the disorders of aging, such as Alzheimer's disease and arteriosclerosis (hardening of the arteries), which lead to changes in behavior that are often called *senility*. Some other personality changes have been demonstrated to be a function of physical destruction of brain tissue caused by tumors, high fever, syphilis, or a severe head injury, as illustrated in the example of Bob.

■■ At age twenty-three, Bob was involved in an auto accident that resulted in the destruction of one-fourth of his frontal lobes, damage to the motor cortex, and a two-month coma. Before the accident, he had a factory job and was engaged to be married. After his primary recovery, he received intensive physical therapy for approximately six months at a rehabilitation hospital. However, Bob's brain damage resulted in major deficits in speech, coordination, and ambulation. Over the next ten years, Bob had numerous hospitalizations in state mental hospitals, usually with a diagnosis of organic brain syndrome without psychosis. Between hospitalizations, Bob lived in various nursing homes. His admissions to the mental hospitals were precipitated by combative behavior. Nursing home and hospital staff members assumed Bob's combative behavior to be due to his impulsivity and a lack of control of rage resulting from his organic damage.

Bob's problem was clearly physical in origin—actual damage to a part of his brain—and was appropriately treated from a medical perspective. Yet in the end, Bob was also helped by a human services approach that did not use the medical perspective.

When seen, Bob was a patient on a medical unit because of his physical infirmity. He spent all his time in a wheelchair, his speech was difficult to understand, and his motor movements were relatively uncoordinated. His "extremely combative" problem behavior consisted of knocking down infirm patients and trying to punch staff. He behaved this way because his various demands for constant attention were not met.

A human service worker instituted a simple behavioral program with Bob. Bob was informed that knocking down other patients and punching staff would result in the loss of privileges. He was also told that the absence of such behavior would result in his receiving a cigarette every thirty minutes, and that one full day of no violence would be reinforced by a thirty-minute meeting with a human service worker (who happened to be a young, attractive female). When the program began, Bob's average frequency of violence was between five and six incidents daily. Within five weeks, no incidents were occurring.

After the aggression disappeared, the human service worker began a similar reinforcement program to encourage Bob to take physical therapy, to practice rehabilitation exercises, and later to practice walking. In four months, Bob was able to walk with crutches, something he had not done for several years. His heightened ability to control his temper, and his physical improvement, allowed him, at the age of thirty-six, to leave the state hospital to live in a long-term community care facility, where he made a good adjustment.

For many years, Bob's use of a wheelchair and his combative behavior were presumed to be due to irreversible organic brain damage. Some of his problems, such as his speech deficit and some motor uncoordination, were certainly due to such damage and continued to be a problem even after contact with the human service worker. However, his aggressive behavior and inability to walk responded to a specific human services approach: behavioral treatment. Certainly, organic disorders such as Bob's original brain damage are appropriately the province of the medical/psychiatric model, but many human service workers are concerned with the model's wider application to problem behaviors, since little evidence exists that they do have a physical cause (see Box 6.2).

The basic assumptions of the medical/psychiatric model can be summarized as follows:

1. Behavioral and psychological disturbances are diseases that have a consistent etiology, cause, and outcome.
2. The diseases have an organic basis.
3. The underlying disease is manifested in symptoms, and changing the symptoms does not cure the disease.
4. Responsibility for the disease symptoms (behavior) is attributed to the disease, not to the person who has it.
5. Cure is a complex process that is a function of treatment administered by highly trained professionals who have medical training or by people who are supervised by physicians.

If eventually these assumptions turn out to be fact (which I consider very unlikely), treatment will ultimately be medical in nature and may include techniques such as genetic manipulation (modification of a person's DNA), chemotherapy (administration of behavior-changing drugs), surgery (removal of damaged brain tissue), or electroconvulsive therapy (modification of brain function through the application of electrical current).

Obviously, a number of "medical" treatments are very effective in changing behavior. Hence, human service workers must be pragmatists; that is, they may be

BOX 6.2   A Culture-Bound Syndrome: Koro, the Disappearing Penis

In the mental health field, "culture-bound" syndromes are unique disorders that are commonly seen only in one (or several similar) cultures. The syndromes are defined by four major characteristics: abrupt onset, short duration, absence of psychotic thinking, and a behavioral pattern that is well organized, even if bizarre (Franzini and Grossberg, 1995).

In Asia, particularly in China, a syndrome called *koro* is a rare but recurrent phenomenon. It consists of a man who believes (falsely) that his penis is shrinking and withdrawing into his abdomen and that, once it has completely withdrawn, he will die. The belief is accompanied by great anxiety and attempts to keep the penis from disappearing by the application of wooden or jade clamps, tying the penis with strings, or other devices.

While the syndrome is rare, there have been epidemics. In one month in 1976, there were 2,000 cases reported in Thailand. As Asian immigration to the United States continues, it is likely that physicians and psychiatrists will encounter more cases of koro.

What cultural explanation might there be for koro? In the traditional Chinese culture, high value is placed on the suppression of negative emotions. It is much more socially acceptable to be physically ill. Therefore, in the face of psychological pressures, the tendency is to hold in the distressing emotions and to express one's reactions in physical symptoms. (In Western medicine, this tendency is called *somatization*.) If a man is bothered by severe sexual anxieties and notices vague or very subtle bodily changes, such as a *slightly* shrunken penis due to cold, he could very well develop a full-scale somatic delusion such as koro. What is crucial is that he is aware of this syndrome and truly believes that it can occur.

According to Chinese medicine, koro is caused by a disturbance in the yin-yang balance. More specifically, it is believed that there has been a great weakening of the yang principle, which can occur as a result of sexual strain. Contributing to the imbalance could be a strengthening of the yin principle, which can happen as a result of extreme chilling or eating cold food.

Briefly, yang signifies not only the excited, upward, forward, aggressive, volatile, hard, bright, and hot but also the abstract and functional. In direct contrast, yin signifies not only the passive, inhibited, unclear, inward, downward, cold, dark, soft, and unaggressive but also the material and concrete.

The theory of yin-yang has broad application in Chinese medicine. It is used to describe anatomic-physiological relations and pathological conditions, but it also details the nature and phase of disease, as well as the categorization of medication, dietary considerations, and other therapeutic measures. The primary concern of diagnosis in Chinese medicine is to delineate imbalance between yin and yang, and treatment is primarily aimed at the restoration of this balance.

The Asian cultural treatments for koro include modification of diet, special herbs, mechanical devices to keep the penis from "disappearing," and the recommendation that fellatio be practiced immediately, which would certainly help to avoid retraction of the penis. The person who exhibits koro is likely to conclude that these treatments work because, of course, the penis does not then shrink into the abdomen, and he does not die!

In the United States, such a person may recover more quickly if treated with anti-anxiety drugs, but, in the long run, the culturally embedded treatment also works.

critical of the medical/psychiatric model but they cannot afford to reject treatments that seem to work.

Common Treatment Strategies of the Medical/Psychiatric Model

The fields of psychiatry and medicine have made a major contribution to human services in the treatment of major mental disorder. The two treatment strategies most associated with this model are electroconvulsive therapy and chemotherapy.

Electroconvulsive Therapy

Electroconvulsive therapy (ECT), sometimes known as electroshock therapy, is sometimes used to treat severe depression. It is usually given in an inpatient setting but sometimes is administered on an outpatient basis. The subject lies prone and is heavily sedated. Electrodes are placed on the temples, and a brief shock is given. The subject immediately becomes unconscious. With the use of a muscle relaxant, the seizure is only slightly noticeable as tremors in the hands and feet. After the treatment, people are confused, and they may lose memory of events immediately preceding the treatment. Treatments are usually given several times a week until the problem behaviors lessen. Maximum benefit is usually obtained in five to ten treatments during a period of two to three weeks.

Electroconvulsive therapy is reported to work particularly well in people who are depressed when there is no evidence of external precipitants for depression, such as loss of a job or divorce. It is particularly well regarded by many physicians in the treatment of depressions occurring during middle age and in depressions that are part of the manic-depressive or bi-polar syndrome. Successful use of ECT for a recurrent depression is illustrated in the case of April.

■■ April, a forty-two-year-old homemaker and mother of four children, had a history of repeated depressions since the age of twenty-eight. She had been in psychotherapy for years and had also been treated with antidepressant medication with little or no benefit. Her depression finally became so severe that April required inpatient treatment.

April described her depressive experience as being "like living in a black hole." Her appetite had disappeared and she had lost twenty-five pounds; her sleep was disturbed; she could no longer concentrate on her housework or reading. April was obsessed with the idea that she had ruined the lives of her family, was racked with guilt, and had threatened suicide. After seven treatments of ECT, April recovered completely from her depression, returned home, and was linked with a community mental health center for follow-up by a psychiatrist and a human service case manager.

A great deal of negative feeling toward electroconvulsive therapy exists among human service workers, owing in part to the abuses of the treatment in the early and mid-1960s. Today, the use of ECT is very closely monitored and reviewed in order to prevent the kinds of abuses that were more common forty

TABLE 6.1   Common Chemotherapeutic Drugs

Category	Generic Name	Trade Name
Antianxiety	Lorazepam	Ativan
	Clonazepam	Klonopin
	Buspirone	BuSpar
	Paroxetine	Paxil
Antidepressant	Sertraline	Zoloft
	Fluoxetine	Prozac
	Doxepin	Sinequan
	Citalopram	Celexa
Antimanic	Lithium	Lithium
Antipsychotic	Haloperidol	Haldol
	Thioridazine	Mellaril
	Thiothixene	Navane
	Chlorpromazine	Thorazine
	Fluphenazine	Prolixin
Atypical Antipsychotic	Clozapine	Clozaril
	Risperidone	Risperdal
	Olanzapine	Zyprexa
	Quetiapine	Seroquel

years ago (Sakauye, 1986). Unfortunately, because of the common misperception about the dangers of ECT, the pendulum may now have swung too far, and people who could benefit from this treatment may now find it hard to obtain.

The Chemotherapies

The most pervasive of the medical/psychiatric model approaches to people in need is the use of chemotherapy (drug treatment), which includes antianxiety agents, antidepressants, antimanics or mood stabilizers, antipsychotics, and the new atypical antipsychotics. Although a number of chemotherapies have been around for a very long time—barbiturates were used in the 1800s—the widespread use of mind-affecting medication dates from the 1950s. These drugs have the effect of modifying affective (emotional) states without significantly impairing cognitive functioning. A number of the more widely used chemotherapy medications with their generic (chemical family) and trade (sales) names are given in Table 6.1. Familiarity with these medications is useful because many human service clients may be taking them.

Antianxiety Agents
These drugs are often called tranquilizers. Physicians commonly prescribe these drugs for individuals who are tense or anxious. The first of the tranquilizers to be

discovered and patented was meprobamate (1952). Many others quickly followed, and their use expanded to the extent that today one of seven Americans is estimated to be using such drugs frequently. The evidence indicates that these drugs are quite effective in reducing the obvious symptoms of anxiety. However, their widespread use has been criticized as merely covering symptoms rather than helping the person deal with problems constructively.

Antipsychotic Agents

The antipsychotic agents, also sometimes called *psychotropics,* were first developed from a class of drugs known as the phenothiazines. The first of these drugs, chlorpromazine (sold under the brand name of Thorazine), was introduced in Europe in 1950. The drug was introduced in the United States in the mid-1950s and quickly became a primary medical/psychiatric model treatment in private and public mental hospitals. Later, it was used with discharged hospital patients on an outpatient basis and with the patients of psychiatrists in private settings.

Alternatively, the use of the antipsychotic drugs is considered by the National Institute of Mental Health (1975) to be one of the two major advances in the treatment of disturbed persons in the last fifty years. The drugs, in effect, mask or cover the stranger patterns of behavior of seriously disturbed persons. Target behaviors that are likely to improve while the drug is being used include combativeness; tension; hyperactivity; hostility; negativism; hallucinations; poor sleep, dress, and appetite; acute delusions; and sociability. Behaviors that are less likely to improve include lack of insight, poor judgment, poor memory, and lack of orientation.

Much of the credit for the tremendous decrease in mental hospital populations since the mid-1950s must go to the antipsychotic drugs. The reduction in severely disturbed behaviors has encouraged many helping professionals to accept the notion that many hospitalized patients could live in the community. However, in order to maintain the behavioral changes resulting from the use of these drugs, patients must continue to take them on a long-term maintenance basis. Unfortunately, often because of unpleasant side effects (see Table 6.2), about 50 percent of the people who are prescribed these medications stop taking them within a year after they are prescribed. Therefore, the strange behavior recurs

TABLE 6.2 Some Side Effects of Psychoactive Drugs

Antianxiety	Antidepressant	Antimanic	Antipsychotic	Atypical Antipsychotic
Drowsiness	Drowsiness	Tremor in fingers	Drowsiness	Agranulocytosis
Weakness	Anxiety/tremor	Nausea	Dry mouth	Seizure
Headache	Headache	Weight gain	Constipation	Dizziness
Nausea	Nausea	Cardic irregularity	Weight gain	Constipation
	Dry mouth	Rashes	Impotence	Weight gain
	Insomnia		Lowered seizure	Drowsiness
	Constipation		threshold	Headache
	Dizziness		Parkinson's reaction	Dry mouth
	Low blood pressure		Tardive dyskinesia	No tardive dyskinesia

after their return to the community, which often requires rehospitalization. In this sense, the drugs are only a temporary measure, although a valuable one. The antipsychotic drugs do *not* cure the major behavior disorders or turn a poorly adjusted, severely disturbed person into a well-adjusted, well-functioning community member.

Some of the side effects of these drugs are very severe. In particular, with the antipsychotics, a disorder called *tardive dyskinesia* sometimes occurs in persons who take the drugs over long periods. This disorder, believed to be usually irreversible, consists of repetitive involuntary facial movements such as smacking and licking of the lips, sucking movements, chewing movements, rolling and protrusion of the tongue, blinking, grotesque grimaces, spastic facial distortions, and body movements such as jerking of the fingers, ankles, and toes and contractions of neck and back muscles.

Atypical Antipsychotics

In the past decade, a number of new antipsychotic medications were introduced. The drugs are called *atypical* antipsychotics because they are just as effective or more so than the older antipsychotics but do not have the same very unpleasant side effects. Of particular importance is that they do not produce the disfiguring and almost crippling tardive dyskinesia. The first of these drugs to be introduced in the United States was clozapine, which is sold under the name Clozaril. The second was risperidone, sold as Risperdal. Both drugs hold great promise in the treatment of severe and persistent mental illness. About 20 percent of persons with chronic schizophrenia do not respond to the older antipsychotic medications. Many (not all) of these nonresponders do have very dramatic positive response to the atypicals.

Clozapine is as effective as the older antipsychotics and also is effective with 30 to 60 percent of nonresponders. It seems to improve social functioning, reduces hostility, and reduces *existing* tardive dyskinesia. Clozapine, however, can cause a *rare* but severe side effect, agranulocytosis, which occurs in about 1 percent of people who begin to take the medication. If this blood disorder is not identified and the person withdrawn from the clozapine, death can result. Because of this side effect, people taking clozapine must have weekly blood tests as a precautionary measure (Buchanan, 1995). Once agranulocytosis is discovered, the person can be taken off the medication and the side effect stops.

The second atypical antipsychotic, risperidone, does *not* have agranulocytosis as a side effect. Risperidone does have more of the traditional side effects than clozapine, but it still produces fewer of the tremors called *extrapyramidal syndrome*. It is at least as effective as the older antipsychotic drugs (Umbricht and Kane, 1995). The atypical antipsychotics to follow had even better effectiveness and less unpleasant side effects (Dawkins et al., 1999).

Antidepressants

Two classes of antidepressants—tricyclics and monoamine oxidase inhibitors (MAO inhibitors)—were developed for use on other disorders, but when their mood-elevating properties were noted, they were given to individuals experiencing depression. The tricyclics seem to be quite effective in combating endogenous depressions—that is, depressions for which there is no observable external stimulus. Less evidence exists for the general utility of the MAO inhibitors, which seem to work well for fewer people. Because they are tricky to use safely—requiring special dietary adjustments—their popularity is limited.

One antidepressant introduced in the early 1990s, fluoxetine, has successfully weathered a storm of controversy. This drug, marketed under the brand name Prozac, lifts the symptoms of depression and has been described as causing significant positive personality change in some people. It has, however, also been accused in the popular media of causing some individuals to paradoxically experience suicidal urges and even to commit suicide. There is, however, no sound evidence that this is actually the case (Kramer, 1993). Other new antidepressants introduced in the 1990s include Sertraline and Cilatopram, sold as Zoloft and Celexa. These new antidepressants are probably no more effective than the older ones but seem to have somewhat less severe side effects.

Antimanic or Mood Stabilizers

Although its use was reported as early as 1949 by an Australian physician, lithium was a highly toxic drug, and it was not in widespread use until the 1960s. At that time, blood tests were developed that allowed the level of toxicity to be measured and monitored. Previously, many subjects experienced severe side effects. Because of its danger, it was not approved for general use in the United States until 1970 (Kornetsky, 1976). Since the blood levels of lithium could be monitored accurately, the treatment has become more common.

The use of lithium seems particularly worthwhile in people who behave in a manner that has been called *manic-depressive,* or *manic type.* Manic individuals are characterized by excessive elation, irritability, talkativeness, accelerated speech and motor activity, and rapidly changing ideas. They often become caught up in wild ventures, squander their resources, and alienate family and friends, and they often lose their jobs. A physician who diagnoses this disorder prescribes approximately 1,800 milligrams of lithium carbonate per day until the subject's blood lithium reaches the required therapeutic level. Once the therapeutic level is reached, approximately 80 percent of the subjects show a distinct improvement. They are no longer highly elated or irritable, are calmer and more concerned with day-to-day functioning, and no longer believe they can do everything they desire. Once the behavior is modified, the subject is usually kept on a maintenance dosage to prevent a recurrence.

Common Usages of Drug Therapy

Although only five types of drugs have been dealt with here specifically, many additional types of chemotherapy exist, such as Antabuse for alcoholics, methadone for heroin withdrawal, and Ritalin for hyperactive children. Mental health, of course, is the system in which chemotherapy is most common. It has been estimated that over 85 percent of inpatients in mental hospitals are on one or more psychoactive medications. In both adult and juvenile corrections systems, psycho-active drugs frequently are given to inmates who are difficult to manage. The drugs are less frequently used in mental retardation facilities but still are common. Even in child care and primary education facilities, the use of drugs, particularly Ritalin, is common in controlling disorderly or hyperactive behavior. Drug use to control hyperactive behavior of children and adolescents may be too common. One large scale study of almost 30,000 school children found that about 1 in 10 was being given medication, and by fifth grade, an astounding 20 percent of white boys were receiving medication for hyperactivity (LeFever et al., 1999).

Prospects for the Medical/Psychiatric Model

The medical/psychiatric model remains a major force in dealing with people in need. Most research on human problems occurs in this model because relatively ample funds are available to its adherents. The drug industry is a multibillion dollar concern, and the American Medical Association is the most powerful of the professional organizations. Many medical/psychiatric model theories have been advanced to account for human behavior, and we can expect many more to be developed.

Summary

1. There are two medically oriented models. The medical approach deals with the physical ailments to which all people are subject. The medical/psychiatric model deals with behavioral, emotional, and cognitive problems that fall in the area of human services.

2. HIV/AIDS appeared to be a deadly disease in a limited group of people. Now that AIDS is spreading through heterosexual contact, the incidence is likely to increase dramatically.

3. Human service workers can play a role in AIDS service programs and, at the minimum, need to be well informed about AIDS issues and facts, as they are almost certain to have clients who are HIV-positive or AIDS symptomatic.

4. Medical/psychiatric approaches have been used in systems as diverse as corrections, child care, early education, mental health, public welfare, and mental retardation.

5. The primary assumptions of the medical/psychiatric model are as follows:

   a. Disturbed people suffer from a disease.

   b. Diseases have an organic basis.

   c. A disease is manifested in symptoms, and changing the symptoms does not cure the disease.

    d. Responsibility for behavior is attributed to the disease, not to the person.

    e. Cure is a complex function of treatment delivered by highly trained professionals.

6. While many human service workers question these medical/psychiatric assumptions, the pragmatic human service worker cannot reject medical/psychiatric treatment. Human service workers must assess these treatments objectively and maintain an awareness of their limitations and benefits because they often must work with followers of the medical/psychiatric model.

7. The common treatments of the medical/psychiatric model include electroconvulsive therapy and chemotherapy. Electroconvulsive therapy is an effective treatment for severe depression. However, severe side effects that were common in the early years of its use and the abuse of the treatment in later years have elicited strong criticism of the technique.

8. In spite of their sometimes dangerous and always unpleasant side effects, the chemotherapies can be of great utility for dealing with serious and persistent mental illness.

9. The medical/psychiatric model is a major force in dealing with people in need. It is, however, unlikely that the medical/psychiatric model theories will be fully confirmed in our lifetimes.

Discussion Questions

1. Why does the human service worker need to understand the medical/psychiatric model?

2. What are the basic assumptions of the medical/psychiatric model?

3. What might account for the negative feelings that many human service workers have toward the medical/psychiatric model?

4. Will HIV/AIDS result in any lasting changes in U.S. society?

Learning Experiences

1. Watch a "doctor" program on television. What does it communicate about the medical/psychiatric model?

2. Ask your acquaintances for their opinions about their doctors or about doctors in general.

3. Find out how many AIDS community support programs there are in your community.

Recommended Readings

Gorenstein, E. E. (1984). Debating mental illness: Implications for science, medicine, and social policy. *American Psychologist, 39.*

Kalichman, S. C. (1998). *Understanding AIDS: Advances in research and treatment* (2nd ed.). Washington, DC: American Psychological Association Press.

7

Behavioral Approaches and the Person in Need

- What are the four models of learned behavior?
- How may disordered behavior be learned?
- What is systematic desensitization?
- How does a token economy help change behavior?
- What is cognitive behavioral therapy?

The behavioral therapies are among the most recent approaches to people in need. The application of behavioral approaches to human service problems began in earnest in the 1950s, and they have gained in popularity ever since. Certain common themes can be identified as hallmarks of behaviorally oriented approaches that distinguish them from other theoretical orientations.

1. The emphasis is on measurable current behavior and its impact on the environment or on the impact of environment on the measurable behavior. *Behavior* is defined as physical actions, current emotions, or specific cognitions (thoughts).
2. Specific behaviors, emotions, or cognitions, once they are identified, may be modified by concrete actions of the person or actions of others that can be clearly or objectively specified.
3. It is assumed that changed behaviors, emotions, or cognitions affect the client's adjustment; that is, the removal of socially maladaptive or distressing personal behaviors or the acquisition of positive social responses leads to reinforcing feedback from the person's interpersonal environment or to self-reinforcement by the person.

The behavioral approaches are based primarily on theories about how people learn. The behaviorist takes the position that all (or nearly all) of people's thoughts,

Modeling the behavior of others is a common process by which children learn.

feelings, and behaviors are a result of learning and that established principles determine how the learning process works. Differences between human beings are seen as the result of the individuals' having learned different behavioral, emotional, or cognitive responses to their environments or culture.

Four Models of Learned Behavior

Although many detailed theories exist on how learning takes place, the following generalizations provide an overview of the process. Behavior can be considered to be either patterned or random. Most human behavior, however, seems to be patterned or goal-directed; that is, it represents a purposeful attempt to obtain something. The goal may be to satisfy physiological needs, such as food, water, and air, or to satisfy secondary needs that have been learned, such as needs for social approval, material objects, or attention.

Many models have contributed to the development of behavioral approaches, but four major conceptualizations can be used as examples: the classical, operant, social, and cognitive models.

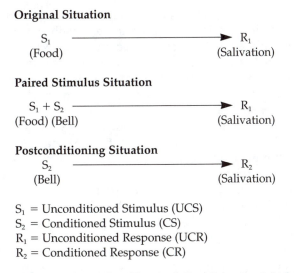

Original Situation

S_1 ⟶ R_1
(Food)   (Salivation)

Paired Stimulus Situation

$S_1 + S_2$ ⟶ R_1
(Food) (Bell)   (Salivation)

Postconditioning Situation

S_2 ⟶ R_2
(Bell)   (Salivation)

S_1 = Unconditioned Stimulus (UCS)
S_2 = Conditioned Stimulus (CS)
R_1 = Unconditioned Response (UCR)
R_2 = Conditioned Response (CR)

FIGURE 7.1   The Classical Conditioning Model

Classical

In the *classical model* shown in Figure 7.1, a stimulus (S) causes an unconditioned response (UCR). For example, food shown to a hungry animal causes the subject to salivate. A second stimulus, such as a bell, light, or gesture, is then paired with the original stimulus through closeness in time or distance and with great frequency. It then becomes associated with the original stimulus (food) and with the unconditioned response (salivation), to the extent that the existence of the second stimulus (bell) elicits the response (salivation), which is then considered to be *conditioned*. One ends up with what appears to be a very strange situation in which the ringing of a bell causes salivation.

Operant

The *operant model* developed by Harvard University psychologist B. F. Skinner is concerned more with the consequences of a response than with the initial stimulus. It takes the approach that all behaviors have consequences on the environment and that the consequences reinforce the response (make it more likely to occur), maintain it, or extinguish it (make it less likely to occur). The consequences of a response may appear to be unpleasant from a commonsense viewpoint but still may reinforce behavior (make it more likely to occur). For example, most parents react very negatively to a child's temper tantrums, but frequently the negative reactions do nothing in terms of stopping the child's tantrums. If temper tantrums are ignored, however, they often decrease in frequency. To explain this, one could suggest that the temper tantrum response is reinforced by the attention the parent gives to the child, even if the attention is punitive. This might be obvious in a situation in which the parents usually ignore the children when they are quiet and occupied in a positive activity. In effect, children may learn that a major way to obtain meaningful extended responses from the parent is to create a scene.

Operant behaviorists, however, are less concerned with identifying the underlying cause of behavior than with determining how to change its consequences in order to increase or decrease its frequency. Along this line, much of their interest has been in the area of reinforcement schedules—determining whether behavior should be reinforced every time it occurs, every second or third time, or on a number of other variable schedules. The main interest is, of course, to determine the most potent approach to changing learned behavior. For a beginning understanding of the behavioral approach to persons in need, several additional concepts must be considered (see Table 7.1).

Generalization is the tendency to perform a response in a new setting because of the setting's similarity to the one in which the response was learned, with the likelihood of the response's occurring being proportional to the degree of similarity between settings. For example, a child is bitten by an angry dog. For quite some time after the experience, the child probably will generalize fear to all dogs, even those that behave in a friendly manner.

Discrimination is the learning of different responses to two or more similar but distinct stimuli because of the different consequences associated with each one. Using the previous example, the child bitten by an aggressive dog first may become frightened by dogs in general. The child may then learn to discriminate

TABLE 7.1   Behavioral Concepts

| | *Process* | | |
Concept	Event or Behavior	Consequence	Outcome
Generalization	Child bitten by dog	Emotional reaction	Fear generalizes to all dogs
Discrimination	General fear of dogs	Encounters friendly dogs (wagging tail, etc.)	Fears snarling dogs or does not fear friendly dogs (discriminates)
Punishment	Child swears at parent	Parent slaps	Swearing decreases
Positive reinforcement	Temper tantrum	Parental attention	More tantrums
Withdrawal of positive reinforcement	Child swears at parent	Parent takes away toys	Swearing decreases
Negative reinforcement	Child picks up clothes	Parent doesn't nag	Picking up clothing occurs more often
Extinction	Temper tantrum	Parent ignores tantrum	Tantrums decrease

between dogs that appear menacing (growling, barking, baring teeth) and those that appear friendly (wagging the tail, offering a paw). The child fears the first and approaches the second, even though the stimuli are similar—both dogs of the same breed and color.

Punishment is the presentation of an unpleasant or aversive stimulus in order to decrease a particular behavior. The occurrence of an unpleasant stimulus leads to the suppression of a behavior. For example, a child who slaps a parent is likely to receive an immediate unpleasant response (a scolding, a spanking), which will, other things being equal, reduce the likelihood of that behavior's recurring.

Positive reinforcement is any consequence of a behavior that increases the probability that a behavior will occur more frequently. As noted previously, a positive reinforcer may appear to be unpleasant, although most positive reinforcers are pleasant events or things, such as money, candy, praise, status, and attention.

Withdrawal of positive reinforcement takes place when a behavior occurs and the usual reinforcement is not offered or is taken away. This is a common strategy in everyday life. A child who misbehaves is not allowed the reinforcement of watching television.

Negative reinforcement is a somewhat tricky concept. It means that the probability of a behavior is increased by the termination of an aversive (unpleasant or painful) stimulus. For example, a child constantly drops his or her clothing on the floor wherever the clothes are taken off. The parent continually nags the child about this behavior (nagging is the aversive stimulus). Finally, the child does pick up some articles of clothing and puts them in their proper place, and the parent doesn't nag (termination of the aversive stimulus). The termination of the aversive stimulus is a reinforcer because it increases the probability of a behavior (picking up clothing), but it is negative (something is subtracted; i.e., the aversive stimulus). Therefore, it is called "negative" reinforcement. Negative reinforcement *is not* the act of applying something that is negative, like a punishment.

Extinction is the absence of reinforcement. If a behavior is being reinforced and the reinforcement stops, eventually the behavior occurs less often and, if the reinforcement does not occur for a long enough period, disappears completely. Be aware however, that when extinction is first begun, the behavior to be extinguished is likely to occur with greater frequency first and then, after some time has passed, will decrease in frequency until extinguished. This initial increase is known as an *extinction burst*.

Although these concepts or procedures appear relatively simple, their effective use requires a great deal of attention to detail and consistency in application. The operant behavior must be clearly defined, the steps leading to change must be clearly specified, and the reinforcement approach must be consistently applied.

Social

Social and cognitive models of learned behavior accept many of the theories of the classical and operant models; their contributions to the understanding of learned behavior have been primarily additive. Social learning theorists such as Albert

Bandura (1977, 1982) have stressed the importance of both environmental reinforcers and internal processes. For example, people seem to be able to learn
without external reinforcers in a process called *modeling* or *observational learning*.
The process occurs because people make a mental or cognitive image of behavior
that later can be copied in physical behavior. In this process, trial and error plays
a negligible role, although reinforced practice refines the behavioral skills. Social
learning theorists believe that the complexity of human behavior precludes the
shaping of each single response through differential reinforcement. In their view,
some other learning processes, such as modeling, must be operative.

Cognitive

Cognitive learning theorists go a step further in emphasizing the importance of
internal processes in learning. Theorists such as Donald Meichenbaum (1977)
emphasize the importance of cognitive events that influence behavior, such as
thoughts, talking to oneself, mental images, self-evaluations, feelings, memories,
and beliefs. The views of social and cognitive learning theorists have led to a more
integrated perspective on human learned behavior. One way of describing this
theory is as a process of reciprocal determinism. Specific behaviors learned
through reinforcement are influenced by the environment and influence cognition, and cognitions affect how people perceive the environment and behave.
Thus, human behavior is viewed as the result of both internal and external factors
that influence people according to established principles of learning.

A range of concepts fall under the label of behavioral approaches. In the material that follows, we shall see in addition that a great variety of techniques have
been brought together under the terms *behavior therapy* and *behavior modification*.

Learning Problem Behaviors

How can disordered behavior be learned? One example shows how a child might
learn a fear that later might appear to be a phobia. In a famous experiment during
the 1920s, an eleven-month-old boy named Albert was presented with a white rat,
to which he showed no fear response. Subsequently, when he was given the white
rat, an extremely loud, sudden noise was made, with the effect that "the infant
jumped violently and fell forward, burying his face in the mattress." Within a
small number of such pairings of the white rat and the unpleasant stimulus of the
loud noise, the presentation of the white rat alone led the infant to react in a terrified manner. Later investigation revealed that Albert's fear had generalized to
rabbits, dogs, and fur coats, and his fear continued after one month with no inter-
vening presentation of the rat or other furry objects.

An additional example of the development of deviant behavior through learning can be seen in the area of crime and delinquency. Many criminals or delinquents
spend their lives in an environment that supports criminal behavior. They are reinforced by the material rewards of their activities (money, possessions) and by the

social approval of associates and friends. But what about the delinquent who comes from a "good" family in the middle or upper class? Here also, delinquency may be a rewarding behavior in that it is certainly a powerful attention-getting device for individuals who feel neglected by their parents. It is, of course, not that simple. In fact, in most cases of delinquent behavior, one must consider the complete variety of behaviors that have been reinforced in a family setting for many years, and the environmental and social reinforcers that the adolescent experiences.

To date, behavioral explanations have been proposed and utilized in the treatment of a broad spectrum of problems, including anxiety, passivity, obsessive-compulsive disorders, depression, alcoholism, criminal behavior, severe mental disorder, and problematic behaviors in the elderly. A variety of behavioral treatments have been developed to deal with such disorders, and a high level of treatment effectiveness has been reported. Space limitations preclude examining the full spectrum of techniques; however, a representative sample of the current behavioral approaches are described in the section that follows.

Representative Behavioral Treatment Approaches

Two general classes of behavioral treatment approaches have been developed. Techniques focus specifically on problems that an *individual* experiences, such as a phobia, passivity, obsessive behavior, obesity, or self-mutilating behavior, or techniques deal with problems from a *group-system* focus, such as so-called token economies in institutional settings or in community group residential settings.

Individually Focused Programs

Systematic Desensitization
Systematic desensitization is a treatment technique designed to help a client overcome irrational fear (phobia) or anxiety reactions to objects or situations. Phobic reactions are presumed to be a result of some traumatic experience in a situation or with an object similar to the one that precipitates the later reaction. In the case of Albert, the original phobic stimulus was a white rat, but the reaction later generalized to a fear of furry objects. Usually the degree of fear or anxiety experienced is directly related to quantitative aspects of the situation: The closer one is to it, the greater the fear. Phobias can be quite disabling. For example, individuals who have a strong fear of elevators would be very disabled if fear prevented them from getting to their workplace on the twenty-fifth floor of an office building.

The process of systematic desensitization is based on the inability of an individual to be both anxious and relaxed at the same time. The goal is to enable the individual to be relaxed (a competing response) rather than anxious in the presence of the phobia situation. Wolpe (1961), an early proponent of the approach, proposes that a response (relaxation) that inhibits anxiety in the presence of the phobic stimulus will weaken the connection between the stimulus and anxiety. This is called the principle of *reciprocal inhibition*.

Treatment of a phobia begins with training in relaxation and the development of an anxiety hierarchy. Clients learn progressive deep relaxation through a process of alternately tensing and relaxing muscle groups. This enables clients to discriminate between feelings of tension and relaxation so that they can learn to relax more completely. The training occurs, of course, under the supervision of a therapist but is structured so that clients can practice the procedure at home.

Along with the relaxation training, the therapist and client create an anxiety hierarchy. The client describes a wide variety of situations related to the phobia and then subjectively rates them according to the degree of distress caused by each one. Ordinarily, twenty to thirty situations are described and ranked from least distressful to most distressful. An individual phobic to dogs, for example, might rank looking at a picture of a puppy as least distressful and standing next to a snarling German shepherd as most distressful, with twenty items ranked between them according to level of distress.

Once the relaxation process is learned and the hierarchy created, the process of desensitization begins. The therapist asks the client to imagine the stimuli, beginning with the least distressful. When tension begins to develop, the client engages in the relaxation procedure to dissipate the anxiety. Repeated presentation of the imagined stimulus with no evoked anxiety decreases its tension-eliciting potential. As the stimulus is counterconditioned, the process generalizes to other stimuli of the hierarchy. The process then moves on to the next higher level of the hierarchy.

After a number of desensitization sessions, the client can ordinarily move up to the highest levels of the hierarchy without experiencing any anxiety. Ultimately, the individual can confront the real-life situations without experiencing the original phobic response. Some therapists, however, believe that the desensitization does not necessarily generalize to the real-life setting. They believe that the therapist must continue to take clients one step further—that is, accompany them into the actual concrete situation and continue desensitization at that point.

Impressive success rates have been consistently reported with the use of this technique to treat phobias. Wolpe (1961) reports that 91 percent of clients were significantly improved after eleven or twelve sessions. In a study on college students who were phobic to public speaking, systematic desensitization proved more effective than attention placebos and insight therapy, and the results were maintained in a two-year follow-up study (Paul, 1967). Systematic desensitization has become a common technique among behaviorists for the treatment of a wide variety of anxiety- and stress-related disorders. The technique can be used as effectively by paraprofessionals as by professionals.

Operant Approaches to an Individual Problem

The operant approach is concerned with the effects or consequences of behaviors on the environment. Treatment involves controlling the consequences of a behavior in an attempt to change that behavior. Through the control of the consequences (rewards), the behavior can be modified. The process is best illustrated through a case example. A famous case illustrating these principles, reported by Bachrach, Erwin, and Mohr (1968), deals with the disorder known as anorexia nervosa.

Anorexia nervosa consists of an extreme refusal to eat or the regurgitation of food to the extent that a severe weight loss occurs. In extreme situations, the problem is life-threatening. Individuals have been known to become so weakened as to die from complications of the debilitation. In the case being described, the patient, at the age of thirty-seven, had slowly lost weight during a period of seventeen years, reducing from a weight of 118 pounds to 47 pounds at the point of hospitalization. On admission, she was completely weakened, suffered from severe malnutrition, and could not stand erect without assistance. A complete physical examination revealed no physiological cause for her inability to eat; instead, it seemed to be psychologically determined.

The treatment program was based on the assumption that her inability (or refusal) to eat was a result of her noneating behavior being *rewarded* (reinforced) by family, friends, and medical staff in previous situations. She was obtaining immediate gains (attention, pity, solicitude) that were more rewarding than the negative consequences of her behavior in terms of ill health. Treatment consisted of placing her in a room devoid of all previous sources of reward. There were no magazines, no radio, no television, no books, and no one to chat with. The restoration of all these pleasant activities became *contingent* on her eating.

The therapist aimed to shape the patient's behavior specifically in the direction of eating. To do this, the therapist broke the process into steps: (1) presenting food, (2) touching a utensil (fork, spoon, etc.), (3) picking up a utensil, (4) picking up food with a utensil, (5) placing food in mouth, (6) chewing, (7) swallowing, and (8) eating increasing amounts of food. At each step, the patient was rewarded by social contact, watching television, praise, or some other desirable (for her) reinforcement. Following implementation of the program, the patient was soon eating normally, and the reinforcers became contingent on weight gain. By the end of the program, the patient's weight had increased to eighty-eight pounds. We now know that operant behavior therapy is useful in the early stages of treating anorexia, but that the best success occurs when it is combined with family therapy.

Another operant approach is used with children who have a problem controlling aggression. Patterson (1971) has become known for his work in this area. School officials and parents see aggressive behavior in children as a particularly important problem. In Patterson's program, parents are taught to observe and record both the child's problem behavior (aggression) and the parents' own reaction to it. It usually turns out that the parents attend more to the disruptions than to the child's positive behaviors.

In the next phase of the program, the parents are taught how to change the contingencies of the child's behavior; that is, they are taught to react differently to the aggression. Frequently, as simple a change as ignoring the aggression and emphatically rewarding competing behaviors (such as cooperative play) results in eliminating or decreasing the aggression. Programs such as Patterson's have been remarkably successful in a variety of settings. In his original work, Patterson reported that the frequency of aggressive behavior was reduced 60 percent in children treated by the method. Of particular interest for the human service worker is that the actual treatment was administered by the parents and, in similar programs, by classroom teachers rather than by a formally trained therapist. In

dealing with children's behavior, school teachers and teacher aides can be particularly effective at using simple behavior therapy techniques (Kaplan, 1998).

Cognitive-Behavioral Approaches

Cognitive-behavioral therapists attempt to improve the client's awareness of
negative self-statements. They focus on teaching the client to use problem-
solving and coping skills and on (1) client's behaviors and the reactions they
elicit; (2) client's internal speech, or what they say to themselves before, during,
and following the behavior; and (3) the cognitive factors (feelings, beliefs, and
attitudes) that give rise to the internal dialogue.

At the beginning of cognitive-behavioral therapy, the therapist encourages the
client to become a self-observer. The client must identify problem behaviors,
thoughts, and reactions in need of change. In the second phase, the client is helped
to create new cognitions, especially inner speech or self-talk, that are incompatible
with the old self-defeating cognitions. In the third phase, the client is trained to
produce new behaviors, first in the therapy session and then in the everyday
world. As the client's new behaviors are trained and practiced, the therapist rein-
forces them and the new inner speech. The extensive rehearsal of new behaviors
distinguishes this approach from simple "positive thinking." Without extensive
reinforced practice, thinking positively is unlikely to have a powerful effect on
behavior. Table 7.2 lists examples of positive self-talk used to train clients who
need help in dealing with stress.

Group-System Focused Programs

Token Economies

The token economy is a system for redesigning total environments to make them
supportive of positive or socially desirable behaviors and capable of extinguish-
ing negative, maladaptive, or socially undesirable behaviors. The initial project of
this type had the goal of improving the functioning of patients on a ward in a
mental hospital. Other workers have since designed and implemented token
economies in settings such as correctional facilities, juvenile detention settings,
and a host of other types of institutional facilities.

The worker develops the token economy by identifying desired behaviors
ranging from those of quite low level (such as brushing teeth, combing hair,
dressing, wearing clothes, proper toileting, and eating with utensils) to those of
a higher level (such as attending meetings, performing work activities, holding
logical conversations, and other activities that make up responsible behavior). A
reward system is then set up in which engaging in a desired behavior entitles the
subject to an immediate reward of a plastic token or paper chit that is redeemable
for material goods such as clothing, magazines, toilet articles, food, drink, or a
variety of other items, including special privileges. In addition, a system of fines
is organized through which the subject may lose tokens for engaging in inappropriate behavior (which is specifically defined) or failing to perform a required task

TABLE 7.2   Self-Talk Rehearsed in Cognitive-Behavioral Therapy
for Dealing with Stress

Preparing for Stress

What is it I have to do?
I can develop a plan to deal with it.
Just think about what I can do about it. That's better than getting anxious.
No negative self-statements: Just think rationally.
Don't worry: Worry won't help anything.
Maybe what I think is anxiety is eagerness to confront the stress.

Confronting and Handling Stress

Just "psych" myself up.
I can convince myself to do it. I can reason my fear away.
One step at a time: I can handle the situation.
Don't think about fear; just think about what I have to do. Stay relevant.
This anxiety is what the therapist said I would feel. It's a reminder to use my coping exercises.
This tenseness can be an ally: a cue to cope.
Relax; I'm in control. Take a slow deep breath.

Dealing with the Feeling of Being Overwhelmed

When fear comes, just pause.
Keep the focus on the present; what is it I have to do?
I should expect my fear to rise.
Don't try to eliminate fear totally; just keep it manageable.

Reinforcing Self-Statements

It worked; I did it.
Wait until I tell my therapist about this.
It wasn't as bad as I expected.
I made more out of my fear than it was worth.
My damn ideas—they're the problem. When I control them, I control my fear.
I can be pleased with the progress I'm making.
I did it!

(Corrigan, McCracken, and Mehr, 1995). Table 7.3 illustrates the types of reinforcement and punishment (fines) that are used for specific problem behaviors in
a community group home.

One may argue that such systems of reward and punishment have existed
before in institutional settings. That is true, but the major differentiation between
the primitive, personalistic systems that existed previously and the token economy is the tremendous emphasis on detail, specificity, and particularly *consistency*
in the token economy programs. Such a brief presentation can hardly do justice to
the involved intricacies of the token economy. Interested students may refer to the
many published works that deal with this subject in depth. It can be reported,

TABLE 7.3   Problems and Behavioral Interventions in a
            Community Group Residence

Problem Behavior	Behavioral Intervention
Bill often urinates in the grass outside the group home.	Bill receives 25 points for showing a staff person that he urinated in the toilet. Bill is fined 10 points for urinating in the yard.
Whenever she sees her case manager, Betty nags him about leaving the hospital.	Betty gets 50 points for writing a request for discharge in the unit log book. She also gets case manager attention and time during the appointment. The case manager ignores Betty when she talks about discharge at any other time. The case manager *does* attend to and talk briefly with Betty about any other topic.
Art brings his lighted cigarette into the bedroom when he reads there.	Art gets 25 points for putting out his cigarette in the ashtray in the outdoor smoking area. He loses one smoking privilege time for bringing a lighted cigarette inside.

however, that as a management system, the token economy has no equal. Impressive evidence exists indicating that a wide variety of strange and bizarre behaviors can be extinguished through its use (Kazdin, 1982).

Token economies are particularly helpful for people who have been institutionalized for many years and have lost most of the self-care skills one takes for granted, including personal hygiene behaviors, eating with a fork and knife, wearing clothing, and appropriate toileting. Programs that combine token reinforcements with training in social skills may be particularly beneficial. Such training involves direct instruction, modeling, performance feedback, and role-playing experiences. It has been effective even with severely disturbed psychiatric patients (Scott and Dixon, 1995). When such group programs are combined with individual treatment focusing on the problem behaviors of individuals, dramatic changes in behavior can occur.

Other Group Approaches

In addition to token economies, which use an operant behavioral approach, the cognitive-behavioral approaches have been used more widely in recent years to deal with persons in groups (Linehan, 1993; Thyer, 1988). For example, Nardone, Tryon, and O'Connor (1986) have reported on a cognitive-behavioral group treatment for reducing impulsive-aggressive behavior in adolescent boys in a residential setting. Ten boys were treated in two groups (five boys in each group) for thirteen sessions over six weeks. Each session was fifty minutes. The first five minutes consisted of an orientation period in which three rules were covered: (1) don't hurt yourself, (2) don't hurt others, and (3) don't damage property. The next ten minutes were spent in a relaxation exercise. The following ten minutes was "talk time." The therapist taught the boys problem-solving skills in a picture story format: (1) defining the problem, (2) developing plans or solutions, (3) acting on plans and solutions, and (4) evaluating the outcome of the action taken. The next twenty-minute period was devoted to a group game or project designed to elicit situations like those presented in "talk time." The therapist spent the final five minutes reviewing the hour with each boy and giving, for positive behavior, reward points that could be exchanged for tangible reinforcers. During the last two weeks, boys could pool their reward points to obtain a group trip (disco roller skating), to emphasize the consequences of each boy's behavior for the group as a whole.

During the course of the project, the frequency of impulsive-aggressive behavior on the part of the boys declined dramatically. During a follow-up period, the therapist discovered, however, that the positive gains slowly eroded and had disappeared within five weeks. This finding emphasizes the need for maintenance reinforcement programs after active behavior therapy programs. The need for follow-up intervention is a common finding with many behavioral approaches.

The Effectiveness of Behavioral Strategies

To some extent, the effectiveness of the behavioral strategies has been considered in the description of the various modalities in this chapter. A major asset of the behavioral strategies is that a majority of their proponents are thoroughly indoctrinated in the scientific method and tend to be extremely concerned with proving whether the techniques work. This has led to a situation in which a large number of controlled studies preponderantly support the claims of significant behavior change from the techniques. These results are in contrast to the usually anecdotal evaluations of the less structured strategies, such as psychotherapy.

Although behavioral approaches to changing human behavior are among the most studied and evaluated, and are demonstrably effective, they have often been criticized as being too mechanistic, and as lacking in "humanism." In reply, proponents argue that effective behavioral treatment is actually empowering for clients, and that it promotes independent decision-making skills. Behavioral interventions:

- provide a setting in which people can consider life decisions;
- reduce the confusing complexity of choices that comprise many of the needed decisions;
- help the person learn behaviors that assist in independent decision making and living;
- teach family members skills, so they can provide more effective support of independent decisions; and
- facilitate self-control over behaviors and the setting in which they occur (Corrigan, 1997).

The effectiveness of the behavioral approaches seems well documented, particularly for clients who have behavior problems that we know can be modified by behavioral techniques. In situations in which the clients' problems seem more global and less easily compartmentalized, other forms of intervention may be more appropriate.

Summary

1. The behavioral approaches to people in need are among the most recently developed therapies. They are concerned more with observable behavior than with underlying causes. Human problems are viewed as primarily learned behavior patterns.

2. If the reinforcement contingencies are modified or counterresponses to learned behavior are conditioned, problem behavior can be extinguished or modified in positive patterns, or entirely new behaviors can be created.

3. Four major conceptualizations of learned behavior have been developed: classical learning theory, operant learning theory, social learning theory, and cognitive learning theory.

4. Several major concepts important in learning theory have been introduced: conditioning, reinforcement, generalization, discrimination, and punishment.

5. Systematic desensitization can be applied effectively to individuals. It has been used successfully in helping clients overcome irrational fears or anxiety reactions.

6. The operant approaches to individual behavioral problems involve controlling the reinforcers in a person's environment. Through control of the reinforcers or modification of the consequences of behavior, the behavior can be changed.

7. Cognitive-behavioral interventions focus on changing behavior through changing cognitive events such as feelings and thoughts, in addition to reinforcing actual behaviors.

8. The token economy is a group-focused behavioral approach. It is a system for redesigning total environments. In token economies, a system of rewards for desirable behaviors and fines for undesired behaviors is maintained consistently.

9. In recent years, the cognitive-behavioral approaches have been used with people in groups with some reasonable success.

10. The behavioral approaches have been effective in helping human service clients. They seem to be efficient.

Discussion Questions

1. Which learning model seems most relevant to human behavior: classical, operant, social, or cognitive? Why?

2. Discuss the concept that "the world is an unplanned token economy."

Learning Experiences

1. Try to identify learned behaviors in your pet. For example, does your dog bother you when you eat?

2. Can you think of behaviors you engage in because they are reinforced?

Recommended Readings

Corrigan, P. W., McCracken, S., & Mehr, J. (1995). *Practice guidelines for extended psychiatric residential care: From chaos to collaboration.* Springfield, IL: Charles C. Thomas.

Follette, V. M., Ruzek, J. I., & Abueg, F. R. (Eds.). (1998). *Cognitive-behavioral therapies for trauma.* New York: The Guilford Press.

Kaplan, J. S. (1998). *Beyond behavior modification: A cognitive-behavioral approach to behavior management in school* (3rd ed.). Austin, TX: Pro-Ed.

Kazdin, A. E. (1989). *Behavior modification in applied settings* (4th ed.). Pacific Grove, CA: Brooks/Cole.

8

Psychotherapy
and the Person in Need

- What are the basic assumptions of the psychotherapeutic approaches to human problems?
- What are the common components of the different types of psychotherapy?
- What are the basic concepts of psychoanalysis?
- What are the characteristics of client-centered therapy?
- Are there advantages to group psychotherapy?
- What is family therapy?
- Does psychotherapy work?

Novice human service workers are not equipped to effectively engage in formal psychotherapy. To do so requires an extensive specialized training and supervision that goes beyond most basic human services training programs. However, when specifically trained to do psychotherapy, human service generalists can be as effective at it as psychotherapists from other professions. The beginning human service worker is likely to work with professionals who do engage in psychotherapy, or with clients who have had, or are in, psychotherapy with another trained professional. Thus, it is important for all human service workers to have some familiarity with systems of formal psychotherapy. All human service workers can and do use many psychotherapeutic concepts and techniques in their work with clients. These concepts, some of which are introduced in this chapter, are also addressed in Chapter 9.

Psychotherapeutic approaches assume that a large proportion of people's problems result from the internal psychology (thinking and emotion) of the individual. Within this broad generalization, there are a variety of approaches to human behavior and ideas about it, from psychoanalysis to gestalt theory. Taking into consideration the major approaches and their many variations, as well as the numerous less common approaches, literally hundreds of different systems exist. Despite the many different approaches, most hold a similar set of assumptions. The following six assumptions constitute the basic framework out of which adherents of these approaches function:

1. Psychological distress or behavioral disturbance is a function of problems in the subject's personality structure.
2. The function of internal psychological processes is more important in determining behavior than the subject's current environment.
3. Usually, past experiences are more important than current experiences in determining behavior or personality because of either the sheer amount of past experiences or the special significance of past experiences, particularly those of childhood.
4. Behavior is overdetermined; that is, the basic personality structure (including problem areas) is so powerful that individual acts of will that focus on changing ingrained patterns (such as New Year's resolutions) are ineffective.
5. There is an optimum personality structure that allows individuals to deal effectively with the environment in a manner that maintains an optimal level of satisfaction.
6. If individuals have not reached the optimal level of personality structure and are experiencing difficulties, they often can be helped to grow through a process of relating to a trained helper who understands human development. This relationship process is almost always verbal.

The helping process these approaches use is called *psychotherapy*. Even though the various subsystems differ in their theoretical formulations of behavior and therapeutic approaches, a number of common elements are apparent.

Two major continuums on which the approaches range are the degree of directiveness and the degree of intensiveness of the process. Psychoanalysis, for example, is considered to be a directive therapy. The determination of issues, such as the content of therapy, its length, and its goals, is more the province of the therapist than of the subject (the therapist directs the client). By contrast, Rogerian client-centered therapy is nondirective; the client or subject has a greater influence in determining its content, length, and goals (the therapist is more a helper than a healer). In addition to the directiveness continuum, one can describe the difference in intensity of the various processes, ranging from five-times-a-week sessions as in traditional psychoanalysis to once-a-week sessions as in most client-centered processes. Despite such differences, certain common elements do appear. Harper (1960) summarizes the common components of psychotherapy along the following lines.

1. One or more persons (clients) have some awareness of neglected or mishandled life problems.

2. One or more persons (therapists) exist with relative lack of disturbance who perceive the distress of the clients and believe themselves capable of helping the clients reduce distress.
3. There is a positive regard of client for therapist and vice versa.
4. The therapist has understanding of and empathy for the client.
5. The client perceives the positive regard for and empathic understanding of him or her by the therapist.
6. The therapist provides corrective information for the client regarding his or her environment.
7. The therapist assists the client in achieving a better self-evaluation.
8. The therapist provides a setting in which the client can experience emotional venting (catharsis).
9. There is a gradually increasing number of tasks for the client to perform between therapy sessions in terms of applying new information about him- or herself and his or her environment.
10. There is a gradual process by which the client learns to become independent of the therapist.

With so many varieties of psychotherapy in existence, it would be impossible to deal with each in depth. In the following pages, let's examine two major approaches that have been cornerstones of the psychotherapy field: psychoanalysis and Rogerian client-centered therapy. We'll also review briefly a number of newer approaches and consider several structural variations, such as group and family therapy.

Psychoanalysis

Psychoanalysis is the grandfather of the current psychotherapies. It was introduced by Sigmund Freud in the 1890s. Freud first treated his patients with hypnosis but later abandoned it for a technique he discovered called *free association.* In this technique, patients are instructed to say whatever comes into their minds without concern for its relevance. No limits are put on what they talk about. In this process, the early experiences of patients and their deeper attitudes and ideas are revealed to themselves and to the analyst. As free association continues, the analyst is particularly concerned about childhood experiences that determine later personality reactions and about the unconscious mind—that part of the mind into which the memories of many early experiences are pushed out of awareness, particularly painful experiences, and from which they still have an effect in determining the individual's reaction patterns. In psychoanalysis, the ability of patients to be well comes through their awareness of the unconscious forces in their personalities and their ability to bring those forces into an orderly arrangement so that they have control over them.

Somewhat similar to free association is the study of dreams. Freud assumed that ego defenses are lowered during sleep and allow repressed material to be expressed symbolically in dream content. The materials are expressed in disguised symbolism because the repressed material is very threatening to the conscious mind. The analyst's role is to assist patients in interpreting the true meaning of the dream symbols.

As unconscious material appears, both in free association and in dreams, the analyst uses the technique of interpretation. Because the goal is to help patients face their repressed and emotion-laden conflicts, the analyst begins to point out to patients the underlying sources of resistance to awareness. If the interpretations are correct and appropriately timed, patients can begin to examine their problems from the perspective of their current reality. They can begin to realize that they no longer must fear their impulses, and this realization leads to a further relaxation of defenses.

Psychoanalysis makes use of *transference.* Transference is the tendency, considered to exist in all human beings, to relate or transfer historical emotions and attitudes developed in childhood to people in the present-day, immediate environment. An example is the person with unresolved childhood difficulties in dealing with a parent, who transfers these residual feelings onto current authority figures such as bosses, teachers, police, and others and behaves toward them as he or she did toward the parent. The transference feelings the patient experiences toward the analyst, both positive and negative, are strong motivations for the patient. The analyst uses these positive feelings to promote change and interprets the negative feelings to assist patients in understanding their origin in early life experiences. As patients begin to understand the origins of these negative feelings, they can work toward making the feelings more positive.

A major factor in analysis is the reenactment of highly emotional, previously repressed childhood memories and feelings, as they are remembered by the patient. The discharge of these repressed emotions and the development of *insight* (understanding of their infantile origin) is called *abreaction.* The reexperiencing of the emotions and the development of insight under the direction of the analyst are considered major factors in the development of personality changes.

In the following excerpt from Wolberg (1977), an analyst deals with transference feeling in the patient. Through judicious questioning and interpretation by the analyst, the patient suddenly discovers something about how her early childhood experiences and feelings influence her current behavior and feelings.

Patient: I want to talk about my feelings about you.

Therapist: Mm hmm . . .

Patient: I get so excited by what is happening here, I feel I'm being held back by needing to be nice. I'd like to blast loose sometimes, but I don't dare.

Therapist: Because you fear my reaction?

Patient: The worst thing would be that you wouldn't like me. You wouldn't speak to me friendly; you wouldn't smile; you'd feel you can't treat me and discharge me from treatment. But I know this isn't so, I know it.

Therapist: Where do you think these attitudes come from?

Patient: When I was nine years old, I read a lot about great men in history. I'd quote them and be dramatic. I'd want a sword at my side; I'd dress like an Indian. Mother would scold me. Don't frown, don't talk so much. Sit on your hands, over and over again. I did all kinds of things. I was a naughty child. She told me I'd be hurt. Then at fourteen I fell off a horse and broke my back. I had to be in bed. Mother then told me on the day I went riding not to, that I'd get hurt because the ground was frozen. I was a stubborn, self-willed child. Then I went against her will and suffered an accident that changed my life, a fractured back. Her attitude was, "I told you so." I was put in a cast and kept in bed for months.

Therapist: You were punished, so to speak, by this accident.

Patient: But I gained attention and love from mother for the first time. I felt so good. I'm ashamed to tell you this. Before I healed I opened the cast and tried to walk to make myself sick again so I could stay in bed longer. (*Pause.*)

Therapist: How does that connect up with your impulses to be sick now and stay in bed so much? (*The patient has these tendencies, of which she is ashamed.*)

Patient: Oh . . . (*Pause.*)

Therapist: What do you think?

Patient: Oh, my God, how infantile, how ungrown up (*pause*), it must be so. I want people to love me and be sorry for me. Oh, my God. How completely childish. It is, is that. My mother must have ignored me when I was little, and I wanted so to be loved. (*This sounds like insight.*)

Therapist: So that it may have been threatening to go back to being self-willed and unloved after you got out of the cast. (*Interpretation.*) Perhaps if you go back to being stubborn with me, you would be returning to how you were before; that is, active, stubborn, but unloved.

Patient: (*Excitedly.*) And, therefore, losing your love. I need you, but after all you aren't going to reject me. The pattern is so established now that the threat of the loss of love is too overwhelming with everybody, and I've got to keep myself from acting selfish or angry.[1]

The course of analysis is, however, by no means smooth. Usually the symptoms that lead people to seek help exist as defenses against underlying anxieties, fears of involvement with others, and fears of really knowing oneself. As the process of free association occurs, patients begin to learn about themselves. They defend against this exposure (to the therapist and to themselves) through forces that tend to slow and thus prevent their growing awareness of their internal processes. The analyst must be aware of such resistances and help patients overcome them.

As resistances are overcome and treatment continues, patients become increasingly aware of their immaturities and begin to attempt to change with the support of the analyst. It is assumed that at some level even resistant patients desire to be better. In fact, the desire to improve is considered a universal trait. The healthy parts of patients' personalities are used at this point as strengths to rely on as new behavior patterns are attempted.

In effect, psychoanalysis is a process involving a gradual breaking down of the personality and a rebuilding of it in changed patterns at the same time.

Patients come to understand the structure of their makeup, their relationships with others become more clear, and their efforts to achieve a more functional life-style begin. The analyst holds a mirror to the patients, helps them adopt more mature reaction patterns, interprets their motivations and the composition of their maladaptations, and assists in their attempts to change.

Rogers's Client-Centered Therapy

Carl Rogers's system of therapy is intimately tied to the notion that each individual has basic potentialities for growth and development. The major role of the therapist is to provide an atmosphere in which the client can engage in self-examination, achieve self-understanding, and reorganize perceptions of the world and his or her place in it. Particularly important in understanding behavior is the concept of the phenomenological field. Each person has such a field, which is an understanding of events as that person *perceives* them. An individual's behavior is a reaction to that field as it is uniquely perceived. The field includes self-concepts, experiences, and perceptions, which are admitted to awareness. When the organism denies to awareness the significant experiences (thoughts, feelings, behaviors) that do not fit the self-concept, psychological tension arises, and the experiences are disowned. It is this lack of fit between what a person *is, thinks* he or she is, and *would like to be* that causes an individual to be distressed and to need help.

For Rogers, the most appropriate source of information about the patient is the patient's self-report. Rogers rejects the notion that true motivation is unconscious and unavailable to self-awareness. Rogerians place little emphasis on dreams, slips of the tongue, and free association. Rather than being concerned with the symbolism of what the client says, the Rogerian is more concerned with creating an atmosphere that is nonthreatening, in which the client can self-explore and try new behavior without fear of rejection or ridicule. The *relationship* is more critical than what is said, and the therapist must have empathy and positive regard for the client and must be genuine.

In addition to empathy, genuineness, and positive regard, characteristic activities of Rogerian therapists (Harper, 1960) include:

1. The therapist makes strong, consistent efforts to understand the client's content of speech and feelings as conveyed by words, gestures, and expressions.
2. The therapist makes an effort to communicate this understanding to the client by words or by a general attitude of acceptance.
3. There is an occasional presentation of a condensation or synthesis of expressed feelings.
4. There are occasional statements on the nature and limits of the therapeutic relationship, the participants' expectations of the situation, and the therapist's confidence in the patient's ability to handle their problems.
5. Question answering and data giving are denied when they seem likely to increase the patient's dependency.

6. Interpretations are avoided unless they are summary in nature.
7. The therapist does not try to promote insight directly, give advice, praise, blame, teach, or otherwise direct the client.

Client-centered therapy is a process of disorganization and reorganization of the self. The primary goal is to assist clients in developing a more accurate conception of a much wider range of sensory experiences based on their own system of values rather than on a system of values borrowed from parents or other significant figures. Clients are able, in effect, to take themselves apart and put themselves back together in a more functional structure, because their contradictory attitudes and behaviors are completely accepted by the therapist.

The experiences of the clients during client-centered therapy are illustrated in the following comments by people who have actually experienced sessions with a client-centered therapist.

Exploring Oneself

■■ At first the inconsistencies between what I felt about myself (and said in the counseling session) and what I thought about myself were the most annoying. I was enjoying the feeling of being honest for the first time, and I didn't like this apparent evidence of untruth.

Discovering Denied Attitudes

■■ I began to think and actually admit things to myself that I had never considered admitting before. I began to see just what was at the root of all my actions.

Reorganization of the Self

■■ Now, after four visits, I have a much clearer picture of my self and my future. It makes me feel a little depressed and disappointed, but on the other hand, it has taken me out of the dark, the load seems a lot lighter now, that is I can see my way now. . . .

Experiencing Progress

■■ It's wonderful how relaxed I can get talking about ideas I couldn't even think about last year, things that just require saying, getting rid of. Last year I kept thinking what a pleasant way out illness would be. This year in my daydreams when the same thing happens I say, "Hell, no, that's not what I want."[2]

From these client reports, the process of client-centered, or nondirective, therapy can be summarized as a series of progressive stages. At first, clients are enabled to explore the discrepancies among their words, attitudes, feelings, and behaviors. Then, clients begin to discover aspects of themselves that have been denied to conscious awareness. With the nonjudgmental, caring support of the therapist, clients then begin to reorganize their experiences into a new and more functional self-concept and discover that progress is being made. Clients finally have new adaptive skills that will help make future behaviors and experiences more satisfying and productive. Rogers et al. (1967) characterize the essence of the therapeutic process as follows:

> *As he finds someone listening to him with consistent acceptance while he expresses his thoughts and feelings, the client, little by little, becomes increasingly able to listen to communications from within himself; he becomes able to realize that he is angry, or that he is frightened, or that he is experiencing feelings of love. . . . As he reveals these hidden and "awful" aspects of himself, he finds that the therapist's regard for him remains unshaken. And, slowly, he moves toward adopting the same attitude toward himself, toward accepting himself in the process of becoming. Finally, as the client is able to listen to more of himself, he moves toward greater congruence, toward expressing all of himself more openly. He is, at last, free to change and grow in the directions which are natural to the human organism.*

Rogers (1957) has described what he feels are the necessary and sufficient conditions to bring about personality change:

1. A psychological contract must be present; that is, both the client and the therapist must be aware of the presence of each other.
2. The client senses a difference between his or her experiences and his or her self-concept.
3. The therapist's experiences support his or her own self-concept.
4. The therapist experiences unconditional positive regard for the client.
5. The therapist experiences an empathic understanding of the client's percepts of his or her own experiences and tries to communicate this empathy to the client.
6. The client *experiences* the therapist as being empathic and having positive regard.

Client-centered therapy has become quite popular since its inception in the late 1940s. Harper (1960) suggests a number of reasons: It fits our democratic tradition that the client is treated as an equal; it appeals to the inexperienced therapist because of its apparent (and deceptive) simplicity; it promises to be a quicker route to personality change than psychoanalysis; and it is American in origin rather than foreign. In the next chapter, it will be seen that client-centered therapy has contributed much to the human services approach.

Transactional Analysis and Gestalt Therapy

The psychotherapies described in this section appear to have fewer followers among the helping professions than the two major approaches that have just been described. These alternative approaches are no less complicated, well developed, or conceptualized than any other, nor do they promise to be any less effective than psychoanalysis or client-centered therapy.

Transactional Analysis

Developed by Eric Berne (1966) as an outgrowth of his experience in group psychotherapy during World War II, the basic concepts of transactional analysis (TA) were first formally published in 1957. The major focus of TA is on an approach to interactional psychology—an approach centering on the interaction processes between two or more persons. As a therapy, it is a contractual form of treatment in which individuals specify as clearly as possible what they want to achieve in the therapeutic relationship. The therapists accept or reject the contract, depending on whether they think it likely that assistance can be provided.

The therapist is an expert in structural analysis, transactional analysis, and script analysis. *Structural analysis* is a fundamental system for describing and analyzing the three basic ego states: parent, adult, and child. Major communication and interaction problems can exist when different states of the egos of different persons determine the content of messages.

For example, as indicated by the solid lines in Figure 8.1, appropriate communication at the adult level would be as follows.

Initiation: "Let's go to the movies." (adult to adult)
Response: "Okay, that would be fun." (adult to adult)

Distorted (crossed) communication or interaction, as indicated by the dotted lines, would be:

Initiation: "Let's go to the movies." (adult to adult)
Response: "All you ever think about is goofing off." (parent to child)

The analysis of such transactions between persons is, of course, *transactional analysis.* Transactions can be grouped in the categories of (1) withdrawal, (2) ritual, (3) pastimes, (4) games, (5) activities, and (6) intimacy. The purpose of transaction is considered to be the satisfaction of needs such as the need for strokes (unit of recognition), the need for structuring time, and the need for excitement. The needs can be satisfied through the six types of transactions; however, the lower-numbered ones are safer, whereas the higher-numbered ones not only are riskier in that they demand more vulnerability to others, but also satisfy more effectively. According to Berne's theory, transactional analysis attempts to give clients the opportunity to *choose* their types of transactions.

Script analysis is a process of assessing the predominant themes in a person's life. A "life script" manifests a decision made by a person as to how he or she spends his or her life. The decision, however, is usually made at an early age, without conscious awareness, and based on simplistic or distorted data. The determinants of the life script include how people see and value themselves

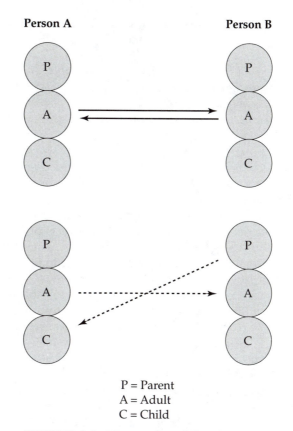

P = Parent
A = Adult
C = Child

FIGURE 8.1   Transactional Ego States

and others in terms of "OK-ness." The TA analyst attempts to assist the client in getting free from self-defeating *scripts* and developing an autonomous self-chosen life-style that can flexibly be changed at any time to a more interesting and rewarding pattern and that allows true intimacy with another person.

Transactional analysis as a total system uses many techniques common to most forms of therapy: querying, reflection, self-analysis, interpretation, modeling, owning up to behavior, homework assignments, and reinforcing (stroking) of positive behavior. Its particular uniqueness includes its emphasis on the group technique and its particular pop language: *parent, adult,* and *child* for ego states; *scripts;* and the names of the games that people play, such as *rapo* and *kick-me.* Its use of everyday language and pop terms has made its concepts popular.

Gestalt Therapy

Gestalt therapy is the creation of Frederick Perls, a physician-psychologist whose concepts were developed in the 1950s. It is a highly experiential approach with little theory, at times seeming very philosophical in its premises. A colleague of Perls, Walter Kempler (1973), exemplifies this approach in his description of *man:*

> *Man may be seen as a momentary precipitation at the vortex of a transient eddy of energy, in the enormous and incomprehensible sea of energy we call the universe. . . . Could man order his energy like gravity, magnetic flow, or the laser phenomenon, we might expect him to disappear from tangible view and exist exclusively as the powerful force that is now only his inherent potential.*

The therapeutic process in this system is focused entirely on the here and now. The gestalt therapist cares little for historical or past data about the client. The total focus is on the relationship between the therapist and client and the client's inherent potential for actualization. Problems are seen as caused by one part of the client's personality refusing to accept another part. Positive change occurs when the two parts recognize and come to appreciate each other to the point where they have no conflict or dissatisfaction. To be able to persuade the patient to confront his or her discordant elements, the therapist must have no internal discord.

The major factor for the therapist is to be able to identify the patient's opposing elements and then get the patient to engage the opposites actively in order to bring them to a resolution. The therapist's attributes are concepts similar to those held by Rogerians: positive regard, empathy, and genuineness. However, a major difference in approaches is the gestalt therapist's willingness to *judge* and the patient's presumed expectation of *being judged.* An approval-disapproval continuum develops in which the patient discovers valued behaviors and is helped to relinquish disvalued behaviors. The basic mechanism of this type of therapy is the creation of a situation in which the patient can show himself or herself to another in order to be able to "find" himself or herself.

Prescriptive Psychotherapy

Prescriptive psychotherapy is a treatment approach based on the assumption that therapy is most effective if it is tailored to the specific problem of the client; that is, a particular treatment is "prescribed" for a particular behavior based on the empirical evidence available in the research literature. In contrast, the other types of psychotherapy that have been discussed are broad-spectrum approaches and, within each type, would approach different problems from the same perspective. In prescriptive psychotherapy, different presenting problems may be treated by very different approaches. Prescriptive psychotherapy holds out the promise of being more efficient and more consistently effective than more general approaches (Beutler and Harwood, 1995) (see Box 8.1).

One example of a prescriptive psychotherapy is multimodal therapy (MMT). It was begun as a behaviorally oriented approach by Arnold Lazarus in the 1950s, but over the years it evolved into an approach that utilizes "what works" from a host of other approaches. It identifies seven domains of experience in which problems might appear and a set of treatment approaches for each domain. The domains are organized into the acronym, BASIC-ID (Behavior, Affect, Sensation, Imagery, Cognition, Interpersonal relationship and Drugs and physiological states) (Lazarus, 1981).

The importance of each of the domains in relation to the patient's presenting problem is identified, and treatment procedures selected that are most appro-

---

BOX 8.1   Some Ethnocultural Issues and Psychotherapists

Since the advent of the Black Power Movement in the late 1960s, the treatment issues of African American men have slowly gained some well-deserved attention. African Americans have made an effort to change their relationships with European Americans, reflected by their change in preference for being called Blacks rather than Negroes. For Black men, to be Negro meant to be the bad, messy, aggressive, willful child; to be Black means to be strong, resilient, mature, warm, sincere, honest, forthright, and attractive (Bell, 1996). As African American men strive to meet this ideal, it has implications for therapy goals and for how therapists interact with African American male patients, particularly when the therapist is White and the patient is Black. In such therapy, one goal for the therapist is to help the patient develop a coping style that admits the existence of racism but keeps it from being the dominant force in the Black person's life. In addition, the patient's self-esteem should be enhanced so it cannot be dissolved by narrow racist perceptions (Brantly, 1983).

The literature on the issue of African American men's needs in treatment suggests that any human service worker, but particularly a psychotherapist who is White and working with Black men, needs to:

- Understand and be sensitive to issues of culture, class, family structure, educational levels, and social activities, and avoid stereotyping.
- Understand barriers and frustrations about denied access as well as the need to achieve and be upwardly mobile.
- Understand the need for strong racial and class identity as well as group identification and mutual dependence.
- Be capable of being active and assertive, when appropriate.
- Understand why some African American men distrust people in authority or have transient paranoid, persecutory, and suspicious feelings.
- Understand issues of self-image that some African Americans bring to treatment, including concerns about skin color, hair texture, facial features, and body types.
- Understand the need to explore potential problems of anger, hostility, and self-esteem.
- Understand why some African American men might feel vulnerable and inferior or feel a need to be submissive and passive.
- Confront anxiety surrounding racial issues and explore their own issues pertaining to race.
- Understand the differences in working with African American men, depending on whether the therapist is African American or European American.

priate for each domain in which the problem is present. If a patient is exhibiting anxious behavior (B), the modality applied might be systematic desensitization, a behavioral technique. If the patient is depressed in affect (A), the technique used might be verbal expression of feelings of sadness. A patient with muscle spasms and tightness has a problem in the sensation realm (S) and might benefit from relaxation training. A poor self-image falls in the imagery domain (I) and might be treated with training in positive coping imaging techniques. If a patient has disturbed thoughts, such as intrusive worries in the cognitive (C) domain, the intervention might be cognitive strategies like cognitive rehearsal or self-instruction. Problems in the interpersonal domain (I) such as shyness might be treated with client-centered counseling. A patient with a problem in the drug or physiological (D) domain might be treated with substance abuse counseling, if the issue was drugs, or behavioral health treatment if the issue was physiological, like overweight.

The MMT therapist uses the seven domains to identify the problems, the proposed treatments, and the timing or staging of the interventions. All these aspects are continually modified with the patient's input and comprise a systematic plan for treatment. Its practitioners believe that prescriptive psychotherapy holds the promise of being more effective because it matches empirically validated techniques with the problems for which they are known to be effective. They are, in addition, likely to be faster in achieving a desired result.

Structural Variations of the Psychotherapeutic Approaches

The five systems of psychotherapy that have been presented are only a few of the many that exist, but they vary greatly in a broad range of areas, including their conceptions of the basic nature of human beings, why people behave as they do, and how to intervene specifically in order to change them. Yet, they maintain the common elements presented earlier in the chapter. As they have been described, the focus has been mainly on the one-to-one verbal relationship between client and therapist. However, a complete introduction to these approaches must also consider certain structural variations on psychotherapy: group and family therapy. In either variation, the underlying theoretical framework may be any one of the systems already described or virtually any other system. Significant differences, however, do exist between these variations and the process that occurs in individual psychotherapy. It is the differences that we focus on here.

Group Psychotherapy

Much of the popularity of group psychotherapy comes from its obvious efficiency. The therapist can work with ten to twelve clients in a session rather than just one. Proponents of the group psychotherapy model, however, focus more on the unique influences of the group process on individuals as a rationale for its use than on the issue of its efficiency (Yalom, 1985).

Understanding the principles of group psychotherapy can assist human service workers in many settings.

Even though group therapists may have a formal background in any of the theoretical systems, most would concur on the specific advantages of the group setting. To begin with, in the group, individuals soon discover that they are not alone with problems, that others have problems as severe. All are encouraged to express themselves freely, often finding reassurance that they are "not too bad." By being able to share problems with others, the individuals not only experience an emotional catharsis or ventilation but also discover that rejection and ridicule are not necessarily a result of openness. Rather than being sanctioned positively or negatively, personal behaviors are analyzed by both the therapist and other group members in terms of their problem components and the difficulties they may cause.

A major force in group psychotherapy is the impact of peer pressure and support as manifested in group standards and values. An incorporation of group standards often neutralizes individuals' self-oriented needs. The therapist sees to it that the standards of the group are not self-defeating and that adaptive patterns become part of the group norm. However, within the norm of the group, the individual is encouraged to behave naturally—that is, without excessive restraint. The person may be competitive, aggressive, submissive, withdrawing, or dominant, for example, so that the group becomes a laboratory for behavior that can then be examined by the members and the therapist.

When problem behaviors are expressed, they are open to interpretation and analysis by the therapist *and* other group members. A major advantage of group treatment is this possibility of a client's behavior's being interpreted and analyzed by more than one person. It is less easy for a client to reject an interpretation or analysis when a number of group members agree that it is correct and provide feedback than when just one person (the therapist in one-to-one psychotherapy) presents it. In addition, for changes in behavior, the individual has the support of a number of persons rather than just one.

A major consequence of group therapy is considered to be the possibility of vicarious learning. Group members can learn how emotional processes function by observing how others react and solve problems and often seem to be able to apply these observations personally. Clients in the group setting have reported that, despite sitting through several sessions without verbally participating, they were experiencing the group ebb and flow and were learning about themselves and experiencing change.

To summarize, group psychotherapy provides a laboratory under the guidance of a trained leader in which the clients may do the following:

1. Discover that their problems are neither unique nor bad.
2. Become involved with others while being supported.
3. Reduce tension and anxiety through ventilation.
4. Study their own behavior in relation to others in order to gain insight and understanding.
5. Receive strong support in their efforts to change self-defeating behavior.
6. See themselves as others really see them, not as they *imagine* others see them.
7. Have a chance to receive the intrinsic reward of helping others.
8. Practice and develop positive self-supporting behavior.

Family Therapy

Family therapy is partially an outgrowth of the observation that family members have tremendous influence on what the client does and is able to do outside the therapy session. It is particularly apparent that the functioning of persons in need is intimately tied to family relationships, and in many cases the clients' problems cannot be effectively dealt with in isolation from the family environment. Therefore, therapists began to see total families. It was soon discovered that the family must often be conceptualized as a unit, that an individual's problem behaviors are often an acting out of interactional problems in the family.

As early as the mid-1950s, Jackson (1957) introduced the term *family homeostasis* to refer to the activities of families operating as a unit in order to maintain a balance in relationships. When family relationships are distorted, disturbed, or pained, members often take on themselves the task of maintaining the family unit by engaging in distorted behavior that acts to cover the family's real problems.

Even though the specific activities of family therapists may be influenced by their theoretical framework, the common tie is the emphasis on intercommunication between family members. The therapist most often meets the family as a unit, with no members excluded from the session. The therapist explores the structure and function of the family, acting as a resource person who is relatively objective. Therapists act as models of communication, teach the members to communicate directly with no hidden meanings or secret agendas, clarify incongruities, and confront double messages. As communication systems in the family become clarified, the family can begin to give up covert or hidden agendas and learn to tolerate differences without fear of disaster (Satir, 1964). The members then can begin to give up the distorted behavior patterns that caused the original identification of one member as being disturbed.

Evaluating the Effectiveness of the Psychotherapeutic Approaches

Do the psychotherapeutic strategies work? If one were to ask any practicing psychotherapist, the answer would certainly be affirmative. Many questions do exist, however, and many criticisms have been leveled at these processes. Foremost of the critics has been Hans Eysenck (1966, 1993), who surveyed the early literature on evaluating psychotherapy and came to a number of negative conclusions.

Eysenck found that most of the studies he surveyed had negative or equivocal results. Many indicated that people who were treated with psychotherapy for psychological problems did not improve any more than people who received no treatment. He also found that people who were treated with behavior therapy based on learning theory improved more and improved more rapidly than those treated with verbal psychotherapy.

Eysenck has received considerable criticism in regard to the methodological soundness of his study. More recent evidence based on controlled quantitative studies (Meltzoff and Kornreich, 1970; Sloane et al., 1975; Smith, Glass, and Miller, 1980) indicates significantly more change in persons who are treated than in those who receive no treatment. In addition, these researchers point out that of seventy controlled studies available when Eysenck drew his conclusions, he included only eleven, and that if he had included all seventy, his conclusions would have been reversed.

One major long-term study of psychotherapy spanned the years from 1954 to 1982. It examined the effects of psychoanalysis and less intense types of psychotherapy on the lives of forty-two people (Wallerstein, 1986). This study found that therapy had a significant impact on most of the forty-two people and that the effects lasted many years. In addition, the study indicates that, in most cases, supportive (less intense) therapies like client-centered counseling were as effective as in-depth psychoanalysis. The study suggests that psychoanalysis has a narrower therapeutic role than previously thought and is most appropriate for the less seriously disturbed person.

One additional study is worth mentioning. In 1994, the popular consumer testing magazine *Consumer Reports* conducted a survey of its readers on the effectiveness of psychotherapy. The survey was a supplement to its annual consumer survey, which consisted primarily of questions about automobile preferences. Of

22,000 responses, 7,000 responded to these mental health questions. Of those, about 3,000 had sought help from friends, relatives, and clergy, while about 4,000 went to a family doctor, a support group, or a mental health professional for psychotherapy. The article concluded that people who reported they had gone through psychotherapy believed that they benefitted substantially from it. It also concluded that long-term treatment did considerably better than short-term treatment, and that psychotherapy alone did not differ in effectiveness from medication plus psychotherapy. Furthermore, no specific modality of psychotherapy did better than any other for any disorder; psychologists, psychiatrists, and social workers did not differ in their effectiveness as treaters; and all did better than marriage counselors and long-term family doctoring (Seligman, 1995). Of about 1,200 people who had been feeling either "very poor" or "fairly poor" when they began therapy, 88 percent moved to "much improved" or "very good" at the time of the survey. As this study suggests, most people who entered into psychotherapy are convinced that it was very helpful.

What does seem clear in the final analysis is that when most psychotherapies work, they work best with the population for which they were designed: reasonably intelligent, often introspective, usually middle-class individuals who can deal with or have the potential to deal with their problems on a verbal-emotional level. Psychotherapy is less likely to work well with individuals who are not highly verbal or introspective and who need to work out their problems by *doing* something rather than by talking about them.

Summary

1. Psychotherapeutic approaches are based on the assumption that many problems result from defects in the internal psychological functioning of the individual.

2. A number of different theories of psychotherapy exist. Although there are substantial differences among the psychotherapeutic approaches, they also share a number of common elements.

3. The oldest of the psychotherapies is psychoanalysis. It is intensive and directive. Important concepts and techniques include free association, transference, and abreaction.

4. Rogerian client-centered therapy is nondirective and rejects the importance of unconscious motivation. It focuses on the importance of the self-concept. It attempts to create a therapeutic atmosphere of nonjudgmental acceptance. The therapist must have empathy, genuineness, and unconditional positive regard for the client.

5. Transactional analysis focuses on the interactions between two or more persons. Important concepts include structural analysis, script analysis, and games.

6. Gestalt therapy focuses on the here and now of the client and avoids dealing with the past. It emphasizes helping the client to be in touch with all aspects of his or her personality.

7. Multimodal therapy, one example of prescriptive psychotherapy, uses the acronym BASIC-ID to organize seven domains in which problems can occur.

8. Prescriptive psychotherapy is characterized by an approach in which specific therapies that have been empirically shown to be valid for specific problems are the ones that are used; one general theoretical approach is not relied on to solve all problems.

9. The structural variations in psychotherapy include group psychotherapy and family therapy. Therapists of nearly all theoretical orientations use these methods.

10. The effectiveness of psychotherapy has been debated for years. Recent evidence indicates that there are significantly more positive changes in persons who have had psychotherapy than in those who have not.

Discussion Questions

1. What are the six basic assumptions of the intrapsychic strategies?

2. What disadvantages can you identify in the psychoanalytic approach in terms of using it with human service clients? What advantages?

3. What advantages can you see in the use of transactional analysis?

4. What advantages does group psychotherapy have over individual psychotherapy?

Learning Experiences

1. Try to recollect an early childhood experience that seems important to the way you behave now.

2. Try to describe a communication experience using the parent-adult-child model of transactional analysis.

3. Reflect on how it feels to talk about your problems to someone.

4. Observe group behaviors. For example, have you noticed how you and your classmates tend to sit at the same desk in a classroom almost all semester? Why haven't you moved around?

5. Identify an event that caused an upset in your family's homeostasis (balance). What effect did it have? How was it resolved?

Endnotes

1. Wolberg, L. R. *The technique of psychotherapy.* 3rd ed. New York: Grune & Stratton, Inc., 1977, pp. 560–561. Reprinted by permission.
2. From Carl R. Rogers: *Client-centered therapy.* Copyright © 1951, renewed 1979 by Houghton Mifflin Company. Used by permission.

Recommended Readings

Ford, D. H., & Urban, H. B. (1998). *Contemporary models of psychotherapy: A comparative analysis* (2nd ed). New York: John Wiley & Sons.

Haveliwala, Y. A., Scheflen, A. E., & Ashcraft, N. (1979). *Common sense in therapy: A handbook for the mental health worker.* New York: Brunner-Mazel.

Yalom, I. D. (1985). *The theory and practice of group psychotherapy* (3rd ed.). New York: Basic Books.

9

Integrating Contemporary Strategies, Personal Relationship Skills, and the Supervisory Process

- How do human service workers integrate contemporary strategies into their work?
- What is meant by *personal relationship skills?*
- What attitudes, values, and feelings are important in personal relationship skills?
- Do verbal communication techniques enhance the helping relationship?
- How can cultural communication barriers be broken through?
- How do people express themselves without using words?
- How do human service workers enhance their skills once they are employed?

Contemporary strategies have much to offer the person in need. Many individuals have benefited or can benefit from medical/psychiatric treatment, behavior therapy, and psychotherapy. For some, these approaches are sufficient for dealing with their problems; for many others, much more in the way of human services alternatives is required.

In some settings, human service workers work with other professionals whose primary role is to engage in the contemporary strategies. Human service workers in these settings may or may not be encouraged to use aspects of those strategies in their work. A more probable situation is one in which the contemporary strategies are used and the human service worker begins to use some aspects of one or more of the approaches through experience, training, and supervision. The human service worker may be employed in a setting that does not offer medical/

psychiatric approaches, psychotherapy, or behavior therapy, yet the worker who has some understanding of the contemporary approaches to therapy may have an advantage in terms of understanding the clients.

In the material that follows, a number of examples illustrate how the human service worker may become involved in the use of medical/psychiatric, behavioral, and psychotherapeutic approaches in human services settings. The importance of some elements of the psychotherapeutic approach to all human services activities is also identified. The human service worker has one particular tool, always available, that can be of great assistance in his or her work: personal relationship skills. Like all tools, these skills must be developed through training and maintained through supervision.

Using Contemporary Strategies

Medical/Psychiatric Approaches

In some settings human service workers may have a close working relationship with medical or psychiatric professionals and may deal with clients who are receiving medical treatment. Such settings include support groups for persons with chronic medical disorders, nursing homes, private or public mental hospitals, senior citizen centers, and community mental health centers. In these settings, the human service worker may need a basic understanding of the medical problems of the client, the medical treatment being rendered, and the impact of the medical problem and its treatment on the client's life.

Individuals with physical illnesses often can benefit from human services approaches. Helping ill or recovering clients, human service workers, like the one described next, need to become knowledgeable about medical disorders and treatment.

■■ Pat Richards is a human service worker at a multiservice community center whose work required her to become familiar with a particular physical disease, its treatments, and its end results. Over a period of a few years, several of the center's clients and one staff member developed cancer and were treated with surgery and chemotherapy at a local hospital. From a medical perspective, the treatment and medical management of these individuals were as good as could be expected. However, it seemed to several staff members that the people who had been stricken with the disease were receiving little support in dealing with the emotional and psychological problems of having cancer and living with its aftermath.

Discussions about the need for support services began among staff members and led to the center director making contact with the hospital. After much planning, the hospital and the community center announced that a joint project would be initiated. Two support groups would be run, one for cancer victims and one for patients and their family members.

Pat Richards, through training, experience, and supervision, had over the years become a good group leader. In addition, she had had direct experience with the emotional and psychological ravages of cancer and its treatment since her eldest sister had been treated for breast cancer. The center director selected Pat as one of the leaders of the support group, and she was enthusiastic about the opportunity.

Planning, organizing, and leading the cancer support groups with a nurse co-leader from the cancer treatment unit was as much an educational experience as a work experience, particularly in the beginning. Pat found that she needed to learn a great deal about various types of cancer, their treatments, the side effects of treatments, and people's psychological reactions to the illness and treatment. Her nurse co-leader was a great help, but Pat also did a lot of reading at the library, made contact with the American Cancer Society, and visited a similar support group in another city.

Pat did not start out in human services with the idea of spending a substantial part of her time working with people with medical problems. She has found, however, that she is becoming a lay expert on a set of medical problems and treatments. She does not do medical treatment, but she does have to integrate her human services work with approaches based on the medical model.

More commonly, psychiatric approaches are an integral part of a human services system. Many human service workers are employed in community mental health centers, public mental hospitals, or other agencies where clients are treated for emotional or behavioral disorders with medical/psychiatric approaches such as chemotherapy. Knowledge of the purpose, effects, and side effects of such treatments can be helpful in dealing with these clients.

■■ Carmen Villalobos is a human service caseworker for a state department of child and family services. Her agency is responsible for the identification, protection, and monitoring of children in families in which child abuse or neglect has occurred. Carmen's role includes making outreach field visits to families in which abuse or neglect has occurred in the past, partly to monitor the welfare of the child but also to provide assistance and support to the parent.

Carmen's caseload includes a single-parent family consisting of a mother, Joan Mitchell, and her children, Ricky, age twelve, and Lisa, age nine. The location of the father is unknown. Three years earlier, Joan had been charged with child neglect. Intervention at that time revealed that the children were being neglected but not physically abused. The home was unheated, the children were unfed and dirty, and Joan appeared very withdrawn and disturbed. Joan's relatives in another city were contacted and temporarily took in Ricky and Lisa. They encouraged Joan to admit herself to a psychiatric unit in a general hospital.

After Joan was admitted to the psychiatric unit, she was diagnosed as suffering from acute schizophrenia. She was treated with short-term psychotherapy and chemotherapy and within seventeen days was discharged as recovered. She was very much her old self again. At discharge, Joan was referred to a local mental health center for outpatient treatment. Within two months, her children returned to live with her.

Carmen Villalobos "inherited" Joan, Ricky, and Lisa from the original caseworker less than two years ago. About six months ago, Carmen became aware of a change in Joan during visits to Joan's apartment. Joan complained of being drowsy and sleeping too much and of always having a dry mouth. She wondered aloud if the medication she was getting was doing any good or was making her sick. Carmen suggested that Joan check it out the next time she went to the mental health center.

A month later, as Carmen was arriving at Joan's apartment, she was already thinking about the last visit. In reviewing her notes, she realized that Joan's drowsiness and dry mouth could be side effects of Thorazine, which she was receiving at the mental health center. Carmen wondered how Joan was doing this time.

Unfortunately, Joan was not doing very well. She was reluctant to let Carmen in but finally did so. Carmen found that Joan was very withdrawn. The apartment was in disorder, dirty dishes were in the sink, apparently from a number of meals, and un-bagged garbage was lying about the kitchen. Both Ricky and Lisa were home on a school day. At first Joan seemed unwilling to talk to Carmen, but Carmen was able to draw her out.

Carmen's suspicions were confirmed. The side effects of the Thorazine had become so unpleasant for Joan that she had completely stopped taking the medication. She also had missed an appointment with the psychiatrist at the mental health center. The deterioration in Joan's behavior, the withdrawal, and the neglect in homemaking and parenting skills constituted an early sign that Joan's disorder was appearing again. Carmen's knowledge of schizophrenia, the effects of Thorazine, and the side effects of medication helped her understand how to help Joan.

Because of her long-standing positive relationship with Joan, Carmen was able to persuade her to go to the mental health center immediately. There, in a session with the center psychiatrist, Carmen was able to act knowledgeably as Joan's advocate and explain the problem with side effects and the changes in Joan's behavior. The psychiatrist was able to administer a fast-acting antipsychotic drug and prescribe a medication with less noticeable side effects.

For the next few weeks, Carmen increased the frequency of her visits. Joan, taking her medication again, became progressively less withdrawn and disorganized. Within a month, she was back to normal and was determined to continue her monthly medication reviews with the psychiatrist at the mental health center.

The agency that employs Carmen Villalobos does not use medical/psychiatric approaches in its delivery of services, yet many of its clients are being treated medically or psychiatrically. Carmen Villalobos's ability to deliver human services was enhanced by the integration of her knowledge of medical/psychiatric approaches into her day-to-day functioning.

Many human service workers are employed in settings where specific medical or psychiatric knowledge is not necessary. Pat Richards and Carmen Villalobos found that they needed to know more about some aspects of medicine or psychiatry than they had expected. Both knew from their training when it was necessary to find out more. In both cases, the needs of their clients dictated the specific knowledge and skills that Pat and Carmen developed.

Behavioral Approaches

Human services systems in which behavioral therapy is used include public school programs for emotionally handicapped children, residential programs for people who are mentally retarded, residential and outpatient programs for children identified as mentally ill, and juvenile and adult corrections facilities. The success of behavioral therapy in diminishing the intensity and frequency of problem behaviors and in helping people develop more functional new behaviors is likely to lead to more use of such approaches in a variety of agencies.

■■ Pauline Erickson is a graduate of an associate of arts degree human services program in child development. She works as an instructional aide with Kathy Turner, a special education instructor, in a public school. The classroom has five children who have behavior problems that prevent their being taught in a regular classroom. The children need more individual attention than would be possible in a class of twenty-five to thirty children.

One of the five children with whom Pauline works is Billy Keller. Billy is a nine-year-old who, along with other problems, is hyperactive. He is extremely active and impulsive, and his motor coordination is below average. He finds it difficult to sit still and concentrate, squirms in his chair, taps his feet, talks loudly to children during class, and often gets up and moves about the classroom instead of listening to the teacher or studying. In spite of his average intelligence, it is hard for Billy to make progress in class because of these behaviors, which also disrupt the general progress of the whole class.

In order to help Billy change his behavior, Pauline, with her supervisor, Kathy, met with the school psychologist. After several meetings, they decided to implement a behavior therapy program. The behaviors they targeted for change were inappropriate speaking out in class and leaving his seat without permission.

Because in this classroom the schoolday was broken down into twenty-five-minute class sessions and five-minute recesses, they decided that the first step would be to use verbal reminders and loss of recess as a consequence for rule breaking. At the beginning of each class session, Billy would be reminded not to speak inappropriately and to stay in his seat. If he behaved acceptably, he would be given verbal praise at the end of the class. If he spoke out or left his seat, he would be told to stay in the room during recess. Pauline, Kathy, and the school psychologist agreed that Pauline would make this behavioral program her special task for several weeks.

On a Friday, Pauline observed Billy and recorded how often he disrupted the class by engaging in the two behaviors. It happened twenty-two times. The following Monday morning, Pauline told Billy about the program and the consequences if he disrupted class. By the end of that week, it was obvious that the program was helping: Billy was down to six disruptions a day. That Friday, Pauline, Kathy, and the school psychologist met again and decided to add another step. After each class period in which Billy did not speak out of turn or leave his desk without permission, Pauline would post a large gold star next to his name on the bulletin board. At the end of the day, Billy would be able to take a gold star home to his mother if he earned stars in more than half the sessions. Once again, Pauline would take responsibility for the program.

The following Monday, Pauline explained the addition to the program to Billy. By the week's end, Billy was down to three disruptions a day. After another week, he was taking a gold star home almost every day. On some days, there were one or two disruptions; on other days, none. More important, Billy's schoolwork was showing a noticeable improvement. Over the course of the year, Pauline and Kathy were able to fade the program. Billy eventually maintained his progress without losing recesses and toward the end of the year did not need gold stars to maintain the behavior.

In many human services settings, behavioral approaches may meet one client's particular needs, whereas other approaches may meet the needs of clients with different problems. For example, one child in Pauline Erickson's classroom was in play therapy with a child psychologist. Another child who, like Billy, had been identified as hyperactive was receiving a medication called methylphenidate that seemed to reduce the problem behaviors. Pauline integrated a behavioral approach into her work because one of the people she wanted to help could benefit from it.

In many human services systems, behavioral strategies are the primary approach. Human service workers who obtain employment in some residential settings often must integrate behavioral approaches into their work with all their clients.

■ ■ Joe Benson works in a juvenile corrections facility that provides residential services for young offenders—that is, a live-in setting for boys who usually have had multiple run-ins with the law. These boys have been arrested and tried in juvenile court for offenses ranging from homicide and major theft to multiple offenses of a less serious nature.

In his four-year human services degree program, Joe Benson took several courses that dealt with principles of learned behavior and behavior therapy. Joe's knowledge of behavioral approaches has helped him in his work because the correctional facility program involves a token economy.

Joe works from 7 A.M. to 3 P.M. in a cottage that houses eight boys in their early teens. The token economy provides a structure for their group life. In this token economy, a variety of positive, or prosocial, behaviors are identified. When the boys engage in these behaviors they earn tokens, called *units,* that they can redeem for commodities such as candy, soft drinks, and snacks and items such as clothing, combs, and radios. The units also can be redeemed for privileges such as attendance at movies or other special activities. The prosocial behaviors for which the boys earn these units include rising on time in the morning, making their beds, good grooming, being prompt, attending counselor sessions, attending school, and helping other students. Thus, the units earned act as positive reinforcement for appropriate behavior.

The units also are used to apply punishment or withdrawal of positive reinforcement. Boys who do not engage in prosocial behavior are not positively reinforced; if they engage in unacceptable behavior, they may have units taken away (they are fined). Unacceptable behaviors that result in fines include foul language, stealing, and fighting.

Joe's duties as a cottage worker are varied. He is involved in counseling the boys under his supervision regarding their day-to-day behavior, their fears and concerns, and their general adjustment to the correctional facility. He also organizes and participates in daily recreational activities. However, the behavioral token economy provides the underlying structure for the group life of the eight boys in Joe's cottage.

When a new boy joins the cottage group, Joe explains the rules and the token system of reinforcers or fines. Joe observes the new boy for several weeks and identifies any particular problems and assets. This data-collection period provides the information for designing an individual program for the boy. In consultation with his supervisor, a psychologist, Joe then develops an individual behavioral program for that boy, involving a plan for reinforcing desirable behaviors and setting up consequences for unacceptable or problem behaviors.

Once an individual plan is developed, Joe collects data on the frequency of the positive and problem behaviors. While this process goes on, it provides the data that

Personal relationship skills are critical tools for the human service worker.

determine whether Joe gives units to the boys as reinforcers or administers fines. Joe also keeps records of the units given, taken away, and spent and notes whether the behaviors change for the better or worse. Joe has found that over a period of time the token economy has had a significant effect on promoting the development of prosocial behavior and reducing problem behaviors.

Joe Benson and the other human service workers at his facility have integrated behavioral therapy into their work with all cottage residents. The correctional facility also requires that Joe and his coworkers be able to interact with the clients as group leaders, activity workers, and counselors. They must be able to relate to the boys in an understanding, caring manner so that each boy realizes that he is seen as a unique individual rather than an object to be manipulated.

Human service workers employed in settings that place a major emphasis on behavioral approaches obviously need to develop skills relevant to those approaches. They must understand the basic principles of learned behavior and concepts such as positive reinforcement, punishment, and negative reinforcement. Like Joe Benson, some human service workers develop a basic understanding of the behavioral approaches through college courses. Many others develop these skills through on-the-job or in-service training.

Psychotherapeutic Approaches

Psychotherapy has been viewed traditionally as a treatment process in which a highly credentialed, trained, and experienced professional develops a helping relationship with a psychologically or emotionally troubled client. The psychotherapist typically engages in a verbal process with the client in order to uncover the psychological causes of the troubles and helps the client change his or her problematic ways of thinking, feeling, and behaving. This treatment process usually occurs on a one-to-one or small-group basis.

For years, the practice of psychotherapy was primarily limited to several professional groups. Psychoanalysts, some psychiatrists, clinical psychologists, and M.S.W. social workers were the primary providers. In the private, fee-for-service sector, this is still basically the case. Traditional professional training and degrees are still required for licensure or certification for the provision of psychotherapy in private practice settings in many states. Some states, however, have created a license category, called a Licensed Clinical Professional Counselor (or other similar title), that allows the private practice of counseling and psychotherapy. These categories allow people with nontraditional human services master's degrees to engage in psychotherapy on a fee-for-service basis just like other more traditional professional disciplines.

Within human services agencies, the situation is somewhat different. For the past twenty-five years, nontraditional workers have engaged in activities ranging from one-to-one intensive psychoanalytically oriented psychotherapy and client-centered counseling to the informal or formal application of psychotherapy principles in a variety of helping relationships. These activities are often called *counseling* to indicate that they are not as intensive as psychotherapy. In practice, a human services counselor may achieve the same ends as a professionally educated and trained psychotherapist (Brown, 1974; Hattie, Sharpley, and Rogers, 1984).

■■ Fred Zimmerman is an alcoholism counselor at a community alcohol and drug abuse agency. He obtained an associate of arts degree in human services, worked for several years, and returned to a university to obtain a bachelor's degree with a focus on addiction counseling.

Fred deals with recovering alcoholics. His case load consists of both inpatients and outpatients. He spends his day doing counseling with individuals on a one-to-one basis, and three times a week he leads a group session with about six members.

The basic philosophy of Fred's agency is that alcohol and drug addictions develop because people discover that chemicals help them avoid the painful realities of living. They feel better when they take drugs or use alcohol. Later, the alcohol or drug use causes problems in living, but the addictive process makes stopping very difficult. The agency's treatment approach is first to find out why clients started abusing drugs (that is, what problems the drugs solved) and then to help the clients change so that they can solve these problems in more adaptive ways. One treatment vehicle that is used to achieve these goals is psychotherapy.

When Fred does psychotherapy with an agency client, he thinks of it as having three phases. In the beginning phase, Fred develops a relationship with the client. During these opening sessions, he gets to know the client, the client's life problems, and the client's addiction problems in some detail. The client also gets to know Fred very well. It is important that the client begin to see Fred as someone who wants to help, who cares about the client, and who *can* help.

During the middle phase, Fred creates an atmosphere of trust and acceptance in which the client can reveal his or her needs, fears, and deepest problems. It is a time when the client can risk change by giving up old behavior patterns and trying new ones. Fred sees this as the most difficult period for the client, who often experiences emotional turmoil. The final phase of treatment is termination. If all has gone as desired, a close relationship has developed between the client and Fred, and the client has been able to change significantly. Now the client must deal with his or her feelings about leaving therapy. At this point, the client is often fearful or anxious about leaving the relationship and becoming independent. During the termination phase, Fred helps the client deal successfully with those feelings.

Fred's work as a psychotherapist requires a number of skills that must be learned and practiced. He learned some of the basic skills in his human services education program but has also had a lot of training at the agency. He continues to be supervised weekly by a more experienced psychotherapist. Fred has become very good at listening. He listens not only to the words of the clients but also for the feelings underlying the words. He also "listens" to nonverbal communication. For example, a client may say, "I'm feeling fine," but her behavior may say that she is anxious or angry.

Fred also has become good at communicating. In psychotherapy, that means much more than being a good speaker and transmitting information. Fred can respond to clients' words and feelings in a way that tells them that he understands what they are saying and feeling. He can reflect back what clients say so that they know whether he understands them. He has learned to confront clients when their actions do not match their words or feelings. Fred also has become skilled at interpretation. He is able to interpret the clients' behavior, words, or feelings in ways that help the clients gain new understanding into why they feel or behave in particular ways. Often, when the clients gain new understanding, they change established problem behaviors.

Fred's listening and communication skills constitute a major part of his ability to do psychotherapy. His knowledge of addiction and its causes and of the problems of alcoholics is also important. Equally important is the fact that Fred cares about his clients. He is able to feel nonpossessive warmth toward them. He accepts them as they are; he does not demand that they be something else but is willing to help them change if they wish. Fred is able to be empathic. He can put himself into the clients' shoes and see the world through their eyes, however bleak that view might be.

Fred also has an air of genuineness. He is not a phony. He is able to reveal his true feelings, and his true feelings are expressed in his behavior. He has no need to manipulate clients or pretend to be something he is not.

Some of the settings in which human service workers may function as psychotherapists are obvious. In public mental hospitals or mental health centers, clients frequently have problems that require psychotherapy. Many human service workers in such settings may be trained to function as psychotherapists or counselors in addition to their other duties. Workers in crisis centers with phone hotlines for people with emotional problems may also need formal psychotherapeutic skills.

In other human services settings, the workers may not have to provide formal psychotherapy. However, the ability to use effective personal helping skills based on general psychotherapeutic principles is likely to be important. The human service worker in a correctional facility, rehabilitation workshop, preschool, senior citizen center, rape counseling center, or public aid office encounters people in need for whom a helping relationship based on psychotherapeutic principles will be helpful.

Most college or university education programs in human services do not train graduates to be psychotherapists. Surprisingly, the same can be said about most graduate programs for traditional professionals. Psychiatrists and clinical psychologists, for example, may take a college course or two on the principles of psychotherapy. However, traditional professionals usually learn to do psychotherapy as apprentices to more experienced psychotherapists during an internship or residency after they have received a graduate degree. Fred Zimmerman became a psychotherapist through much the same process. He learned by doing psychotherapy under the supervision and training of an experienced psychotherapist at his agency.

In human services agencies that do not offer formal psychotherapy, the integration of some of the principles and skills of the psychotherapeutic approach may still be useful. Even when clients' needs consist of such things as housing, money, medical care, job training, or education, clients enter into a personal relationship with a human service provider that is often very important in finding solutions.

■■ After graduating from a two-year associate of arts degree program in human services, Irene Thomas found employment directing an activity program in a county nursing home. It was challenging and rewarding to work with the elderly people who needed the support services of the county residence. Most of the residents seemed to respond very favorably to the activities Irene organized and to her relationship with them.

Irene remembers one resident who needed individual attention. Mrs. Wilson was seventy-six years old and widowed. Her son and daughter-in-law had brought her to the county home because she could no longer maintain herself in her apartment and needed a limited amount of nursing care for a chronic illness.

Mrs. Wilson did not seem to adapt to the home. She stayed by herself in her room, staring out the window. She refused to be involved in activities. The nursing staff described her as angry, critical, and complaining. When Mrs. Wilson's son and daughter-in-law visited, she berated them for putting her in the home, begged tearfully for them to take her out, or sat without speaking.

Irene began to drop by Mrs. Wilson's room several times a day. For weeks, Mrs. Wilson had little to say, and Irene would just sit quietly with her. On occasion, Irene would tell Mrs. Wilson that she enjoyed sitting quietly with her. Soon, Mrs. Wilson began to talk about her life with her husband and how much she missed him. Irene reflected those feelings back to Mrs. Wilson and shared how she felt about losing people she had known. Mrs. Wilson began to share more of her life with Irene. They talked about the meaning of friends, home, and family. Irene's genuine interest in Mrs. Wilson helped Mrs. Wilson share her fears, concerns, interests, and beliefs.

Irene and Mrs. Wilson began to talk about what it meant for a person to have to go to a nursing home. Mrs. Wilson was able to share her feelings of abandonment and her anger toward her son and daughter-in-law. Talking about these things with Irene helped Mrs. Wilson sort out her mixed feelings, and she soon was able to talk about how much she loved her son, his wife, and their children.

The growing relationship between Mrs. Wilson and Irene seemed to help Mrs. Wilson see the nursing home as a friendlier place. With Irene's urging, she began to get more involved in the activities and made friends with the other residents. The nursing staff began to notice that Mrs. Wilson was more talkative and friendly and complained less. Mrs. Wilson began to relate more positively to her son and daughter-in-law again.

For the next several years, Irene continued her relationship with Mrs. Wilson. Each respected the other, and Mrs. Wilson knew that Irene could understand her feelings. It seemed to Mrs. Wilson that often, after she had talked to Irene, she had a better grasp of how she really felt about things. Mrs. Wilson never really did like being in a nursing home, but Irene helped her make the best of the situation.

The relationship between Irene and Mrs. Wilson was not psychotherapy. Irene used her personal relationship skills to create an atmosphere in which Mrs. Wilson could examine her situation and change her way of dealing with it. But Irene Thomas was more than a friend who sympathized with Mrs. Wilson's plight and took her side. Irene, in fact, took no sides. She did not support Mrs. Wilson's early attitudes about how terrible it was to be put in the home and how terrible the son and daughter-in-law were to do that to her. Irene did show that she understood how Mrs. Wilson felt and that she cared about her, and she helped her see things from a different perspective.

Using Personal Relationship Skills

A common thread runs through the case examples in this chapter. Although each human service worker described is unique and each works in a different setting with different roles and functions, all use effective personal relationship skills in their work.

What characterizes effective personal relationship skills? Although the question cannot be answered in absolute terms, sufficient study, research, and experience in psychotherapy suggest what some of the important factors may be (Danish and Hauer, 1973; Runyan, 1999; Truax and Carkuff, 1967; Zingale, 1985). Effective personal relationship skills can be divided into two broad categories: being (Moustakas, 1986) and doing. *Being* refers to the attitudes, values, and feelings a human service worker holds that color his or her actions. *Doing* refers to the observable skills or activities that enhance relationships. They are, of course, intimately related.

Being

You probably encountered people whom you found easy to talk to, who you felt cared about you, who accepted you as you are with all your faults and strengths, and who valued your uniqueness rather than what you have, whom you know, or your social status. Such individuals have developed a sense of being that helps them create positive relationships with others. Some develop this sense naturally; others have to work to achieve it. To a greater or lesser extent, the human service workers described in this chapter have cultivated this quality.

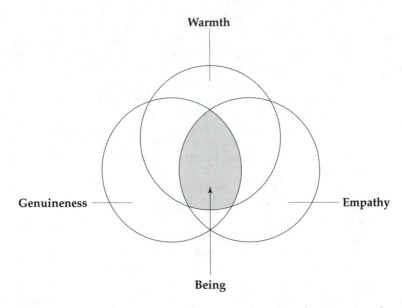

FIGURE 9.1   The Truax Triad: Distinct but Overlapping Attributes
                    of Being

For the human service worker, three aspects of this sense of being have been
identified as particularly important: warmth, empathy, and genuineness. These
terms are used to describe interrelated and overlapping attributes that are sometimes called the *Truax triad*, named for a counselor who emphasized their importance (Truax and Carkuff, 1967). Although they are described separately, they are
closely related and interdependent (see Figure 9.1).

Warmth
Warmth is a fuzzy concept. It consists of a subtle communication of tender, caring
feelings. People who lack warmth are described as cold, uncaring, or uninvolved.
Thus, warmth implies involvement. The expression of warmth requires a nonjudgmental attitude and an avoidance of blaming. Warmth involves acceptance of
the equal worth of others. It is necessary for a sense of closeness toward others and
the ability to be open and revealing of oneself to others. The feelings of warmth
one has toward others are most fruitful when they are nonpossessive. Possessive
warmth may occur when one person maintains a relationship with another in
order to manipulate that person or to meet his or her own needs rather than the
needs of the other. Nonpossessive warmth entails a feeling of caring and concern
without placing conditions on the relationship.

Empathy
People often want to help others out of sympathy, which is sorrow over the
distress and misfortune of others. Empathic feeling goes a step further. Rather

than feeling *for* someone, empathy means feeling *with* someone. The empathic process in helping relationships has been described as having four aspects (Marcia, 1987):

1. *Identification*—paying attention to another and allowing oneself to become absorbed in contemplation of that person.
2. *Incorporation*—making the other's experience one's own via internalizing the other.
3. *Reverberation*—experiencing the other's experience while simultaneously attending to one's own cognitive and affective associations to that experience.
4. *Detachment*—moving back from the merged inner relationship to a position of separate identity, which permits a response to be made that reflects both understanding of others and separateness from them.

Empathy has often been described as walking in another's shoes. Empathy involves experiencing another's point of view, experiences, and feelings. Empathy allows one to know the world as another knows it. To the extent that one can do this, one's understanding becomes deeper. To the degree that one has empathic understanding of another human being, one is more able to accept that person. Empathic feelings, acceptance, and openness are reflected in behavior and allow others to feel that one understands them.

Genuineness

Being genuine means that what a person says, does, or thinks reflects what that person actually feels. It is a condition of congruence among all aspects of the individual. To be genuine requires that the human service worker be aware of his or her feelings and accept them. It involves the ability to express those feelings accurately in words and behavior. In order to be genuine, one must be self-aware: aware of one's emotional responses and habitual patterns of behavior. One must be aware, for example, of the inability to say no or the need to avoid conflict. In addition, human service workers must be aware of their values, prejudices, and stereotypes. Awareness is the first step toward achieving congruence between internal experiences and outward behavior. Genuineness also, however, requires the maturity and skills to be able to express these feelings in the context of a warm and empathic relationship. Genuineness helps differentiate between feelings that are appropriately due to relationships and feelings that derive from one's inaccurate perceptions.

Is Being All That It Takes?

Warmth, empathy, and genuineness are described as critical aspects of helping relationships. Some experts go so far as to suggest that if these three characteristics are present, effective helping relationships develop naturally. There is some research to support this view. In one study, researchers selected college students who were experiencing anxiety, depression, and a sense of isolation (Strupp and Hadley, 1979). The students were assigned for counseling to experienced psychoanalytically oriented psychotherapists, trained experientially oriented psychotherapists, or untrained therapists. The study also compared the students with a waiting-list control group selected from the same student sample. The untrained therapists were college professors with no special knowledge or training in human services. They were selected because they were reputed to be interested in and available to students with problems and had been described as warm, caring, and trustworthy.

The study found that the students who had received counseling had improved more than the students in the control group. More important, the students seen by the untrained but warm, caring, and trustworthy professors had improved as much as those seen by highly trained specialists.

Although some research and a great deal of practical experience suggest that things such as warmth, empathy, and genuineness are important factors in effective helping relationships, other factors also may be important. Before any conclusions can be drawn in this regard, we must await further study; (Rutan, 1992). In the meantime, developing warm, empathic, and genuine qualities will continue to be important for human service workers.

Doing

We have seen that warmth, empathy, and genuineness are important qualities of effective personal relationship skills. These factors constitute personal attributes of human service workers that are expressed in the things they do. In later chapters, we examine many of the things human service workers do. Within the specific context of one-to-one personal relationship skills, though, there are a number of things worth identifying.

The *doing* skills that enhance personal relationships involve a particular way of communicating. In typical social intercourse, communicating most often involves a sharing of data or information. Although information sharing is often important in human services, a deeper form of communication is more desirable: the expressive communication of understanding, caring, warmth, empathy, and genuineness. The vehicles for this expressive form of communications include paraphrasing, reflection, confrontation, and interpretation, as well as nonverbal communication. Before we consider these techniques, a word of caution is in order. Techniques such as these cannot be learned through reading any more than warmth, empathy, and genuineness can. They *can* be learned, but it takes supervised practice.

Paraphrasing
Paraphrasing is putting a person's words into a new form in order to clarify what has been said. It may involve simply repeating a word or phrase that captures the essence of the communication or using entirely new words.

Client: Sometimes I feel like I'm being choked. There's too many demands that people are putting on me. I can't swallow them fast enough.

Counselor: Choked? (*Repeating the client.*) Like you're being force-fed. (*Restating, substituting new word.*)

The repetition of important, emotion-filled words or the rephrasing of the content of the communication serves two functions. First, it communicates to clients that they have been heard and encourages them to continue. Second, it gives the client the opportunity to correct the counselor if the counselor has missed the meaning of the communication.

Reflection

Reflection involves the identification and expression of the client's feelings. If the client's feelings are reflected back to the client, those feelings will be brought to the forefront of the client's awareness. Becoming more aware, the client is more likely to be enabled to deal with those feelings.

Client: Things just don't seem to be going right. I'm in a dead-end job, I can't seem to concentrate on my studies. . . . I just don't know how to grab ahold of things.

Counselor: Feeling trapped and helpless.

A client's feelings may at times be obvious both to the client and to the human service worker. At other times, clients may be less aware of the feelings that they are experiencing and that are influencing their behavior. When the counselor is able to hear between the lines and accurately reflect those feelings back, clients often perceive that they are deeply understood. Clients are encouraged to look more closely at themselves. This opens the possibility of exploring the relationship between the new feelings of awareness and client behaviors. Through this process, reflection increases the consistency between what clients feel and their words and behavior. Reflection has the potential of increasing congruence and genuineness.

Confrontation

Confrontation involves bringing clients face to face with their denials, discrepancies between feelings and behavior, or unpleasant realities. Because many clients also deny their strengths and assets, confrontation is also used to help them recognize these positive aspects of themselves. The purpose of confrontation is not to attack but to push clients toward self-awareness and change within a supportive atmosphere.

Client: Well, that last job I got canned from . . . . I couldn't get along with the foreman. Nobody could. He had some kind of problem.

Counselor: But the others didn't get fired. *You* did. How's that similar to the other jobs you lost?

Confrontation is a risky technique when used improperly or to excess. Clients who feel attacked or demeaned may become alienated from the human service worker. Confrontations that are improperly timed or too aggressive may undo previous progress in the development of a helping relationship. Confrontation must be used sparingly and within a supportive atmosphere.

Interpretation

Interpretation involves the human service worker in a process of placing clients' communication and behavior in a broader or different framework. It is an attempt to enable clients to see their behavior from a different perspective. Effective interpretation results in new self-understanding for the client, and that understanding may help the client see underlying motivations for particular behaviors or reasons for particular feelings. Effective interpretation requires that the human service worker have a deep and accurate understanding of the client.

Client: God, what is it with me? Every time I get involved with a guy, he's married to somebody else!

Counselor: You know, Judy, that's one way of protecting yourself from a relationship that can grow.

Client: Huh! Yeah, I see it. If a guy was single, I'd have to take responsibility for the long term! Wow, that's something to chew on!

When interpretations are appropriately timed and based on an accurate understanding of clients' reasons for behavior, clients are able to integrate the counselor's views into their own self-perceptions. The resulting change in self-perception allows clients to try on new ways of behaving or feeling with the continued support of the counselor. The ability to make effective interpretations requires substantial training and experience.

Nonverbal Communication

The personal relationship skills discussed so far have been described as verbal processes of communication. Another significant aspect of communication involves nonverbal behavior. All people can communicate volumes about themselves and their reactions to others without the need for spoken dialogue. Sensitivity to our own and others' nonverbal communication can facilitate the development of effective helping skills. The reverse is also true. A person who is not aware of nonverbal communications may transmit incomplete or even discrepant messages.

Some forms of nonverbal communication are obvious. The clenched hand with thumb up in the air or pointing down to indicate that things are good or bad is a case in point. Arms spread wide and extended toward a person represent an invitation to closeness. The arm stretched toward a person with the palm upraised indicates that the other person should stop or stay distant. Such gestures often cut across cultural boundaries, but some gestures mean entirely different things in different cultures (see Box 9.1).

Posture and body movement may communicate feelings that cannot be expressed verbally, perhaps even things of which a person is not consciously aware. A slouching posture may indicate depression, hopelessness, or lack of interest on the part of a client. The counselor who sits leaning slightly toward the client communicates interest. Clients who sit stiffly and rigidly may be unaware of their own tension and discomfort, but the observant counselor still can "hear"

BOX 9.1   Cross-Cultural Communication Barriers and Strategies for Breaking Through

Human service work requires personal relationship skills, which are manifested through communication. When human service workers have clients from another culture, the cultural difference may pose barriers to communication that must be broken through. Here are some of the barriers and strategies for the human service worker to use in breaking through.

1. Other cultures may use different language or other dialects of the same language. The breakthrough strategy:
   a. Learn the language or dialect.
   b. Always ask for clarification if you are not sure about the meaning of a phrase or word.
   c. Use an interpreter (one with interpreter training and experience, preferably).
2. Nonverbal communication may be very different in other cultures. The same or similar gestures may have *very* different meanings. The breakthrough strategy:
   a. Don't assume you understand the gesture, posture, or facial expression. Observe closely; develop a confidant from the culture who is open to teaching you about it.
   b. Become self-aware of your own cultural meaning for gestures and how they may be misinterpreted by another culture. Explain respectfully if you become aware that you have insulted someone from another culture.
   c. If a person from another culture engages in a behavior or gesture that is confusing or insulting to you, don't take it personally, express your confusion, and try to get clarification.
3. Stereotypes and biases we may have learned from childhood can interfere with our ability to understand others, to communicate accurately, or to develop a respectful relationship. Deep-seated beliefs like "they're all uptight," "they eat weird stuff," "they're not smart," "they're all violent," "they have no will power," or "they're all filthy" may linger in us in spite of our good intentions. The breakthrough strategy:
   a. Make a commitment to the ongoing struggle to become aware of the preconceptions, stereotypes, and perhaps even prejudices that you have been taught about other ethnic and cultural groups.
   b. Be open to accepting new experiences and new ways of viewing the people of other cultures.
4. Superficial cultural awareness can be the result of brief self-education, training events, or lack of in vivo experience: a little knowledge can be a dangerous thing. If we think we "know it all" about another culture, we're sure to get some embarrassing and perhaps unpleasant surprises. The breakthrough strategy:
   a. Be humble. Accept that you always will need to learn more.
   b. Be wary. Broad generalizations are often *wrong* about individuals.
   c. Be open. Get to know some people from the different culture *very* well, especially some you don't see professionally.

Learning about other cultures is a mind-opening experience. It may help us in our work, but it has value in its own right. Besides, it's fun!

the communication and respond to it. Squirming, tapping fingers, wringing hands, pacing, and rocking the body are all behaviors that carry messages about the feelings and attitudes of clients and counselors.

The face is a very expressive body part. People communicate joy, concern, fear, anxiety, anger, and depression through facial movement. Smiles, frowns, widened eyes, a dropped jaw, narrowed eyes, tears, and slack features all contain messages that must be heard and reflected and perhaps confronted and interpreted.

The human service worker who is sensitive to both verbal and nonverbal communications has a greater opportunity to understand a client fully. Counselors who are aware of their own nonverbal communications have a greater degree of awareness of their own feelings about the client. A nonverbally aware counselor can also use nonverbal communication to respond to the client.

Client: (*Enters room with a bounce in his walk and a beaming smile.*) Hi, John!

Counselor: Hi, Bob. You seem to be feeling *up* this morning.

❖ ❖ ❖

Client: (*While discussing his relationship with his wife, begins to slouch forward, drops his head, and stares at the floor.*)

Counselor: Jim, you're beginning to look pretty sad. How do you feel?

❖ ❖ ❖

Client: (*In the middle of a session, talks about a painful, emotional interaction with her husband. Her voice trails off.*)

Counselor: (*Leans forward and nods in an understanding manner.*)

Client: (*Exhales breath heavily, looks at counselor, and in a tremulous voice continues to talk about feelings.*)

❖ ❖ ❖

Client: I really have a hard time speaking up in meetings at work. Everyone else seems to have something to say, but I . . . I . . . I don't think people pay much attention when I talk.

Counselor: (*While the client talks, furtively glances at the clock on the wall. Although neither is consciously aware of it, the counselor is not involved with the client, the client doesn't feel like he is being heard, and the nonverbal behavior of the counselor shuts off the client. The session lurches to a strained conclusion with both parties feeling uncomfortable and unsure why they feel that way.*)

Nonverbal communication can both add to and detract from personal relationships. All people are aware to some degree of their own and others' nonverbal messages. Through training and experience, human service workers can improve their sensitivity to these messages. As one's awareness increases, personal relationship skills are enhanced.

Developing Personal Relationship Skills

It may seem that developing effective skills requires attributes that are difficult to describe, much less develop. Let us briefly look at them again:

Being

Warmth
Empathy
Genuineness

Doing

Paraphrasing
Reflection
Confrontation
Interpretation
Nonverbal communication

Does acquiring these attributes and skills seem to be an insurmountable task? As they begin their careers, many human service workers wonder whether they will be able to achieve an adequate level of functioning in these areas. Be assured that most do. However, reading about these attributes in a book does not prepare a person to employ effective personal relationship skills. How are such skills developed?

Each human service worker brings something with him or her into the field. Each brings a desire to be involved, along with many motives, beliefs, attitudes, and feelings. Many aspects of oneself are strengths; others are weaknesses. It is on this foundation—the personal equation factor—that human services training builds.

Human service educators have begun to identify the characteristics that human service workers need to cultivate. Among those that have been identified are personal qualities that benefit the human service worker and values that effective human service workers appear to embrace (Clubok, 1999; Littleton, 1999; Long and Doyle, 1999). Human service workers who have these personal qualities and values or who cultivate them appear to have an easier time learning or enhancing personal relationship skills.

1. *Acceptance of criticism.* Tolerate critics and be open about mistakes. Learn from all experiences, both positive and negative. Cultivate the habit of taking personal responsibility for self-growth, both in personal aspects and in terms of professional activity.

2. *Awareness of your fears.* Fear is a powerful blocking agent, but awareness is a first step toward surmounting it. Fear can be a challenge that we can meet, or it can result in self-defeating attitudes.

3. *Understanding of yourself.* Know your strengths and your weaknesses. You can capitalize on strengths and work on weaknesses. One person, for example, may

be great at relating to children but a poor writer; this person could aim at specializing in children's programs and work toward improved writing skills. Know who you are, what your problems are, and how you handle them. Know your goals and dreams and how you want to get there. Know what motivates you. All of this requires a fair degree of personal reflection and introspection.

4. *Know your limits, and take care of yourself.* Especially early in human service work, it is easy for people to get overinvolved, set goals for themselves *and clients* that are too ambitious, and set themselves up for failure. Separate your personal life from your work life, develop off-the-job interests and satisfactions, and be as committed to yourself in your *personal* life as you are to your clients in your *work* life.

5. *Acknowledge differences.* Be aware of who your clients are and where they are coming from both personally and culturally. Be culturally and ethnically sensitive. Seek ways to break through your cultural barriers and your clients' cultural barriers, while still valuing the diversity.

There are five critical but simple values that human service workers should hold.

1. Put the client's needs first.
2. Do not discriminate; that is, do not avoid helping people because of race, color, or creed. More difficult, do not avoid helping people who are unpleasant, dirty, angry, or unpretty.
3. Value clients' privacy. Share information with other workers and agencies *only* when you have to and never with friends or relatives.
4. Be honest. Unfortunately, sometimes agencies or other workers do things that you will see as not in a client's best interest. Give your opinion about the matter, but do not be a martyr.
5. Do no harm. Do your best, do what you know how to do, do not get in—or stay in—over your head, and do not take advantage of a client for your own needs.

The personal characteristics and values described here can be honed through experiential training and supervision. A college-level human services program will teach students the basic knowledge required in human services. In addition, some courses involve actual practice of personal relationship skills. Such practice usually involves events such as role playing and supervised feedback aimed at increasing warmth, empathy, genuineness, and communication skills. No one expects the novice to have all these attributes and skills fully formed and ready to go.

The development of personal relationship skills is an ongoing process. After completing college training, human service workers find employment in settings that usually require supervision. It is exceedingly rare for inexperienced or even experienced human service workers to be thrown into a situation where they must rely only on their own resources. Under the supervision of more experienced professionals, human service workers can continue the process of developing and sharpening personal relationship skills.

Who Helps the Helper? Supervision and Teamwork

For some period of time, the novice and even the experienced human service worker can expect to function under the supervision of a more experienced professional. The focus of the supervision, its intensity, and the nature of the supervisor vary from setting to setting. To a great extent, these aspects depend on the type of agency, the needs of the client population, the approaches used to deal with the clients' needs, and the training of the supervisors.

The issue of supervision is usually first encountered by human service students in their field practicum (Simon, 1999). The practicum student is assigned to an agency and an agency supervisor, usually called a *field instructor*. The student's assignment is a hands-on experience under the watchful eye of the field instructor. The field instructor's responsibility to the school is to provide three major functions: (1) administrative tasks such as linkage, accountability for the student's experience, and evaluation of the student; (2) education of the student through a tutorial or mentoring role; and (3) actual observation and supervision of the student.

The student in what is perhaps a first experience in being supervised is given much attention in the early stages of practice but, as ability is demonstrated, may have less direct supervision as time passes. Early supervision experiences can be anxiety-provoking for students who feel put on the spot. Most field supervisors, however, are well aware of this and try to be supportive of the students and open to dealing with their concerns.

For graduate employed human service workers, supervisors come from many disciplines, including education, social work, psychiatry, and psychology (see Table 9.1). However, the generic human services field has been growing for a long enough time that there are now many supervisors who began as human service professionals. In some settings, the novice is supervised by both a traditionally trained specialist and a senior human service worker.

Supervision for the beginning human service worker generally falls into three categories: housekeeping factors, role-specific factors, and personal relationship skills. Housekeeping factors include things such as use of time. The supervisor deals with such issues as worker absenteeism, tardiness, keeping appointments, and other factors that are important in any type of employment. Role-specific factors are relevant to a particular job in a particular agency. The supervisor may be concerned with, and give guidance on, the worker's understanding of the specific knowledge and needed skills. Behavior therapy, group dynamics, brokering, outreach, interviewing, activity therapies, and data collection are a few examples of the functions in this category on which supervisors may focus. In terms of relationship skills, supervisors often provide guidance and feedback on the human service worker's warmth, empathy, and genuineness with clients and on the effectiveness of the worker's verbal and nonverbal communication.

Many of the issues in effective personal relationship skills are relevant to making good use of supervisory sessions. The effective supervisor acts as a role model; warmth, empathy, and genuineness are attributes that the good supervisor should express toward the supervisee. As in the counseling relationship, growth is promoted

TABLE 9.1   Examples of Supervisors of Human Service Workers

Discipline	Education and Training	Settings
Educator	Bachelor's or master's degree in education or special education, practice teaching, supervised practice	Schools, preschools, special education programs, mental retardation programs
Psychiatrist	Medical degree (M.D.), psychiatric internship, psychiatric residency	Mental health clinics, mental hospitals
Psychologist	Doctorate in philosophy (Ph.D.), doctorate in psychology (Psy.D.), or master's in psychology, plus one year internship	Mental health clinics, mental hospitals, school systems, mental retardation programs
Social worker	Master of social work degree (M.S.W.), bachelor of social work (B.S.W.), plus practicum training	Mental health clinics, mental hospitals, family service agencies, wide variety of human services settings
Activity therapist	Bachelor's or master's degrees in activity therapy (A.T.), recreation therapy, and so forth; practicum experience	Work rehabilitation programs, mental hospitals, mental retardation programs
Human service worker	Associate of arts, bachelor's degree, or master's degree in human services program, plus experience	Virtually all human services settings

by an atmosphere of acceptance, involvement, and concern. The supervisor should also engage in effective communication, giving the supervisee clear feedback on strengths and weaknesses, positive behaviors, and errors in a supportive atmosphere (Cohen, 1999). Supervisors who are rated highly typically allow workers to raise issues about clients in their own way. They identify and track workers' emotionally charged concerns without digression to unrelated topics (Shanfield, Matthews, and Hetherly, 1993). Technical terms and jargon are used sparingly and then specifically linked to the material brought up by the worker. Often focus is placed on relationship issues, directed toward understanding the client's point of view. The supervisor focuses on helping the worker understand the issues the worker is raising with the intent of improving his or her ability to work with the client.

The human service worker has an equal responsibility for making the supervisory relationship work. In order to benefit from supervision, it is important to be as self-disclosing and open as possible. Being supervised is an active rather than a passive process. Employees who cover their mistakes will not be able to discover better ways of functioning. The most functional approach to receiving supervision is to adopt the attitude that behavior can be openly examined and modified. Human service workers who are helped by a supervisor to be aware of their own motives or behaviors have the opportunity to enhance their skills (Atwood, 1986).

Whether a novice or an expert, the human service worker usually does not work in isolation but as a member of a team that is a highly organized group of specialists or a looser group of generalists. Whatever the type of team, the members have the opportunity to develop a mutual support system. Like formal supervision, membership in a team provides a vehicle for enhancing skills. People can learn from peers and coworkers just as they learn from experts. To the extent that people can share their experiences, are self-disclosing, and listen to others, they can grow and develop as human service workers.

While the supervisory relationship is usually positive and helpful, on occasion a human service worker may find himself or herself with a supervisor who does not provide the supervision that is needed, or with whom a serious personality conflict develops. At times, this type of situation can be resolved by the efforts of the two persons to deal with the situation. But what of the human service worker who has this type of problem with a supervisor and who has been unsuccessful in resolving it with that supervisor? At the least, the human service worker should discuss the situation with peers for the support they can provide, and he or she must seriously consider taking the problem to a higher level of the organization (the supervisor's own supervisor). Additional strategies for dealing with this type of situation and other personal problems that human service workers face, such as handling personal values when working with clients, professional stress, burnout, and a variety of ethical issues, are covered in specific detail in an excellent text by Schneider-Corey and Corey (1989), *Becoming a Helper.*

Summary

1. Human service workers often are employed in settings in which the contemporary strategies constitute major treatment approaches. Human service workers then need to become familiar with whichever of the approaches is used in the setting: medical/psychiatric, behavioral, or psychotherapeutic.

2. Effective personal relationship skills fall into two broad categories: being and doing. *Being* refers to the attitudes, values, and feelings that have an impact on human relationships. *Doing* refers to observable skills or activities that enhance relationships.

3. Three aspects of being that have been identified as important are warmth, empathy, and genuineness. Warmth consists of the expression of tender, caring feelings and implies the ability to be involved with others. Empathy refers to the ability to tune in to another's point of view, feelings, and experience. Genuineness refers to congruence among behavior, feelings, words, and thoughts. Warmth, empathy, and genuineness are interrelated and important in forming effective helping relationships.

4. Doing involves particular communication techniques that enhance the expression and reception of information and feelings. These techniques include paraphrasing, reflection, confrontation, interpretation, and nonverbal behavior.

5. There are a number of techniques for breaking through cultural barriers to meaningful communication.

6. Five personal qualities that human service workers need to cultivate are identified along with five basic values.

7. Both novice and experienced human service workers can expect to be supervised by more experienced professionals. These supervisors may be traditionally trained specialists or more experienced human service workers.

8. Supervision usually deals with three categories of functioning. Housekeeping factors include routine issues such as employee use of time. Role-specific factors are specific to a particular job. Relationship factors are warmth, empathy, genuineness, and communication.

9. The supervisory relationship focuses on enhancing the supervisee's functioning. Ideally, supervisor and employee collaborate to increase the employee's awareness of personal strengths and weaknesses.

Discussion Questions

1. Is it necessary for human service workers to understand the contemporary strategies?

2. Should every human service worker be required to demonstrate competence in the relevant skills of each of the strategies?

3. Are warmth, empathy, and genuineness absolutely necessary for a person to work effectively in human services?

4. What might be an appropriate way of dealing with a supervisor with whom it seems impossible to develop a working relationship?

Learning Experiences

1. Listen to the content of your conversations with others. How much is focused on information transmission? How much on feelings?

2. Because paraphrasing is nonthreatening, practice the technique in daily conversations. Do not overdo it; a little bit goes a long way. Does it facilitate an interchange that clarifies what people say?

3. With another student, spend some time observing people's nonverbal behavior in different settings (in the classroom, cafeteria, or student union). Share your impressions about what the nonverbal behavior might mean in terms of people's communicated feelings.

4. In your interactions with others, try to analyze how their verbalizations and nonverbal behaviors are affecting you.

5. Discuss cultural differences and cultural barriers with someone from another culture.

Recommended Readings

Albronda Heaton, J. (1988). *Building basic therapeutic skills: A practical guide for current mental health practice.* San Francisco: Jossey-Bass.

Schneider-Corey, M., & Corey, G. (1989). *Becoming a helper.* Pacific Grove, CA: Brooks/Cole.

Truax, C. B., & Carkuff, R. R. (1967). *Toward effective counseling and psychotherapy.* Chicago: Aldine.

Wehrly, B. (1995). *Pathways to multicultural counseling competence: A developmental journey.* Pacific Grove, CA: Brooks/Cole.

10

Problem Assessment, Planning, Brokering

- Why is it important to make an accurate assessment of a client's presenting problem?
- What general principles govern the assessment and planning process?
- What types of assessment data should be gathered from clients?
- What is linkage, or brokering, of services?

The human services deal with a wide variety of people problems, and no single treatment, technique, or program can meet the needs of all persons. Specific problems require specific solutions or responses, and before a solution or response can be provided, the problem must be identified accurately. The human service worker must sort out the important problem or problems that the people in need are experiencing and link them to the appropriate services or experiences that will assist the clients in changing themselves or their environments. To list all the problems a human service worker will encounter is virtually impossible, but a number of illustrative problems can be presented to sensitize the worker to the types of issues in question.

Typical Problems Seen by Human Service Workers

1. *Problems of personal dissatisfaction.* Large numbers of individuals from all classes of society suffer from a sense of personal dissatisfaction; that is, they feel incomplete, unhappy, aimless, anxious, and lost. They are not "making it." It is not unusual for such people to walk into a human services center seeking relief.

■ ■ Betty Wilson is a forty-two-year-old mother of three. For several years, she has felt a lack of fulfillment in her life. Her relationship with her husband seems routine, and he seems more involved with his work and friends than with Betty and the children. For about six months, Betty has felt increasingly depressed about her life. No one seems to care how she feels, and she spends a lot of time tearfully recollecting "better times." Her painful feelings have become so pronounced that she has talked about them with her minister. He suggested that she make an appointment at a community women's center to talk to a counselor.

2. *Problems of isolation.* A major problem for human service workers is the social isolation of many individuals: the elderly in retirement homes, ex–mental patients in sheltered-care homes, and vagrants in skid row transient hotels, among others.

■ ■ Ethel Warren is seventy-one years old. Her husband died three years ago, and her children live in distant cities. Ethel lives alone in a two-room apartment in a large rundown urban building. Her friends are long gone, and she sees no one but the clerk at the grocery store. Ethel feels lonely and uncared for. She is frightened of going out because of the dangers of her neighborhood. Her days are bleak and uninteresting, each blending into another. Ethel often wishes that death would overtake her.

3. *Problems of poverty.* It has been estimated that there are approximately 36 million people living below the poverty level in the United States. Most human services programs thus require tax support to serve this needy group. When poverty strikes, there are often associated psychological experiences of distress and turmoil.

■ ■ John Selton is twenty-eight and unemployed. He was laid off from his job at a Detroit automaker and drove to Dallas because he heard that work was available in the Sunbelt. His grade school education and lack of technical skills did not make him a good candidate for employment, and he now lives in his car in a tent city along a ravine outside Dallas. He survives on handouts from a charity group and feels demeaned and desperate.

4. *Problems of addiction.* Alcoholics and drug abusers are commonly seen as clients at human services centers.

■ ■ Miguel Hernandez is thirty-two years old and separated from his wife and two children. He is on his third job in seven months as a manual laborer. Miguel has lost his family and his jobs because of excessive drinking. Most of his paycheck is spent in bars. In the past half year, he has been arrested four times for drunk and disorderly conduct. On the verge of being fired again for drinking on the job, Miguel still denies that he has a problem with alcohol abuse.

5. *Problems of crisis.* Individuals experiencing a crisis often become human service clients. Loss of a loved one through death, divorce, or abandonment; loss of a job; or any number of severe stress situations can lead to an inability to cope with day-to-day events.

■■ Mary Jo Brandt is a young farm widow whose husband recently died from a heart attack. Mary Jo is losing the heavily mortgaged farm to foreclosure by the bank. She has trouble sleeping and caring for her school-age children. Mary Jo feels guilty over her inability to function but is unable to keep from slipping into inactivity and depression. She feels that things are hopeless and does not know where to turn for help.

6. *Problems of severely disruptive behavior.* Many people end up in human services settings because they engage in extremely disruptive behavior that is long-standing in nature.

■■ Larry Teal is twenty-three years old. His middle-class parents are extremely distraught about his behavior. Larry dropped out of college after one semester because he could not handle the work load, even though he had been a B student in high school. His behavior has been very strange. He recently was apprehended by the police after he created a disturbance on a city bus. Larry had disrobed in front of the other passengers while screaming that he was the new Christ and that nakedness could open the doors to heaven. When police tried to take him into custody, Larry fought them and claimed that they had been sent by Satan.

In Table 10.1, these typical problem areas are presented with common responses for each problem. Unfortunately, individuals who have only one problem are rarely seen in human services centers; rather, we see multiproblem persons. For example, one might encounter individuals who have lost their jobs because of drunkenness; who have no friends or family, no money, and no place to live; who have bleeding ulcers; and who think everyone is out to get them. In other multiproblem cases, the issues may not be so clear. It becomes the human service

TABLE 10.1   Typical Problems and Common Responses

Problem	*Response*
Personal dissatisfaction	Psychological counseling
Isolation	New social network
Poverty	Public financial assistance Vocational training Employment counseling
Addiction: alcohol	Alcoholism counseling Alcoholics Anonymous Residential treatment
Addiction: drugs	Methadone maintenance Synanon program
Crisis	Crisis counseling
Severe behavior problems	Medication Psychotherapy Residential program

worker's responsibility to identify the problems accurately so that appropriate responses can be made.

The Need for Assessment

Why is it so critical to identify the problem areas accurately in the multiproblem person? We have already touched briefly on one major reason: the need to tailor services to the problems the client experiences. Not only does it not make good conceptual sense to use, for example, the psychotherapies as a shotgun approach for all human problems but also it is not likely to work. Problem identification is a process to be used to expedite linkages. Effective, accurate problem identification assists the human service worker in directing the client to the appropriate services and resources. Figure 10.1 depicts the flow of clients through a hypothetical human services system based on this triage (sorting out) process.

Physical and psychological crises are dealt with first: food, medical problems, money, housing, and crisis feelings. The client then can be linked with psychotherapeutic services if the problem is psychological, with social or environmental support systems if those are sufficient, or with both, if necessary. If maximal impact systems are required (such as a residential treatment program), the client can ultimately be linked to those that are appropriate and available. At any point in the system flow, clients can exit if their identified problems have been resolved or can enter new services if new problems appear.

A second rationale for this process involves maximizing resource use and determining priorities. As discussed earlier, funding for human services is not unlimited. At times, the human service worker must make very unpleasant decisions about which of the potential clients should receive the services. Using the common example about the middle-class housewife who is mildly depressed about her place in life and the ghetto mother on public aid, it would seem that it is more critical to provide services to the latter because the middle-class housewife usually has alternative resources (for example, she may be able to pay for private services). This is not a hard-and-fast statement, of course. Obviously, such decision making must rest on the situations and data of individual cases. One can propose, however, that the greater the need, the more likely that services should be provided.

Principles of Triage

A few general principles govern the effective application of the triage process. The following discussion clarifies the importance of each.

1. Not all people are alike; different problems demand different solutions. Even though this principle may seem obvious, in practice the same type of solution (such as psychotherapy) is often applied to widely different problems.

190

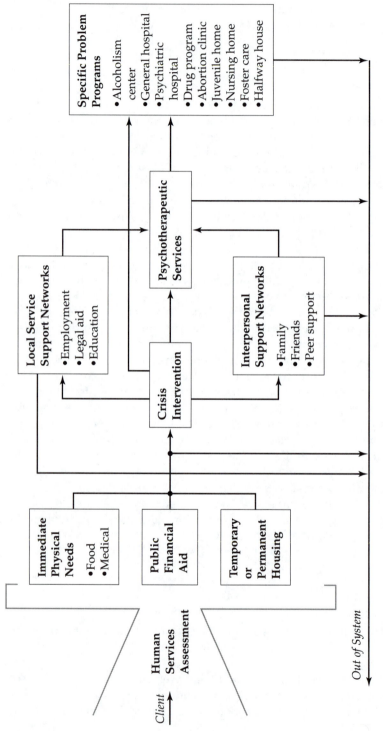

FIGURE 10.1 Human Services Flowchart

2. The more specific to the problem the solution is, the more effective and efficient it will be. The child who is phobic (frightened and anxious) about going to school usually can be treated more quickly and with better results through a behavior therapy program than through verbal family therapy.

3. The less intrusive the solution, the better. A common occurrence in the identification of problems and their linkage with solutions is a tendency to "oversolve" the problems; that is, the service provider does not let the client *go* when the identified problem is solved or handled. Rather than just dealing with the specific problem, the service provider attempts to revamp the psychological and behavioral makeup of the client completely. Such an approach tends to create in clients unnecessary dependency on the services being provided and links clients into the system for an inappropriate length of time. In effect, this principle suggests that only services that are absolutely necessary be provided—if an individual needs a job, help him or her get one but do not attempt to remake personality through psychotherapy.

4. Solutions are more effective if applied soon after the development of the problem. Strong evidence supports this principle (Follette et al., 1998; Fraser, 1986; Myers, 1994). As time passes, individuals often develop inappropriate ways of trying to cope. The more they use these inappropriate coping strategies, the more difficult it is for them to change. This principle implies that human services centers should not have waiting lists of clients and that there should be no delays in linking clients to services once the problems have been identified in the triage process.

5. Problems must be identified (assessed) accurately if appropriate solutions and resources are to be linked to the client. Obviously, if one cannot identify the client problem accurately, there is a greater likelihood of offering inappropriate and ineffective services. For example, a chronic alcoholic arrives at a human services intake program having just lost his job. The intake worker accepts that problem at face value and links the client to an employment counselor. The odds are that the problem will be repeated (the client will lose the new job) because the critical issue (the drinking pattern) has not been modified.

Issues in Assessment

When individuals ask for help, there are four basic ways to gather data in order to assess the problem and its severity. The human service worker can (1) ask the client, (2) ask someone who knows the person, (3) observe the client in his or her natural setting, or (4) observe the person in certain standard test situations. By far the most common assessment technique is interviewing the client. The interview generally can be described as a structured conversation that has the goal of eliciting specific types of information.

In the triage process, the goals are ordinarily to identify the client's problems, determine what factors have led to the development of the problems, and, most important, determine the severity of the problems. The interview is important, but it is only one part of the assessment process, which also includes (1) learning the client's problem, (2) data collection (interviewing, formal testing, talking to collaterals, observing behavior), (3) organizing and interpreting the data, and (4) action (decision making, including possible referral, brokering of services, or the direct provision of services).

Effectively completing the four steps in the assessment process assumes that the human service worker is able to develop a beginning trustful relationship with the client and has accurately gathered the information that is necessary for problem identification, planning, and brokering of services. This may be particularly difficult when the human service worker and the client are of different cultural backgrounds. The dynamics of difference can be most problematic at the assessment phase of service (Cross, Bazron, Dennis, and Isaacs, 1989).

When assessing a person of another culture, the human service worker must be prepared by having learned what types of behavior are accepted and common in the client's culture. The worker must also be sensitive to the behaviors that are typical of this type of bicultural encounter (Paniagua, 1994). For example, when a minority family or individual encounters a system or helper that is unlike them, they may exhibit adjustment behaviors; that is, they're likely to be more reserved than usual, they may be apprehensive and fearful, or they may display a false sense of bravado as a defense against the possible threats in the novel situation. The presence of these behaviors may obscure the underlying problems, and the human service worker may identify one of these behaviors as the problem or as a complicating factor.

Assessment can be biased by misinterpretation of language and emotional expression. Eye contact, firmness of handshake, tone of voice, and greeting are culturally dependent, and workers who rely on what these things mean in their culture may draw incorrect conclusions. The human service worker must be aware of various forms of etiquette important in different cultures. Home visits in a Black or Native American community usually involve offers of food, with *refusal* of the food considered a personal rejection. In Hispanic encounters, a period of social contact is considered polite before conducting business. Asian clients expect the human service worker to answer polite but personal questions. Rebuffs of these social conventions impair the worker's ability to effectively communicate and obtain information. If the human service worker can thread a path through these obstacles, the assessment process can continue through the formal interview.

The interview is so important and common an assessment tool that numerous human service books devote most of their material to its discussion and presentation. Here, we must limit ourselves to a broad consideration.

The process of effective interviewing is clearly a skill, the acquisition of which requires hands-on practice, training, supervision, and experience. It cannot be learned from books. What can be considered here is the type of information or data a human service worker may need to make reasonable decisions during the triage process. The following outline contains the major types of data human service workers have found helpful in the triage process. Not all the data are necessary in all cases, and the choice of particular areas of data collection for a particular client is dependent on the individual situation.

Client Care Data

I. Current life status
   A. Major life setting. Describe major life systems the client interacts with (work, family, school). How adequately is the client functioning in these systems?
   B. Problem behaviors
      1. From the client's perspective, what are the problems?
      2. What do significant others consider to be a problem for the client?
      3. From the human service worker's perspective, what are the problem behaviors?
   C. History of presenting problems
      1. A chronological description of the reasons for and events surrounding present status
      2. Special attention may be paid to the duration and onset of the problems, especially in making efforts to quantify the problems, circumstances, and events in frequency and time
      3. A brief review of past and present treatment: involvement in social service agency or agencies
      4. A report of the antecedents to the problem behavior(s) and the subsequent consequences
      5. What the client has tried to do to solve the problems and how he or she has been coping with them
   D. What does the client want out of this contact?

II. How does the client present himself or herself?
   A. Physically: healthy, sick, attractive, unattractive, slovenly, neat
   B. Emotionally: depressed, nervous, energetic, angry, quiet, loud, controlled, impulsive, mature
   C. Client's self-description
   D. Intellectual assets

III. Social determinants
   A. Group membership
      1. Referent groups
      2. Occupational identity
   B. Family
      1. Structure
      2. Relationships
   C. Education
   D. Work
   E. Ecology
      1. Type of community
      2. Community involvement
   F. Cultural factors

IV. Major stress and coping
   A. Type of stress
      1. Social
      2. Interpersonal
      3. Situational
      4. Intrapersonal
   B. Current coping styles
      1. Withdrawal
      2. Aggression
      3. Internalization

V. Development: Analysis of the client's significant past experiences that have led to this client's current "being"

VI. The conceptualization: Bring together all the information into a relatively concise conceptualization of the person as he or she is and can be

VII. The plan
   A. Identify the needed changes in order to assist the client
      1. Environmental or social
      2. Intrapersonal
   B. Outline the necessary steps to effect the changes, including the linkages to other personnel or agencies
   C. Develop a criterion for successful implementation of change agentry

After the human service worker has gathered the critical data and identified the client's problem areas, several important decisions must be made. The first, of course, is whether the client needs the available services. If the client does, the services must be specified, the goals for the services defined, and the client linked to those services. (In the outline, this occurs in section VII.) In other words, the human service worker develops a service plan, in writing, that can follow the client along as he or she receives help. Such a plan is important in that it (1) provides a baseline around which services can be organized and (2) specifies desired results so that the human service worker knows whether the original goals are being reached. It is possible and even likely that as the client receives the initially identified services, new data will be discovered or new problems may arise, and the original service plan may be modified (Stout and Jongsma, 1998).

The final product of the process is the actual linkage or brokering of services for the client. In the ideal system, all services are available under one agency; therefore, the worker can link the client to the needed service with a minimum of effort. Unfortunately, few human services systems are organized in such a manner. Much more commonly, in order to provide needed services for clients, the human service worker must refer them across agency lines. Figure 10.2 illustrates this system, with two hypothetical human service clients: an individual having a psychotic episode (broken line) and an alcoholic (solid line).

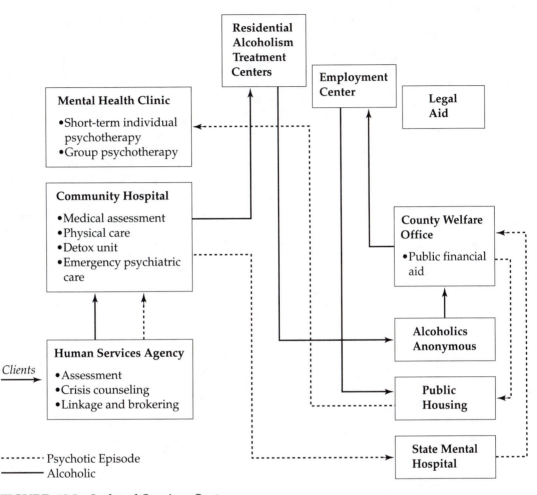

FIGURE 10.2   Isolated Services System

In this example (Figure 10.2), the human services agency staff members function mainly as problem identifiers. Thereafter, they serve as advocates and brokers for the client, following the client through the maze of services and assisting the transition between services when such transfers are necessary. Most community service systems function along these lines. Many services are available, but they are functionally isolated from each other. Unfortunately, most communities do not have a central human services agency to play the advocate-broker role for the client. This coordinating role is just now being developed in most communities. It is often up to individual human service workers to act as advocate-broker-coordinators for their clients.

The situation becomes even more problematic for the client who has two major disorders, each of which is traditionally addressed by a separate system. Look again at the example in Figure 10.2. This time think of it as an example of one person who suffers *both* from severe mental illness and substance abuse at the same time. This dual problem is such a common occurrance that service providers have developed acronyms for it: MISA (mental illness and substance abuse) or MICA (mental illness and chemical abuse). The service systems for these two disorders are often organized, administered, and funded separately.

The seriously mentally ill and substance-abusing client presents several challenges to the mental health and the alcohol and substance abuse service delivery providers. During the course of this decade, an increasing number of researchers have explored the the nature and problems of MISA clients in the professional and research literature (Drake & Mueser, 1996a). Treatment difficulty and poor outcomes are consistently reported in the literature for the MISA client. Anecdotal reports from the field support these findings. Dual-diagnosed clients are often excluded or expelled from drug treatment settings because they are on psychotropic medication or are difficult to manage. These treatment interruptions are often due to knowledge, attitude, and philosophy differences between alcohol and substance abuse counselors and mental health providers, a sort of professional "cultural" bias (Mehr, 1999).

A second presumed cause of treatment failure is the referral of these clients from one system to the other. As clients are referred back and forth between the mental health and substance abuse systems—"Ping-Pong therapy"—conflicting treatment plans are developed by service providers. This lack of coordination between the two service delivery systems often results in the client's confusion and frustration, and a large number of these clients give up on serivces. The MISA client, in addition, generally presents a severe level of dysfunction and is beset by multiple problems. These additional problems may include homelessness, unemployment, other medical needs, and legal difficulties. Finally, the person typically comes to the attention of either the alcohol and substance abuse or the mental health systems in crisis (for example, a psychiatric or medical emergency or acute intoxication). Intervention at this time typically involves observation, management of withdrawal or management of acute psychiatric symptoms, and stabilization. Although the immediate symptomatology is addressed, a coordinated, comprehensive approach for ongoing treatment is absent. The end result is that people in need of services from both systems receive appropriate services from neither.

Estimates of the scope of the problem vary dramatically. For example, survey samples drawn from a number of psychiatric settings across the country indicate that from 25 percent to 40 percent of all psychiatric patients suffer from both mental illness and substance abuse disorders. Further, a number of studies suggest that substance abuse is more frequent among the chronic mentally ill than in the general population. In fact, the reported substance abuse rate among chronic mentally ill patients approaches or exceeds 50 percent, depending on the definitions used and the substances studied. One survey reported a history of marijuana abuse among 37 percent of young adults with chronic mental illness. An earlier study of an outpatient chronic population found the 37 percent abused alcohol and

37 percent abused drugs—not necessarily the same individuals. Two other surveys reveal an incidence of both alcoholism and substance abuse as high as 74 percent among younger psychiatric patients, eighteen to thirty-five years of age .

Because mental health, substance abuse, and other professionals tend to become extremely focused on specialty training in their areas of interest, they tend to be subject to "diagnostic overshadowing," a sort of assessment and problem identification blind spot. The mental health professional tends to underdiagnose mental illness in the mentally retarded and underdiagnose substance abuse in the mentally ill. The mental retardation professional tends to overdiagnose mental illness in the person who is mentally retarded and having a behavior problem. The substance abuse professional tends to underdiagnose substance abuse and overidentify mental illness in people who present with behavior problems. This phenomenon often assures that individuals with multiple problems that may be unrecognized do not get the services they need.

Human service workers must be alert to these issues of major dual diagnoses because they may have to become broker-advocates in order to access dual services for their particularly needy clients. Obviously, to function in this role with this particular group of individuals or with any multiproblem client, workers must *know* their community, know the services available, and know the contact person in the corresponding agencies (Petrie, 1986; Whittaker et al., 1983). Human service workers must assess the community and develop a community resource directory with a list of the resource agencies, the services each provides, and their client requirements, cost, intake process, and contact person. In addition, it might include the informal systems that would benefit the client, such as clubs, organizations, transportation, and recreational systems. Without knowing community resource data, human service workers cannot effectively assist their clients.

Summary

1. Human service workers are confronted with a wide variety of people problems, including personal dissatisfaction, isolation, poverty, addiction, crisis, and severely disruptive behavior.

2. Human service clients often have combinations of problems. It is critical to identify the problems accurately so that appropriate services can be rendered in a manner that maximizes resources.

3. A number of principles have been identified that govern the triage or assessment and linkage process.

   a. Different problems demand different solutions.

   b. Solutions should be specific to the problem.

   c. Solutions should not be intrusive.

   d. Solutions should be rapid.

   e. Assessment should be accurate.

4. The assessment process includes preparation, client input, data processing, and output (decision making).

5. Interviewing is a major assessment technique that must be learned experientially. Many types of information must be obtained in an assessment interview.

6. The human service worker must become familiar with the culture of the client to be able to conduct an effective interview and collect valid data.

7. The client care data gained in the assessment process are used to identify problems or client needs in order to develop an individual service plan that provides the basis for organizing services. The plan specifies desired results so that service delivery can be evaluated.

8. The final product of the assessment and planning process is the actual linkage, or brokering, of services. This often places the human service worker in a coordinating role among various community agencies.

9. Identifying and assessing multiple problems of the client, as illustrated by the dual diagnosis of MISA, presents a special challenge for the human service worker.

Discussion Questions

1. Why is it important to identify problems accurately?
2. What are the principles of assessment, planning, and brokering?
3. Why is it important to have a service plan?

Learning Experiences

1. Practice an assessment interview on a friend with the friend's permission.
2. Develop a hypothetical service plan for a make-believe client (or a real client if you have access to someone and permission to do it).
3. Identify the formal human services resources in your community (hot lines, mental health clinics, and employment offices) by name and address.

Recommended Readings

Cormier, W. H., & Cormier, L. S. (1985). *Interviewing strategies for helpers: Fundamental skills and cognitive-behavioral intervention* (2nd ed.). Monterey, CA: Brooks/Cole.

Mehr, J. (1999). Human services in the mental health arena: From institution to community. In H. S. Harris and D. C. Maloney (Eds.), *Human services: Contemporary issues and trends* (2nd ed.). Boston: Allyn and Bacon.

Paniagua, F. A. (1994). *Assessing and treating culturally diverse clients: A practical guide.* Thousand Oaks, CA: Sage.

11

Case Management
Cornerstone for Human Services

- How is *case management* defined?
- What core functions describe case management?
- What are the different case management models?
- What are the three high intensity models?
- How does case management vary across several different settings?
- What are some important case management issues to consider?

Case management is only one of a number of roles that human service workers fill, but the probability is high that an entry-level human service worker's first paid position will be in case management. In just a few decades, *case management,* or as it is now sometimes called, *service coordination,* has become a cornerstone service or process in most human services systems. Today case managers are found in such areas as community mental health agencies, childrens' services, public welfare agencies, long-term care programs for the elderly, alcohol and substance abuse treatment agencies, vocational rehabilitation services, agencies for people with mental retardation, and the community criminal justice system, to name but a few.

Case management is critically important for many people who have any of a variety of human services problems. Despite its simplicity, this statement belies the complexity of issues that surround case management services. In considering the application of a case management approach to human services, a number of factors must be taken into account, including the model of case management, the level of intensity, the critical elements that must be present, and the requisite skills that are needed by a case manager. Our understanding of a variety of such issues has grown substantially over the past ten to fifteen years (Drake and Mueser, 1996). The use of case management services was an early feature of the human services movement, dating from its very inception more than thirty years ago (Woodside and McClam, 1998). In one form or another, elements of case management practice can be traced back to the beginning of modern social welfare (Trattner, 1986; Weil and Karls, 1989).

In its general form, case management has been defined in a variety of ways. Geron and Chassler (1994) have defined case management as a "service that links and coordinates assistance from both paid service providers and unpaid help from family and friends to enable consumers to obtain the highest level of independence consistent with their capacity and their preferences for care." In another example, the National Association of Social Workers (1992) defined it as "a method of providing services whereby a professional social worker assesses the needs of the client and the client's family (when appropriate), and arranges, coordinates, monitors, evaluates, and advocates for a package of multiple services to meet the specific client's complex needs." More recently, the National Association of Case Management defined it as

> A practice in which the service recipient is a partner, to the greatest extent possible, in assessing needs, obtaining services, treatments, and supports, and in preventing and managing crisis. The focus of the partnership is recovery and self management of . . . life. The individual and the practitioner plan, coordinate, monitor, adjust, and advocate for services and supports directed toward the achievement of the individual's personal goals for community living. (Hodge and Giesler, 1997)

The application of case management to people with serious human service problems began in the 1960s and became widespread in the 1970s and 80s. Like many human services endeavors, it became prominent as the main focus for treatment of the tens of thousands of severely mentally ill people who had been discharged from state hospitals into the community during the deinstitutionalization era. Case management was ultimately designated as an essential service within the influential federal Community Support Program (CSP) model of services in 1978 (Rapp and Kisthardt, 1996). In these same decades, human services programs of many different types were developed, and case management was often viewed as the foundation for delivering the service to the identified clients. All across North America, case management has been incorporated in child welfare, mental health, child protection, substance abuse, mental retardation, adult and juvenile justice, teen pregnancy, youth employment, aging, AIDS, welfare to work, rehabilitation, and managed care programs.

During the past thirty years, several different models of case management have emerged, reflecting different approaches to differing types of need and intensity of problem. Originally, *case management* meant to arrange for services for one's client, essentially to act as a broker-advocate and help the client negotiate a complex system of care (Southern Regional Education Board, 1969). Over time, the original brokering approach was joined by approaches to case management that differed in intensity, underlying theory of focus, and clinical involvement.

Approaches to Case Management

A fairly comprehensive categorization of case management models includes the brokerage model, the clinical model, the strengths model, the rehabilitation model, Assertive Community Treatment (ACT), and Intensive Case Management (ICM) (Hodge and Giesler, 1997; Kuno, Rothbard, and Sands, 1999; Mueser, Bond, Drake, and Resnick, 1998; Winarski, 1996). While these various models differ substantially, they share similar core functions. Lists of core functions vary only slightly from expert to expert, and most lists include something similar to the following (Moxley, 1989; Stroud, 1995):

- *Assessment:* Gathering information about the person's circumstances, assets, problems, needs, and goals. Assessment often involves convening and facilitating a multidisciplinary or multiagency team to complete a broad-based ecological assessment.
- *Planning:* Identifying activities that will further the achievement of the consumer's goals, promote problem solving, meet needs; identifying who will do what. Planning often involves input from significant others, such as a child's parents.
- *Service Implementation:* May involve linkage to services and provision of services. Case managers may procure and broker services, including informal and nontraditional supports. May involve resource development or the provision of direct clinical services by the case manager.
- *Service Coordination:* Linking various agencies or individuals involved with service provision to the client. The case manager acts as the hub of all service-related interaction for the client; he or she should be the one person who knows all the critical information regarding the client.
- *Monitoring:* Ongoing regular contact with the client. Monitoring often results in formal reassessment and change of the plan, and is directed toward ensuring the continuity of service provision.
- *Evaluation:* Assessing the effectiveness of the plan and activities based on attachment of the client's goals.
- *Involvement:* Staying engaged with the client in a helping relationship per the client's desire and need. The relationship represents the core of the case management process.

The core functions of case management in human services may be expressed in different ways and to differing degrees, depending upon the particular case management model.

The Brokerage Model

The brokerage model of case management has the longest history of the identified models. It is a rather generic model that has been applied in many of the human services fields (Austin and McClelland, 1996). The generic functions of brokerage case management include outreach, screening or intake, assessment, case planning, service arrangement, monitoring, and, when necessary, reassessment. The term *brokerage* refers to the service arrangement function, since historically, in this model, much emphasis has been placed on acting as a so-called broker of services for the client. Prior to the development of the Community Support Program (CSP) approach by the National Institute of Mental Health (NIMH) in 1978, brokerage case management was probably the dominant model in community mental health agencies, and it continues to be in many social welfare agencies.

The brokerage model focuses on problem identification, plan development, and brokerage to services that will solve, or assist the client in solving, the identified problems. The model does not incorporate the notion that the case manager must necessarily provide clinical services to the client or even that the case manager have some advanced clinical understanding of the client's problems in behavior. This exclusive focus on the brokerage role distinguishes this model from those that were developed as alternatives to it. The brokerage model is the dominant case management model in many social welfare programs, such as Transitional Aid to Needy Families (TANF). Human service workers who are employed as case workers in such programs are likely to function like John in the following illustration.

■■ John Mateson is a case worker in the regional office of a midwestern state's main social service agency, the Office of Transitional Services. It is this agency that handles requests for state financial assistance for persons who need public aid. John's job is to process requests for public financial assistance as they are assigned to him. With the new federal and state regulations limiting eligibility time for assistance and requiring people to move off welfare into competitive employment, case workers such as John have to do more active case management of people on their case load. John screens applicants for eligibility and, if the client is eligible, assesses the client's needs for supportive services including, for example, screening whether the individual has an alcohol or drug problem or a mental illness that would interfere with job training or job placement. John then brokers services for the client. He refers the person to ancillary services that the person needs, and even links the person to those services (arranges an appointment at a drug treatment center, for example). John will link the person to a variety of supports based on the assessment and joint planning that is captured in a written service plan (in this agency called an *Independence Plan*). John schedules periodic follow-up meetings, which he will use to monitor the client's involvement in services, the impact of the services, and reassess whether any additional service needs must be addressed in order for the client to obtain work. In this brokerage case management role, John does almost no direct behavior change work himself with the client other than occasionally attempt to increase the motivation of the client.

Engagement of client
Assessment of strengths and deficits
Planning
Linkage to resources
Consultation with family, other service(s)
Social network maintenance and expansion
Collaboration with other providers (especially physicians)
Advocacy for the client and the system
Intermittent psychotherapy or counseling
Social skills training
Psychoeducation
Crisis intervention
Monitoring progress

FIGURE 11.1   Tasks or Components of Clinical Case Management

Source: Based on Kanter, 1989

Clinical Case Management

The CSP, promulgated by the National Institute of Mental Health in the 1980s, identified case management as an essential service for people with severe and persistent mental illness. It was promulgated as the glue that holds the service system together for the mentally ill.

Experience with providing case management for such individuals stimulated a number of clinicians to advocate for a more clinical approach to case management than the prevailing brokerage model (Bachrach, 1982; Lamb, 1980; Rapp and Chamberlin, 1985). Clinical case management has been succinctly defined by Kanter (1985, 1989), as an approach that addresses the maintenance of a person's physical and social environment, with the goals of facilitating his or her physical survival, personal growth, community participation, and recovery from or adaptation to mental illness. It is a model that emphasizes the principles of continuity of care (treatment over extended periods of time); the use of the relationship with the client, the family, and significant others, for collaboration; the variation in the intensity of support and intervention based on client's needs; the flexibility of intervention strategies; and the facilitation of self-determination and resourcefulness on the part of the client. Kantor has identified a number of component tasks that the clinical case manager engages in (see Figure 11.1).

Unlike the brokerage model, in this approach the expectation that the case manager will provide clinical services is made very clear. Case managers must thus have some significant level of clinical training. For example, although case managers might not schedule formal psychotherapy sessions, as would a client's psychotherapist, the skills involved in dealing with issues such as housemates, family, or work conflicts are substantially the same as those required to do psychotherapy (Kanter, 1989). It requires the ability to build a relationship, identify and respect defenses, explore relevant defenses and make appropriate reflective, clarifying, or interpretive comments. Clinical case management is particularly prevalent in service systems for people with significant behavioral problems, such as mental health, substance abuse, and child welfare. The first and perhaps most critical task in clinical case management is the engagement of the client into the helping relationship, as illustrated in the following example (Able-Peterson and Bucy, 1993).

■■ Trudee Able-Peterson is a human service case manager working with homeless-runaway youth on the streets of a U.S. city. She works "in a poor neighborhood filled with hustlers preying on children, youth, and other vulnerable human beings. She has walked the streets; rocked the raped, beaten, child to sleep; educated a bewildered twelve-year-old about AIDS and buried a teenager who died of that disease; she's knocked on doors to ask for money to keep the program alive; pleaded with politicians to develop laws to protect children; shared her vision with hospital workers, police, lawyers and church groups, of a society that does not exploit and harm children but rather halts the injustices against them, recognizes their talents and their dreams and builds on them".

Trudee follows four rules while doing outreach and trying to engage street youths in a relationship. Rule 1 is to state simply who you are, and Rule 2 is to learn their name. Trudee describes that process: "'Hi, my name is Trudee and I'm a counselor with The Streetwork Project.' At this point, I hand the youth a business card with the name of the project, a 24-hour hotline number, and the services listed at the drop-in center a few blocks away—food, showers, clothing, counseling, AIDS education, and so forth. 'I noticed you hanging around here, and it's kind of dangerous in the area. Is everything all right?' Usually by now the kid is reading the card. 'This is my partner Ilene. We come out in this area and talk to kids, just to make sure they're okay, or if they need anything. What's your name?' In a nonjudgmental way, streetworkers slip into the lives of young people. 'Did you have anything to eat today? Are you still living at home?' Intersperse these questions throughout the first contact as if they were the most natural questions in the world, in a quiet, calm voice. Keep your body language respectful of their space. Offer a hand shake, but no other touching in this early stage. If you are offering a drop-in center or van/office services, tell them the location, hours, and services available. Stress food, clothing, and showers. They are always hungry in these rapid growth years and are often experiencing malnutrition. A shower and clean clothing offers them a bit of dignity in a world where they're often stripped of it. If you offer to buy them food immediately, let them suggest their favorite fast food restaurant nearby. They will be less wary on known turf. A meal for one or two kids may be an opportunity to have a longer conversation. If they seem reluctant, buy them the meal, tell them to be careful tonight, let them know you'll be around again, and repeat your name and theirs when you say goodbye."

Rule 3 is "be patient and consistent," and Rule 4 is "trust the process." It takes a long time and is difficult for a helper to be recognized as such by youth on the street who have experienced rejection and violence in their families, and broken promises and more rejection from workers and caretakers in their downward spiral through

Case managers often need to use engagement strategies wherever the potential client is located, even in the street.

placements to the degradation of the streets and the assaults of street predators. Trudee says, "When I met Nancy she had been on the streets for two years. She left home at age 13 after she was raped by her stepfather. She was addicted to street drugs—angel dust, speed, downers, and alcohol. Every time I spoke to her, she would snarl back at me, and even when some of her girlfriends began responding to me, she totally ignored me. I said hello to her every night anyway. I kept my voice open and friendly, and told her to be careful each night. After I knew her for about six months, I realized that she was pregnant. A few months later she disappeared from the streets. The other kids were vague about what happened to her. One day, sitting at my desk in the Street-work Project office, I heard someone call my name. When I looked up, there was Nancy. Her head was hanging as if in shame and embarrassment. I stood to greet her and said how glad I was to see her, noticing that she was no longer pregnant. 'My baby died and it was my fault,' she mumbled as she began to cry. Her baby, born with severe medical problems, had died a few hours after birth.

"After so many months of trying to reach Nancy and being rebuffed constantly, she finally turned to me for help. She was able to do this because I was never judgmental with her in the past. We worked together for the next two years. Nancy has been living off the streets now for many years. It had taken almost a year for her to begin to trust me, but she finally was able to become engaged in case management relationship that could help her change her life."

The Strengths Model

The strengths model of case management grew from a view that treatment and services (including case management) for people with severe human service problems such as mental illness were overly focused on the deficits and disabilities of the person, rather than on the strengths that the person may be able to capitalize on in order to reach personal goals. This negative or pessimistic approach was seen as hampering clients' adjustment and recovery. The strengths model rests on two basic assumptions about human behavior (Rapp, 1996, 1997). The first underlying assumption of this model is that people who are successful at community living are able to develop and maximize this potential, and that they have access to the resources needed to do so. The second assumption is that effective human behavior is mostly a function of, and dependent on, the amount of resources available to individuals. Thus, the strengths model identifies people's strengths and actually creates situations where those strengths can lead to personal successes. For people who are severely mentally ill, for example, this means providing assistance in securing important resources such as employment skills, housing, education, medical care, social skills, and in developing social networks. There are several defining characteristics of the strengths model:

1. Strengths are focused on, rather than deficits (Rapp, 1993, 1996, 1997)
2. Interventions are determined by the client.
3. Community is seen as the locus of resources rather than of obstacles to overcome.
4. Active enrichment of strengths and client self-identity are focused on.
5. Clients are connected to resources for improving their quality of life.
6. Environmental support is provided to assist the client in moving closer to her or his personal goals.
7. The case manager–client relationship is viewed as the primary essential tool in the helping process.

■ ■ Joanie May Cotton, a case manager in a child service agency in Chicago, has adopted a strengths case management perspective. She's working now with a nine-year-old boy, Damon, and his single mother, Sarnia. Damon has been truant from school and Sarnia feels overwhelmed with "Just one more problem to deal with, with this child." She feels too intimidated to be able to effectively talk with the school administrators about Damon's problems at school. After exploring the family history, structure, relationships, and individual issues of the boy and his mother, Joanie May begins to focus on strengths revealed in the assessment process. First, Damon has an avid interest in science (robots and space ships). Joanie May will use that as a strength to encourage Damon to return to school to satisfy his desire to know more about those things. Second, Sarnia is a Licensed Practical Nurse (LPN). Joanie May will work with Sarnia to help her transfer her skills at doing a complicated job and her ability to relate to intimidating physicians to relating to the school administrators. These strengths will become the foundation of an extensive plan of care that focuses on Damon and Sarnia's goals, rather than on problems. Damon's desires will be the foundation for determining his goals, and Sarnia's goals will focus on the resources that she needs in order to provide supportive care to her child. The plan will identify specific steps or tasks necessary to acquire needed resources or to learn a specific skill.

The Rehabilitation Model

The rehabilitation model of case management has primarily been promulgated by psychiatrist William Anthony and others of the Boston University Center for Psychiatric Rehabilitation (Anthony, Cohen, Farkas, and Cohen, 1988; Anthony, Forbes, and Cohen, 1993). This model shares many similarities with the strengths model. In the rehabilitation model there is primary concern with identifying the individual client's unique needs and goals, rather than with having any focus on the overall goals of the formal human services system (such as reducing expensive hospital utilization). A characteristic of a rehabilitation case management model is an emphasis on assessing skills deficits and the remediation of instrumental and affiliative skills (for example, housekeeping skills or skills of social conversation or dating), that could prolong community stays and promote the attainment of the client's personal goals (Okpakus et al., 1997). Rehabilitation case management focuses on helping clients find success and satisfaction in the social environment of their choice with the least amount of intrusion by clinical professionals necessary in order to support clients' strengths and remediate skills deficits (Rapp and Kisthardt, 1996).

■■ Kathy is a case manager in a community psychosocial rehabilitation program run under the administrative umbrella of a community mental health center. She, like her coworkers, emphasizes the identification of her twenty-two clients' goals and objectives and the specific skills deficits that hinder each client in achieving his or her goals. Kathy spends a substantial portion of her time as a case manager teaching specific skills to clients and then supporting them as they put those skills into practice. One of her clients is Jerry, a forty-something man who had a large number of psychiatric hospitalizations during a decade-long period, ending about five years ago. He had recently told Kathy that he wanted to leave his current board and care home residence because there was too much drug trafficing going on in his neighborhood (an accurate assessment) and he felt it was too risky for him to be exposed to it.

Kathy, in individual talks with Jerry, helped him clarify the steps he would need to take to identify an alternative and to set up an appointment with a new landlord. She helped him role play an interview and identify the tasks necessary in moving. Kathy used direct teaching skills, modeling and role playing to help Jerry prepare for this transition, and supported his efforts once he began the process. She monitored his effectiveness during counseling appointments while the move was taking place, and provided Jerry with encouragement and support when the move began to get a bit hectic. These individual skills building efforts built on previous small group social skills training that Jerry had experienced in the program. Throughout the process Kathy focused on goals, objectives, and skills, and never needed to refer to supposed symptoms or mental illness.

High-Intensity Case Management Models

Three case management models, referred to as PACT, ACT, and ICM, share an emphasis on a high intensity of service. This is represented by a recommended case manager to client ratio of about 1 to 10. These high-intensity case management programs are almost always reserved for people who have severe and persistent mental illness combined with homelessness and substance abuse (Johnson et al., 1999). In contrast, brokerage case management systems usually operate with ratios of 1 case manager to 30 or 40 clients, and even the clinical, strengths, and rehabilitation models usually have a ratio of about 1 to 20. The Program for Assertive Community Treatment (PACT), was first implemented by social worker Mary Ann Test and psychiatrist Leonard Stein in Dane County, Wisconsin, in the 1970s (Stein and Test, 1980). This was the original model for later Assertive Community Treatment (ACT) programs around the country. The original PACT model, and later strict ACT models, combine case management and clinical service by merging direct assistance for symptom management of mental illness with meeting basic needs and the improvement of social, family, and instrumental functioning. PACT emphasizes, as major case management functions, the development of clinical relationships with the client and family, individual instruction about symptoms, and assistance in managing those symptoms so the client can function maximally in the community.

The original PACT model and ACT model (similar to the clinical model of case management) require provision of clinical services by case managers. However, in PACT and ACT the case managers are on a team consisting of a full- or part-time psychiatrist, a nurse, and multiple case managers. The basic principles of a strict ACT model include:

1. Caseloads are shared across clinicians rather than individually assigned. Thus clients get to know well, and can rely on, more than one clinician.
2. There is twenty four-hour availability for crisis intervention by someone who knows the client fairly well.
3. Most services are provided in community settings such as client homes, clubs, parks, or on the street, rather than in clinician office.
4. Most, if not all, services are provided by the team and are not brokered out.
5. There are no artificial time limits for service—it is available indefinitely, as long as needed.
6. ACT programs have *high-intensity* ratios of staff to clients of approximately 1 to 10, not high ratios such as 40 or more clients to 1 case manager (Bond, Salyers, and Fekete, 1996; Test, 1992).

It is important that to note that the first five principles are workable only when the final principle is adhered to.

Since the early 1980s, many case management programs have been developed and implemented that have varying degrees of conformity with the critical defining components of the PACT/ACT model. Programs have been developed that call themselves ACT programs, yet don't have a psychiatrist. Some programs don't have a nurse; for others, the case manager client ratio is 1 to 15 or 1 to 17 or perhaps even greater. In some programs there are no shared case loads; in others, particularly rural programs, distances are too great to achieve high-frequency contacts. In some programs, supposed family treatment or education is involved; some do not offer twenty four-hour availability of team members. By a strict definition, most programs such as these should not be called ACT programs. More appropriately, these types of case management programs should be called Intensive Case Management (ICM) programs when they depart from the strict PACT/ACT model. To add confusion, however, while some call themselves ACT programs, although very different from the PACT model, others that *are* identical call themselves ICM programs.

The National Association of Case Management (NACM) has developed a description of case management based on three levels of intensity. NACM would consider PACT, ACT, and ICM all as forms of *Level I* case management (Hodge and Giesler, 1997). NACM describes Level I case management as the most intensive level of case management. NACM proposes that Level I is designed for people with the most acute (severe) and disabling problems from mental illness. Intensive case management may be provided by individual case managers organized into teams for accessibility and supervision, similar to the ACT model. Case loads are usually ten to thirteen persons per case manager. A team member is available for contact by recipients twenty-four-hours a day, seven days a week through on-call arrangements made within or by each team. Based upon current provider experience, the number of contacts for participants in ICM will vary, based on individual need, from daily to weekly (Bond, Salyers, and Fekete, 1996). It is an approach in which most contacts occur outside the clinician's office and in the community.

A significant feature of ICM case management is the availability of psychiatry and nursing services. Individuals and their case managers are in collaboration with a psychiatrist and nurse to assure consistency in the approach to symptom reduction and to the minimization of the side effects of medication. In addition to regular psychiatric visits by appointment, time is set aside by the team every day for emergency walk-in medication capability. Another feature of ICM is a result of the flexibility provided by small case loads, which allows case managers to provide direct services. ICM case managers may teach independent living skills and social skills, provide supported housing and employment services, facilitate psychoeducational groups, and provide day services that assure the ability to tailor the offerings in order to assist in meeting the unique goals of the people served. They may also provide family education, family groups, and supportive counseling directed at solving day-to-day problems with community living as well as many other tasks (see Figure 11.2).

Due to the frequency with which substance abuse co-occurs with severe mental illness, NACM specifies that case managers practicing Level I case management (PACT, ACT, or ICM) should have training in providing support and treatment to people with both mental illness and substance abuse. The following example describes an individual with multiple problems who benefitted from an Intensive Case Management (ICM) program for dually-diagnosed people with a history of mental illness, drug abuse, and criminal justice system involvement.

■■ Nikki's prognosis was poor when she was referred by the probation department to the community mental health center for case management. In her late thirties, she was

Make phone calls
Make visits in the community
Talk to client's family
Contact other agencies where client is to see how client is doing
Visit client at home, on the job, at other agencies, in jail
Discharge planning at state hospital
Set up appointments
Help with the night program
Facilitate a self-help group
Arrange appointments and transportation
Consult with supervisor
Lead recreational group
Go to other agencies, such as the department of public aid, with client
Meet with probation officer, or discuss a case with the public defender
Financial management: write checks, handle money
Attend art therapy with client
Watch client take psychotropic medications
Transport clients
Travel to client's home for meeting
Attend staffings
Paperwork

FIGURE 11.2   Case Management: Typical Activities

Source: Based on Godley, 1995.

unemployed with a tenth-grade education. A debilitating battle with AIDS had left her with serious medical problems. She had been taking a half-dozen different prescribed medications, including two psychotropic drugs. Her only income was from Social Security Disability Insurance based on her illness. At the point of referral Nikki was under court supervision due to violation of probation for her fourth offense of writing bad checks to support her crack cocaine habit of ten years. The judge felt that Intensive Case Management might work with Nikki and would be an alternative to a jail sentence.

Nikki was diagnosed with cocaine dependence and depression. Like many felons, she was also often diagnosed with a personality disorder. Nikki had a history of using many different drugs including alcohol, marijuana, hallucinogens, and inhalants of various types. She had once attempted suicide. Her most recent treatment history consisted of twenty-two days in a residential rehabilitation substance abuse program about a year before. After entering into the case management program, Nikki intermittently attended outpatient counseling sessions, but never missed a scheduled visit with her case worker. She stayed drug free for eight months, with the exception of relapsing for six days on cocaine, when she encountered a couple of "old friends" from her street days. As Nikki's depression grew worse, she talked to her case manager about detoxification and more residential rehab for her substance abuse. She was referred to several different substance abuse agencies, but none would accept her for treatment because of her AIDS status. She finally was admitted to a hospital for treatment of her growing medical problems and while there was also prescribed a new antidepressant that might be more effective for her. During the next month, she suffered from many physical complications and had numerous visits to the hospital's urgent care service.

Nikki's mental state improved even as her physical condition continued on its slow decline. The new antidepressant medication seemed to help. She was less depressed, attended counseling sessions, and participated in a community support group. Nikki no longer used street drugs. She saw her case manager both in the office and in her natural environment several times a week. After another six months, Nikki's physical health began to fail more rapidly. In spite of that, Nikki, with the support of her case manager, was able to avoid clinical depression. She attended her AIDS support group daily. Nikki began to mend what had been a long-term estrangement with her family. Throughout this period there was no criminal activity and Nikki completed her terms of probation.

As Nikki neared death, she received continued support from her case manager and her family. Nikki often said that she was sure she could not have stayed off drugs without the daily support of her case manager. Nikki remained in the program until her death.

Case Management in a Variety of Settings

Case management is utilized in a variety of human services systems. However, as there has been increasing growth in the complexity of service systems and financial reimbursement processes, obtaining access to services has become more difficult for the client. Each service system has different fiscal, structural, environmental, and political constraints that shade how case management is developed and implemented (Quinn, 1996). In addition, over the past few decades a very different kind of case management has been developed, one that has a much different focus than those described earlier. That different brand of case management is described in Box 11.1.

The various routes to the implementation of human services case management are illustrated in the following examples. These examples show both the differences and the similarities in the range of case management practice.

Alcohol and Substance Abuse Treatment

The use of formal case management as a framework within which alcohol or substance abuse treatment can be delivered is a relatively recent phenomenon. As we have recognized that the struggle against addiction is a lifelong issue and that many life factors can work against recovery, it has become more obvious that the holistic approach to change that is characteristic of case management can be useful in this human services system. Case managers in substance abuse treatment programs view addiction and recovery through a wider lens than most other alcohol and drug abuse therapists, and work toward a diverse range of goals in collaboration with consumers. Case managers in substance abuse systems can offer services that do not focus directly on the abuse behavior, but instead attend to those areas of social functioning in which settings, events, or client behaviors contribute to or maintain abusing behaviors. In addition, case management seems particularly well suited to addressing the needs of diverse populations that have been historically underserved by traditional alcoholism or drug treatment programs, such as women, youths, and minorities (Sullivan, 1996).

For some years, alcohol and substance abuse treatment agencies (and whole systems) were quite resistive to the introduction of case management approaches. Treatment of the addiction was predicated on the presence of high levels of motivation for change on the part of the client, and treaters screened out people who could not, would not, or simply did not express that motivation. As it has become clearer that many external factors influence motivations, practitioners in the addiction field have come to recognize that treatment systems have an obligation to motivate people to change harmful practices. That has increased the willingness of the alcohol and substance abuse treatment field to accept case management models as a practical approach to the provision of treatment to difficult to serve individuals.

Child Welfare

There is a long tradition of utilization of case management in the child welfare system, both in traditional child welfare services and in newer family preservation approaches. From the current family preservation perspective, the child welfare system consists of the areas of social services aimed at protecting children from abuse and neglect and on improving opportunities for child development by improving family functioning. In the past, and unfortunately still today in some systems, case loads have been high. In child welfare, case loads are sometimes in excess of one hundred cases per worker (Zlotnik, 1996). When case loads are that high, it becomes exceedingly difficult to provide effective case management, even of a brokerage type.

When case loads are of moderate to large size, case managers must focus on brokerage functions—the linkage of clients to other services (Zlotnick, Kronstadt, and Klee, 1999). The case manager cannot spend the amount of time with individual children and families that is necessary if behavior change is the goal. Linkage to other services may, however, include referral to a more intensive level of case management often known as Intensive or Family Focused Case Management. These types of programs limit case load sizes, generally to less than ten or fifteen children. The approach is guided by the principle that programs should be family focused, community based, culturally sensitive, and comprehensive. The model of case management utilized is usually a clinical or strengths type.

Child and Adolescent Mental Health Services

Case management is viewed as a critical component of organized services for severely emotionally disturbed (SED) children and adolescents. In 1984, Congress authorized the federal Child and Adolescent Service System Program (CASSP) to fund grants to states to improve services for youths. One of the CASSP principles stated that "Children . . . should be provided with case management or similar mechanisms to ensure that multiple services are delivered in a coordinated and therapeutic manner" (Stroul and Friedman, 1994). This federal funding effort stimulated virtually all states to fund and require the development of clinical case management services for seriously emotionally disturbed children and adolescents. Today, in this particular human services system the term *case management* is being supplanted by the phrase *service coordination,* to communicate that people in need are not *cases,* but that they need services.

In both the child welfare system and the child and adolescent mental health system, the provision of case management services to the client is complicated by the needs of one or both parents, or other adult caretaker. Parents or other caregivers want case managers to support family preservation, to accept parents' lifestyles, to ask parents what they need, to build on family values and strengths, and to be flexible. They want case managers to have small case loads and flexible work schedules, to be available, and to be parent centered (Zlotnik, 1996). While these interests on the part of parents are understandable, it remains important to keep at the forefront that the seriously emotionally disturbed child or adolescent is the primary client, and that meeting the needs of the child or adolescent may not necessarily meet the needs of the caretaker.

Long Term Care for the Aging

Dramatic growth in the aging population, which is even expected to accelerate between now and the year 2050, has contributed to the innovation of case management services for the elderly who have unmet needs (Austin, 1996). There has been a particular emphasis on the development of case management programs whose primary objective is to keep the elderly out of nursing homes for as long as possible. Public funding for such programs has often been made available because it has been thought that this would reduce overall tax-supported costs of care. This view is premised on the notion that many elderly who are placed in nursing homes are there because community alternatives have not been developed, and those alternatives, including case management, would cost less than the twenty-four-hour residential care that is the hallmark of the nursing home. In addition to this fiscal incentive, these types of case management programs are well received by consumers, few of whom wish to go into a nursing home for any longer than is absolutely necessary. Case management for the elderly focuses on three general principles: it takes a holistic approach to the consumer; it is a problem solving approach; and it is dynamic—a process of involvement among the case manager, the consumer, and other caretakers such as the family, friends, agencies, and health care providers. Case management programs for the aging may be provided by a variety of agencies such as community hospitals, senior centers, adult day care centers, or local aging services agencies.

HIV/AIDS Services

As the numbers of people with HIV or AIDS multiplied, it became apparent from a public health perspective that the disease was so catastrophic that a comprehensive array of services, both medical and psychosocial, would be necessary if for no other reason than to provide adequate symptomatic care and to reduce transmission of the disease. HIV/AIDS involves every area of functioning—physical health, mental health, financial stability, family interactions, child welfare, and social relationships. The available medical treatments are costly and often ineffective (Ho, 1999). Case management services were applied to HIV/AIDS management not long after the disease was recognized in 1981. The use of a case management approach allowed the effective development of a continuum of care for HIV/AIDS victims, and demonstrated reduction in the costs of care for people with AIDS receiving case management services. The demonstrated effectiveness resulted in federal guidelines that described case management as one important *best practice* in HIV/AIDS disease management (Agency for Health Care Policy and Research, 1993).

Case managers who work with individuals who have HIV/AIDS, or other deteriorating terminal illnesses, face an issue that case managers working with people with other types of problems face only rarely: the death of the individuals one is working with. In HIV/AIDS work, literally all the people on one's case load will die while still a client. Case managers in these programs will experience the loss of clients with whom relationships have been developed for years and will see rapidly declining health and abilities of people who were once healthy and vital. Case managers working with terminally ill individuals have a particular need for emotional support to deal with burnout. Supervisors, peers, and outside consultants will be needed to provide direction, encouragement, and acceptance.

Issues in Case Management

Although the practice of case management is an "idea whose time has come" (Woodside and McClam, 1998), it is a methodology that is not without issues or controversy. Three such issues seem particularly important: unrealistic expectations, advocacy versus social control, and human resource development.

Unrealistic Expectations

Case management has become an extraordinarily popular methodology for dealing with human services public policy issues. During the course of implementation, the various models or approaches to case management have often been modified in practice for a variety of reasons, most frequently for reasons of lack of adequate program funding. Yet expectations for the results of case management may be unrealistically high when the models are compromised. A good example of this is in regards to Intensive Case Management (ICM) for individuals with severe and persistent mental illness. As ICM programs have been implemented by various entities, the ratio of clients to case managers has often been increased from the model's recommended 10 to 1 up to nearly 20 to 1 or more. This can reduce the cost of the program substantially, or double the number of clients served for a given cost. This can be almost irresistable to program planners—yet in this situation, the expectations for outcomes remain undiluted: reduced hospitalizations, reduced homelessness, reduced symptomatology, and improved quality of life. Substantial research demonstrates that when such programs are watered down,

---

BOX 11.1   That Other Kind of Case Management

If you belong to a Health Maintenance Organization (HMO) and have ever needed more than routine care, you have probably experienced that *other* kind of case management. In response to spiraling health care costs in the United States the so-called managed care industry has developed with promises to slow the growth of, or reduce the costs of, health care. Managed health care is a system for controlling the delivery and quality of health care, and for managing its costs. Health care is unique as a purchased service, since most consumers rarely pay for the service out of their own pockets. The consumer has insurance, pays (or their employer pays) for that instance, or pays to belong to some type of prepaid health care plan. Managed care is also utilized in public tax-supported systems such as medicaid or medicare, and so is relevant to services for the poor. These insurance plans, the HMO, or other managed health care system specifies benefits (services), co-payments, and system requirements. Many limit who the medical provider (physician) can be, limit the services or treatments that will be paid for, may limit the setting in which certain services can be delivered, and may limit how much treatment (visits, days of hospital care) can be reimbursed. The limits are usually defined in *protocols* that are managed by case managers.

In these systems, the work of case managers is quite different from that which most human service case managers perform, but there are some similarities. Case loads are very large, ranging from one case manager to 15,000 clients up to 40,000 clients. Active cases are of course less, but number in the many hundreds or thousands. Case managers coordinate in the sense of arranging specialty services (brokerage), but often act as gatekeepers by being the authorizing agent for the more expensive services. In some systems or for some more expensive procedures, the case manager may need to obtain authorization from a higher-level gatekeeper, such as a physician.

Managed care systems are most prominent in medical services, but have been and are being applied to other human service arenas such as public mental health services, rehabilitation services, correctional systems (prisons), and child welfare. Within all these systems there is a significant tension between saving money and providing effective quality services. Critics point to the apparent dominance of the motives of fiscal cutbacks, profit, and the lack of client advocacy as major flaws in the managed care approach.

---

they cannot achieve the range of outcomes generally expected of them (Bond, Salyers, and Fekete, 1996; Mueser, Bond, Drake, and Resnick, 1998).

A similar issue may be developing in the welfare reform movement. As states implement the changes in welfare regulations that are an aspect of the Transitional Assistance to Needy Families (TANF) program of the federal government, case management is one methodology being touted as an effective approach to getting people off of welfare and back to work. The reliance on case management and the belief that case management can be extremely effective in this role neglects to consider that there are hundreds of thousands of individuals on welfare who will need extensive services *beyond* case management in order to get and retain employment. Unrealistic expectations for case management on the part of policy-makers and funders can allow them to ignore the need for other resources and programs. Human service professionals have an obligation to constantly remind policymakers that goals and expectations for case management must be kept within resonable bounds.

Advocacy versus Social Control

Advocacy for the client has been described as an important, if not critical, role in case management for decades. Advocacy defines and promotes the well-being of the individual client, the group, and the community. Yet, case managers soon discover that the programs, agencies, or systems that fund case management create written protocols for service delivery that are intended to identify the eligible clients (in other words, limit access), and to specify (limit) funded services. These protocols may be rules, regulations, laws, or a combination of all three. Unfortunately, the role of advocacy in case management is, more often than not, simply given lip service in formal systems of care particularly when funded or operated by governmental agencies. In fact, it is not at all unlikely that case managers may be faced with the dilemma that to do the so-called right thing for or with the client would involve the violation of an agency rule, or, more critically, it might involve the violation of a government regulation or law. For example, welfare systems usually prohibit single mothers from having a live-in male friend. If that occurs, case mangers are to report it, and welfare payments are to be stopped. Some case managers believe that doing the right thing means that they must look the other way on this issue and ignore the violation of the regulation.

In particular, it may be the case that advocacy conflicts with social control interests in some systems when agencies find that cost containment requires program cuts. When cost containment becomes an important goal of a human services system, as it has in medical care and welfare, there tends to be a proliferation of rules that have the effect of limiting advocacy. During times of cost containment it often becomes the case manager's responsibility to implement the increasingly restrictive limits on services. In the environment of cost containment, programs may require the case manager to identify more strongly with the agency and its goals than with the client, and thus may focus on social control issues rather than advocacy. Advocacy by case managers may even be met with hostility in these settings (McClelland, Austin, and Schneck, 1996). A primary role conflict in case management surfaces when advocacy conflicts with social system control. In case management systems where it is clear that advocacy is not an expectation of the case manager's role, the conflict may not exist. However, when the conflict between advocacy and social control is intense, case managers must rely on their conscience to be the guide. Some case managers believe that advocacy is the most important thing they do—a social activist position. Others believe that their responsibility is to the institution or system that funds the services—they are team players. The obligation to follow regulations needs to be weighed on a case-by-case basis (Woodside and McClam, 1998). Case managers who include rule- or law-breaking in their advocacy efforts will need to be prepared for the potential consequences.

Human Resource Development

The work of case management can be extremely intense. It can be a demanding methodology, but typically a case manager job is an entry-level position within an agency. Agencies usually employ people with associate's or bachelor's degrees as case managers, preferring degrees with a human services focus. People with advanced degrees may be employed as case management program team leaders or as supervisors. There are few comprehensive academic training programs focusing on case management, so most job preparation occurs after employment, as preservice or inservice training. The National Association of Case Management recommends that a new case manager receive at least forty hours of preservice training before the assignment of a case load, and another forty hours of inservice specialty training each year thereafter (Hodge and Giesler, 1997). Many states specify their own qualifications for case managers in their community agency reimbursement rules (for example, state medicaid regulations), and some have developed state-sanctioned training materials. Usually these curricula require training in issues such as engagement strategies, interviewing, assessment, service planning, community resources, local, state, and federal rules and regulations, family process, team process, and advocacy strategies. In spite of the efforts at training and preservice orientation, turnover among case managers is somewhat high, with as many as 30 percent leaving each year (Bond, Salyers, and Fekete, 1996). Many leave for higher-paying positions, some simply discover that they don't care for the work, and some leave because of burnout, a concept also dealt with in Chapter 12.

Burnout is not unique to case management or to human services. It is most common in people who work with service recipients of all sorts, but can happen in many occupations. *Burnout* refers to a sense of emotional and physical exhaustion that can result from intense relationships that place stress on those responsible for the provision of services to others (Sweitzer, 1999). Its symptoms can be severe enough that they seem much like the signs of a crisis response in any individual. The incidence of burnout is heightened in case management systems if case managers are likely to be working with difficult, demanding clients, if they are working in a bureaucratic system, if case loads are high in numbers, if they have few resources to access, if they have little autonomy, and if supervision is poor. These risk factors are complicated by the probability that case managers have a particular vulnerability to burnout due to a greater degree of empathy and sensitivity to the problems of others, which arises from the human service worker's training and background. Burnout need not be inevitable, however; a number of factors can help case managers avoid it: variety in case load problem intensity, smaller case load, adequacy of resources, an increase in autonomy, and adequate supervision. In addition, the individual case manager can be helped to adopt several strategies that are useful for combating feelings of burnout. These include sharing feelings with coworkers and supervisors, modifying one's approach to the job to have more "little victories," developing non–job related interests, changing priorities, learning to accept one's limitations, and scaling back expectations of clients. Human resource development issues have no easy solution; for the individual case manager, membership in a professional organization that has a targeted focus, such as the National Association of Case Management (NACM), is a wise move.

Summary

1. Case management is a significant methodology for the provision and coordination of interventions in human services, and is often the first type of position occupied by new human service workers.

2. To a greater or lesser degree, various models of case management share a number of core functions, including: (a) assessment, (b) planning, (c) service implementation, (d) service coordination, (e) monitoring, (f) evaluation, and (g) involvement.

3. Several different models of case management have been described in the human services literature. The most common of these models include (a) the brokerage model, (b) clinical case management, (c) the strengths model, (d) the rehabilitation model, and (e) the high-intensity case management models.

4. The high-intensity case management models consist of the Program for Assertive Community Treatment (PACT), Assertive Community Treatment (ACT), and Intensive Case Management (ICM).

5. PACT, ACT, and ICM share an emphasis on high-intensity service, as represented by a recommended case manager to client ratio of about 1 to 10, although, in practice, programs called PACT, ACT, or ICM may depart from the models' recommendations.

6. Case management is a common methodology for delivering or coordinating services in all human services settings. Examples of case management approaches are given in the areas of alcohol and substance abuse treatment, child welfare, child and adolescent mental health service, long-term care for the aging, and HIV/AIDS services.

7. Three important issues in human services case management are (1) unrealistic expectations, (2) advocacy versus social control, and (3) human resource development.

8. Program planners, administrators, or politicians sometimes expect case management to be an effective solution to any problem, even when case management is implemented in a watered-down version.

9. Case managers may find themselves in conflict over whether and to what degree they can be advocates for their clients, or must act as agents of social control and cost containment.

10. Case management can be a stressful occupation, at times resulting in high turnover of employees due to burnout. Case management programs and case managers can practice strategies that can reduce the incidence of burnout.

11. Membership in a national organization such as the National Association of Case Management (NACM) is important for human service workers doing case management.

Discussion Questions

1. What do you think is the most important function of case management?
2. What was the most important reason that case management became a cornerstone of human services?
3. How would you go about selecting a case management model for a specific human service issue (for example, for juveniles who have committed several crimes)?
4. Should a case manager break an agency rule or regulation if it would help a client?
5. Debate whether cost containment is an appropriate role for a human service case manager.

Learning Experiences

1. Arrange a visit to your local public mental health center Intensive Case Management (or ACT or PACT) program, and also a visit to your local Transitional Aid to Needy Families (TANF) office. Meet with a few case managers at each site to find out how their training, skills, and function differ.
2. Interview several case management clients to find out how they view their case management experience. What do they believe was most important and of greatest help?

Recommended Readings

Stroul, B., & Friedman, R.M. (1994). *A system of care for children and youth with severe emotional disturbances.* (Revised edition). Washington, DC: Georgetown University Child Development Center.

Swietzer, H.F. (1999). Burnout: Avoiding the trap. In H. S. Harris and D. C. Maloney (Eds.), *Human services: Contemporary issues and trends* (2nd ed.). Boston: Allyn and Bacon.

Woodside, M., & McClam, T. (1998). *Generalist case management: A method of human service delivery.* Pacific Grove, CA: Brooks/Cole.

12

Crisis Intervention

- How is a *crisis* defined?
- What are the signs of crisis states?
- What are some examples of common crises?
- What common reactions are seen in major disasters?
- What principles guide most crisis intervention programs?
- What impact does crisis work have on the human service worker?

When people in need seek help, they are often in a state of crisis. Most people have a strong desire to see themselves as able to handle life's problems without outside assistance. Our culture has given people the expectation that they should be strong, independent, and self-reliant. When someone begins to be overwhelmed by difficulties, a common first reaction is to feel that one has let oneself and others down, that one has failed because of personal weakness. Many people are unwilling to reveal that sense of personal weakness to others. To seek out help is often seen as an admission of failure, and many people avoid taking that step until no other solution seems possible.

Unfortunately, when people try to solve serious problems on their own, they are often unsuccessful, and the problems become more severe. As the problems become complex and disabling, the individual's problem-solving capabilities become even more impaired. Events reach crisis proportions before the individual can admit to a need for outside assistance. To deal with the emotional turmoil of people in such crises, a major development has been crisis intervention programs.

The concept of crisis intervention is an outgrowth of attempts to deal with acute psychological problems resulting from major environmental stress. Much of the early work in crisis intervention was done during World War II, when men experienced a reaction to combat called *combat neurosis* or *battle fatigue.* Additional knowledge about reactions to stress and techniques for dealing with crisis experiences were gained from the study of reactions to natural disasters. Today we call those reactions *Posttraumatic Stress Disorders* or *PTSD*.

Understanding Crisis States

One of the first studies of crisis states was Erich Lindemann's report on the Coconut Grove nightclub fire in Boston during 1942, in which 492 people were killed (Lindemann, 1944). Lindemann studied the psychological reactions of the survivors and their families and the reactions of the family members of those who had died. He found that half the families needed psychological help in dealing with their reactions to the loss of loved ones. Lindemann found, as have others, that some people appear to adjust remarkably well shortly after the disaster, but that problems surface later on (Lindemann, 1944):

> *A girl of seventeen lost both parents and her boy friend in the fire and was herself burned severely, with marked involvement of the lungs. Throughout her stay in the hospital her attitude was that of cheerful acceptance without any sign of . . . distress. When she was discharged at the end of three weeks she appeared cheerful, talked rapidly, with a considerable flow of ideas, seemed eager to return home and to assume the role of parent for her two younger siblings. Except for slight feelings of "lonesomeness," she complained of no distress.*
>
> *This period of griefless acceptance continued for the next two months, even when the household was dispersed and her younger siblings were placed in other homes. Not until the end of the tenth week did she begin to show a true state of grief with marked feelings of depression, intestinal emptiness, tightness in her throat, frequent crying, and vivid preoccupation with her deceased parents.*

One early crisis specialist (Caplan, 1964) formulated a classic definition of a crisis state: "a short period of psychological disequilibrium in a person who confronts a hazardous circumstance that for him constitutes an important problem which he can for the time being neither escape nor solve with his customary problem-solving resources." A major premise of crisis intervention theory is that a crisis can be resolved adaptively or maladaptively, positively or negatively. During the disruption characteristic of the crisis state, individuals are thought to be vulnerable to intervention by others. They are especially sensitive to their own inability to cope and look for ways to reduce their discomfort. If at this point they receive support from a human service worker, their changes can be positive. If, however, alternative coping mechanisms are unavailable, the *disruptive* behaviors of the crisis state can be incorporated into the person's personality structure, and the person may stabilize at a level of functioning that is even less adaptive than the precrisis behavior. Figure 12.1 illustrates this crisis phase sequence.

Before a crisis-producing event occurs, most individuals maintain an adjustment level whose effectiveness varies only slightly from time to time. However, as

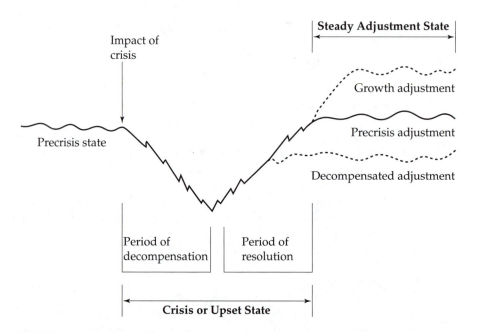

FIGURE 12.1   Crisis Phase Sequence

Source: Reproduced with permission of Robert J. Brady Co., Bowie, MD 20715, from 1975 copyrighted work titled, "Emergency Psychiatric Care: Management of Mental Health Crisis."

the crisis makes its impact on the subject, a period of decompensation occurs, during which the usual coping mechanisms fail and behavior becomes relatively disorganized and ineffective for solving problems.

Individuals who experience crisis decompensation as a result of stress eventually bottom out in the behavioral decline, and because crisis states seem to be somewhat self-limiting, they enter a period of crisis resolution. After the resolution, these persons once again enter a steady adjustment state that has only slight variations in levels of effectiveness over a period of time. What is particularly significant about the postcrisis adjustment level is that it may be at a higher-functioning level than the precrisis state, a lower level than the precrisis state, or the same level as the precrisis state.

People who make a moderately successful adjustment to a crisis, who regain their normal coping mechanisms, return to the precrisis level. People who are relatively unable to deal with the crisis decompensation period and who have few coping mechanisms and resources are likely to end up with a decompensated adjustment level. In other words, they have learned maladaptive responses during the crisis, and afterward they are less able to deal with stress and day-to-day living than they were before. However, people may resolve the crisis state with a growth adjustment and be able to function at an even higher level after the crisis period. For such to occur, the individual in crisis usually needs assistance in the form of crisis intervention strategies in order to learn highly adaptive coping techniques.

Successful crisis resolution that results in a return to precrisis behavior or a growth adjustment requires (1) correct perception of the situation, furthered by seeking new knowledge and keeping the problem in consciousness, (2) management of emotion through awareness of feelings and verbalizations leading toward tension discharge and mastery, and (3) development of patterns of seeking and using help with actual tasks and feelings by using interpersonal and institutional resources (Rapoport, 1962).

A major element of the crisis state, of course, is the client's *perception* of an event as so extremely stressful that it interferes with the individual's normal coping patterns (Parad and Resnik, 1975). To an objective observer, the stress may appear to be high or low. To most people, high-stress events such as divorce, natural disasters (tornadoes, earthquakes, floods), or the death of a loved one are easily accepted as crisis-developing situations. But even what appear to be relatively low-stress events to an outside observer can be crises for some. What makes an event stressful? Four characteristics of stressful events are often noted in the literature on stress and coping resources.

1. People feel a sense of loss of control over the events in their lives. They feel helpless to change what is going on or to intervene successfully in the process.
2. There is an anticipation or occurrence of physical or psychological pain. For example, the individual fears being injured or killed (as in a disaster) or is threatened with a loss of self-esteem (as in a divorce).
3. There is a loss of social and emotional support. In a disaster, friends and relatives may be missing or killed. Less dramatic events such as divorce, job loss, or marriage may separate individuals from family members and old friends.
4. The event or some aspect of it is perceived as unpleasant or aversive, and the individual tries actively to avoid the unpleasantness.

Some people appear to be unable to deal with common events such as a child going to school for the first time or marrying and leaving home. For these individuals, these common experiences interact with other variables to fit the four characteristics noted previously. Such events are able to produce crisis in some individuals due to their personal vulnerabilities: they may not be resourceful, for example, or perhaps they might have an already existing emotional disorder, such as depression or anxiety. In contrast, some events can precipitate crisis in the great majority of people, if not in everyone. The destruction of the city of Armero, Colombia, by a volcanic eruption on November 13, 1985, is an example. In this tragedy a double eruption of built-up molten rock and trapped gases melted tons of ice and snow that covered the top of the volcanic peak. A steaming, mile-wide avalanche of ash, mud, and rocks roared thirty miles down mountain valleys and buried the city under 50,000 million cubic feet of boiling mud. The catastrophe left 22,000 people dead or missing and many thousands more injured, orphaned, or homeless (Cohen, 1987).

Another example is the December 1988 earthquake that struck Soviet Armenia (DeAngelis, 1990; Goenjian et al., 1994). An estimated 25,000 people were killed, according to the Soviet government, but European sources estimated that as many as 100,000 died and 530,000 were left homeless. Interviews with residents of the Armenian city of Gumri regarding their worst experiences during and after the earthquake consistently revealed similar traumatic experiences, such as seeing mutilated corpses on sidewalks or hanging from buildings, hearing the screams of people in agony trapped under the rubble, and seeing the terrified expressions on the faces of people frantically seaching for loved ones. A year and a half after the earthquake, one fourteen-year-old girl who was the *only* survivor from her entire school class felt so guilty about being the only one left alive that she tried to kill herself by throwing herself in front of a car. She is one example of tens of thousands of Armenians who continue to suffer the psychological, behavioral, and physical effects of the disaster. Because of the overwhelming impact of these types of disaster, a crisis response was generated in all the immediate survivors, no matter how effective their problem-solving abilities prior to the event. In fact, in disasters of this severity, crisis responses often occur in rescuers and human service workers who arrive later to give assistance following the disaster event.

Signs of Crisis States

Whereas some individuals can withstand more stress than others, all individuals have a breaking point. Whatever the level of stress an individual can withstand, once the stress is great enough to set off a crisis, certain common signs of the crisis experience usually appear:

1. The individual seems preoccupied.
2. The person experiences guilt over his or her inability to resolve the problem.
3. He or she feels hostility toward others or toward the world in general.
4. He or she experiences physical distress: nervousness, stomachaches, inability to sleep, and so on.
5. Established patterns of conduct may change: personal hygiene slips, routines are disrupted.
6. The person may become apathetic.
7. There may be a lot of aimless activity.
8. Relationships with others change; the person may become more dependent or withdrawn.
9. Behavior may appear that is detrimental to the individual's self-interest.

It is not unusual for human service workers to encounter the *same* individual over and over again manifesting the signs of crisis. Parad and Resnik (1975) have identified a list of problems that may maintain such persons at a point at which they are particularly vulnerable to crisis:

1. Difficulty in learning from experience
2. A history of frequent crises ineffectively resolved because of poor coping ability
3. A history of mental disorder or other serious emotional disturbance
4. Low self-esteem, which may be masked by provocative behavior
5. A tendency toward impulsive acting-out behavior (doing without thinking)
6. Marginal income
7. Lack of regular, fulfilling work
8. Unsatisfying marriage and family relations
9. Heavy drinking or substance abuse
10. History of numerous accidents
11. Frequent encounters with law enforcement agencies
12. Frequent change in address[1]

Such a list clearly suggests that the more problems individuals have, the less likely they are to be able to handle a crisis situation. In addition, the multiproblem person is less likely to benefit from crisis intervention without additional support systems that can deal with the long-standing problems.

The Crisis of Major Disasters

It is clear that an overwhelming majority of people exhibit crisis behavior during events such as major disasters. Events that can be considered major disasters include any sudden, unexpected loss of life or damage to property involving relatively large numbers of persons, such as earthquakes, floods, tornadoes, train wrecks, and major aircraft crashes. In the aftermath of such occurrences, the victims manifest a wide variety of problem behaviors that are compounded by the physical security problems of fiscal aid, housing, food, and medical care. How do you imagine you would react in a disaster situation?

Imagine, for example, that on May 18, 1980, you are vacationing at a campsite on the slopes of Mount St. Helens in the state of Washington. On that date, a volcanic eruption destroyed a large area of land and forest, killing sixty-three people and injuring others. Many of the dead have never been found. What would it have been like to be there and survive? Imagine yourself there. A deafening roar, the earth shaking, day turning into night from the falling ash, the air almost unbreathable from gases, extreme heat, roads blocked—helpless against the threat of injury or death, you think only of escape. In terror for your life, you and your companions start for safety, which you hope exists miles away through the wilderness. Abandoning your camp, you try to walk out; your car will not run. After marching continuously for thirty-six hours, you yourself are finally found and rescued. But a vivid memory remains of your companions being swept away by a flood of mud as the group tried to cross a ravine, their screams echoing in your ears. You are certain that they are dead and their bodies maimed, but they are never found. Few of us would handle such an experience well; we would manifest crisis behavior almost immediately and for some time afterward.

In one study of the Mount St. Helens disaster, reported in 1989, two rural communities in the Northwest, one of which was affected by the volcanic eruption, were analyzed to determine the lifetime rate of crisis behavior. The lifetime rate was found to be about 3 percent (Shore, Vollmer and Tatum, 1989). The rate for crisis behaviors (also known as *posttraumatic stress disorders*) was found to be substantially higher in those people who had the highest degree of exposure to the volcanic eruption. Other studies have discovered extremely high rates of human services problems in previously emotionally normal people who have been victims of disasters. Overall, about 5 percent of men and 10 to 12 percent of women will experience events in their lifetime resulting in posttraumatic stress disorder (Solomon and Davidson, 1997).

Norman Farberow (1977), in a survey of reports on nine major disasters between 1971 and 1974, indicates a long list of problems seen by human service workers doing crisis counseling in the periods after such disasters. The problems included nightmares, hostility, depression, phobias, guilt feelings, amnesia, eating problems, agitation, immobilization, alcohol intoxication, marital problems, inability to concentrate, and psychosomatic reactions. In one study (Taylor, 1976) of the Xenia, Ohio, tornado disaster, 56 percent of the victims were depressed afterwards, 27 percent had sleeping problems, 19 percent experienced eating problems, 15 percent had psychosomatic difficulties, 25 percent had headaches, 19 percent had respiratory problems, 28 percent reported marital problems, and 81 percent of the children showed greater fear of storms (see Figure 12.2).

Children seem to be particularly vulnerable to crisis experiences, and may show symptoms of crisis either at home or at school. They are also quite resilient and many recover within a month, though some do not. The responses of children to disasters are to some extent age related (see Box 12.1 on page 228). Thus, crisis interveners must consider the child or adolescent's age when assessing the extent of the crisis impact (Friedman et al., 1995).

The many problems that numerous studies have identified as common aftereffects of major disasters or crises can be categorized as follows:

Psychosomatic

Vomiting, diarrhea, insomnia, loss of appetite, headaches, allergies, ulcers, bladder problems, extreme tiredness, weakness, and rashes. A physician should determine that symptoms are not of primarily physical origin but are related to stress.

Loss

Bereavement (loss of loved ones); separation from loved ones (especially children); loss of limbs due to trauma; loss of familiar objects, possessions, lifestyle; loss of independence; loss of home, farmlands, or livelihood.

Social Stresses

Divorce, separation, delinquency, alcoholism, drugs, family discord. These reactions most often appear in later periods after the disaster.

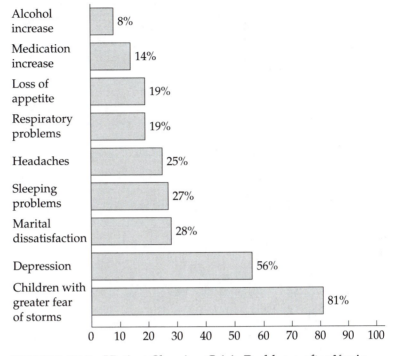

FIGURE 12.2   Victims Showing Crisis Problems after Xenia,
Ohio, Tornado (Percent)

Sequelae of Physical Trauma

Broken bones, burns, pain, toxicity, changes in body image caused by disfigurement and invalidism, loss of memory.

Psychological

Nightmares, unreasonable anticipation of another disaster, difficulty in concentrating, severe depression, extended dazed feeling, nervousness, crying spells, hopeless feelings, irritability.

More formal classifications are:

a. *Depression:* Severe sadness, feels hopeless, can't get out of bed, won't eat, cries, apathetic, unable to engage in usual activities, sleep disturbance, feelings of helplessness, unshakable feelings of worthlessness and inadequacy, withdrawal from others, does not respond to others.

b. *Disorientation:* Confusion, doesn't know where they are, what's happening, what time it is, unaware of surroundings, memory loss, dazed.

c. *Hysteria:* Uncontrollable crying and upset, screaming, can't be left unattended, agitated, may show paralysis or numbness of parts of the body.

BOX 12.1   Differences in Children and Adolescent
Responses to Disasters by General Age Group

Toddlers and Preschoolers

regressive behavior
decreased appetite
vomiting, constipation, diarrhea
sleep disorders (nightmares, insomnia)
tics, stuttering, muteness
clinging
reenactment through play
jumpiness and irritability
posttraumatic stress disorder (PTSD)

School-Age Children

fear and anxiety
hostility with siblings
complaints of physical sickness
sleep disorders
school problems, social withdrawal, or apathy
reenactment
PTSD

Preadolescents

hostility with siblings
complaints of physical illness
sleep disorders
eating disorders
apathy
rebelliousness
PTSD

Adolescents

complaints of physical illness
sleep disorders, eating disorders
apathy
rebellion or risk-taking behavior
change in activity level
confusion or lack of concentration
reduction in acceptance of responsibility
PTSD

Adapted from Friedman et al., 1995.

d. *Psychosis:* Marked personality change, irrational thinking and highly un-usual behavior, may report sensations for which there is no determined cause, and may have delusions of grandeur or persecution. The frequency of psychosis is very low compared to the other aftereffects.

The emotional problems experienced by victims of disasters may be quite severe, even when they are not immediately apparent. They may not appear until months after the actual physical disaster. Hartsough (Farberow, 1977) has devel-oped a tentative set of postdisaster phases that identify the sequence of reactions of victims of disaster:

- *Heroic phase:* Most individuals respond to the immediate disaster with posi-tive action to save their own and other lives and property. A sense of shared community and altruism develops that may last up to several weeks. During this phase, many people manifest the initial crisis behavior reactions.
- *Honeymoon phase:* Efforts focus on cleaning up and establishing new sites of residence and are accompanied by a strong sense of shared experience. Much help is promised by officials and expected by victims. This phase lasts one week to six months after the disaster, and behavioral problems continue to appear.
- *Disillusionment phase:* From two months to twelve months after the disaster. A loss of the feeling of shared experience and bitterness and anger over the delays or failure in promised aid. Many behavioral problems previously hid-den now appear.
- *Reconstruction phase:* From six months to several years following the disaster. Victims realize they need to solve their own problems and attempt to do so; most are successful. Some behavioral problems are still apparent during this phase.

The evidence from studies such as those surveyed by Farberow clearly demonstrates that crisis behavior is a common response to unexpected high-stress events. Efforts must be directed to dealing with these behavioral problems in addition to the life-support problems created by the major disasters. Differences do exist in the levels of stress that are required to produce crisis behavior in dif-ferent individuals.

Common Crisis Situations

It is relatively easy to understand that a major natural disaster can lead to diffi-culty in adjustment among its victims. However, even more common events can result in a crisis response among essentially normal people. A variety of events are experienced as more or less stressful by different individuals.

1. *Family and marital problems.* A problematic marriage is stressful for both partners and for any children who may be involved. If the marriage is dissolved, the members of the family must deal with new relationships, old and new feelings, and the impact of divorce on self-esteem. Children frequently develop problem behaviors in response to the disruption of family life.

■■ At the age of thirty-two, John married Ann, a twenty-nine-year-old schoolteacher. The first year and a half of the marriage appeared to be relatively uneventful. By their second anniversary, things were no longer going well. Ann told John that she felt that the marriage was not working. She felt tied down by John's desire that she spend all her time with him. Ann began going "out with the girls" several times a week. During the next year, Ann and John fought more and more often. As the problems escalated, they finally came to a mutual decision to divorce.

John felt bad about the upcoming divorce. During a separation while waiting for the divorce to become final, he was preoccupied by thoughts of how he had failed as a husband. All he seemed able to do was to think about Ann. As the filing of the final divorce papers came near, he became very depressed. He was unable to complete his work satisfactorily and dropped out of an evening graduate course that he had been taking. His unusual behavior alarmed his parents, who had never seen him become depressed over setbacks before. They encouraged him to enter counseling to "get his head straight." In counseling sessions, John finally expressed his anger at Ann for "dumping him" and his sense of helplessness about the situation: "Nothing I did, none of the changes I made, seemed to make any difference to her."

Over six months John's depression lifted, and he began to date again. He was no longer preoccupied with "what [he] did wrong" in his marriage to Ann. He was again able to work energetically and enthusiastically. Three years later John married again, and he has had a successful relationship with his second wife for the past seven years.

2. *Death of a loved one.* Most people handle this loss reasonably well. They experience sadness and grief but soon go on to lead their lives as before. At times, though, the loss is accompanied by depression and despair, guilt and anger. These reactions are particularly common when the loved one has died unnaturally (suddenly in an accident, or violently) (Rynearson, 1986).

3. *Criminal victimization.* Millions of individuals are victims of crime each year. People are subjected to muggings, beatings, robbery, burglary, and rape. Some are killed, and their families must deal with that difficult loss. It's hard for anyone to cope with the effects of criminal events. A number of studies have found that, after criminal victimization, there is an increase in anxiety, fear, nightmares, anger, social withdrawal, and depression. The reaction of children may be particularly problematic. For example, in February 1984 a sniper opened fire with a rifle and two shotguns on a crowded elementary school playground. One child was killed, and one staff member and thirteen children were wounded. Nineteen of the children on the playground were studied by mental health experts shortly afterward and fourteen months later (Nader et al., 1990). The children who had the greatest exposure to the threat (those on the playground) all experienced serious adjustment difficulties such as reexperiencing the fear, emotional detachment and

jumpiness, and sleep disturbances. Even fourteen months later, they described continued thoughts and images of the deceased child, bullets striking the pavement, and cries for help, and occasionally intrusive nightmares of the event.

The findings in that study were similar to those in an event known as the Chowchilla schoolbus kidnapping (Terr, 1981). In July 1976, a schoolbus, carrying twenty-six children aged five to fourteen and a bus driver, was hijacked by three masked men. The children were driven around for eleven hours in darkened, enclosed vans and then transferred to a truck trailer buried underground. Sixteen hours later, two of the older children were able to dig an escape route. The kidnappers were never caught. Twenty-three of the twenty-six children were studied, and each one manifested disturbed behaviors in the year afterward. Twenty-one developed unusual fears of mundane experiences (e.g., anxiety attacks when riding in the family car) including Mandy and Johnny described below. All the children feared another kidnapping and became extremely suspicious and frightened of any event that reminded them of the ordeal.

■ ■ Mandy, age seven, twice screamed that her little brother had been kidnapped when he was actually playing next door or trying on clothes in a store dressing room. Exactly one year after the kidnapping, Johnny, age eleven, refused to sleep in his bedroom for many nights because he believed the ceiling was collapsing.

Adults also experience crisis reaction to criminal victimization. In March 1994, a van carrying fifteen yeshiva (Jewish religious school) students aged sixteen to twenty-two was on an entrance ramp to the Brooklyn Bridge when it was ambushed by a gunman who fired thirty shots into the van. One student was killed instantly, and three were wounded, one critically. The surviving students were provided crisis intervention services. When first assessed, seven of the eleven students who received the services had serious crisis reactions, such as intrusive recollections, recurrent nightmares, and intense distress when reminded of it, and some also had symptoms of clinical depression and anxiety (Trappler and Friedman, 1996).

4. *Employment.* Job stresses may lead to a crisis reaction, but job loss is an even more stressful event. Chronic unemployment often leads to feelings of hopelessness, defeat, and apathy. Many people find unemployment compensation or the receipt of welfare to be very damaging to their self-concept.

5. *Retirement.* Although most people look forward to retirement, it can be quite stressful. Retirees often feel useless, engage in boring busywork, and encounter a loss of status and economic support. They often become depressed and anxious. In addition, the elderly must deal with a decline in physical ability, loss of friends and relatives, the threat of sickness, and children who are busy leading their own lives.

The five examples given here of common crisis situations are just a few of the many that could have been used. Human service workers will see people experiencing these types of crises and many others.

Intervening in the Crisis

Crisis work is a high-intensity human services function. It is often composed of long periods of idleness or quiet, interspersed with short intervals of tense situations that can be anxiety provoking for the human service worker. Experience has taught us that not all human service workers are suited for crisis work, and personal qualities of potential crisis workers appear to be more important than advanced formal education and training (Stroul, 1993). Box 12.2 lists a number of characteristics and skills of effective crisis workers identified in actual work situations.

In crisis counseling, as in all types of counseling situations, client and counselor expectations are of great importance. As Getz et al. (1974) note, "In crisis counseling, if the counselor and client establish the expectation that the client can regain control over himself and his environment, there is an increased opportunity to assist the person in regaining a sense of mastery over what has happened to him." In addition to the expectations, however, a broad range of specific intervention techniques may be brought into play. The intervention may range from advice giving and assertiveness training to ventilation and interpretation of psycho-dynamic processes.

At times, the crisis intervener is fighting a holding action, trying to maintain an individual until more formal structured intervention can be arranged. The first contact with an individual in crisis is usually by telephone, especially since

---

BOX 12.2   Desirable Characteristics, Skills,
             and Abilities of Crisis Workers

Personal Characteristics

calm, cool, and collected
good judgment, common sense, flexible, mature, responsible
empathic, perceptive, intuitive, intelligent, resourceful, creative
assertive, independent, decisive, self-confident, motivated, ethical
good sense of humor, emotionally stable, high energy

Skills

listening, communication
assessment, counseling, decision making, problem solving

Abilities

tolerate stress, handle conflict
make decisions quickly, manage multiple tasks simultaneously
establish rapport with many types of people
interact effectively with many different systems
function as part of a team

Adapted from Stroul, 1993.

In recent years, emergency shelters have become a setting for intervention into many types of crisis experienced by people who are homeless.

telephone crisis lines have been organized in major cities. The human service worker who handles calls on a crisis line has a demanding job, as illustrated in the following excerpt.

> *I settle down at my desk and just then comes the soft chime of the suicide line. As always, I feel the familiar tightening in my throat and a sinking sensation in my stomach.*
>
> *I answer: "Suicide and Crisis. Can I help you?" I hear a click and then a dial tone. Entry in Log Book: 4:12—Anon. Hung up.*
>
> *Stephanie hands me a file and says: "Here's one you ought to call back. She gave us permission. Marilyn was pretty worried about her and Marilyn's judgment is sharp."*
>
> *I skim the file. Evelyn J. is fifty years old, has a husband and two grown sons. Deeply depressed and threatening suicide. Husband harsh and unsympathetic. She calls him "Daddy." She says her poodle is the only one that cares about her anymore and that's all that is keeping her alive. I call the number.*
>
> *"Mrs. J.? I'm calling from the Suicide and Crisis office. I was just reading your file and I'm a little worried about you. How are you feeling now?"*
>
> *Her voice is light and airy, in fact unnaturally so. "Oh, really? Isn't that nice!"*
>
> *I answer, "Is it difficult for you to talk right now? Is there someone there?"*
>
> *Her response comes in the same light tone. "That's right."*
>
> *"Okay, Mrs. J. I'd really appreciate it if you would call back when you can. We want to know how you're doing."*
>
> *"Fine, I'll do that. Goodbye."*
>
> *Log Book Entry: 4:15—Called Evelyn J. She'll call back.*

Betsy has come in by now and we chatter awhile about her date last weekend. Again come the chimes of the suicide phone.

"I'll get it," says Betsy as she settles down at the other desk. It is a student requesting information about our service for a paper he is writing. I do some more filing and chat with Stephanie. Again the phone rings on the second suicide line.

I answer and it is Evelyn J. calling me back. This time there is no airy quality in her voice. She is crying softly while she talks to me. She is at the end of her rope. She has tried so hard to please Daddy but nothing she does is right in his eyes. . . . The one son at home has turned against her, too, because she has started drinking a little to ease her depression. Only her poodle cares. I find out that Evelyn has a bottle of sleeping pills she is saving for the big step to oblivion, and I urge her to go to a psychiatrist. It seems Daddy doesn't believe in psychiatrists and would never approve. I ask her about menopause symptoms and learn that she is beginning to have them. When I tell her she should go to a gynecologist for hormones, she seems surprised. Daddy doesn't believe in doctors for all that nonsense either. I tell her I'm forty-eight years

---

BOX 12.3   Myths about Suicide

If suicidal feelings are not one of the most common reasons that people call crisis lines, they are one of the most anxiety-provoking for human service workers. Human service workers who deal with suicidal clients learn early in their training that there are many myths about suicide. Here are ten that are commonly believed.

1. Myth: *Most people do not ever think about suicide.*
   Fact: Most studies suggest that at least 40 percent and as many as 80 percent of nonclinical populations admit to having thought about killing themselves at least once in their lives.
2. Myth: *Suicidal people obviously really want to die.*
   Fact: Most people who kill themselves leave evidence that they were ambivalent about death. Some people who are saved at the last moment are grateful. Many who are helped through a suicidal crisis are grateful that they were prevented from taking their own lives. Some people, however, are so determined to kill themselves that no one can save them, no matter what is done.
3. Myth: *Everyone who commits suicide is depressed.*
   Fact: Many people who commit suicide are, in fact, depressed. However, some are not. They are matter-of-fact, calm, and seemingly at peace with themselves. Of course, the vast majority of people who are depressed do not kill themselves.
4. Myth: *People who talk about suicide will not follow through and really do it.*
   Fact: About 75 percent of people who commit suicide have communicated their intentions to others. It pays to be responsive to those warnings.
5. Myth: *People who kill themselves must be crazy.*
   Fact: People who kill themselves may be unhappy, sad, and depressed, but the vast majority are completely rational, know what they are about to do, and understand the consequences.

old and know what I'm talking about; she gets interested and asks about me. I urge
her to go to a doctor or therapist or both, regardless of what Daddy thinks. I point out
that she has been a doormat long enough.
  I tell her: "If he objects, tell him to go to hell!"
  This brings a giggle from her and she stops crying.
  "Oh, that's so funny! I think I'll just do that." She giggles off and on throughout the
rest of our conversation whenever she thinks of the prospect of telling her husband off.
She says she will call for an appointment and promises me she will do nothing drastic
until I call her again next week. She tells me I'm a darling girl and she's very grateful.
  Entry: 4:55—Evelyn J. called back on follow-up. OK for now.[2]

The goal of the first contact, in addition to preventing deterioration in the
client, is to obtain a commitment from the client to seek substantial help. Once the
client enters into a more formal crisis intervention relationship, we can aim for significant change in the problem behavior (see Box 12.3).

BOX 12.3—continued

  6. Myth: *The reason people kill themselves is usually obvious.*
     Fact: The reason is usually not very clear. Even when it seems to be, like a
             suicide after a badly ended love affair, the actual reasons for taking
             the route of suicide depend on the influence of many factors; that is,
             an ecological prospective is needed to understand the event.
  7. Myth: *Suicide is a middle-class or upper-class behavior.*
     Fact: Suicide occurs all too frequently in all classes of society. It is correct
             that some cultures are less negative toward suicide. Japan perhaps is
             the prime example of a culture with a tradition of honorable suicide.
             Japan's suicide rate is substantially higher than that in other coun-
             tries, possibly in part because of this cultural variation. However,
             even in Japan there is much concern because most suicides do not fit
             the culture's parameters for ritual suicide.
  8. Myth: *Suicidal tendency is inherited.*
     Fact: There is no evidence for this in terms of biological inheritance. Suicides
             do have a *slight* tendency to run in families. That means that they
             may occasionally occur more than once over several generations in a
             family. It is more likely that what may be inherited is a predisposition
             to *depression,* not suicide.
  9. Myth: *If a person has been depressed and suicidal, and their emotional state*
            improves noticeably, you can stop being concerned about an attempt.
     Fact: Actually, this can be the riskiest time. People often commit suicide
             when they are coming out of a deep depression because they have
             more energy to act.
 10. Myth: *Asking a depressed person about suicide will push him or her over the edge*
            into a suicidal act that would not have happened otherwise.
     Fact: One of the *best* things you can do is inquire into possible suicidal feel-
             ings if a person is depressed. It is likely to encourage the person to
             reveal the feelings, if they exist, and allow them to be dealt with.

In general, the crisis counselor provides a setting in which clients can ventilate their feelings, discuss their problems, examine their approaches to the problems, receive feedback (both positive and negative) on their coping methods, receive support in their coping attempts, and obtain resources to help them solve current problems and learn better ways of solving future problems. As discussed earlier, during a crisis, people seem particularly open to developing new positive response patterns with the proper guidance, in relatively short periods of time. The intervention process is guided by a number of principles embraced by most crisis intervention programs.

1. *Interventions are made with a minimum of delay.* It is generally accepted that crises are self-limiting from a time perspective. The period of crisis (see Figure 12.1) is usually four to six weeks in duration. Once the person has reached the postcrisis stage, the pressure to resolve the crisis has dissipated, and the crisis worker is left with little to work with. This fact requires rapid intervention and *no* waiting lists. The effective crisis worker must work fast.

2. *Interventions are time limited.* Most crisis programs adhere to short-term programs for the reason just described. Interventions beyond the crisis phase tend not only to waste resources but also to promote dependency. Referral to other programs is, of course, a separate issue when their purpose is to deal with long-standing problems such as personality malfunction or job training.

3. *The client's social network is used.* Frequently, clients have resources that they have been unable to tap, such as friends, family, employers, and ministers, who can be drawn in to provide support and assistance.

4. *The client is usually seen by more than one worker.* The use of more than one worker helps avoid dependency relationships and brings broader experience to bear on the problem.

5. *Intervention is focused on the current life situation.* Because the disorganized crisis state, during which the client is particularly open to change, often lasts only four to six weeks, the intervention attempts must focus on the current life situation if for no other reason than economy of effort. Yet, since the crisis is generally precipitated by a specific problem situation, it is that problem that must be the focus of problem solution strategies.

6. *Trust and rapport must be established.* To develop a working relationship between the worker and the person in crisis, the client must have trust that the worker is operating in the client's best interest, is really concerned, understands the client's problems, and is willing to help.

7. *The client's self-esteem and self-reliance must be supported.* Not only do the crisis workers focus on the client's maladaptive problem-solving efforts but also they reinforce the positive behaviors and aspects of the client. The workers do not solve the client's problem for him or her, which would support the client's personal helplessness and dependency, but, instead, they help the *client* to solve them.

Crisis Intervention for the Crisis Worker

The proliferation of formal crisis intervention programs and the systematic study of the effects of major disasters have brought to the fore the problem of *burnout* among those responding to major disasters (Myers, 1994). Workers in all phases of disaster relief expose themselves to unprecedented personal demands in their desire to meet the needs of the victims. Many workers devote all their time to the disaster-created tasks, at least in the immediate postimpact period. Then, as order returns, some of the workers, especially volunteers, return to their regular jobs and at the same time attempt to continue with their disaster work. The result of the overwork is the burnout syndrome—a state of exhaustion, irritability, and fatigue that markedly decreases the worker's effectiveness and capability (Sweitzer, 1999). The best way to forestall the burnout syndrome is to expect it, to be alert to its early signs, and to act authoritatively to relieve the stress. Four areas of symptomatology have been identified:

- *Thinking:* Mental confusion, slowness of thought, inability to make judgments and decisions, loss of ability to conceptualize alternatives or to prioritize tasks, loss of objectivity in evaluating own functioning.
- *Psychological:* Depression, irritability, anxiety, hyperexcitability, excessive rage reactions.
- *Somatic:* Physical exhaustion, loss of energy, gastrointestinal distress, appetite disturbances, hypochondria, sleep disorders, tremors.
- *Behavioral:* Hyperactivity, excessive fatigue, inability to express oneself verbally or in writing.

Obviously, the symptoms of burnout are signs that the disaster crisis is having an impact on the human service worker. The first step in dealing with burnout is to be alert for and aware of and to recognize the symptoms when they begin to appear. The earlier they are recognized, the better. All personnel need to be aware of the early symptoms so they may recognize them not only in themselves but also in their fellow workers. Any such observations, either about themselves or about others, should be reported to supervisors. Supervisors also need to be alert to any early symptoms in their staffs so that they can intervene.

The supervisor should talk to the individual and try to get him or her to recognize the symptoms. The supervisor should relieve the person of duties for a short period of time. Guilt over leaving the activity is relieved by giving official permission to stop and by pointing out that the worker is no longer helping because of the loss of effectiveness. The human service worker can be reassured that he or she can return and then will have improved greatly as a result of a short recuperation. The supervisor should at first attempt to persuade the helper to take the time off but, if necessary, should order it. The burnout syndrome may appear early or well into the postdisaster period, from two weeks to a year. On the average, it seems to take about four to six weeks for most of the symptoms to appear.

The Goal and Setting of Crisis Intervention

Because crisis is often associated with extreme change in interpersonal or environmental functioning, stabilization is a primary goal in crisis intervention (Aguilera and Messick, 1993). Thus, a primary goal of crisis intervention is emotional-environmental first aid. Its goal is definitely *not* to resolve all the problems of the client. The actual intervention activity may occur in a variety of settings, including the following:

1. The field site of a disaster.
2. Transportation vehicles.
3. The emergency room while the patient waits or receives needed medical care.
4. The walk-in clinic offering crisis counseling to ambulatory patients.
5. Hotlines (or rap lines) offering suicide prevention and other crisis-intervention telephone services to troubled individuals. (These services may be independent of or part of emergency medical services. They rely mainly on telephone counseling by trained volunteers, ideally with professional consultation available on a backup basis.)
6. Mobile services (often called *home treatment teams* or *emergency teams*), usually staffed by two or more team members.

Once the client is identified as being in crisis, the concepts discussed in this chapter come into play. However, at the termination of the crisis intervention process, the human service worker returns to the assessment approach: What additional problems does the client have, if any, and what additional services may the client need? Three obvious possibilities exist, as illustrated in Figure 12.3. The client's crisis may be resolved, and no additional services may be necessary. The client's crisis may be resolved, but additional services may be necessary. And the client's crisis may *not* be adaptively resolved, and additional longer-term interventions may be necessary. In succeeding chapters, we deal with strategies available for clients with whom crisis intervention was not successful, was not available, or was successful but uncovered further problems in addition to the crisis state.

Summary

1. People in need often postpone seeking help until their problems have reached crisis proportions.

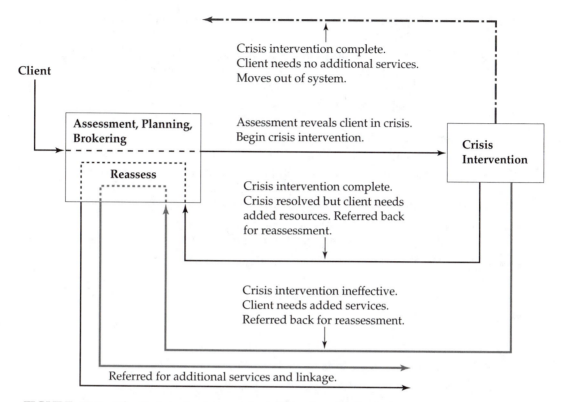

FIGURE 12.3   The Return to Assessment, Planning, Brokering
after Crisis Intervention

2. Crises usually follow a similar pattern of disorganization of behavior, slow recovery, and reorganization.

3. Individuals usually resolve crises in four to six weeks by reorganizing their behavior at a higher, lower, or equivalent level of functioning than the pre-crisis period.

4. Crisis intervention is employed to assist in the reorganization of behavior at a higher or equivalent level of functioning and to prevent reorganization at a lower level of functioning.

5. Some human service practitioners have identified a crisis-prone type of client whose resources are so limited that the client is likely to experience stress as crisis-provoking.

6. Common signs of crisis states have been identified; they range from preoccupation to behavior that appears detrimental to the person's self-interest and from bewilderment to discomfort.

7. A crisis can be set off in almost any person by extremely stressful events such as natural disasters.

8. Workers who respond to major disasters are likely to develop signs of crisis themselves, called *burnout,* and may need intervention from supervisors or others.

9. Many people respond with a crisis reaction to more common events, such as family dissolution, death of a loved one, criminal victimization, loss of employment, and retirement.

10. The principles under which crisis intervention programs operate include promptness of service, time limits on treatment, use of social networks, prevention of dependency, focus on current problems, and development of trust, self-reliance, and self-esteem by the client.

11. Though crisis periods may be resolved effectively, the crisis worker must be alert to longer-term problems and must be prepared to link clients to additional services.

Discussion Questions

1. What might it take to develop a crisis state in *everyone?*
2. What are the characteristics of a crisis-prone person?
3. What are some of the common crises that people experience?
4. What are the principles of crisis intervention programs?

Learning Experiences

1. List the crises you have gone through. How did they affect you?
2. If your community has a crisis intervention program, visit it and find out what kinds of problems it deals with and how it deals with them.
3. Make a list of events that you think could precipitate crisis behavior in yourself.
4. Explain how you usually cope with high stress.

Endnotes

1. H. J. Parad and H. L. P. Resnik, "The Practice of Crisis Intervention in Emergency Care." Reproduced with the permission of the Charles Press Publishers, Bowie, MD 20715 from their copyrighted work *Emergency Psychiatric Care,* © 1975.
2. E. Atkinson, "Four Hours on the Suicide Phone." *Bulletin of Suicidology,* No. 7, 1970, pp. 38–39.

Recommended Readings

Aguilera, D. C., & Messick, J. M. (1993). Crisis intervention: Theory and methodology (7th ed.). St. Louis, MO: C. V. Mosby.

Follette, V. M., Ruzek, J. I., & Abueg, F. R. (Eds.). (1998). *Cognitive-behavioral therapies for trauma.* New York: The Guilford Press.

Gist, R., & Lubin, B. (Eds.). (1989). *Psychosocial aspects of disaster.* New York: Wiley.

13

Culturally Favored Approaches

Indigenous Workers, Peer Therapy, Parahelpers, and Mutual Self-Help

- Are there advantages to the use of indigenous workers and parahelpers?
- What is an indigenous worker?
- What is peer therapy?
- Who are parahelpers?
- What are some functions of indigenous workers and parahelpers?
- What are mutual help or self-help groups?
- What similarities do these groups share?
- What potential hazards exist in the use of mutual help and self-help groups?

In this chapter, four human service approaches are described that are particularly amenable to culturally sensitive human service practice. Of the four, the first three to be discussed are virtually by definition culturally or ethnically sensitive to the minority cultures in which they may be used. The fourth approach is not *necessarily* culturally or ethnically sensitive but certainly has the potential to be so, depending upon the mix of persons involved (Simoni and Perez, 1995).

The notion that only highly educated and intensively trained professionals from the traditional disciplines of medicine, psychology, and social work can effectively help others is obviously rejected by followers of the human service approach. In fact, in many settings, the highly trained traditional professionals may be in extremely short supply or experience cultural barriers in applying their specialty training to the client population. The absence of enough professionals and early recognition that cross-cultural services are difficult to deliver contributed to the development of four similar but unique human service approaches. They are indigenous workers, peer therapy, parahelpers, and mutual self-help approaches.

Indigenous workers are members of the cultural community that is being provided with services and are employed by the service agency to provide those services. *Peer therapy* consists of the activities of a naturally significant other from a person's social support network, such as a parent, sibling, close friend, classmate, or recovered client, that are directed toward developing positive changes in the person. *Parahelpers* are individuals in the community who already provide informal helping services or who have the potential to do so by virtue of their social, cultural, or community role. *Mutual self-help* is the activity of two or more otherwise unrelated people who band together for mutual social support in order to receive help *from* others and to provide help *to* others.

All four of these approaches rely heavily on social support systems to facilitate client change, problem resolution, or client stabilization in the community. The importance of social support networks for effective personal functioning has been touched upon in prior chapters. It remains unclear exactly how social support networks enhance human functioning, but it is obvious that they can have important effects both positive and negative (Galinsky and Schopler, 1995).

When social support networks are intact, people in trouble have others to whom they can turn for help, advice, guidance, and expressions of concern. The psychological and social support offered or available from one's social network appears to provide a buffer against stress or the experience of psychological or even physical crises (Stephens et al., 1987; Throits, 1986). For many human service clients, the absence of a viable social support network compounds already present problems or is in itself the problem. It must be recognized, however, that a strong social support network may also have a *negative* influence on a person (Scheffler, 1984). If a person's social support network is dominated by a manipulative or malevolent person, damage can certainly be done. As a case in point, consider the Reverend Jim Jones, who in the 1970s convinced his large flock to leave the United States and emigrate to South America, and who, not long after, presided over the mass suicide of hundreds of his followers and himself. That particular social network was clearly destructive. This unusually tragic example suggests the possible negative effects of problematic social support networks, which may exist on a smaller, less dramatic scale. The key for human service workers is to be sensitive to the possible negative impacts of social support systems while working to encourage and develop social support networks that have positive impacts on people.

Indigenous Workers

The indigenous worker is employed by an agency from a particular subcultural group that the agency serves. The individual is almost always initially untrained, may have been unemployed, and is trained by the agency to do one particular job. Common subcultural groups from which indigenous workers have been selected are Hispanics, Blacks, Native Americans, and Asians. The use of indigenous

Indigenous workers and volunteers can maximize the impact of human service programs.

workers originally grew out of the realization that there would never be enough traditional professionals to provide the required services. Additionally, a body of evidence strongly suggests the advantages of using such workers in the human services (Gartner, 1971; Gartner and Riessman, 1982; James, 1979; Kestenbaum and Bar-On, 1982; Nash et al., 1978; Smith and Meyer, 1981).

The indigenous worker has the advantage of relating to the client as a peer rather than as an outsider. These workers tend to share the values, customs, language, and problems of the client group, which puts them in a better position to understand real-life problems and gain clients' trust (Bokan and Campbell, 1984; Westermeyer, 1987).

In many cases, the indigenous worker has specific skills or attributes that the professional human service worker may not have. Blum (1966) reports that such a group had an "exceptional ability to reach out and establish initial contacts with clients whom professional social workers were unable to reach." Meyer (1969) has stated, "The strength of the nonprofessional as a link stems from his (or her) double position as a member of the community and its groups, on the one hand, and a member of the agency, on the other hand."

Not all indigenous workers make a career of human services. Many, however, do. They discover that helping others brings meaning to their own existence, in addition to the financial rewards of employment (Riessman, 1965). Indigenous workers become career human service workers at a point of transition in self-perception. That transition involves seeing their helping activities as an important part of their long-term self-perception and seeing themselves as having a career orientation of helping others, rather than just performing a job.

Peer Therapy

Unless they are extremely isolated and alienated, most individuals have strong bonds to some other people. The prime example of such a relationship is that between child and parent. Other examples include the relationships between siblings, spouses, and close friends. In addition, certain types of settings encourage the development of strong attachments that maximize the effects of peer relationships, as in the relationships between barrackmates in the military service, classmates in a schoolroom, or cellmates in prison.

In peer therapy, the relationship is clearly intended to be advantageous for one member of the peer dyad and usually is advantageous to both. A significant other interacts with the person in need in such a way as to modify the person's problematic behavior or to provide general support or assistance to help the person meet his or her needs. The distinguishing feature that sets peer therapy apart from other important relationships between significant others is that the peer therapist typically functions under the supervision of or is trained by a human service worker who is experienced in the peer therapy approach.

Peer therapy seems to be effective for three reasons:

1. Naturally significant others are usually strongly motivated to learn how to help the person in need to change his or her behavior.
2. By virtue of his or her inherent role, the significant other is already linked to the physical and psychosocial need systems of the client.
3. Significant others naturally function as models or identification figures for the client.

In the human services, the use of peers as therapists or change agents seems to have the potential to be a powerful, cost-effective approach. By their very nature, peers have strong influences on each other, and their helping attempts are usually formalized into their natural relationships.

An excellent example of the use of significant others as change agents is in the Regional Intervention Program (RIP) in Nashville, Tennessee, a professionally administered, parent-operated, therapeutic preschool for children who have severe behavior problems. In this program, parents are trained to act as change agents. Services are free, but once the child has completed the program, each parent must volunteer his or her services to the program for three mornings a week for six months.

The RIP program described here represents programs that use significant others (such as parents) as change agents. It illustrates the helper-therapy principle: Not only does the child's (client's) behavior change but also the parent's (helper's) behavior changes positively.

Community crisis lines are often staffed by trained peer counselors.

The Regional Intervention Program: A Typical RIP Experience

■■ Mr. and Mrs. James Pruden with their four-year-old son, Paul, came to RIP at the suggestion of their pediatrician. Paul was unmanageable. Rather than eat he preferred to throw his food on the floor. He still wet his bed. He was reckless with his toys and those of other children, and he had no young friends because he preferred to pinch his playmates instead of play with them. . . .

A parent "intake worker" interviewed the Prudens with a checklist of questions. She comforted them with the admission that she had been through similar kinds of problems with her daughter and that it sounded as though Paul could be helped by the RIP program if one of his parents could work with the child there at least three mornings a week for several months.

Since Mr. Pruden worked, and Mrs. Pruden had quit her job, it was agreed that Paul and his mother would immediately start in the program. In a few weeks another parent from RIP would visit the Prudens at home to see how things were going there, and then Mr. Pruden could learn directly some of the techniques taught at RIP. At the conclusion of the interview, Mr. and Mrs. Pruden watched a twenty-minute movie about RIP which simply explained the program's organization. Paul and his mother returned to RIP the next day to begin the initial observation sessions in the Generalization Training Module for children with behavioral problems.

Behind the One-Way Mirrors

The Generalization Training Module has a simulated three room apartment—living room, bedroom, and kitchen—where RIP staff can observe a parent with child. Here Paul and his mother were to meet for twenty minutes every day for several months in a highly structured format. Two RIP parents would observe their relationship, systematically rating behaviors that they would interpret for Mrs. Pruden after each session.

In the first session, Mrs. Pruden was asked to play with her child as she would play at home, with one exception. The living room in the apartment had ten toys, and Mrs. Pruden was to change the toy her child was playing with every two minutes. (An observer from behind the window tapped the window with a pencil as a signal that two minutes were up.) Because most children want to keep certain toys for more than two minutes, this procedure brought out Paul's frustrations, and quickly allowed the RIP staff to observe parent-child behavior in frustrating situations.

"Without this kind of specialized procedure," says Judy Horowitz, the professional staff person responsible for the Generalization Training Module, "it might take a long time for Paul to exhibit his typical problems in front of strangers. Instead we try to see the oppositional behavior quickly so we can begin to train the parents quickly."

Paul's frustration level was quickly reached in the first session of toy changes. As toys were taken away he kicked and cried, even threw one toy at his mother. And the greater his aggressive behavior, the more attention, albeit negative, he received from his mother.

In a conference after the first twenty-minute session, Mrs. Pruden was shown the checklist and graph reflecting Paul's aggressive actions, recorded by two observers. In twenty minutes, six kicking tantrums, four punching actions, etc.

"This is what we call 'baseline information,'" says Ms. Horowitz. "After two or three baseline sessions, after we've had a chance to see what is happening between parent and child, we begin to teach a parent new ways of handling her child. We begin to teach some of our 'tricks.'"

RIP's tricks belong to the repertoire of popular procedures used by behavior modification technicians. They are special "interventions that help a parent control a preschooler's behavior," says Ms. Horowitz. . . .

The Interventions

. . . "In your next play session," a trained parent told her, "you are to bring a toy down as you have done before, but this time you must add a definite command as you hand it to Paul. Say to him, 'Now it's time to play with the truck.' You have to tell a child what you want him to do before you can expect him to do it. If Paul listens to you and begins to play with the toy, play with him. Give him lots of attention. We call this 'turning on.' Talk to him, hug him, describe to him what he is doing, talk with him about the toy you are playing with. But if your child does not listen to what you've told him to do, ignore him. We call this 'turning off.' Do not talk to your child. Do not look at him. Don't shake him to make him obey. Simply sit or stand with your back to him and play quietly with the toy. If Paul then comes to you and wants to play with the toy, it's time to turn on and talk to him."

She emphasizes: "This is the general rule: when you like what your child is doing and would like him to do it more often, give him lots of attention. But when you don't like it, ignore him."

To those familiar with behavior modification theory, this may sound elementary. What's stressed at RIP, however, is not theory but experience. Mrs. Pruden learned the concept of differential reinforcement—rewarding desired behavior and ignoring undesirable behavior—by doing it. And she learned it under the observing eyes of those skilled in the technique.

The Generalization Module is like a laboratory, one mother explains. "We experiment until we find out what works for us."

What Works

For the next several sessions, Mrs. Pruden and Paul looked as though they were acting in a melodramatic silent film. Mrs. Pruden would animatedly encourage her son when he played actively, but not aggressively, with his toys. She turned away stonily when he tried to get her attention through tantrums, tears, and toy throwing.

All during these sessions, *raters*—observers with checklists of behavior—were tabulating the kinds of behavior exhibited by Paul from behind the one-way mirror. After a couple of weeks, a graph of Paul's behavior sharply depicted his changing behavior patterns. As a RIP staff person read the graph to Mrs. Pruden, it sounded like a kind of behavioral Dow Jones report: kicking and crying down 50 percent; toy involvement and appropriate behavior up 75 percent.

By the time of this graph report, however, Mrs. Pruden really didn't need the data to know that Paul was getting more manageable. She could see it. But she did need to learn that what she was doing was directly responsible for it. Perhaps, she said, he was just growing out of bad habits.

"It's important at this point," says Ms. Horowitz, "that a parent fully understands and experiences the changed interaction pattern as the reason for a child's improved behavior habits." Thus, in what behaviorists and RIP staff call "reversal" sessions, Mrs. Pruden was instructed to go back to her old ways of dealing with Paul: she was asked to pay lots of attention to him when he cried, and to be passive when he played quietly. In other words, the reinforcement techniques which she had learned were turned around and, consequently, so was Paul.

"It was a nightmare experience," says Mrs. Pruden. "Paul was back to his kicking tantrums in only two reversal sessions. I got the point which I don't think I'll ever forget. Techniques taught to me at RIP had worked in helping Paul become a less hostile, aggressive child." The effects of the reversal sessions were, of course, temporary. The second phase of differential reinforcement was instituted immediately. . . .

Positive reinforcement becomes much more selective after a parent learns the basic behavior modification techniques. As Ms. Horowitz explains, "Nobody is continually reinforced in real life for good social behavior. Nobody gets constant praise or attention every time they behave well. What we call 'intermittent reinforcement,' therefore, is more practical. When you're making dinner, you don't have time to pay constant attention to your child."

The practice of intermittent reinforcement begins behind the one-way mirror where a parent is asked to read a magazine while the child is playing, or she pretends to cook something in the module kitchen. Sometimes RIP arranges to have someone visit the module living room. Mrs. Pruden began to learn intermittent reinforcement when a RIP staff person visited with her in one of the module units. Paul also had a visitor that day; another preschool child came to play with him. . . .

In the eight months that Paul spent at RIP, he played in preschool classes after his one-way mirror sessions. First there was the initial intake classroom where he was observed for placement. That was followed by the community classroom which was designed to prepare him for a public school kindergarten. In each of these classes, he participated in routine activities of preschool—coloring, drinking juice, eating cookies, building with blocks. Lots of free time was spent in a big indoor sandbox laden with toys. Classroom teachers continually applied the same kinds of techniques taught to Mrs. Pruden.

Periodically Paul's classroom behavior was rated in checklists similar to the ones used behind the one-way mirrors, so that his aggressive actions toward other children—pinching, biting, kicking—were monitored for change. Raters in the classrooms, as those behind the one-way mirrors, are parents or special education students from local colleges who are getting their practicum experience. . . .[1]

Peer therapy is not limited to children and parents. Hawkinshire (1969), for example, discusses the application of peer therapy to criminal offenders. Craighead and Mercatoris (1983) have described the use of mentally retarded residents as peer therapists, and Byers-Lang (1984) has reported on the use of peers for building networks for blind older adults. Even children may be used as peer therapists for other children. Sancilio (1987) describes the use of programmed child-child interactions as a method of intervention in the social and behavioral difficulties of children. In the approach he describes, adults program the interventions of children as peer therapists. The children function as social reinforcers and social initiators in group interactions and social skills training. Sancilio demonstrates that, with adult supervision, environments can be changed so that a problem child's peers interact with him or her in such a way as to bring about a desired behavior change.

Common to a majority of such programs is a recognition that the peer therapists must be given assistance in becoming change agents. The prospective peer therapist must be trained for that role. Hawkinshire (1969) has identified issues that must be faced when peers serve as change agents:

1. *The peers must be trained in the activities they are to engage in.*
2. *The peers need at-the-elbow support from the trainer or supervisor so that they can develop confidence in the new behavior and have someone to turn to when problems arise.*
3. *The peers must have the opportunity to give feedback to the trainer or supervisor in terms of their feelings about what is happening.*
4. *The peers are most effective when a support group of other peer therapists is available as a source of critique and new ideas.*[2]

These four points are certainly not unique to the use of peer therapists, but they are clearly important in the use of any type of change agent. They may, however, have special significance for peer therapists, who are often relatively naive in dealing appropriately with the person in need and most likely will initially need extensive assistance and supervision.

Parahelpers

A major human services system resource appears to be individuals in the community who already supply informal helping services to persons in need or those who have the potential for doing so. Until recently, such community resources remained relatively untapped, but more efforts are being expended in the direction of their utilization. In many cases, such persons are identical to the indigenous worker in that they share subcultural beliefs and values with the person in need. The major difference is that they are usually not *formally* employed by a human service system to provide helping services. The range of parahelpers is broad, including ministers, police, teachers, bartenders, hairdressers, babysitters, retired persons, relatives, neighbors, college students, and folk healers. The types of services such persons can provide vary from information giving and referral to major therapeutic interventions.

That parahelpers can provide major human service assistance is relatively well accepted. The chief issue today involves the creative use of these persons in programs that work. The following examples show how some types of parahelpers are used.

Beauticians/Bartenders Learn Mental Health Helper Role

■■ Students in a Grand Forks, North Dakota, beauty college got a taste of their future roles as unofficial mental health aides during a "people helpers' workshop" sponsored by the Grand Forks Mental Health and Retardation Center.

"In most American communities, people with emotional problems can easily seek help from an agency or therapist," says Pam McLean, center staff member, who supervised the student beauticians' workshop. "But in North Dakota, with its many small isolated communities, this is not always feasible. To help solve the problem, the North Dakota Mental Health Association suggested a program that would enlist the aid of beauticians as mental health helpers." . . .

Ms. McLean designed a six-week course, with the group meeting for two hours each week. The first meeting, which was lecture style, was not as successful as the later ones, which directly involved the students in role playing and small group discussions, Ms. McLean says. Communication, the role of a beautician, aspects of mental health versus mental illness, and community resources available for referral were some of the topics discussed. In addition to Ms. McLean, a group therapist and the consultation and education specialist from the mental health center participated in the course.

Participants completed evaluation sheets at the group's final meeting: "I didn't realize how important I could be to a customer," "Now I understand the importance of good listening," "I didn't know there were so many resources in this area," and "I understand better the feelings of people in need of help" were some of the students' comments. Ms. McLean plans to do a follow-up evaluation six months after the end of the course and is investigating the possibility of setting up similar workshops for bartenders and practicing beauticians.[3]

Texas Trims Some Red Tape

■■ The sixty-eight-year-old Black woman—let's call her Eloise Denton—was severely depressed. She didn't need a psychiatrist to tell her that much. For days she stayed inside her small frame house near a noisy Houston freeway and watched the cars go by. She didn't bother to change her dirty nightgown because, she said, "There's no one who cares what I look like." She cooked a thin chicken broth for herself and not much else. "Food is expensive," she complained, "and anyway my dentures are hurting so there's not much I can eat." . . .

Mrs. Denton's husband died six months ago. She felt alone and isolated without him. Her Social Security payments had been cut in half since he died, and she worried a lot about money. Her daughter tried to help out, but she didn't have much money left over from her own family expenses. She also complained that her mother was unpleasant to be around. "When I visit her she makes me feel that I'm just not there," she said.

When someone suggested that her mother see a psychiatrist, she laughed. "Don't you think she's a little old for that?" she asked. "My mother's not crazy, she's sad and poor. What's a psychiatrist going to do about it?" Nevertheless, she was persuaded to call the geriatric clinic at the Texas Research Institute of Mental Sciences. Within a week the clinic had sent Mrs. Lenora Driver, seventy-four, a Black outreach worker, into Mrs. Denton's home to see if she could be of any help.

"You've come because you think I'm crazy," said Mrs. Denton to the outreach worker. "No," said Mrs. Driver, "I've come because I have lots of information I think will be of interest to you."

Mrs. Driver was a walking encyclopedia of information that was of interest to Mrs. Denton. She told her where she could get new glasses free, what clinic offered dental care free, which forms to fill out to get supplemental Social Security income payments. She told her about the local nutrition center, one of a number of county-run senior citizen activity centers where free lunches are served, and where she would meet other people her age who sew, knit, play dominoes, watch television, and plan group outings. Mrs. Driver explained the bus routes or walking directions to all the places she mentioned.

In a couple of months Mrs. Denton seemed transformed. She could see the stitches on a bright red scarf she was knitting. She could chew the chicken in her soup. She was neither alone nor lonely at the nutrition center. She never had to see a psychiatrist, but if her depression had persisted, Mrs. Driver would have arranged for that, too. . . .

In a two-week training course, followed by weekly training meetings at TRIMS, the outreach workers learn about federal, state, and local programs for old people—Social Security supplements, food stamps, nutrition programs, special medical and dental care services. The only criteria for the outreach workers are that they be able to read and write and enjoy older people. They range in age from twenty-three to seventy-four.

Most of them grew up in the neighborhoods they now serve, and know the indigenous landmarks and language. Spanish-speaking neighborhoods have Spanish-speaking outreach workers. . . .[4]

Innovations in Foster Care

■■ Jason Alexander, a four-year-old boy, was found strolling the streets of a major city at four A.M. by police officers. Investigation by Child Protective Services (CPS) workers revealed that Jason Alexander (J.A., as he was called) was frequently neglected by his crack-cocaine-addicted mother. CPS initiated steps to remove custody of J.A. from his mother, with the intent of placing him in foster care. Through a new culturally sensitive program, CPS relied on the strong extended kinship bonds of African American families and placed J.A. in foster care with his grandmother. J.A.'s grandmother received training in foster care requirements and a monthly stipend to support the cost to care for J.A.

In the same Midwestern city, there is a large Native American population (in fact, larger than on any existing tribal reservation). In this city, CPS is using Native American spiritual leaders to counsel problem parents, to mediate placements, and to recruit foster parents. Decisions about removal of Native American children from their parents' custody is no longer made exclusively by non–Native American CPS workers, but only after consultation and input of the Native American spiritual leaders.

These brief program descriptions depict beauticians, relatives, and elderly women as parahelpers. The programs range from Texas to New York to North Dakota. Similar programs are in operation in most areas of the country, particularly in large metropolitan areas. Other types of parahelpers, such as families of penal offenders, foster grandparents, teenage volunteers, and daytime baby-sitters for working mothers are common. One resource that is often overlooked is alternative healing or folk healing (Box 13.1). Discouraging the involvement of traditional helpers such as Mexican curanderas, Puerto Rican espiritistos, Cuban santeros, or Native American shaman is one sure way to lose the confidence of clients who are immersed in those cultures (SAMHSA News, 1999).

It should be obvious that parahelpers are of critical importance to the maximum use of resources. Because parahelpers can provide valuable services with the proper training and most operate on a volunteer basis, it seems most feasible to use such services in the human service system.

Mutual Help Groups

Two broad functions for mutual help groups exist. Some provide support for people who have personal problems, and others provide advocacy for groups of people who view themselves as disenfranchised from the broader society. The first function has emerged from a concern with the individual problems or behavior of the group members. In contrast, social advocacy groups are marked by a belief system that assumes dysfunctional social structures. Membership consists of committed community activists with a broader, recognized constituency. The emphasis of these groups tends to be on the acquisition of services, resources, and access for their constituencies, and their strategies revolve around changing social, political, economic, and service-delivery systems to obtain equity and control over resources. In this chapter, the emphasis is on mutual help groups that focus on providing support for people who have personal problems. In actuality, though, most mutual help groups that focus on members' personal problems also, to a lesser or greater extent, have a social advocacy function.

Within the type of group that focuses on members' personal problems, two subtypes can be distinguished (Lieberman and Borman, 1979). There are groups that effect change in their members and groups that *enable* their members' behaviors, attitudes, and affects. Examples of the first type include Alcoholics Anonymous, Parents Anonymous, Recovery, Inc., and Take Off Pounds Sensibly

BOX 13.1   Traditional Cultural Helpers and Human Services

In many cultures, there are figures who are highly regarded by a large portion of the populace as healers. In the industrialized, Western countries, these types of healers or helpers were considered "unscientific" and of little value for many years. However, as their *results* have been followed by some researchers, respect has developed for their ability to help members of their culture.

Western medical science recognizes that many of what people believe are purely physically caused medical problems have strong psychological components, and many psychological approaches are now being applied in physical health care. The usefulness of traditional cultural helpers probably derives from this concept. The traditional cultural helper can be of assistance as a parahelper in dealing with persons whose problems are culturally embedded.

In the Hispanic Caribbean, especially in Puerto Rico, *espiritismo* has a long tradition of sanction and practice. It is a philosophy that is based on the belief that many of life's misfortunes and conflicts can be helped by contact with the world of spirits that is said to surround the material world. An *espiritista*, or spiritual healer, is consulted by a person in crisis and determines whether the client's suffering is caused by his or her spirit's need for "evolutions." This spiritual evolution takes place with the help of the healer and the healer's contacts with the spirit world, which may direct the sufferer to atone for a presumed misdeed in order to relieve the suffering.

Santeria is a belief system native to Cuba that has been born of a melding between the religion of African slaves and the Catholic beliefs of their Spanish slave masters. A number of Yoruba gods have been imbued with some of the qualities of particular Catholic saints, out of similarities perceived by the adherents and perhaps out of the slaves' need to disguise beliefs regarded as pagan by their masters. These saints/gods are utilized by *santeros* for the purpose of counseling, managing crises, and, in general, securing an improved lot in life for those who need it. Sacrifices and offerings can be made as attempts to improve one's prosperity, to reduce outbursts of anger, to enhance one's sexual ability, and to remove illnesses that may have been occasioned by ill will.

In Brazil, similar mixing has occurred between Yoruba beliefs and the Catholic credo in the cults of Umbanda and Candomble. Although the healing practices of these systems vary, both are united by beliefs in the duality of spirit and body, the ability of spirits to contact the material world, and the assumption that spirits can be used in healing.

Some European Americans, of course, find the same kind of assistance and relief from their own organized religions. There are the examples of the miracle of Lourdes and Protestant "laying on of hands" for healing. Not too many decades ago, medical and mental health professionals scoffed at these other healers, but today it has become obvious that they *are* effective helpers. It is wise for human service workers to respect their practices even if they may not accept the underlying beliefs. They can be effective parahelpers for human service workers.

(TOPS). These organizations provide intensive support systems that uphold the importance of the members' change and behavior. Support is available, not just at regularly scheduled meetings but as often as the members need it. Such groups often specify clear and concrete guidelines through which to obtain desired change. The second type of self-help group focuses much more on *adaptation* and *coping* through internal behavioral, attitudinal, or affective changes. These groups provide a variety of helping methods to their members, their goal being adapting to major life changes that may range from a medical condition to the catastrophic event of parents' coping with their child's terminal illness.

The principles that seem to be important in the effectiveness of mutual help or support groups are beginning to be identified (Citron, Solomon, and Draine, 1999; Long, 1999). They include (1) a person who has successfully survived a difficult experience may be a positive and powerful role model for someone who is currently dealing with the same issues, (2) a person in need who tries the role of helping another becomes stronger from the experience, (3) becoming a helper confers a degree of status that helps the person supersede the stigma of the condition (for example, of "being" mentally ill) that led to the need for help to begin with, (4) belonging to a self-help group provides emotional support and a social network, (5) having an active role in helping others and oneself combats the dependent and passive role that is not only unacceptable in U.S. culture but also attributed to those who are in need, and (6) the best way to challenge stigma is for those who experience it to show their strengths by advocating for themselves.

Who can benefit from a self-help or mutual help group? Many people may find that the concern and assistance of their peers in a small-group setting helps them deal with important life problems. The individuals in the examples below represent just a few of the types of people who might benefit.

- ■■ Margaret and Bill are the parents of a young child with cancer. For two years, they have shared suffering, dashed hopes, and heartbreak. In spite of caring friends and professional support, they feel alone in their grief.

- ■■ Jean is a divorced mother who has custody of her three children. She now finds herself overwhelmed by the problems of single parenthood. Her teenage son has become difficult to handle, and she is increasingly discouraged in trying to provide for her children's needs and the demands of her job.

- ■■ Roger has a serious drinking problem. He has been fired from two jobs in the last year and is deeply in debt. He has lost the respect of his family and friends. He entered treatment at an alcoholism clinic but began to drink again two months after the treatment ended. He realizes that his addiction is ruining his life but feels helpless to control it.

- ■■ Paul is very bright, but he has a poor opinion of himself because of his stutter. When he sees people with speech problems who are successful, he wonders how they did it.

- ■■ Marilyn's doctors consider her physically recovered from breast surgery, but she cannot escape the feeling that she is disfigured and may develop cancer again. She becomes more and more depressed as she withdraws from friends who "just can't understand."

■■ Jim is a heavy man whose overeating has caused him great personal unhappiness. After years of unsuccessful attempts to control his weight with medical help, fad diets, and pills, he sees himself as a hopeless victim of his own weak will.

To individuals engaged in human services activities, it has become clear that alienation and isolation from significant others is a major factor in the development and maintenance of problem behaviors. Some have gone so far as to suggest that most human services problems are a result of people feeling adrift and unlinked from each other because of the disruption of the traditional institutions of home, family, church, school, and neighborhood (Hurvitz, 1975; Mowrer, 1971; Van der Avort and Van Harberden, 1985). In what appears to be a response to this situation, in recent years there has been a fantastic growth in what has been called the *small-group movement.*

Although the small-group movement includes the formal group psychotherapy type, the most significant aspect for human services is the growth of mutual help groups or peer groups (Katz, 1981). Voluntary small groups of persons gather together in a relatively ongoing relationship in order to satisfy a common need, to overcome a shared problem, and to bring about social or personal change. The groups commonly deal with issues that existing social institutions or service agencies neglect (Macht, 1999).

Self-help groups are of a variety of general types (Schensul and Schensul, 1982):

1. Conduct reorganization or behavioral control (for example, Alcoholics Anonymous).
2. Common predicament (for example, the Alliance for the Mentally Ill (AMI), a support group for family members of individuals who are mentally ill).
3. Survival or self-esteem (for example, Reach to Recovery, a support group for women who have had mastectomies).
4. Personal growth or self-actualization (for example, Parents without Partners).

Often, mutual or self-help groups do not fit neatly into this type of categorization, and their goals or focus may overlap. By whatever scheme they are categorized, it is characteristic of all these groups that the participants have banded together for mutual help in the sense that they are seeking help in changing themselves or their environments, often without resorting to outside professional assistance. In fact, some groups are openly antagonistic or hostile to trained professionals, who have for many years rejected the mutual help groups as interlopers and amateurs in a highly complex field (Emrick, 1990). This rejection by professionals has weakened dramatically in the last decade, mainly because of the persistent success of many of the mutual help group activities (Riessman and Carroll, 1995).

To give some sense of the extent of the mutual help movement, an example is the prototype mutual help organization, Alcoholics Anonymous. Since it was founded in 1935, Alcoholics Anonymous has grown into an organization with 41,000 chapters and over 800,000 members in the United States and Canada

TABLE 13.1   A Sampling of Mutual Help Groups

Name	Focus
Candlelighters	Peer support for parents of children with cancer
The Compassionate Friends	Peer support for parents whose children have died
Gamblers Anonymous	Peer support to help people stop gambling
Gray Panthers	Advocacy and support for older adults
Mended Hearts, Inc.	Peer support for those who have had heart surgery
Narcotics Anonymous	Peer support for recovered drug addicts
National Alliance for the Mentally Ill	Peer support and information about and advocacy for seriously mentally ill people
Overeaters Anonymous	Peer support for overweight people and programs to combat overeating
Parents Anonymous	Peer support and crisis intervention for abusing or ex–abusing parents
Reach to Recovery	Peer support for women who have had mastectomies
Theos Foundation	Peer support for the widowed and their families

(Hurley, 1988). Worldwide, it has 87,000 groups and 1.7 million members in 150 countries (Maisto, 1995).

Mutual help groups are being developed for new population groups on a constant basis. For example, the development of self-help groups for mentally retarded citizens has been an important new community approach (Browning, Thorin, and Rhoades, 1984). Nationwide, there are over 150 self-help groups for mentally retarded people; they focus on activities such as socialization, fund raising, political lobbying, and group advocacy. Across the United States, there are over 500,000 self-help groups of different types currently in operation, with an estimated 14 million members (Steinburg, 1997). Obviously, the range of mutual help groups is quite broad. The examples that follow are illustrative of the types of mutual or self-help groups in existence or in the process of being developed around the country. An additional sampling of the broad range of targeted issues dealt with in self-help groups is given in Table 13.1.

Self-Help for the Widowed

■■ A self-help group for widows and widowers, an outgrowth of a "Workshop for the Widowed" sponsored by the Rockland County (New York) Mental Health Association at the local community college, has been meeting weekly since May 1974.

The widowed workshop offered each semester at Rockland Community College is one of several programs designed by the association to provide preventive intervention at critical transitional periods in people's lives, according to Pat Thaler, director of the association's Educational Service.

Participants reported that while the workshop was extremely helpful to them in dealing with their new life situation, they wanted to meet with an ongoing group of widowed persons because they felt their problems were quite separate and distinct from those of divorced persons—who have groups such as "Parents Without Partners."

"The Widowed Group" meets each week at the Rockland Community Mental Health Center in Pomona. More than 125 men and women have participated in the program, with each meeting attracting between thirty and forty persons. Membership is limited to those under the age of fifty-five because it is felt that the problems of widowed people in the early and middle adult years are different from those experienced by older individuals who lose their spouses toward the end of the life cycle—the younger widowed have problems related to helping children deal with the death of a parent, untimely loss of a spouse, moving into the world of singles, anger and grief, extrusion by society. Ms. Thaler is consultant to the group, and is the only professional involved. There is no other expense to the association since the group collects dues and is self-sustaining.

"This is a self-help educational and social organization," Ms. Thaler says. "A strong family feeling exists among group members, who frequently help each other out in times of sickness or other distress. The group sponsors many social events that may or may not include children. Recently the group has taken a bus trip with children to New York City to see the Nutcracker Ballet; sponsored a members' Sunday morning brunch; and organized a Christmas/Hanukkah party with everyone bringing a dish."

Each meeting is planned in advance, with speakers on subjects of interest invited once or twice a month. Recent speakers have included a woman attorney discussing wills, trust funds, and providing for children when the widowed remarry; a psychiatrist on the special emotional needs and the new identity of the widowed; and a travel agent on trips for the single.

In addition to these programs, one or two meetings a month are devoted to group "raps" led by Ms. Thaler. Subjects have included the impact of death on children; relationships with in-laws; starting again; and the special problems of widowed men.

The group has initiated a telephone service for widows and widowers who need practical information or an understanding ear. Persons calling "The Widowed Group Line" speak to someone who takes the caller's name and telephone number. A return call is made to the caller by a helpful widowed person as soon as possible. This service is provided with the cooperation of the Rockland Community Mental Health Center's Crisis Telephone Service.[5]

Alcoholics Anonymous (AA) is one of the oldest mutual help organizations and has been a model for many of the groups that have followed. Alcoholics Anonymous was started in 1935 by two alcoholics as a way for *them* to stay sober. It has grown into a major approach to alcohol addiction but retains the mutual help character of its early beginnings.

As a prototype, AA demonstrates that in order for the self-help or mutual-help process to work with the major problems of living, the person in need must make a major commitment, *with the support of others,* to changing the problem behavior. In AA in particular, the commitment includes a spiritual flavor, as illustrated in its "twelve steps." These twelve steps are the core of the AA program and describe the attitude and activities that AA members believe are important in helping them achieve sobriety (Alcoholics Anonymous, 1955):

1. *We admitted we were powerless over alcohol—that our lives had become unmanageable.*
2. *Came to believe that a Power greater than ourselves could restore us to sanity.*
3. *Made a decision to turn our will and our lives over to the care of God as we understood Him.*
4. *Made a searching and fearless moral inventory of ourselves.*
5. *Admitted to God, to ourselves and to another human being the exact nature of our wrongs.*
6. *Were entirely ready to have God remove all these defects of character.*
7. *Humbly asked Him to remove our shortcomings.*
8. *Made a list of all persons we had harmed, and became willing to make amends to them all.*
9. *Made direct amends to such people wherever possible, except where to do so would injure them or others.*
10. *Continued to take personal inventory and when we were wrong promptly admitted it.*
11. *Sought through prayer and meditation to improve our conscious contact with God, as we understood Him, praying only for knowledge of His will for us and the power to carry that out.*
12. *Having had a spiritual awakening as the result of these steps, we tried to carry this message to alcoholics, and to practice these principles in all our affairs.*

One extremely common arena for the development of self-help groups is in the area of medical illnesses, particularly for chronic illnesses. The lack of assistance from medical professionals for information, support, and coping skills for people with medical problems has stimulated the formation of large numbers of self-help organizations and local groups.

Home Dialysis Club for Patients, Families

■■ A "Home Dialysis Club" for patients and their families coping with the stresses of using an artificial kidney machine at home offers a way for families to get together and support each other, without feeling they are stigmatized as members of a psychotherapy group. "Patients had resisted the idea that they in any way needed psychiatric treatment, and had greatly feared being seen as emotionally sick. It was burdensome enough to cope with being physically sick," says author Helen Kress.

Kress began the club . . . when she was with the VA hospital in New York City. It began as a club for wives of patients, where they could gain support and understanding for what they were experiencing. Now both the patient and spouse are included in the monthly three-hour meetings, and sometimes children are invited to attend also.

In addition to sharing problems and feelings, club members plan social events and act as "sponsors" for new people entering the home dialysis training program. Thus, new trainees have someone in addition to staff members to whom to turn for support, and they see club membership as the norm for home dialysis couples.

"The club approach (is) an unconventional but effective means of offering services to home dialysis patients and their families consonant with their needs for dignity, self-respect, and more control of the structure than is needed by some clients," concludes the author.[6]

Other mutual help groups that have gained a great deal of public awareness include Synanon, Gateway House, and Daytop Village. These programs have become models for approaches to dealing with people who are trying to escape from chemical addictions other than alcohol, and similar mutual help programs for addicts have grown up all around the country. Such programs require great commitment on the part of their members in order to be successful, greater than in the case of most other mutual aid groups.

What Makes Mutual Help Systems Successful?

Although mutual help groups have been in existence formally for more than sixty years and informally for much longer than that, many questions remain as to why they function effectively. Systematic attempts to examine their processes and their effectiveness have only recently been started. Unfortunately, the little information that is available in regard to what makes them tick is speculative in nature. Some clues, however, are emerging (Steinberg, 1997).

1. Self-help group members learn about common aspects of their problems from other group members. A predominant activity is information sharing.
2. Members may be enabled to reattribute the cause of their problem from a personal failure to an impersonal issue. For example, parents of a schizophrenic may learn that their child's faulty biochemistry is the problem, not the parents' child-rearing skills.
3. The member experiences strong group acceptance and shared understanding.
4. The member develops a sense of normalization: "There are many others just like me."

O. H. Mowrer (1971), an early proponent of the mutual help concept, suggested that people become alienated (lose their sense of community) because of dishonesty, irresponsibility, and uninvolvement. The mutual help group uses the opposite approach to become in effect a substitute for the extended family.

In surveying mutual help groups, it appears that the principles of honesty, responsibility, and involvement are common to all, even though the phraseology describing the concepts may differ from one group to another.

Honesty is defined as being straight with oneself and with others, not being self-protective or self-indulgent at the expense of others, disclosing one's being, not rationalizing, and not deceiving oneself or others. *Responsibility* means accepting the consequences of one's behavior and one's effect on others, making amends when necessary, keeping commitments, keeping one's word, not blaming others for what happens to oneself, and gaining control over one's behavior. *Involvement* is emotionally opening up to the group, in effect "buying in," not holding oneself aloof from the process or from one's *own* feelings, letting the group, its process, and its goals have meaning for oneself, and being available for the needs of others.

To what extent each of these factors contributes to the functioning of mutual help groups is unclear. Certainly, many other factors are likely to be involved. But with the increasing emphasis on the use of mutual help groups in the human services sector, we can expect more interest in determining the critical factors in their use as a social policy option (Newsome and Newsome, 1983).

Mutual help or self-help groups obviously provide significant assistance to many people in need. It appears that this approach can be expanded to many other people problems. However, this approach is not without problems and dangers. One obvious problem is that a group may be organized or structured in such a way that the group will fail in its purpose, perhaps leaving the group members in worse straits than before the group was begun. Lemberg (1984) has identified a number of factors that may lead to ineffectiveness in a self-help group process:

- Lack of external support
- Few intact members
- Lack of sharing of leadership and responsibility
- Passive members
- Communication only between leaders and members, not member to member
- Superficial meetings, avoidance of "hot" or emotional issues
- Noninvolved members
- Leaders who do not admit the need for support
- No risk taking or involvement

If these factors are avoided and the group becomes successful as an ongoing social support system, a number of other possible dangers may develop. Gartner and Riessman (1977) break down dangers into two sets, one set relating to the professional human services system and one set relating to consequences to the client.

Dangers Relating to the Professional Human Services System
1. *The mutual help system may be used to justify the reduction of other services.*
2. *It may be used to avoid responsibility by the appointed service providers.*
3. *The mutual help approach may be taken over by the "establishment," which would negate a major focus of the current systems.*[7]

Dangers Relating to the Mutual Help Group Client
1. *Emphasizing mutual-help approaches leads to the possibility of "victim blaming."*
2. *Participation rather than real help may be a resultant, and there are few controls over the delivery of the services.*
3. *Mutual help may interfere with persons obtaining needed* professional help *when it is appropriate and useful.*
4. *Mutual help may foster an unnecessary dependence on the part of the members.*[8]

Even though such problems and dangers exist, it is very likely that judicious use of and emphasis on mutual help systems can avoid many of the problems, and the existence of such dangers certainly does not justify the neglect of the possible benefits by human service workers.

Mutual Help Groups and the Human Service Worker

The human service worker can use the mutual help concept in at least two ways. The first and most obvious is referral. If the mutual help groups in the community are known, clients can be referred to such groups as an additional or sometimes primary support system. The best example here is Alcoholics Anonymous. If the human service worker identifies problem drinking as a major issue for a client, it makes sense to refer that person to AA. Even though most mutual help systems do not use professional help, they are ordinarily receptive to referrals from formal human services systems and maintain good working relationships with them.

The second way in which the human service worker can utilize the mutual help process is more complicated and difficult but perhaps more rewarding and meaningful in the long run. That is, the human service worker may be able to initiate and set up entirely new mutual help systems. By no means is it being suggested that the human service worker attempt to replicate a national organization on the scale of Alcoholics Anonymous; rather, limited mutual help groups on a local level should be the target. The widowed group and the dialysis club described earlier are prime examples of such projects; an identified problem at a local level was met through the creation of a limited mutual help approach. The possibilities of types of mutual help systems are limited only by the creativity of human service workers.

Summary

1. Indigenous workers are people employed by an agency who share the subcultural values of all or part of the agency's clientele. Indigenous workers have thus far included Hispanics, Blacks, Native Americans, and Asians.

2. Peer therapy has been demonstrated to effectively use the naturally significant persons in the client's culture to stimulate and maintain significant adaptive behavior change.

3. Peer therapy seems to be effective for three reasons: (a) Naturally significant others are strongly motivated to help the person in need; (b) the significant other is already linked into the physical, cultural, and psychosocial need system of the client; and (c) significant others act as natural models or identification figures for the client.

4. When peers are used as change agents, they must be trained and have supervision available. Peers must have the opportunity to give feedback and receive support from a more experienced human service worker or another peer therapist.

5. Parahelpers are individuals in the community who supply or have the potential to supply informal helping services to people in need. Parahelpers are not

usually formally employed to provide helping services but do so in the context of other employment, as in the case of a police officer or minister.

6. The use of indigenous workers and parahelpers grew out of the realization that there would never be enough traditional professionals to provide the required services and a growing awareness that the subcultural values and customs shared between indigenous workers and clients could facilitate the helping role.

7. A mutual help or self-help group is composed of people who share the same concerns or problems and have banded together to give and receive help and support.

8. Mutual help or self-help groups share the principles of honesty, responsibility, and involvement.

9. The effective functioning of a mutual help or self-help group may be compromised by a number of factors, such as lack of external support, a majority of disturbed or passive members, lack of shared leadership, lack of member involvement, or an absence of risk taking.

10. Even effective mutual help groups may present dangers to the professional human services system, such as using the self-help movement to justify reducing funded services, as well as dangers for the client, such as victim blaming or fostering unnecessary dependence.

11. Human service workers can use the mutual help or self-help approach in at least two ways: (a) referring clients to existing groups and (b) developing entirely new groups for needy target populations.

Discussion Questions

1. What are the advantages of using indigenous workers, peer therapists, parahelpers, and mutual help groups?
2. What is the difference between peer therapy and mutual self-help?
3. Why is peer therapy effective?
4. What issues exist in using peer therapists?
5. What are the common elements of mutual help systems?
6. What other factors may be operating in mutual help groups?

Learning Experiences

1. Interview an indigenous worker and find out what he or she does.
2. Interview a bartender, beautician, or police officer. Find out if people tell them their problems, what the problems are, and what the parahelper does about them, if anything.

3. Identify the self-help groups operating in your community by name and address. Keep the list for future reference. (A good starting point is the telephone directory.)
4. Ask a self-help group if you can observe meetings or participate.
5. Try to determine what new self-help groups your community needs.
6. Join a self-help group if you think you need to (for example, to stop smoking, to lose weight, and so on).
7. If your community has a peer therapy program, ask if you can observe it or perhaps join (for example, a campus hotline).

Endnotes

1. Reprinted by permission from *Innovations* (Vol. 2, No. 3, Fall, 1975), published by the American Institutes for Research, P.O. Box 1113, Palo Alto, CA 94302, under a collaborative grant from the National Institute of Mental Health.
2. Adapted from F. Hawkinshire. "Training Procedures for Offenders Working in Community Treatment Programs." Published in Guerney, Bernard G., Jr. (Ed.), *Psychotherapeutic Agents: New Roles for Nonprofessionals, Parents, and Teachers.* New York: Holt, Rinehart and Winston, 1969. Reprinted by permission of the publisher.
3. Reprinted by permission from *Innovations* (Vol. 2, No. 2, Summer, 1975), p. 30, published by the American Institutes for Research, P.O. Box 1113, Palo Alto, CA 94302, under a collaborative grant from the National Institute of Mental Health.
4. By Suzanne Fields. Reprinted by permission from *Innovations* (Vol. 4, No. 1, Spring, 1977), pp. 19–20, published by the American Institutes for Research, P.O. Box 1113, Palo Alto, CA 94302, under a collaborative grant from the National Institute of Mental Health.
5. Reprinted by permission from *Innovations* (Vol. 2, No. 2, Summer, 1975), pp. 32–33, published by the American Institutes for Research, P.O. Box 1113, Palo Alto, CA 94302, under a collaborative grant from the National Institute of Mental Health.
6. Reprinted by permission from *Innovations* (Vol. 3, No. 3, Fall, 1976), p. 40, published by the American Institutes for Research, P.O. Box 1113, Palo Alto, CA 94302, under a collaborative grant from the National Institute of Mental Health.
7. A. Gartner and F. Riessman. *Self-Help in the Human Services.* San Francisco: Jossey-Bass, Inc., Publishers, 1977, p. 20. Reprinted by permission of the publisher.
8. A. Gartner and F. Riessman. *Self-Help in the Human Services.* San Francisco: Jossey-Bass, Inc., Publishers, 1977, p. 21. Reprinted by permission of the publisher.

Recommended Readings

NMHA. (1999). *Directory of self-help groups.* Alexandria, VA: National Mental Health Association.

Riessman, F., & Carroll, D. (1995). *Redefining self-help: Policy and practice.* San Francisco: Jossey-Bass.

Steinberg, D. M. (1997). *The mutual-aid approach to working with groups: Helping people to help each other.* Northvale NJ: Aronson.

14

Social Intervention

Prevention through Environmental Change

- How do personal and general environments contribute to the difficulties experienced by human service clients?
- What processes are involved in improving a person's immediate environment?
- What are some historical and current examples of attempts to change personal environments for the better?
- What can be done to change general social systems in order to reduce human services problems?
- What current trends are apparent in social change?

Many of the problems with which human service workers deal do not reside in the individual client as much as in the fabric of society.

■■ Carmen V. is the seventeen-year-old mother of three children between the ages of seven months and three years. During her first pregnancy she dropped out of high school, where she had been a failing student, and lived with her mother in order to care for Carmen's younger brothers and sisters while her mother worked. Carmen was shortly thereafter thrown out on the streets when her mother found her using drugs in the home. Carmen had been introduced to drugs by her boyfriend, the father of her first child.

During the next few years, Carmen held several short-lived jobs in fast-food restaurants. Because of Carmen's lack of punctuality and reliability, associated with her drug use and her successive pregnancies, none of the jobs lasted for more than a few weeks. Carmen's boyfriend began to criticize her about her use of drugs and the inadequate care he thought she was providing for the children. About a year ago, during Carmen's third pregnancy, her boyfriend (common-law husband) left the area, and Carmen has not heard from him since.

Although young and bright, Carmen projects a sense of helplessness and hope-lessness. She sees little in her future that is more satisfying than her past and appears overwhelmed by the responsibilities of caring for three young children. The one thing that she experiences as positive in her life is her association with her "friends" who are deeply involved in drug use. The few times she has tried to quit using drugs, her lack of social support has led her back to that same group of associates.

If we see Carmen's problems as residing within her personality, our approach will focus on changing her so she can deal with the many problems she has. In this example, we might conclude that Carmen needs remedial education and job train-ing at some point but that the immediate problem is lack of motivation (dropped out of high school), poor frustration tolerance (cannot hold a job), withdrawal (uses drugs to escape from the harsh realities of life), poor human relations (boyfriend was fed up and left), and sense of helplessness (does not have the strength to get out of the inner city). Because we perceive the problems as caused by Carmen's lack of inner capacities, we may try to make drastic changes in her psychological processes. If we are successful, the other problems can be solved by Carmen: She can get an education and a good job and income, leave the inner city, and develop a loving relationship with a new spouse.

Another way of looking at the problems of an individual is to consider the impact of social factors on the person's life. Certainly, Carmen needs individual help, and that help involves working on problems such as motivation, frustration, withdrawal, addiction, and feelings of helplessness. Of course, he also may need more education and job training. But what about the social environment from which she comes? What can we do about the social factors that contribute to poor education, lack of jobs, drug abuse, unstable families, and substandard housing? Perhaps these are the most critical reasons why Carmen is in a needy state. If she had been born and raised in different circumstances, would she be the same? If we could have provided good schools, jobs, and a safe environment, would we still see her as needing helping services? These are questions that can-not be confidently answered. We do know, however, that broad social problems have profound effects on the people who must suffer with them.

Many human service workers are involved in activities designed to prevent the development of further damage to people in need. These activities involve changing the immediate environments of people who already need services and, on a broader scale, working toward major social changes that will reduce our society's production of the psychosocially walking wounded. Human service workers may act as change agents through the process of social intervention. When human service workers try to change the environment of a person or that of a small group of clients, the process can be called a *limited social intervention.* Some broad social factors, such as poverty, may cause a wide variety of human problems. When we try to change these broader aspects of society, the process is one of *comprehensive social intervention.* Whether social interventions are conducted on a limited scale or are more comprehensive, in essence, the goal is *prevention* of human service problems.

Prevention in Human Services

A team of human service workers, working in an area of the country where job-lessness is everywhere, knows that for some people job loss leads to marked symptoms of depression and other mental health problems. Additional studies have revealed that those who have experienced especially severe financial hardships develop signs of mental disorder. Moreover, their vulnerability is increased because they are tempermentally shy and uncomfortable in asserting themselves in new social situations—presumably including the challenge of a stressful job search as unemployed people.

The team of human service workers set out to develop strategies aimed at a dual goal: to reduce the toll of depression among those experiencing job loss and to restore them to productive employment as quickly as possible. Their subsequent efforts produced positive results. A program of interventions—notably, guidance, counseling, and support in the job search process—turned out to be effective in both economic and human terms by increasing family income, reducing dependency, and diminishing rates of depression even when workers are followed for two and a half years. The efforts of these human service workers unwittingly fall into the realm of prevention services. They were dealing with the immediate problem of joblessness, but the programs they instituted had long-term effects in reducing another human service problem, the incidence of depression in a community (Reiss et al., 1993). They were engaging in a proactive rather than reactive approach to human services (Heckman, 1999).

Prevention in the human services has traditionally been conceptualized similarly to prevention in medicine and public health. In this view, there are three levels of prevention effort: primary prevention, secondary prevention, and tertiary prevention.

Primary prevention includes efforts intended to prevent a disorder from occurring to begin with. These efforts include two broad strategies: (1) system-directed approaches, such as social policy development and modification of social environments designed to reduce sources of stress and to enhance life opportunities, and (2) person-centered strategies, such as educational programs to impart adaptive skills and competencies, as well as preventive interventions for specific risk groups (for example, for children of divorce). A core quality that links primary prevention efforts and sets them apart from other approaches is their intentional targeting to well people (Price et al., 1988).

Perhaps the best example of a major nationwide primary prevention program in the human services is Project Head Start. The rationale for intervening in the lives of disadvantaged children by providing high-quality early childhood education emerged from a growing mass of scientific evidence gathered starting in the 1950s. Guided by social concerns and intellectual inquiry, the scientific community developed experimental preschool programs designed to enhance intellectual performance through the enrichment of early experience. The beneficial effects to the children, their families, and communities have been extensively documented (Zigler, 1999).

On the basis of the initial findings of sharp increases in intelligence test scores for the children in the experimental programs, Head Start was begun in 1965 as part of a large-scale community action program legislated by the Economic Opportunity Act. The act mandated the creation of comprehensive child development programs, more commonly known as Head Start, as well as several other antipoverty programs, and a new federal agency, the Office of Economic Opportunity. As you have seen elsewhere in this text, Head Start continues to this day to serve children and their families in most communities across the country, and it illustrates the process leading from basic research to prevention research and from prevention research to clinical and social services implementation.

Secondary prevention consists of the early detection of dysfunction and immediate intervention. With early detection and immediate treatment or intervention, disorders or dysfunctions are believed to be more easily and effectively treated. Some would argue that this is not really prevention but simply treatment. Others point out that what is being prevented is long-term chronic disability.

Tertiary prevention includes those strategies we use to reduce the severity or level of disabilities once a disorder or dysfunction has chronically impaired an individual. Most of those activities that are called *rehabilitation* fall into this category.

The areas of secondary and tertiary prevention have received the lion's share of available resources in the human services. Only relatively recently have more attention and resources been directed toward primary prevention. However, in comparison to the resources directed toward secondary and tertiary prevention, primary prevention is only just beginning to be seen as important (Newton, 1988).

Limited Social Interventions

Limited social interventions attempt to make significant formal changes in the personal environments of needy people, and this can have a beneficial effect on those individuals' abilities to adjust to life in the broader society. In this sense, one-to-one therapies, group therapies, peer therapy, and mutual help groups, when first developed, would fit under this concept. However, in this chapter the focus is on modification of current environments or development of new environments in such a manner that they become inherently positive or supportive of adequate functioning on the part of persons who experience them. The stimulus for changing the immediate environments of persons in need has grown out of the recognition by human service workers of two related major issues:

1. Most environments of people in need support—and, in fact, stimulate—*problem* behavior.
2. For many people in need, providing one hour of *treatment* contact per day or week is not sufficient to generate positive behavior change.

A prime example of the first issue is the negative effect of short- and long-term imprisonment on lawbreakers, and on those who guard them (Chaneles, 1987;

Haney and Zimbardo, 1998). The penal setting has been found to be so negative to the process of rehabilitation that many sources have described prisons as schools for crime. Prisoners, particularly first offenders, learn little during their imprisonment other than how to do better the type of crime they have committed or how to engage in new types of criminal activity. For the most part, for people who have or will have contact with the corrections system, this problem also exists in the community. In the clearest example, lawbreakers or potential lawbreakers tend to relate mainly with other lawbreakers, and their problem behaviors are reinforced through social acceptance by their peers. In addition, once labeled as a delinquent or criminal, such people tend to be treated by society as if they must inevitably again behave criminally.

Obviously, many personal environments have a negative effect on people and may well be a major factor in otherwise adequately functioning individuals' *becoming* persons in need. As possible examples of negative personal environments, one could consider the following:

- The friendless, resourceless life of many elderly citizens without families
- The stimulus-deprived environment of the infant or child in a ghetto
- Overcrowded, underfunded poverty-area schools
- The unstable environment of the migrant worker
- The delinquent gang peer-group culture
- The skid row environment of the chronic alcoholic

Certainly, such a list could go on and on, with examples from formal helping systems such as mental hospitals, prisons, and schools and from society at large. It is clear that many such negative environments exist, and there is virtually total agreement among human service professionals that such environments can have significantly negative effects on a person's behavior, even when the primary problem of the client is not considered to be a function of environmental causes.

The second major factor that has stimulated social intervention approaches is the recognition that limited direct contacts, such as one hour of treatment per week, are often not sufficient for generating positive behavior change. This observation has been made for prisoners in penal systems, patients in mental hospitals, and students in mental retardation facilities. The failure of such systems is often attributed to this problem. Ex-convicts return to their criminal subcultures, discharged mental patients return to their old problem-generating environments, and mentally retarded people return to their nonsupportive life situations, with the result that many of these people must go back to the institutions they came from because they "can't make it on the outside."

A further complicating factor is the chronicity of the problems that people in need experience. Very frequently, human service clients present with problems that have existed for many years, often since their childhood or adolescence. It is not uncommon to encounter clients who have manifested the same difficulties for five, ten, twenty, or thirty years. It seems highly unrealistic to expect such longstanding problems to be resolved by one-to-one or group counseling or by psychotherapy on a once-a-week basis in a relatively short period of time. Rather, what is needed is the creation of an *environment* in which the client can exist and in which all activities, occurrences, and events have a positive effect on the problem behavior.

Changing Institutions versus Changing Persons

The major problem in human services today may be that the person in need is provided with only partial services. For the most part, the focus has been on changing people so that they can adjust to society's stresses, with the assumption that the problem most frequently lies within the client. Traditional human services approaches have focused on one-to-one or small-group treatment approaches, which are labor intensive in that one treatment provider can provide services to only a small number of clients. The traditional approaches by and large require intensive efforts directed at achieving significant change in how an individual client relates to an established social system. The recognition that labor-intensive intervention systems use costly resources in dealing with relatively small numbers of people has led us to a growing awareness of the need to intervene in social systems in order to provide alternative change strategies for people in need.

What appears to be required in the human services field is a major investment in discovering or developing natural growth experiences that will have a positive effect on the behavior and adjustment of clients. Obviously, no one such experience would be appropriate for all persons; rather, a range of experiences would have to be available.

These types of limited social interventions are becoming more common and focus on changing the immediate social systems and organizations that impact on people in need, including social welfare agencies, institutions, facilities, and programs. The goal is to promote positive growth on the part of people in need by changing the systems with which they must interact, so that the social systems themselves do not produce or maintain problem behavior. (See Box 14.1 for a culturally embedded intervention.) Whatever problems are present in social systems, limited social intervention involves a similar process:

1. Identifying environments that have significant negative effects on a client or clients
2. Identifying the aspects of the environment that can be changed
3. Determining how the negative aspects can be changed in a positive direction
4. Implementing the changes or creating entirely new environments that will have an ongoing positive effect

Historical Examples

Several examples can be given of environmental changes that have had important impacts on human services. Such examples could be drawn from any of the

BOX 14.1   The Ethnic Agency

For many decades, ethnic communities have had difficulty in accessing adequate and culturally sensitive or appropriate human services. This has led in many locations to the founding of "ethnic agencies" (Iglehart and Becarra, 1995). Ethnic agencies are human service agencies that (1) serve mostly or exclusively one ethnic group, (2) are mainly or only staffed by one ethnic group (the same group as that being served), (3) are controlled by the ethnic community power structure, and (4) promote ethnic identification by the agency clients. The presence of ethnic agencies circumvents the cultural barriers that are present when services are controlled, provided, and staffed by one (dominant) culture within another (minority) culture ethnic community. Thus, a Cuban American–operated and –staffed community mental health center in Miami's ethnic Cuban American neighborhood is more likely to be sought out for services by ethnic community members than one operated and staffed by European Americans (or, for that matter, by Asian Americans). An African American–operated and –staffed Head Start program in Chicago's Englewood neighborhood is more likely to provide useful educational experience to Black children than one operated by White, middle-class, suburban European Americans.

   The disadvantage of ethnic agencies is that they are no better prepared to deal with clients from outside their ethnic group or cultural background than any mainstream agency. In fact, they might be less prepared because most mainstream agencies are making at least some effort to become multiculturally sensitive, and an ethnically identified service agency is not likely to be concerned with that. This is not really an issue unless the ethnic character of the community begins to change, but that does seem to be happening in some places. There are now ethnic agencies funded by public tax dollars in areas where more than one ethnic group resides (e.g., Korean immigrants moving into previously all African American neighborhoods), and the minority ethnic group (the Koreans, in this example) are not able to access culturally sensitive services from the community agency.

subfields of human services: corrections, retardation, mental health, education, and child care. However, we shall focus on two of the larger systems: corrections and mental health.

   As early as 1913, the corrections system of Wisconsin innovated a work release program (Clare and Kramer, 1976). In such programs, prisoners are allowed to seek and maintain gainful employment in the community while serving a sentence. The underlying premise of such programs is that they allow prison inmates to begin an appropriate transition to community life before the end of the sentence. The transition allows them to develop new social networks that will be supportive of the "straight" life after the sentence is complete.

   In a similar vein, prerelease halfway houses for felons have been developed around the country. Their focus is to assist in the transition from prison life to life in the community. The emphasis in such settings is on employment, talking out problems, and sharing the difficulty of reentry into community life. Such settings have as major goals the breaking of old patterns of behavior and the development of new support systems. Unfortunately, there are simply not enough slots in the existing work-release programs and halfway houses across the country to handle the explosive growth in prison population that has occurred during the past fifteen years, when the number of prisoners in jails and prisons combined has soared from about 400,000 to nearly 2,000,000 (Gearan, 1999).

In the mental health system, an environmental manipulation that has had both positive and negative results occurred in the early 1960s. At that time, many people were considered inappropriately admitted and retained in mental hospitals. The criteria for admission to these very restrictive settings were not stringent, and few community services were available. Because admission was easy and other resources were absent, mental hospitals became swollen with residents. Changes in treatment approaches, new legislation, and funding for increased community resources, combined with a changing viewpoint about the desirability of restrictive settings, led to the phenomenon we now call *deinstitutionalization:* the movement of patients and the responsibility for their care into community settings. This approach resulted in a steady reduction of inpatient population from a peak of 559,000 in 1955 to under 70,000 in 1996 (see Figure 14.1). Federal and state monies that were made available to support ex–mental patients in community settings led to the growth of a major new industry: nursing homes and sheltered-care facilities for discharged mental patients.

The process of deinstitutionalization was a success in part (Mehr, 1999; Minkoff, 1987; Torrey, 1989). It resulted in many improvements in services in public mental hospitals. With lower census levels, the institutions' funding could provide more services to the fewer remaining inpatients. In addition, many people who had been locked away were able to move into less restrictive community settings.

However, it is clear that many abuses occurred.[1] In fact, in many community mental health centers, the severely mentally ill people who were discharged did not receive adequate and comprehensive care. The increase in patient care episodes reflected a broadening of the clientele to new groups that in the previous years had no access to the mental health system—persons with problems of crisis, problems of satisfaction, and milder psychological problems rather than severe mental illness (Grob, 1994). More typically, the chronically and severely mentally ill person discharged from the public mental hospital was placed in a nursing home or entered a cycle of short-term stays in the public mental hospital, discharge, and readmission. To be sure, many community mental health centers did provide adequate service that would maintain a severely mentally ill person in the community, but the reality did not approach the dream.

A compounding problem for the vision of a reformed mental health system was the impact of declining fiscal support from government entities. In 1981, federal support for comprehensive community mental health centers was eliminated after only slightly more than 600 of the proposed 2,000 were established (Kiesler, 1992). Medicaid did not keep pace with the growth of the number of poor people, and Congress required states to review SSI and SSDI eligibility, resulting in 500,000 people losing benefits, which disproportionately affected the mentally ill, for a time losing benefits until the eligibility changes were reversed. In general, the Reagan-Bush White House years saw significant cuts in funding for social

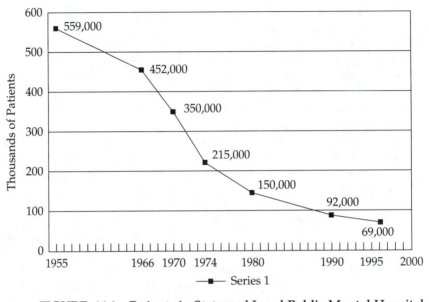

FIGURE 14.1   Patients in State and Local Public Mental Hospitals
from 1955 to 1996, Based on National Institute of
Mental Health Figures

programs—though the federal deficit continued to soar. In addition, a general anti-tax, anti–government-spending sentiment at local levels resulted in social service funding stagnation at state levels. By the late 1980s, only a few state systems had seen any increases in funding for mental health services.

The plight of the mentally ill in the community was further compromised by a general loss of housing availability. Federal housing programs suffered cutbacks, low-cost housing units were converted to middle-class housing through gentrification in most cities, and single-room-occupancy (SRO) hotels virtually disappeared. Homelessness has become a problem of much greater magnitude, highly visible on the nightly news and present in every city in the country. Many view the growth in homelessness as a sign of the failure of the deinstitutionalization of public mental hospitals and the community mental health movement (Torrey, 1989). In fact, the two groups, the homeless and mentally ill, are quite different populations even though they do overlap. Only about one quarter of the homeless have ever experienced prior psychiatric hospitalization (Rossi, 1990).

A number of factors came together in the 1980s to result in a bifurcated system consisting of continued use of and need for public mental hospitals and a community mental health system substantially lacking the full range of services for the neediest of the mentally ill population. With a lack of new or expanded fiscal sources, the two sides of the system competed for the same funds. In most states, the downsizing of public mental hospitals continued. The fiscal savings from the downsizing in some states was put into funding new community programs. In other states, unfortunately, the savings were lost to the mental health system (Mehr, 1999). They were used to cover state deficits in other areas. The bifurcated system was characterized by weak institutional linkages or mechanisms to ensure continuity and coordination of services. Severely mentally ill people were often released from public mental hospitals after relatively brief periods of time, into communities without adequate support mechanisms (Grob, 1994).

The late 1980s and early 1990s saw a reconsideration of the overly optimistic promises of the original community mental health movement. Few authorities still believe that public mental hospitals can be entirely eliminated. However, they will continue to be smaller, and the total available beds will be even fewer than the 69,000 reached in 1996 (Mehr, 1999). Although plagued by the negative stereotypes of decades past that are reinforced by occasional scandals in the popular media, most public mental hospitals are consistently improving as they get smaller and become better staffed. The pendulum has swung to a somewhat more centrist position with a goal of a system of mental health care that not only is balanced between public mental hospitals and a comprehensive community mental health system but also in fact integrates public mental hospitals into the community mental health system.

In this particular example of an environmental manipulation, it is clear that even though the negative aspects of the original situation (a reliance on institutionalization of the chronically mentally ill) were relatively obvious, the results of the intervention were not clearly thought out, and no one was able to foresee the problems that would occur. It has taken several decades to begin to resolve the unexpected effects of what began as a grand plan to solve a social policy problem.

Does Limited Social Intervention Really Work?

The notion that changing an individual's environment for the better will prevent future problems is appealing. But does it work? Let us look at examples of what happened when such an approach was studied closely. The examples involve attempts to reduce the effects of a deprived environment on intellectual functioning in children.

A great deal of evidence indicates that mild mental retardation in children is much more prevalent in lower socioeconomic classes than can be accounted for by genetic or other organic reasons. We suspect that much of this mild retardation is due to psychosocial deprivation. If at least some of the children who are at risk for this type of mild retardation could be kept functioning at a higher intellectual potential, a major victory would be accomplished. Based on an early intervention program organized in Milwaukee in the 1970s, it appears that this may be possible.

The Milwaukee project focused on children in one geographic area of the city. That area contained only 2.5 percent of the children in the city but produced more than 30 percent of the mildly retarded children for the whole metropolitan area (Garber and Heber, 1977). The families at risk for producing these retarded children were those in which the mothers had IQs of 80 or below. The staff of the Milwaukee project decided to try to enrich the environment of these families to see if they could intervene in the retarding process. Because they were concerned about finding out if they had been successful, they wanted to compare the families with whom they worked with families who were similar but for whom they could not provide services.

Forty children of mothers with IQs of 75 or lower were identified, and half the children and their mothers were worked with. The other half were periodically evaluated but did not receive environmental intervention. The environmental change that was implemented for the families who received services was quite comprehensive. An indigenous human service worker entered each child's life and spent five days a week, most of the waking day, with the child, enriching the environment. This "teacher" was responsible for feeding, bathing, and cuddling the child and for providing exciting, interesting activities. The staff organized group activity programs for the children to provide intellectual and social stimulation. They taught the mothers these child care skills and instructed them in job skills, reading, and homemaking. At the end of this program, the mothers of the intervention groups were more positive in their self-concept and more verbal and responsive to their children than the mothers who had not received the social intervention, and more were employed.

The differences in the two groups of children were even more noticeable. The program began when the children were three months old, and direct involvement ended when they were about eighteen months old. The mothers continued in their training until the children were six. At the beginning, the children who received the intervention and those who did not were very similar in intellectual performance. The children were followed up until they were nine years old. At that age, children who had received the intervention had maintained their level of intellectual functioning, whereas children who had received no intervention had declined in intellectual functioning. The environmental changes that were provided to the intervention groups led to an average 20-point difference in IQ between children who had received services and those who had not. Although the supporting data for this study have been questioned, it appears that the program of limited social intervention did have important effects on these children (Garber, 1984).

A similar, more recent project conducted with children who had a wider range of intellectual levels also had lasting results. This project, called the Carolina Abecedarian Project, provided a group of youngsters with enriched environments from early infancy through preschool. By age two, IQ scores of the project children were already higher than those of comparable children in a control group, and remained higher ten years later. The children in the enrichment group also outperformed the control group in academic achievement (Neisser et al., 1996). Even less intensive interventions can have an impact. Follow-up studies of Head Start and similar programs show that children who participate are less likely to be assigned to special education class, are less likely to be held back a grade, and are more likely to finish high school than are similar children who do not participate (Zigler, 1999).

Will the effects last? We do not know. Children in the intervention group began to score less well as time went by after the program ended because of a lack of funding. These data, however, also demonstrate the positive impact of environmental enrichment as an early intervention for deprived children.

Current Examples of Limited Social Intervention

The following examples of limited social intervention provide some sense of the range of environmental changes that have been tried and can be attempted today. The changes in a client's environment made by human service workers can vary from changing one simple element to a complete overhaul of the client's life space.

For Ex-Offenders

■■ After its first two years in operation, DESEO, a program for convicted public offenders in Albuquerque, New Mexico, can point to a recidivism rate of less than 10 percent among its active participants. National statistics, on the other hand, show that approximately 75 percent of all parolees commit new crimes during the first two years of parole.

DESEO ("I desire," in Spanish) got its start when ex-offenders involved in a weekly therapy group at the Bernalillo County Mental Health–Mental Retardation Center developed the concepts for the program, and obtained the support of the center and funding from the Law Enforcement Assistance Administration, the state of New Mexico, and the city of Albuquerque.

Joanne Sterling, Ph.D., the center's assistant director of special programs, and Robert W. Harty, a former offender who is the program's coordinator, attribute much of the success of DESEO to the fact that offenders have been involved from the beginning in its design. In addition, two of the three field office staff are ex-convicts themselves.

DESEO is housed in a community-based facility as accessible as possible to the client population and the judicial and correctional components of the city, county, and state. Harty says the site has an added advantage because individuals who are hesitant to seek services at the main center are considerably less hesitant to visit the satellite center.

DESEO has active programs in a number of areas, with emphasis on strengthening the family support structure, both while the offender is incarcerated and during the crucial three to six months after his reentry into the community.

Essential components of the DESEO program include prerelease groups; counseling-treatment groups; a women's group for wives, girl friends, and mothers of offenders; bus service to the penitentiary; employment and training; and public education.

DESEO works hard to establish relationships with prisoners before they are paroled in Bernalillo County. One prerelease group meets weekly at Los Lunas Correctional Center, and another meets monthly at the New Mexico State Penitentiary. "At the same time, we are involved with his family, so both the inmate and his family are becoming more realistic about what to expect of each other, and themselves, before release," Harty says. The State Parole Board has begun requesting recommendations from DESEO staff about parole status and planning.

DESEO works to strengthen the ex-offender's social support system by holding weekly women's group meetings to provide socializing and discussion of mutual problems, and by providing weekly transportation for family members to the penitentiary.

Other ways in which DESEO helps its clients' families:

- It acts as advocate to helping agencies the family may know nothing about or is reluctant to approach.
- It sponsors, with local churches and civic clubs, recreational programs for clients' children, such as Little League Baseball and Big Brother type of activities.
- It intervenes in crises, whether they are emotional or practical needs for assistance with housing, welfare benefits, utility bills, or transportation.
- It utilizes the specialized treatment resources available through the mental health center.

Another area in which DESEO has a deep commitment is employment and training. "Research completed elsewhere has shown that a key factor in reducing recidivism is placement in a satisfactory job setting," Harty says. "Thus the program's staff has established links with all available resources within the community in this area, including the Division of Vocational Rehabilitation, the Employment Security Commission, and so on. In addition, a high percentage of the 2,400 hours provided to individual client services in the first year were devoted to this area."

Harty has these suggestions to anyone thinking of starting a similar program:

- Don't negate input from clients. The ex-offender must know that it is his program and he can get out of it whatever he puts in.
- The program must actively seek public exposure and gain public support through all forms of media.
- A close liaison must be maintained with agencies that might perceive the program as "radical" or a threat to them.
- For maximum delivery of services, a team approach is by far more effective than a hierarchical one.
- It is essential, unless the program is a nonprofit corporation, that it receive strong administrative support from the sponsoring agency, and that this agency also have strong community support. This is especially true in the area of devising funding methods for the program's continuation.
- Continuing efforts for minimal staff expansion must be made or a steadily increasing client load will eventually erode the energy, enthusiasm, and productivity of staff personnel.
- Probably most important is that the program not become an "institution" that drifts in the direction of meeting needs as they are perceived by professionals and administrators, rather than as they in fact are, and as they are perceived by the clients they serve.[2]

The environmental changes that have been made by DESEO and similar programs include maximizing social support networks for ex-offenders, employment, community involvement, crisis intervention, and residential services (Davis et al., 1984). In systems where such programs are unavailable, the ex-offender is likely to return to an environment in which the most supported response is renewed criminal activity. One would expect that programs like DESEO would by now be common all over the country, given its apparent effectiveness. Unfortunately, rehabilitation and community programming seem to be taking second place to an attitude of retribution and punishment in the populace and among our politicians, beginning in the 1970s and accelerating from the mid-1980s to today (Haney and Zimbardo, 1998). This so-called hard line approach toward crime is reflected in the astonishing increase in people in prisons and jails in the United States (see Figure 14.2). The United States has the dubious distinction of imprisoning far more people per capita than any other modern nation, with the exception of Russia. In fact, by 1998, the number of prisoners in federal and state prisons, combined with those in county or city jails, had soared to nearly 2 million (Gearan, 1999).

Another group of individuals for whom social intervention has been and will continue to be necessary are the tens of thousands of people who are mentally retarded and who need assistance in living independently in the community. For several decades, the mental retardation field has embraced the philosophy of "normalization," which includes the view that the social roles of individuals with mental retardation are enhanced by age-appropriate activities in the settings in which those activities usually occur, by having friends and other associates who are themselves valued socially in the community, and by participating in typical social, cultural, and economic roles in the community (Lakin, 1996). Social inter-

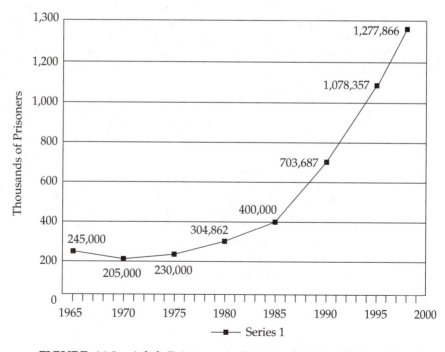

FIGURE 14.2   Adult Prisoners in State and Federal Prisons (Excluding County Jails), 1965 to 1998

ventions that promote normalization, personal autonomy, and self-determination have become a formal part of the instructional approach of many special education and community living programs today. More than twenty years ago, however, normalization approaches were quite rare, and a program in Minnesota was given some national attention for an innovative approach to teaching life skills and personal autonomy. The program involved providing an environment that encouraged self-reliance: wilderness camping.

Who Can't Canoe?

■■ A five-day, twenty-five-mile canoe trip into the Boundary Waters Canoe Area in Northwestern Minnesota has been a summer highlight for mildly and moderately retarded citizens from the northwestern region of the state for the past two summers. . . .

The program was initiated because many persons, especially staff and participants of the area's sheltered workshops, were concerned with the lack of an appropriate summer recreational experience for educable retarded citizens.

"The Northwestern Region of Minnesota had, for a number of years, provided a relatively structured camping experience for trainable mentally retarded," says Dan Wilson, developmental disability specialist at the Northwestern Mental Health Center in Crookston. "Initially, educable mentally retarded were also included in that camping experience. However, in many cases, mildly retarded adult citizens found themselves being counseled by high school age and young college people at this camp in areas of arts and crafts or beginning waterfront activities. These retarded persons felt that this particular camping experience was beneath them. As a result, they lost interest and few continued in subsequent years."

A representative of the local National Association for Retarded Citizens, together with a representative of the sheltered workshop and the Northwestern Mental Health Center, worked out a camping package that would meet the levels and the challenges necessary to stimulate these higher functioning mentally retarded persons as well as to help them on the road to independent living, Wilson says. . . .

"The screening process," according to Wilson, "involved a simple sampling of the kinds of behaviors that each of the participants would be expected to demonstrate once in the Boundary Waters Area. During the screening process, the participants were trained to get in and out of a canoe, to paddle a canoe, to select a paddle, to load and unload a pack sack, to roll and unroll a sleeping bag, to carry or help carry a canoe, to load and unload the canoe, to roll and unroll a tent, and to help set up a tent.

"As was previously suspected, the screening process revealed that it would be difficult to train mentally retarded persons to function as a sternsman in a canoe. The skill required to adequately steer a canoe was more than could be acquired in a relatively short period of time. For this reason, the staff ratio was predetermined at one staff person to two participants. In other words, one counselor would steer the canoe from the stern and the mentally retarded participants would paddle from the bow and the middle of the canoe.

"One of the keys to the success of this project was the staffing pattern. Throughout the camping trip, everything was done in threes by canoe: the counselor stayed with the two occupants of his canoe while traveling across the water, cooking, dishwashing, woodcutting, or setting up the tent. Each counselor was responsible for the supervision of only two other persons. In this way, no single person carried a greater supervisory responsibility than any other; and as a result, the trip was a vacation for all. Camping chores were broken down into modules and rotated three times a day. Each of the participants was trained in each of the modules and took equal responsibility for such tasks as woodcutting, dishwashing, cooking, etc."

These goals were achieved on the trip, Wilson says:

- Participants from both the sheltered workshop and the day activity center were provided with a five-day independent camping experience, totally apart from "civilization."
- A number of workers from both the state hospital and the county welfare departments were trained in the special needs of retarded persons, as well as made aware of their heretofore untapped potential.
- Workers from many agencies were able to work together on an immediate goal from a team approach; this has since helped in planning for larger and more difficult goals.
- The mentally retarded persons who participated in the camping experience did, in fact, become more independent. Seven of the ten participants on the first canoe trip were later placed in community employment and have continued to maintain themselves independently.
- The participants have learned to save money for their own interests as a result of this trip.
- The governing board of the regional camp for retarded has incorporated the EMR camping program as a part of the regular summer camping experience.

[According to Wilson,] ". . . Our experience here has demonstrated that these handicapped persons showed the wisdom to recognize their own limitations, and as a result, we had no accidents of any sort either year. The assumptions that we have held, that any skill which we as 'normal' persons find difficult at first, is impossible for the retarded, is quite untrue. I believe that if we tried we would find that most of the experiences that we find gratifying to ourselves and by which we grow intellectually and emotionally, would also be growing and gratifying experiences for the developmentally disabled.

"Our challenge is to dare to help these people to not need us anymore."[3]

The early wilderness camping program was a model for many programs to follow. Another program much better known that illustrates the benefits of normalization and self-reliance is the Special Olympics, which receives national attention each year and has participants from all across the country. The full integration of mentally retarded citizens into society, however, remains a challenge with many opportunities for contributions by human services workers.

In the examples of DESEO and wilderness camping, the change of environment was relatively minor although still important. In the example that follows, a major reconstruction of the environment of a group of clients was attempted. This microenvironmental change is fully described in two texts: *Community Life for the Mentally Ill: An Alternative to Institutional Care,* by Fairweather, Sanders, Cressler, and Maynard (1969), and *Creating Change in Mental Health Organizations,* by Fairweather, Sanders, and Tornatzky (1974).

The Community Lodge Program

In the mid-1960s, a group of researchers attacked the problem of lack of appropriate environments into which chronic mental patients could be discharged. At this time, it had become clear that many people were hospitalized mainly because there was no place for them to go, rather than because their behavior was so extremely deviant that they required protection and treatment. Such patients did express strange behaviors, including delusions, hallucinations, extreme mannerisms, and other eccentricities. Their premise was that such persons could live fairly productively if the appropriate circumstances were arranged.

The group embarked on a very ambitious project—in essence, they decided to create a new environment in the community in which these chronic patients could live a self-determined life. Funding was obtained to lease an entire motel, in which the patients would live, and a business was set up that was to be completely operated by them. The patients were trained and supervised by several staff supervisors who slowly withdrew their support and control over the course of about one year.

The patients (all men) were discharged from the hospital and had responsibility for their own self-care, personal hygiene, medication, food, and government (making and keeping rules) and for the operation of their groundskeeping and janitorial business. In addition, each took responsibility for his own behavior and the behavior of his fellows because they knew the community would not tolerate them if they became too "disturbed."

In many ways, this communelike living experience for ex–mental patients was a remarkable success. Although not all the members were able to remain out of the hospital, many did. They became relatively self-supporting and self-directing and were able to operate a functional business venture for several years. The results of the project have been considered so significant that similar community lodge programs have been started around the country.

Changing Personal Environments

The simplest aspect of the process of changing personal environments is identifying environments that one considers bad or in need of change. One need only examine the human services literature to find many situations that are considered to be detrimental to the adjustment or growth of persons in need. Once an environment is selected to be changed, the real difficulty begins (Reppucci and Saunders, 1983).

Fairweather, Sanders, and Tornatzky (1974) made an extensive study of the process of changing environments that have detrimental effects on people. Many of these environments are part of human services systems. For example, the mental hospital has often been criticized as having detrimental effects on patients in spite of providing treatment. Fairweather and his colleagues suggest principles to follow to succeed in changing some aspect of an organized service system. Implementing change is not an easy task.

Guidelines for change include these hints:

1. *Have perseverance.* Change is never easy, and it will not occur overnight. The human service worker must persevere in order to obtain change.
2. *Change is independent of resources.* Even resource-poor systems can change. Change is more a function of the involvement of people than of the availability of resources.
3. *Outside intervention is best.* People who are external to an agency are more likely to have success as change agents.
4. *Change requires action.* Doing is better than planning because planning can be a way of avoiding taking action.
5. *Start small.* Early changes should be nonthreatening.
6. *Use a grassroots approach.* Change is likely to be resisted by those in power.
7. *Obtain wide involvement.* The greater the number of people who feel that the change is their project, the more likely success will be.
8. *Act as part of a group.* Partners can provide each other with mutual support.
9. *Plan on continuous effort.* Once change has occurred, it has to be monitored. If it is not working, other changes may be necessary.

Even if one successfully follows these guidelines, success is not guaranteed. If the guidelines are not followed, however, success is very unlikely.

Comprehensive Social Intervention

The concept of comprehensive social intervention can be defined as (1) the process of identifying broad social problems that contribute to or possibly cause maladaptive behaviors and (2) the subsequent modification of the social systems or policies that contribute to the problems, in a planned attempt to eradicate those problems. A prime example of a broad social problem that is currently of great concern is the issue of poverty. What can be done to ease the plight of the nation's poor? It is clear that poverty in and of itself is a major contributor to human services problems. Crime rates are high among the urban poor, there is a higher incidence of drug abuse, infant death rates are higher, and most other types of major behavioral problems tend to have a higher incidence in poverty-stricken individuals. Using the concept of comprehensive social intervention, the approach to the problems exhibited by the nation's poor would be to discover a solution to *poverty* rather than attempt to help *individual* clients by means of direct assistance to them or through the modification of their immediate environments.

Most of the major behavioral changes in humanity have been a function of broad socioenvironmental restructurings, including changes in economy, political systems, social systems, and religious systems (Fisher, Mehr, and Truckenbrod, 1974). The philosopher-historian Bertrand Russell suggested that major changes in social systems have influenced the level of deviance in various societies. For example, he suggested that in Renaissance Italy traditional moral restraints and controls became weak because they were felt to be a result of superstition. As a result, liberation from such controls fostered the genius of energetic and creative individuals (such as Leonardo da Vinci) while leading to an era of anarchy and treachery, with little regard for human life.

Fried (1964) has developed a definition of social change:

> *For a working definition of social change, we can speak of gross alterations in the institutions of a society such as the structure of the family, the organization of occupational activities, the patterns of economic exchange or the political system. However, the specific effects of social change on the individual derive more directly from changes in the criteria for social role performance or fulfillment and in the expectations people have of one another with respect to any form of interaction.*

It should be pointed out that Fried and many others speak of social-environmental change in regard to its negative effects; that is, they describe its disruptive effects on individuals, which include anxiety, fear, confusion, and disturbed behavior. These effects on individuals do often occur, especially when the change is rapid and unexpected. However, the broader view shows that major social changes also have positive effects.

Riessman and Miller (1964), writing at about the same time as Fried, pointed out that the concept of social change has been largely neglected since the 1930s in favor of dealing with people problems on an individual basis. However, they provide examples of socioenvironmental changes that have had a major impact on the behavior patterns of large groups of people, for example, racial integration and the desegregation of schools. It is difficult to predict the totality of effects of large-scale changes in society and the environment, and often the results are both positive and negative, depending on one's viewpoint. In fact, frequently the effects of major changes are totally unforeseen and perhaps impossible to expect. However, if major changes are to occur in the incidence of problems such as poverty, crime, delinquency, drug abuse, unemployment, and a host of other issues, major environmental changes are probably needed.

Examples of Early Comprehensive Social Intervention

Prohibition

Shortly after World War I, the United States government prohibited the manufacture and marketing of alcoholic beverages. The impetus came from concern over the negative effects of alcohol consumption, including alcoholism. Unfortunately, in this comprehensive social intervention, the "solution" was ineffective and, in fact, created other problems. Not only did the constitutional amendment not have the desired effect (most people still drank) but in addition an unexpected side effect was to provide a major source of revenue and growth for organized crime through the creation of an environment conducive to bootlegging. The amendment was so ineffective that within a few years it was repealed with another constitutional amendment. Nevertheless, alcohol use continues to create problems for our society. Each year, 25,000 people die in alcohol-related automobile accidents, and hundreds of thousands of people are injured; about 18 million people in the United States are alcoholics.

Social Security

A comprehensive social intervention that has been moderately successful has been federal involvement in elder welfare services, dating from the Social Security Act of 1935. Before that time, national social policy fell far short of recognizing any broad responsibility to assist the needy members of society. Since then, major strides have been made in assisting these populations. However, far too many of our citizens remain in financial need for the social welfare system to be considered a major success; further changes are clearly necessary.

A major current problem is the danger of bankruptcy of the Social Security Administration. Not long after the year 2020, there will not be adequate funding to support even the current level of benefits for people over the age of sixty-five and those below age sixty-five who are disabled, unless major changes in social welfare policy occur. Already, the age at which one qualifies for full Social Security retirement benefits is being raised in order to reduce the number of people eligible for the benefits.

Trends in Comprehensive Social Intervention

It is difficult, if not impossible, to transcend one's environment and accurately predict major social change events that will occur in the future. One can, however, note recent changes that may have an important impact on our society and therefore on the field of human services. The four examples that follow illustrate the types of occurrences that currently fall into this category.

Civil Rights Legislation

Since the 1950s, major changes have occurred in our society as a result of a strong governmental concern over the issue of equal rights for all people, regardless of race, color, religion, or gender. Obviously, discrimination and prejudices continue to exist in spite of the changes; however, most people would agree that progress has been made—more school systems are desegregated, and more members of minority groups are entering the middle class. As larger numbers of the disadvantaged minorities gain access to the mainstream, we can expect some reduction in the problems that are a function of membership in disadvantaged classes.

Women's Movement

An extremely interesting social change in recent decades has been the evolution of the women's movement. This movement, which reflects changing attitudes and also is a prime force in the changing of attitudes, has had important effects on society. Even though only a small percentage of women actively belong to groups such as the National Organization for Women (NOW), the basic concepts and attitudes of the movement have almost imperceptibly become part of the thinking of large numbers of American women and men. The consciousness-raising aspect of these attitudes has affected the style of life of many members of our society. The effects of the movement appear in styles of family life, occupational patterns, leisure activities, and so on. The movement has, to some extent, affected the human services field directly, in that some have suggested that male human service workers, when dealing with female clients, tend to perpetuate the male dominance role in the relationship, to the client's detriment. Even though such assertions are speculative, they provide food for thought.

Gay Rights

Is homosexuality a disease? Is it a human services problem? Members of the gay rights movement would undoubtedly answer these questions with a resounding No. The prevailing attitude among "straight" society has been that homosexuality is a psychological problem and that one who is "normal" psychologically is not a homosexual. The basically negative attitude of society toward homosexuals has been challenged by the homosexual liberation movement. The major message of the movement is that they are the same as anyone else (with the exception of their sexual preference) and should be accepted as they are. The consciousness-raising efforts of the movement have led many closet homosexuals openly to declare their sexual preferences. It also seems to have made some inroads in changing popular attitudes.

It should be pointed out, however, that the sociopolitical aspects of the gay rights movement may in the long run tend to polarize attitudes about homosexuality. This already seems to be occurring in some parts of the country. Those whose attitudes toward homosexuality are negative may end up mobilizing against the movement. In several areas of the United States, legislation against discrimination toward homosexuals has been defeated by a wide margin, and in others, there have been attempts to take away rights previously achieved by gay activists. The issue of polarization of attitudes may be an important one in social change events, no matter what the area of concern.

Medicare-Medicaid and National Health Insurance

The Social Security Act was changed in 1968 to provide increased benefits through the programs called Medicare and Medicaid, which fund health care services for aged persons and the medically disabled. Before this change, most aged and disabled people were in dire straits because of their inability to afford health care. As an outgrowth of the change in attitude from the belief that acceptable-quality health care is a privilege of the rich to the belief that such care is a *right* of all citizens regardless of economic status, we have seen major emphasis recently placed on the issue of national health insurance (health care insurance funded by tax dollars that would provide funding for basic health care for *all citizens* regardless of economic standing).

Shortly after being elected to his first four-year term in office, President Bill Clinton announced that First Lady Hillary Rodham Clinton would chair his administration's efforts in health care reform. The idea was to achieve a system with universal health care coverage so that all Americans had access to health care. After several years of hearings, planning, and acrimonious debate, it became clear that universal health coverage for all would not be possible anytime soon. While national health care reform was a nonstarter, however, the states continue to move very rapidly in that direction. Unfortunately, the driving force behind the states' health reform movements is to save tax dollars.

Through a variety of different approaches, states are moving Medicaid services from a fee-for-service system to a health maintenance organization (HMO) system. This privatizing of state Medicaid funds demonstrates a desire, if not to reverse the increasing medical cost spiral, at least to drastically slow it down. The HMO penetration of this market means restrictions in clients' choice of provider, restriction in providers' choice of services to be delivered, and the distinct possibility that health care quality could suffer. At least, that is the warning of opponents of this managed care approach. The counterargument is that health care quality will be monitored so it will be as good as ever, yet cost will be reduced for the state government and the taxpayer. It will be some time before we can clearly see all of the ramifications of this social change process.

Examples of Comprehensive Social Interventions

As an example of the possibilities that may result from intentioned (rather than unplanned and unexpected) social change, one can consider the areas of poverty and social welfare. Poverty has been identified as a major human services problem.

Poverty and Welfare Reform

The application of comprehensive social interventions to the problem of poverty is quite simple in its broad design. It consists basically of a plan for the implementation of a federal *guaranteed income.* That is, the establishment of an economic survival level for families, based on their size, would ensure that the families' minimum economic needs would be met. If a family were without resources to maintain this level, it would be aided by the federal government. An alternative system would provide every family with this income and then collect a proportionate amount in return from families with incomes above that level.

The implementation of such a program is hindered by a number of problems (Reischauer, 1986; Wittman, 1972), including the following:

1. Change in public attitudes
2. Cost requirements and the inevitable increase in taxation
3. Development of adequate delivery systems

In the late 1990s, we saw just how difficult dealing with poverty and the concept of welfare can really be. Currently, it seems to be very popular to decry the failure of welfare "as we know it" to solve the problem of poverty. The public statements of members of Congress harken back a hundred years to the philosophy of the Charity Organization Society, with its notion that the deserving poor did *not* include able-bodied persons who could otherwise work. The social policy focus of welfare reform seems directed at stamping out welfare dependency. That is a noble notion.

Human services certainly promotes the idea that people should have the opportunity to become self-sufficient and that they should receive the assistance they need in order to achieve that self-sufficiency. The concern about the current welfare reform is that people may be moved off welfare—may lose their entitlement to it—but the helping services that are required for people to move to self-sufficiency may not be made available.

As of 1997, the current welfare reform enacted by Congress and signed into law by President Clinton included the following:

1. Aid to Families with Dependent Children (AFDC) is eliminated. It is replaced by block grants to states under the name *Temporary* Assistance for Needy Families (TANF).
2. Employment, work, and school requirements
   a. All TANF recipients must be engaged in state-defined work activities within 24 months.
   b. Teenage parents on TANF assistance must attend school and live at home or in a supervised arrangement.
   c. Lifetime limits: Most nondisabled adults will be able to receive TANF for no more than 60 months during their lifetimes.

In implementing and administering TANF, states have the responsibility to provide programs that will prepare people currently on welfare for the world of work. It is on this point that critics of TANF's strict requirements express concern. Are states able or willing to mount the necessary services to give people a reasonable chance of successfully getting off welfare? Past history forecasts a gloomy future. Then again, this may prove to be as grand and successful an experiment as was Social Security in 1935. So far, the welfare to work initiative seems to have been very successful from an economic or political point of view. States have pushed very hard to get welfare recipients into competitive employment, and many states have developed new work placement training programs and other forms of assistance to help recipients succeed. The U.S. economy during the 1990s was strong, with very low unemployment, which was a definite assistance in achieving the goals of the reform. From 1994 to 1998, there was a 45 percent reduction in the number of families receiving welfare, from a high of about 5 million in 1994 to 2.7 million as of January 1999 (Fagnoni, 1999). Around 80 percent of those leaving welfare became employed, about 65 percent of those maintained employment, and about 20 percent returned to the welfare rolls. However, as people reach their time limit on benefits, the option of returning to welfare will not be there. The reduction in welfare case loads across the country have been held up as an illustration of a successful social policy and program change, but TANF and welfare reform remains controversial (Withorn, 1998). The vast majority of those leaving welfare for work earn minimum wage or slightly more. They have simply entered the ranks of the working poor. Large amounts of tax money are being saved, but many continue to be concerned that the "welfare to work" reform will leave millions of people without a safety net down the road.

Human Services and Social Advocacy

A significant role for human service workers has been and will be that of an advocate: one who pleads and fights for services, policies, rules, regulations, and laws for the clients' benefit (McPheeters, 1999). A human service worker in the role of an advocate generally can exert more influence on the powers that be than can individual disadvantaged people. How does one do that? McPheeters (1999) suggests that human service workers must become very familiar with governmental processes and the realm of civics—the study of how government works from elections to lobbying to legislation. He proposes that we should become political activists, talk to candidates, contribute to causes we value, testify on legislation at hearings, and build coalitions. It is clearly an important arena, and one we have clearly neglected. However, changes in services, policies, laws, and rules that advocacy can achieve may have a positive impact on large numbers of people in need. It is within this advocacy role that individuals or small groups of human service workers have engineered the types of limited social interventions described in the first part of this chapter. Yet, even in that context, the efforts of one or a few human service workers are limited in their effect.

A more powerful approach appears to be the mobilization of the disadvantaged themselves into groups as advocates or activists on their own behalf (Schensul and Schensul, 1982). This mobilization of the disadvantaged as their own advocates not only maximizes the numbers of people agitating for social change but also has an impact on the self-perception of the needy. This process of social mobilization is an empowerment activity, and empowerment should be a major focus of human services (B. Cohen, 1999; Runyan, 1999). The power to work for change is shared with (given to) those whom the change can benefit. The human service worker in effect says, "I will not decide for you and do for you, but rather I will help *you* decide what you need and want, and help you find ways to achieve it." When the needy or disadvantaged discover that they can be involved in changing not only their own lives but also the very society in which they live and discover that they have more control over their destiny than they believed, they develop a sense of empowerment and worth not present before. Thus, like the mutual help groups that focus on dealing with personal problems, social advocacy groups can have an impact on the individual functioning of their members. Social advocacy groups' primary goal, however, is social change.

The development of social advocacy groups is based on a specific viewpoint about the development of social problems and the behavior of individuals, which

Disadvantaged individuals often feel empowered by making their needs known in public demonstrations.

can be called the *social structuralist viewpoint*. Social structuralists seek to account for individual behavior in terms of the organization and distribution of resources within the societal framework. Structuralists blame oppressive institutions, inequitable systems of distribution, and systematic discrimination for negative social and economic conditions among members of subgroups within a society. They believe that aspects of the existing social order must change to facilitate more effective individual adaptations. Thus, the action-oriented structuralist will seek to change the institutions that seem to have an impact on individuals and that shape their lives.

The widely accepted competing view, as has been discussed, sees behavior primarily as a product of individual biopsychological development. The individual must change in order to adapt more effectively to the existing social order. The action-oriented individualist seeks to identify and provide services and support that will change personal or individual inadequacies believed to account for negative behavior. While support may come from individual or group-oriented services, the focus is on the individual's need for changing behavior. As noted earlier in this text, these views are not necessarily mutually exclusive, and individual behavior is a product of interactive factors, both personal and environmental.

However, a focus on one or another of these general viewpoints in the organization of an intervention group will play a role in determining the group's actions and objectives. For example, the interpretation of the condition of Blacks in

American society as a product of White racist institutions and inequitable distribution of resources resulted in the Black Power movement of the late 1960s—an attempt to change institutions to promote more access for Blacks. But a view of that condition as a result of the intrinsic inadequacies of individual members of the Black American population generates a much different set of activities aimed at affecting the individual behavior—economic, social, educational—of Black people in a White-oriented and -dominated society.

It is the thesis of this book that it makes much more sense to work on social and economic problems from a social advocacy approach. Social advocacy groups must address attention to creating changes in access and distribution of resources in relation to economically and socially oppressed peoples. Social advocacy groups already include organizations linked to the nationally known Black, Brown, and Gray Power movements, as well as neighborhood collectives focused on more immediate and local concerns. They use the tools of mobilization and collective action to communicate in the sociopolitical arena. Their abilities to reflect accurately the needs of their constituencies and to mobilize members of those constituencies for collective action are frequently their only resources.

A wide range of social advocacy groups exists; they may differ significantly, depending upon the perceived needs of their respective constituencies. Despite their differences, social advocacy groups do share certain basic commonalities.

1. The primary goal of each is to represent the service needs of a larger constituency in the public/social sector. Participants believe that because they either are deeply involved in or are residents in their community constituencies, they have the right to speak for them. Social advocacy groups recognize that they do not have access to sufficient information about their constituencies to fully defend the need for services or to argue for appropriate services. This often leads a group to sponsor research on its constituency, which shapes and confirms the beliefs of the group concerning inadequacy of service provision in its community.

2. Their objective is to change the current pattern of distribution of resources. Members of advocacy groups believe that sufficient access to service resources is selectively denied their constituencies. Their strategies, therefore, revolve around identifying these resources in the public sector, on the one hand, and establishing and developing the strength of the social advocacy/citizens' group, on the other.

3. The groups organize in the belief that united action will be effective in the demand for resources. They believe that no single individual has the right to speak for his or her constituency, but that collective groups with open membership can take such responsibility. They also believe that community- or constituency-based groups, when clear about their objectives, can have a significant impact on the wider system of health or other service delivery. Groups meet regularly, spend much of their time working out differences of opinion within the group itself, and consistently present a united front when arguing in public in support of financial or service resources.

4. Social advocacy groups often use the outside expertise of human service workers and others to assist in the achievement of their objectives. At the same time, they maintain basic control of direction and decision making.

This chapter has given numerous examples of successful and not-so-successful attempts at both limited and comprehensive social interventions. The manner in which human service workers may be able to have impact as a change agent on the personal environment of their immediate clients is clear (though definitely not simple).

In contrast, the individual human service worker is unlikely to be able to make a significant impact on changing the major social and economic systems through individual efforts. What, then, can human service workers do about these broader issues? At the least, human service workers can become vocal advocates of the social changes they believe in. Individually, one can, of course, engage in written correspondence with legislators on the local, state, and national levels and join organizations that can exert political leverage to create social change. The really ambitious individual can follow McPheeter's (1999) advice and become an informal (or formal) political lobbyist.

On a more immediate level, a human service worker can join local or national social advocacy groups that are trying to generate social change in which the worker believes. Some human service workers who have the necessary leadership qualities, expertise, and energy may focus their careers on developing and nurturing new social advocacy groups in order to address current and future social problems.

Summary

1. Many of the problems of people in need are due to or complicated by societal factors such as poverty. The immediate environment of the individual may contribute substantially to the development and maintenance of problem behaviors such as apathy, joblessness, drug use, and criminal activities.

2. Major social ills also may lead to problem behavior among people who suffer the brunt of social problems such as discrimination, poor health care, or poor housing. Changing the person is unlikely to help much unless the individual's environment, the relevant social systems, and the social ills are modified. Thus, for the human service worker, social interventions are an important facet of helping services.

3. The phrase *limited social intervention* describes the attempt to make significant formal changes in the immediate environment of a client or group of clients that will have a remedial effect on the problems of that client or group.

4. The concept of limited social intervention has grown out of the virtually universally recognized fact that the environment of people in need often supports or stimulates problem behaviors and that single treatment contacts, whether in an institution or in the community, tend not to be sufficient in generating lasting major changes in a person's behavior.

5. Limited social interventions involve a four-step process: (a) identifying negative environments, (b) identifying environmental factors that can be changed, (c) de-

termining how negative aspects can be changed in a positive direction, and (d) implementing the changes or creating entirely new positive environments.

6. The effectiveness of limited social intervention is demonstrated in the description of community intervention programs that focus on the intellectual enhancement of children. Children who received services were better off after the intervention than similar children who received no services.

7. Examples of limited social change include the areas of community corrections, deinstitutionalization of people who are mentally ill or retarded, community programs for retarded people, and a community program for ex–mental patients.

8. A number of principles of social change have general applicability to the concept of limited social interventions. Even though the principles do not constitute how-to instructions, they illustrate important issues that must be considered by human service workers who contemplate environmental change strategies.

9. The concept of comprehensive social intervention has been defined as (a) the process of identifying broad social problems that contribute to or cause maladaptive behavior and (b) the subsequent modification of social systems or policies that contribute to the problems, in an attempt to eradicate them.

10. Many experts have focused on the negative effects of social change. However, it is clear that social change can be a positive factor in the reduction of social problems.

11. Examples of major social system and social policy change events demonstrate both effective and ineffective attempts to deal with social problems. Examples include the prohibition of alcohol and the Social Security Act.

12. Four examples of currently ongoing social change are civil rights legislation, the women's movement, gay rights, and Medicare-Medicaid and national health insurance.

13. An attempt at implementing a comprehensive social policy intervention for reforming social welfare and reducing poverty, called *welfare to work,* has been described.

14. The individual human service worker is unlikely to be able to engage in comprehensive social interventions because of personal, social, and political powerlessness. However, membership in and support of social advocacy groups appears to be a powerful strategy for the implementation of comprehensive social change.

Discussion Questions

1. What advantages are there for limited social interventions over direct interpersonal intervention if a choice must be made between them, and vice versa?

2. What are the positive and negative effects of social change?

3. Why do you think Prohibition failed?

4. What is the likely result of welfare reform and time limits on eligibility for benefits?

5. Should illegal immigrants be allowed to receive TANF?

6. How can human service workers become involved in comprehensive social interventions? Should they?

Learning Experiences

1. Have any limited social interventions been developed in your community? If so, visit the setting and try to find out why the intervention was developed, how it was developed, and whether it is working.

2. Contact your federal legislators to find out what they think about a guaranteed annual income or national health insurance.

3. Talk with a doctor to find out what he or she thinks of managed care and HMOs.

4. Survey your acquaintances about what they think are the major social problems facing our country and what should be done about them.

Endnotes

1. *Returning the mentally disabled to the community: The government needs to do more.* Reports to the Congress by the Comptroller General of the United States, January 1977.

2. Reprinted by permission from *Innovations* (Vol. 2, No. 3, Fall 1975), pp. 5–7, published by the American Institutes for Research, P.O. Box 1113, Palo Alto, CA 94302, under a collaborative grant from the National Institute of Mental Health.

3. Reprinted by permission from *Innovations* (Vol. 2, No. 2, Summer, 1975), pp. 32–33, published by the American Institutes for Research, P.O. Box 1113, Palo Alto, CA 94302, under a collaborative grant from the National Institute of Mental Health.

Recommended Readings

Newton, J. (1988). *Preventing mental illness in practice.* London: Routledge & Keegan Paul.

Price, R. H., Cowen, E. L., Lorion, R. P., & Ramos-McKay, J. (1988). *Fourteen ounces of prevention: A casebook for practitioners.* Washington, DC: American Psychological Association.

Reiss, C., Liner, L., Harrison, R., & Harrison, C. (1993). *The prevention of mental disorders: A national research agenda.* Washington, DC: National Institute of Mental Health.

15

Social Control, Human Rights, Ethics, and the Law

- What impact does the law have on human behavior?
- How have psychological, social, and medical viewpoints influenced the application of law to human behavior?
- What are the legal rights of human service clients?
- What are the ethical standards followed by human service workers?

The law of the land has both direct and indirect impacts on human behavior and human services. In a direct sense, the law tells us what it is legal to do, what behavior is illegal, and what the consequences are for illegal behaviors. Thus, the law codifies many of society's rules of conduct. Indirectly, the existence of laws that proscribe certain individual behaviors influence some people to behave prosocially—that is, for the common good. The law also influences the behavior or functioning of groups or of society as a whole in regard to its individual members. It defines individual rights and society's obligations. The laws we work and live under in the United States derive from English common law, and the origin of some date back a thousand years. It is worth keeping in mind that many other cultures do not follow this tradition. They may share many similar laws, but there may be differences that can cause cross-cultural discord when a person from one culture tries to live with the legal system of another culture (see Box 15.1).

Law serves at least two specific functions. First, of course, it defines certain behaviors as wrong or unacceptable and subject to social sanction. The second function is to protect the individual's *rights* in a free and democratic society. For example, law not only defines certain behaviors as criminal but also protects those who are accused of those behaviors. In both of these functions, the law and the legal system overlap with the human services sector in dealing with human behavior.

BOX 15.1   A Lack of Cultural Sensitivity?

In 1996, in Lincoln, Nebraska, two brothers aged 29 and 32, refugees from Iran, sought and received permission from a fellow Iranian refugee to marry his two daughters. Shortly afterward, the two brothers married the two sisters in a small Muslim ceremony held within this tiny Iranian community in this Midwestern city set in the cornfields of Nebraska. Neither the two brothers nor the two sisters' parents spoke English. Only the two sisters could directly communicate in the language of their adopted country.

This otherwise celebratory event soon received national publicity. The sisters were 13 and 14 years old. After one sister revealed to a non-Iranian friend in her eighth-grade class that she was married and having sex with her new husband, the brothers were arrested and charged with statutory rape. The parents were investigated and threatened with charges of neglect by the state's child protective agency.

In this clash of cultures, the *common* practice in Iran of arranged marriages between older Iranian men and girls is not only *not* acceptable but also can result in felony charges in the United States, where in most states it is illegal to be married under the age of 15.

A local university professor, who also had emigrated from Iran but who speaks English and has lived in the United States for years, points out that in the one week of training given to refugees prior to resettlement the cross-cultural issues and the difference in laws between Iran and the United States are not addressed. He himself was not aware that marriage and marital intercourse would be illegal with a young girl of childbearing age. The expression of deeply held, highly valued beliefs may not be acceptable in a different culture from one's own, even if that new culture accepts and even promotes cultural sensitivity.

We have seen in recent decades an increase in the interaction between the legal system and the human services system. This increased interaction has developed as a result of a number of factors (Slovenko, 1973).

1. Increased density of urban and suburban population increases the probability that people will infringe on the rights of others.
2. Behaviors that once were considered sinful or unlawful now are explained by human service professionals as being due to psychological or social causes for which an individual has no responsibility.
3. Under the *parens patriae doctrine* (the doctrine of society acting as a responsible parent for its citizens), the state is seen as having the obligation to intervene in the lives of minors (or in the lives of others who are considered unable to make decisions that are in their own best interest) who might become community problems.
4. There has been increased financial support by public, private, and charitable organizations for lawyers to become involved in litigation over human service issues.

Laws governing the conduct of human services and human service funding are determined by state and federal legislators. Human service workers need to make their views public on these matters.

5. Over the last half-century, much media attention has been given to legal groundbreaking human service cases.
6. There has been an increased familiarity among judges and lawyers with the subfields of human services and a corresponding increase in their interactions with those systems.
7. Recent years have seen an increased concern with the constitutional rights of our citizens, particularly in the human services sector, in regard to the concepts of involuntary treatment or incarceration, paralleling the concern over civil rights issues such as racial discrimination.

The Therapeutic State

Much of the concern of the judiciary system regarding human services has focused on the development of the phenomenon called the *therapeutic state*. This term refers to a legal system based on the notion that socially proscribed behavior (including illegal acts) is often not a function of free will but rather is determined by psychological, social, or medical causes, so that it should not be punished but *treated* or *rehabilitated*. Although such a notion seems enlightened, its critics have pointed out that it results in a number of abuses of personal liberty of the people to whom it is applied.

A major problem with the therapeutic state approach is that it has led to a situation in which indeterminate sentences of incarceration in restrictive human services settings have supplanted determinate sentences in jails or prisons. To illustrate, there is the following example (Arens, 1964):

> *In the District of Columbia, Frederick C. Lynch was charged with passing bad checks. Although Lynch maintained that his behavior was an act of free will, psychiatrists testified that he was mentally ill at the time of the crimes. The court found him not guilty by reason of insanity and confined him to a mental hospital. If he had been found guilty, he would have received a maximum sentence of twelve months in jail. Lynch, facing a lengthy period of hospitalization against his will, committed suicide.*

The Lynch case is not unique. Thousands of individuals around the country are incarcerated in mental hospitals, juvenile detention homes, and mental retardation facilities for an indeterminate period until they are "cured" of whatever problem supposedly led them to engage in criminal behavior. In addition, many people are locked up because there is a *threat* that *in the future* they will engage in behavior that *may* be dangerous to themselves or others. The reality of this threat has been criticized by many who have been involved in such cases.

The issue of involuntary treatment is an important one because each state government has a body of legislation that sets up the requirements for involuntary admission to human services facilities such as mental hospitals, juvenile detention facilities, and mental retardation facilities. In all cases, these statutes are much less well defined than the criminal codes and therefore much more subject to abuse.

Human Rights Issues and Human Services

Experience with the current human services systems has demonstrated that a series of issues in regard to the rights of the clients must be considered by all human service workers:

1. Voluntary versus involuntary services
2. Due process and equal protection
3. The right to services
4. The right to refuse services
5. The issue of the least drastic or restrictive alternative
6. The privilege of confidentiality

Because most issues that have arisen are particularly critical for those who are involuntarily confined, that issue must be examined before others can be dealt with.

Voluntary versus Involuntary Services

There are clear differences between voluntary and involuntary services. The concept of voluntary service implies that clients make an informed decision that help is needed and that they want to change. Clients set their own goals and objectives and enter into a written or verbal contract (a services plan) with the service provider on what will happen. Finally, clients can terminate the relationship and services at will. Service is involuntary if people other than the clients decided that the client needs services and the client is *required* to have the service. In addition, it is involuntary if the clients are powerless in deciding what kind of services they will receive and some authority figure sets the goals and objectives for how and when the service will be terminated.

Opinions on involuntary service run the gamut from the "abolitionists" who believe that it should be eliminated to those who recognize that it can be abused but feel it is not only necessary but also beneficial (Hoaken, 1986). For some time, the "abolitionists" lobbied with great success for a tightening of criteria for involuntary hospitalization. In all states, it became extremely difficult to treat people against their will. This increase in the protection of clients' rights was warranted, but the results illustrated that it is difficult to balance the rights of individuals against the safety needs of society.

■■ Mr. and Mrs. Donner, the parents of 32-year-old Jeremy, were concerned that he might injure himself or someone else. He had ceased taking his antipsychotic medication, and the symptoms of his schizophrenia were getting much worse. Years ago, he had threatened them with harm when he thought they were spying on him and trying to control his thoughts and sexual behavior. He had just recently accused them of the same thing but also told his father that he knew his parents were going to put "saltpeter" in his food to "chemically castrate him."

Mr. and Mrs. Donner took Jeremy to the local hospital under false pretenses in order to get him evaluated. The unfortunate result was that the psychiatrist there could not get Jeremy to reveal any reason for the psychiatrist to believe he would act on his beliefs and hurt the parents. It was obvious that Jeremy refused to be admitted. Without actual evidence of violence or evidence of serious threats, the psychiatrist could not do an emergency admission or start commitment proceedings.

The Donners returned home with a now enraged and very suspicious Jeremy on their hands. They retired for the night, falling asleep with great difficulty due to their anxiety and concern about how to get treatment for their son. Several days later, a neighbor who knew the situation became concerned over not having seen Mrs. Donner in her garden for a few days. He entered the Donner home and found both parents dead in their beds with hundreds of stab wounds. Jeremy was in his bedroom, naked, confused, and disoriented. He informed the neighbor that he finally solved his problem and had "gutted" the devil and her keeper. They would no longer keep him from being able to have sex. Jeremy was finally hospitalized as unfit to stand trial, a few years later he was tried and found not guilty by reason of insanity.

Cases that end this badly are fortunately rare, but many members of the National Association for Mental Illness, who are parents or siblings of adults with serious and persistent mental illness, have many similar, though less dramatic, stories. They find it exceedingly difficult to get their relatives hospitalized against their will, even when they feel it would prevent very serious deterioration and possible danger to themselves or others. The current restrictiveness of commitment codes prevents abuses of power but now sometimes fails clients and those who care for them when involuntary treatment could have helped prevent deterioration or worse. Human service workers (and society in general) have been left with the very real problem of balancing individual human rights against the need to protect society against harm from its members.

Due Process and Equal Protection

Even though involuntary service is a major issue of contention, it *is* currently a fact of life, and a number of issues revolve around its use. Among these are due process and equal protection. The due process clause of the Constitution provides that if government activities affect citizens in a way that would deprive them of liberty or property, this must be done with due process of law. The courts have ruled that due process requires a hearing before an impartial entity, with the opportunity for witnesses to testify, with representation of the client by an attorney (or other counsel), and with the opportunity for the client to appeal. In order to provide this due process, state statutes provide for a hearing before the court before a client can be committed for involuntary services.

The due process clause impacts on all human services systems. For example, interpretations of the due process clause require school administrators to specify in writing those offenses for which children can be disciplined (Guttesman, 1982). They must notify the children that the rule is going to be applied and must conduct a hearing at which the children and their parents can be present when an action such as expulsion is considered. Similar requirements pertain to the use of punitive action such as isolation in prisons.

The Constitution's equal protection clause provides that citizens cannot be denied the equal protection of the law. In this sense, a state agency cannot treat one group differently from another when both are entitled to the same treatment. This clause is quite important in the right to services issue, as we shall see, but it also prevents certain groups from being dealt with in a *harsher* manner than others; for example, psychosurgery cannot be applied only to Blacks in a prison setting. However, these laws (and others) do not prevent abuses in and of themselves; they provide the means of protection only if they are enforced.

The Right to Services

It is now an accepted assumption of litigation in the United States that individuals who are involuntarily deprived of freedom because they have engaged in some activity that demonstrates that they are unable to care for themselves or are dangerous to others have the *right* to helping services (Stone, 1975). The right to service has become an issue due to the problem of persons' being confined in restrictive settings and languishing there with little but food, lodging, and tranquilizing medication; in effect, this is a situation that amounts to little more than imprisonment. It has now become clear that facilities must demonstrate that they really are providing the service for which the client was committed, or the commitment itself becomes ludicrous.

In recent years, the right to receive services has been extended to community settings. Even when people are not involuntarily deprived of their right to freedom, their membership in a disadvantaged class may entitle them to demand services from society in the form of civil government (Herr, 1983).

The Right to Refuse Services

For many years, it was a common assumption that helping professionals could administer services even when the patients or clients resisted. It was assumed that the services were in the clients' best interest and that their objections were a function of a disordered mind. Recent case law has confirmed, however, that clients *do* have the right to refuse service. If, for example, patients in a mental hospital refuse to take a prescribed medication, it is illegal to force them to do so unless a court of law judges the patients to be incompetent to make such a decision. Unfortunately, this patient right is routinely violated in most current systems, and the problem is compounded by the fact that many courts seem to be overly willing to declare persons incompetent. The extent to which an individual has the right to refuse services that will change behaviors depends on the behaviors in question and continues to be a controversial issue (Michels, 1981).

The Least Drastic or Restrictive Alternative

Patients or clients have the right to be helped in an effective manner that is the least restrictive. For example, a client who can manage in the community while receiving outpatient services should not be hospitalized because hospitalization is more restrictive of personal liberty and freedom. Few would argue this point, but until community alternatives are available, this may simply mean that the least restrictive alternative results in no service at all. This right is particularly applicable to the many people who are in correctional settings, mental retardation facilities, mental hospitals, residential nursing homes, or sheltered care settings simply because there are no less restrictive alternatives in the community.

The Privilege of Confidential Communication

Trust between client and service provider is of prime importance in most helping relationships, and a major ingredient of such trust is confidentiality. The principle of confidentiality requires that human service workers maintain a confidential relationship with their clients—that is, that the clients' identities be protected *unless* they agree (in writing) that their identities and personal information may be shared with other professionals or agencies. Client confidentiality is respected even in court settings such as criminal or civil trials *unless* this information bears directly on the issues being tried. Thus, confidentiality is not a right; it is a privilege. Some human service workers (Dubey, 1974) feel that confidentiality should be an absolute privilege (that is, under no circumstances should helping professionals have to testify in court about their clients); others believe that in some situations confidentiality *must* be breached. Under some circumstances, in fact, there appears to be a legal duty to breach confidentiality, such as the duty to warn others of a dangerous threat made by a client or the duty to report evidence, allegations, or suspicion of child or (in some states) elder abuse (Blair, 1999).

The Duty to Warn

The *duty to warn* is based on the notion that helping service providers who have good evidence that a client intends to harm someone must warn the person in danger. A number of court cases have established that a human service worker does have a legal duty to warn others of a client's threats if the human service worker in good conscience believes the threats may be acted upon (Kermani and Drob, 1987). If the worker does *not* warn a potential victim of physical danger and the client acts on the threat, the human service worker may be sued for negligence. Some professionals object that the requirement to warn is fraught with problems, particularly the difficulty of being sure that the client really means the threats. Another problem area is that the duty to warn may compromise the trust relationship with patients who make threats (many do) but who actually would not act upon them because therapists will warn more often than necessary out of fear of being sued if they make a mistake. In spite of these issues, the duty to warn remains a legal requirement.

A Human Services Bill of Rights

The redefinition of the rights of human service clients and the legal responsibilities of human service workers and systems has not grown out of a vacuum. It is clearly responsive to problems and injustices that have existed for many years but that in some cases have only recently been recognized. The concern over these issues has led to the development of a number of model *human services bills of rights* for clients (Blair, 1999). The following generic sample is based on a variety of models:

1. No person shall be *compelled* to receive services except for their own safety and the safety of others.
2. People have the right to be free of excessive forms of human modification.
3. No person shall be subjected to involuntary incarceration or services on the basis of a general condition or status alone.

4. No official sanctions, whether designated criminal, civil, or therapeutic, may be applied without the right to a judicial or other independent hearing, appointed counsel, and the opportunity to confront those testifying about one's actions.

5. An involuntary client shall have the right to helping services that are judged clinically reasonable.

6. Any compulsory services must be the *least* required to reasonably safeguard society.

7. Persons receiving involuntary services shall have unimpeded access to legal counsel and the right to petition the court for relief.

8. Individuals receiving voluntary services shall *not* be transferred to involuntary status without due process.

9. Individuals' personal information shall not be shared without permission unless mandated by law in judicial proceedings.

Such bills of rights clearly reflect the growing concern for the rights of individuals of whom society *requires* behavior change if they are to return to ordinary community life. The fact that such bills of rights have been proposed and that there is a major concern for the rights of human service clients provides evidence that such rights have been violated significantly in the past. If they are to be effective advocates of the client, human service workers must retain a healthy respect for the rights of the client in order to prevent the possible abuse that can occur (Rubenstein, 1986).

Ethical Standards for Human Service Workers

Any profession, regardless of its other characteristics, maintains standards that guide its members' functioning. These standards, called *ethical guidelines,* are important in guiding our professional practice since there are deep divisions in our society about what constitutes acceptable behavior (Rhodes, 1998). There are fundamentally different beliefs in our society on issues such as abortion, gay marriage and parenting, and welfare reform. Ethical standards help us deal with these conflicting views.

The standards that human service providers follow, while recognizing the basic minimal rights of clients as set down in law, go beyond these rights to suggest broader guidelines in regard to human service worker-client relationships. For the first three to four decades of the development of the human services, generic human service professionals and human service workers have relied on the ethics statements of other helping professions to guide their professional behavior. In one more large step forward in professionalization, the field of human services now has a proposed set of ethical standards. These standards, jointly developed by the National Organization for Human Service Education and the Council for Standards in Human Service Education, capture the essence of human services (NOHSE, 1994). It seems fitting to conclude this book, then, with the ethical standards of human service professionals.

The Human Service Professional's Responsibility to Clients

Statement 1 Human service professionals negotiate with clients the purpose, goals, and nature of the helping relationship prior to its onset as well as inform clients of the limitations of the proposed relationship.

Statement 2 Human service professionals respect the integrity and welfare of the client at all times. Each client is treated with respect, acceptance, and dignity.

Statement 3 Human service professionals protect the client's right to privacy and confidentiality except when such confidentiality would cause harm to the client or others, when agency guidelines state otherwise, or under other stated conditions (e.g., local, state, or federal laws). Professionals inform clients of the limits of confidentiality prior to the onset of the helping relationship.

Statement 4 If it is suspected that danger or harm may occur to the client or to others as a result of a client's behavior, the human service professional acts in an appropriate and professional manner to protect the safety of those individuals. This may involve seeking consultation, supervision, and/or breaking the confidentiality of the relationship.

Statement 5 Human service professionals protect the integrity, safety, and security of client records. All written client information that is shared with other professionals, except in the course of professional supervision, must have the client's prior written consent.

Statement 6 Human service professionals are aware that in their relationships with clients power and status are unequal. Therefore, they recognize that dual or multiple relationships may increase the risk of harm to, or exploitation of, clients and may impair their professional judgment. However, in some communities and situations it may not be feasible to avoid social or other nonprofessional contact with clients. Human service professionals support the trust implicit in the helping relationship by avoiding dual relationships that may impair professional judgment, increase the risk of harm to clients, or lead to exploitation.

Statement 7 Sexual relationships with current clients are not considered to be in the best interest of the client and are prohibited. Sexual relationships with previous clients are considered dual relationships and are addressed in Statement 6 (above).

Statement 8 The client's right to self-determination is protected by human service professionals. They recognize the client's right to receive or refuse services.

Statement 9 Human service professionals recognize and build on client strengths.

The Human Service Professional's Responsibility to the Community and Society

Statement 10 Human service professionals are aware of local, state, and federal laws. They advocate for change in regulations and statutes when such legislation conflicts with ethical guidelines and/or client rights. Where laws are harmful to individuals, groups, or communities, human service professionals consider the conflict between the values of obeying the law and the values of serving people and may decide to initiate social action.

Statement 11 Human service professionals keep informed about current social issues as they affect the client and the community. They share that information with clients, groups, and community as part of their work.

Statement 12 Human service professionals understand the complex interaction between individuals, their families, the communities in which they live, and society.

Statement 13 Human service professionals act as advocates in addressing unmet client and community needs. Human service professionals provide a mechanism for identifying unmet client needs, calling attention to these needs, and assisting in planning and mobilizing to advocate for those needs at the local community level.

Statement 14 Human service professionals represent their qualifications to the public accurately.

Statement 15 Human service professionals describe the effectiveness of programs, treatments, and/or techniques accurately.

Statement 16 Human service professionals advocate for the rights of all members of society, particularly those who are members of minorities and groups at which discriminatory practices have historically been directed.

Statement 17 Human service professionals provide services without discrimination or preference based on age, ethnicity, culture, race, disability, gender, religion, sexual orientation, or socioeconomic status.

Statement 18 Human service professionals are knowledgeable about the cultures and communities within which they practice. They are aware of multiculturalism in society and its impact on the community as well as individuals within the community. They respect individuals and groups, their cultures and beliefs.

Statement 19 Human service professionals are aware of their own cultural backgrounds, beliefs, and values, recognizing the potential for impact on their relationships with others.

Statement 20 Human service professionals are aware of sociopolitical issues that differentially affect clients from diverse backgrounds.

Statement 21 Human service professionals seek the training, experience, education, and supervision necessary to ensure their effectiveness in working with culturally diverse client populations.

The Human Service Professional's Responsibility to Colleagues

Statement 22 Human service professionals avoid duplicating another professional's helping relationship with a client. They consult with other professionals who are assisting the client in a different type of relationship when it is in the best interest of the client to do so.

Statement 23 When a human service professional has a conflict with a colleague, he or she first seeks out the colleague in an attempt to manage the problem. If necessary, the professional than seeks the assistance of supervisors, consultants, or other professionals in efforts to manage the problem.

Statement 24 Human service professionals respond appropriately to unethical behavior of colleagues. Usually, this means initially talking directly with the colleague and, if no resolution is forthcoming, reporting the colleague's behavior to supervisory or administrative staff and/or to the professional organization(s) to which the colleague belongs.

Statement 25 All consultations between human service professionals are kept confidential unless to do so would result in harm to clients or communities.

The Human Service Professional's Responsibility to the Profession

Statement 26 Human service professionals know the limit and scope of their professional knowledge and offer services only within their knowledge and skill base.

Statement 27 Human service professionals seek appropriate consultation and supervision to assist in decision making when there are legal, ethical, or other dilemmas.

Statement 28 Human service professionals act with integrity, honesty, genuineness, and objectivity.

Statement 29 Human service professionals promote cooperation among related disciplines (e.g., psychology, counseling, social work, nursing, family and consumer sciences, medicine, education) to foster professional growth and interests within the various fields.

Statement 30 Human service professionals promote the continuing development of their profession. They encourage membership in professional associations, support research endeavors, foster educational advancement, advocate for appropriate legislative actions, and participate in other related professional activities.

Statement 31 Human service professionals continually seek out new and effective approaches to enhance their professional abilities.

The Human Service Professional's Responsibility to Employers

Statement 32 Human service professionals adhere to commitments made to their employers.

Statement 33 Human service professionals participate in efforts to establish and maintain employment conditions that are conducive to high-quality client services. They assist in evaluating the effectiveness of the agency through reliable and valid assessment measures.

Statement 34 When a conflict arises between fulfilling the responsibility to the employer and the responsibility to the client, human service professionals advise both of the conflict and work conjointly with all involved to manage the conflict.

The Human Service Professional's Responsibility to Self

Statement 35 Human service professionals strive to personify those characteristics typically associated with the profession (e.g., accountability, respect for others, genuineness, empathy, pragmatism).

Statement 36 Human service professionals foster self-awareness and personal growth in themselves. They recognize that when professionals are aware of their own values, attitudes, cultural background, and personal needs, the process of helping others is less likely to be negatively impacted by those factors.

Statement 37 Human service professionals recognize a commitment to life-long learning and continually upgrade knowledge and skills to serve the populations better.

Summary

1. The law has both direct and indirect impacts on human behavior. It proscribes certain behaviors and assigns consequences in order to maintain social order. It also protects the rights of individuals against unjust actions by the social group.
2. The judicial system has become more involved in considering the rights of human service clients and the obligations of the human services system.
3. The therapeutic state sees misbehavior as a problem that is due to psychological, social, or medical causes. It sometimes can result in abuses of liberty in the name of helping services.
4. A number of issues have been raised regarding the delivery of human services from the viewpoint of the therapeutic state:
   a. The issue of voluntary versus involuntary helping services
   b. Due process and equal protection

  c. The right to services

  d. The right to refuse services

  e. The issue of the least drastic or restrictive alternative

  f. The privilege of confidentiality

5. A human services bill of rights has been presented that specifies the proposed obligations and limits of society in the rendering of services.

6. Human service workers have certain obligations and limits in the delivery of helping services that go beyond the written laws. Guidelines for ethical standards have been developed for human service workers.

Discussion Questions

1. Do we, in your view, have a "therapeutic state"?

2. Should we make it easier for clients to be treated involuntarily?

3. Is it really all right to tell friends and relatives stories about clients as long as you change the name?

4. Why shouldn't I date my ex-client? We have not seen each other professionally in two years.

Learning Experiences

1. If the opportunity is available, visit and observe a mental health court and record your reaction.

2. Interview a committed (involuntary) client. How does the client feel about it?

3. Interview a lawyer or judge about the issues presented. What is his or her opinion?

4. What is your reaction to being *forced* to do something? Considering your reaction, how would *you* feel if you were forced to have *services* or *treatment* that would change you "for your own good"?

5. Reflect on how you felt when someone you confided in told others what you said. How did you feel? Did you still trust that person? Will you ever confide in him or her again?

Recommended Readings

Finkel, N. J. (1988). *Insanity on trial.* New York: Plenum Press.

Herlihy, B., & Corey, G. (1996). *ACA ethical standards casebook* (5th ed.). Alexandria, VA: American Counseling Association.

Rooney, R. H. (1992). *Strategies for work with involuntary clients.* New York: Columbia University Press.

Woody, R. H., & Associates. (1984). *The law and the practice of human services.* San Francisco: Jossey-Bass.

Glossary

Achieved role   A social role that individuals are able to obtain through their efforts, such as the role of doctor or police officer.

Acting out   Expressing problems through behavior rather than holding problems within.

Actualization   The process of achieving one's full potential.

Addiction   Strong dependence, usually both physical and psychological, on a drug or chemical.

Advocacy   The process of being for and supporting some person, object, or idea.

Alienation   A feeling of being separate from something, of not belonging.

Ancillary variable   A factor that accompanies an event and has an impact on it.

Antabuse   A drug used in the treatment of alcoholism that causes a very unpleasant physical reaction when alcohol is ingested.

Arteriosclerosis   A gradual narrowing of the inner diameter of the body's arteries caused by the deposit of fatty tissue, which decreases blood flow to various parts of the body, including the brain.

Ascribed role   A social role that is given to the individual as a result of natural circumstance such as birth or genetics. *Ascribed roles* include man, woman, husband, child, and parent.

Atavistic   Reappearing after an absence of several generations.

Battle fatigue   A psychological disorder presumed to be a function of the stress of combat experience.

Behavior modification   The systematic attempt to change behavior, usually using principles of learning theory.

Behavior therapy   See *Behavior modification.*

Behavioral dysfunction   The lack of functioning of appropriate behavior.

Behavioral sciences   Those sciences concerned with the study of human functioning.

Behavioral technologies   The techniques related to changing human behavior.

Behavioral treatment program   A treatment program that applies the theories of learning to a systematic attempt to change human behavior.

Behaviorists   People trained as behavior changers using learning theory.

Bromide   An early sedative.

Catharsis   The expression of intense feeling leading to a sense of relief.

Change agent   One who attempts to change ongoing situations.

Chemotherapy   The use of chemicals to treat physical or emotional disorders.

Clientele   A group of persons who receive a set of services.

Combat neurosis   See *Battle fatigue.*

Commitment   A legal process in which individuals are placed in mental institutions, often against their will.

Compulsion   An irresistible impulse to act regardless of the rationality of the motive.

Concordance   A statement of agreement.

Conditioning   The linking of stimulus with response.

Correctional institution   An institution that attempts to correct the behavior of those who reside in it.

Credentialed   Having credentials (evidence) that indicate that one is specially educated or trained.

Crisis-prone   Particularly sensitive to stress that results in a crisis state.

Cultural expectations   The expectations of one's culture, for example, the expectation that one will dress within certain bounds of modesty.

Custodial approach   An approach to service delivery in the mental health system. Little treatment is given; the focus is primarily on providing food and shelter.

Debilitation   The process of becoming weakened or feeble.

Decompensation   A process in which a system operates less effectively than in the past.

Deinstitutionalization   The process of removing or assisting the removal of persons from institutional settings, such as mental hospitals, and placing them in the community.

Delinquency   Failure to do what is required; often used to label the law-violating behaviors of youth.

Delusion   A strong belief held in spite of adequate evidence to the contrary.

Deviance   Behavior that differs from an acceptable standard.

Diagnosis   The act of identifying the nature of a disease through examination, or the label applied to a disease process.

Diminished responsibility   A concept that implies that an individual cannot be held accountable for behavior that results from psychological disturbance.

Discordancies   Things that are not in agreement with others.

Disenfranchise   To deprive an individual of a privilege of citizenship previously granted by a government or state or of a statutory or constitutional right, such as the right to vote.

Due process   The formal legal proceedings required by the Constitution before an individual may be deprived of any rights or liberties.

Dysfunctional   Not functioning as it should.

Ego defense   A psychological mechanism that protects the self from experiencing anxiety.

Empathic understanding   Understanding accurately the feelings, thoughts, and motives of another.

Enuresis   Involuntary urination.

Extended family   The members of the family beyond parents and siblings, such as uncles, aunts, and in-laws.

Facilitator   One who assists the occurrence of something.

Feedback   Data relating to output that are put back into the system as a control process.

Fixation   A strong attachment to a person, thing, or event in one's past history that influences current behavior.

Foster care   Organized formal care given to children by persons unrelated to the children, especially when controlled and organized by a governmental agency.

Gay liberation   An organized movement of homosexuals that attempts to change attitudes expressed toward them and to obtain full legal rights.

Genetic   Affecting or affected by genes (the mechanism of biological inheritance).

Ghetto   A city section occupied primarily by minority group members who live there as a result of social or economic pressure.

Grandiose   Characterized by greatness of scope; usually used to describe one who presents an unrealistically grand self-impression.

Grassroots level   Society's basic local level.

Gray Panthers   A social-political organization of elderly citizens who work actively for their rights.

Habilitation program   A program that attempts to supply people with the resources they need, including personal skills.

Hallucination   A perception for which there is no external stimulus.

Heredity   The totality of characteristics transmitted from parents to offspring by genes.

Homosexuality   Sexual behavior involving members of the same sex.

Human services   All those services designed or available to help people who are having difficulty with life and its stress.

Huntington's chorea   A degenerative brain disease that is irreversible.

Hyperactive   Excessively or abnormally active.

Hypnotism   The practice of inducing an artificial condition in which an individual is extremely responsive to suggestions.

Identification figure   A person with whom one identifies—that is, to whom one tries to be similar.

Incontinent   Incapable of holding back; often used to describe persons who cannot control the bowel or bladder.

Indigenous worker   A worker native to an area or group.

Inner person   Those aspects of a person that occur within the personality and influence the person's behavior.

Inpatient   One who receives treatment while living in the treatment facility.

Insanity   A legal term describing a state in which persons are not legally responsible for their actions.

Insight   A state of self-awareness of one's motives and the causes of one's behavior.

Instinctual   Arising from inborn characteristics that are unlearned.

Insulin shock therapy   A psychiatric treatment that consists of administering insulin to persons until they enter an insulin coma.

Intrapsychic   Within the mind.

Introject   Take into one's personality the characteristics of another person.

Introspection   The state of turning one's thoughts inward and examining one's feelings.

Irresistible impulse   An impulse toward behavior that one does not have the ability to resist.

Jargon   The specialized or technical language of a trade, profession, or other group; it often is obscure to nonmembers.

Journeyman   An experienced, competent worker, often one who has finished an apprenticeship.

Layperson   One who does not have specialized training in a field.

Learning theory   The body of theory or theories that proposes how the process of learning takes place.

Libido   Psychic and emotional energy associated with instinctual biological drives.

Life matrix   The combination of factors that influence how one leads one's life.

Major tranquilizer   A chemical that quiets major emotional upsets.

Manic-depressive syndrome   A psychological disorder characterized by extreme mood swings of elation and depression, sometimes accompanied by disorders of perception and belief.

Mediator   One who resolves or settles differences by acting as an intermediary between two conflicting parties.

Medical/psychiatric model   An approach to behavior disorder that conceptualizes problems as diseases with medical causes and treatments.

Mental deficiency   Below normal intellectual development.

Mental disorder   A broad term used to refer to any disorder of intellect, emotion, or behavior.

Mentally ill   Having an intellectual, emotional, or behavioral problem caused by an illness of physical or psychological origin.

Mentally retarded   Having subnormal intellectual functioning.

Methadone   A drug used as a substitute for heroin in the treatment of heroin addicts.

Metrazol shock   A treatment comprised of the induction of a convulsive seizure through the injection of a camphor derivative.

Minor tranquilizer   A chemical that quiets or tranquilizes mild to moderate emotional states, primarily anxiety.

Molar   Pertaining to a body of matter as a whole.

Mood elevator   A chemical that causes one's mood to rise or be more positive.

Motivational state   A state of an individual that acts as a motivator toward action.

Mutism   A state of not speaking, either voluntarily or involuntarily, for long periods of time.

Naturalistic observation   Observing the world (nature) as it is in order to find out facts.

Neurological   Pertaining to the nervous system.

Neurosis   A functional disorder of the mind or emotions without organic lesion, which is characterized primarily by anxiety.

NIMH   National Institute of Mental Health.

Norm   A standard of behavior regarded as typical of a specific group.

Normal curve   A statistical model of the probability of frequency distributions. Also known as a *bell-shaped curve.*

Operant   Characterizing a response elicited or changed by an environment rather than a specific stimulus. The environment "operates" on the behavior, and the behavior operates on the environment.

Operant conditioning   The establishment of a behavior, or its modification, by manipulating the environmental effects of that behavior.

Organic brain syndrome   A disorder that is a function of damage to the brain tissue.

Organismic energy   The energy of the living organism.

Outpatient   An individual who is being treated for a disorder while not a resident of the treatment facility.

Parahelper   An individual who provides helping services although not employed specifically for that service.

Paranoid schizophrenic   One who exhibits the symptoms of extreme suspiciousness, deluded beliefs, and, frequently, hallucinations.

Paraprofessional   A worker trained to engage in helping services who has not reached a professional level of education or function.

Pathology   The anatomic or functional manifestation of disease.

Patient government   A system in which residential patients are given the opportunity to make large numbers of decisions in regard to things that affect them through a democratic process.

Phenylketonuria   An inherited disorder of metabolism that, if uncorrected, can cause mental retardation.

Phobia   An unreasonable fear of an object or situation.

Placebo   A substance or treatment having no medical or remedial value.

Psychiatric nurse   A nurse with special training and education in psychiatry.

Psychiatrist   A medical doctor with special training in psychiatry.

Psychoactive chemical   A chemical that affects the mind or emotions.

Psychodynamics   The psychological processes that govern behavior, especially those proposed by Freudian theorists.

Psychological dynamics   The psychological processes that govern behavior.

Psychologist   An individual with advanced training and education in psychology, usually having a Ph.D. degree.

Psychopathy   A condition in which individuals act as if they had no conscience, that is, feels no guilt or anxiety.

Psychosexual stages   Stages of development as defined by Freudian theorists in which sexual energy is centered in various zones of the body, depending on the person's maturation and growth.

Psychosomatic   Pertaining to phenomena that can be both physical and psychological in origin, such as ulcers and hypertension.

Psychosurgery   Surgery on the brain for the purpose of changing behavior.

Psychotherapy   Treatment of disorders of thinking, emotion, and behavior, which is usually verbal (the talking cure).

Psychotic   Manifesting psychosis, a severe disorder that is characterized by extreme withdrawal from reality.

Psychotropic medication   Medication that affects the thinking and emotional processes.

Rationalizing   Developing self-satisfying but inaccurate reasons for behavior.

Reality contact   The process of accurately perceiving and relating to one's environment.

Referent group   A group that contributes to one's sense of identity.

Reinforcement program   A program that provides positive reinforcement for behaviors defined as appropriate and withholds positive reinforcement or applies negative reinforcement for behaviors defined as inappropriate.

Repression   The exclusion of painful thoughts and memories into the unconscious.

Schizophrenia   A severe mental disorder characterized by lack of contact with reality, withdrawal, and bizarre behavior.

Self-mutilating behavior   The act of causing physical damage to one's own body, usually short of causing death.

Senility   The mental deterioration of old age, which includes forgetfulness.

Shaping   A process of sequential modifications of behavior, each step of which more closely approximates the desired result.

Sheltered living facility   A facility that provides supervised living situations for individuals who are unable to be independent.

Significant others   Persons who have special important meaning to an individual.

Social support network   Social systems that support independent living, such as friends, employers, unions, and religious congregations.

Social worker   A trained worker who usually has a master's degree in social work and who focuses on the social systems of clients.

Sociocultural   Pertaining to society and culture.

Socioeconomic class   The social and economic level to which a person belongs.

Socioeconomic strata   See *Socioeconomic class.*

Socioenvironmental   Pertaining to social and environmental factors.

Somatic   Pertaining to the body.

Stigmatize   To characterize as disgraceful or unacceptable.

Substance abuse   The excessive use of a substance to cause psychological or physiological change, such as alcohol, heroin, cannabis, LSD, and so on.

Suicide center   A program whose prime goal is to prevent suicide or to reduce its incidence through providing counseling and other assistance to persons who are suicidal risks.

Symptom   A phenomenon usually regarded as a characteristic of a condition or event.

Total institution   An institution in which the great majority of decisions are made *for* the members without their input, such as hospitals, prisons, and the military service.

Triage   From the French language, meaning "to sort." A process of identifying problems, determining their severity, and making a decision as to whether resources should be provided to deal with the problems.

Unconscious motivation   Motivations that lead people to act but that are not in their conscious awareness.

Vicarious learning   Learning that occurs when one is not the focus of the instruction, for example, when one is a bystander or onlooker.

Visceral   Pertaining to the internal organs of the body, for example, a "gut feeling."

Vocational rehabilitation   The training or retraining of job skills in individuals who have been unemployed because of illness or disability.

Vulnerable   The state of having lowered defenses so that one is more open to injury; also more open to intimacy.

References

Able-Peterson, T., & Bucy, J. (1993). *The street-work outreach training manual*. Washington, DC: Substance Abuse and Mental Health Services Administration. Center for Mental Health Services.

Advisory Panel on Alzheimer's Disease. (1991). *Second report of the advisory panel on Alzheimer's disease* (DHHS Publication No. ADM 91-1791). Washington, DC: U.S. Government Printing Office.

Agency for Health Care Policy and Research. (1993). *Guidelines for best practice in HIV/AIDS disease management*. Washington, DC: Department of Health and Human Services.

Aguilera, D. C., & Messick, J. M. (1993). *Crisis intervention: Theory and methodology* (7th ed.). St. Louis, MO: C. V. Mosby.

Aiken, L. S., Lo Sciuto, L. A., & Ausetts, M. A. (1984). Paraprofessional versus professional drug counselors: The progress of clients in treatment. *International Journal of the Addictions, 19*.

Albee, G. W. (1961). *Mental health manpower trends*. New York: Basic Books.

Alcoholics Anonymous. (1955). New York: Alcoholics Anonymous World Services.

Alley, S., Blanton, J., & Feldman, R. E. (Eds.). (1979). *Paraprofessionals in mental health: Theory and practice*. New York: Human Sciences Press.

Andreasen, N. C. (1984). *The broken brain: The biological revolution in psychiatry*. New York: Harper & Row.

Andreasen, N. C. (1998). Editorial: Orphanages: An idea whose time has come again? *American Journal of Psychiatry, 155*.

Anthony, W. A., Forbes, R., & Cohen, M. R. (1993). Rehabilitation oriented case management. In M. Harris and H. Bergman (Eds.), *Case management for mentally ill patients: Theory and practice*. Chur, Switzerland: Harwood Academic.

Anthony, W. A., Cohen, M. R., Farkas, M., & Cohen, B. F. (1988). Clinical care update: The chronically mentally ill. Case management—more than a response to a dysfunctional system. *Community Mental Health Journal, 24*.

Arens, R. (1964). Due process and the rights of the mentally ill: The strange case of Frederick Lynch. *Catholic University Law Review, 13*.

Atwood, J. D. (1986). Self-awareness in supervision. *Clinical Supervisor, 4*.

Austin, C. D. (1996). Aging and long-term care. In C. D. Austin and R. W. McClelland (Eds.), *Perspectives on case management practice*. Milwaukee: Families International.

Austin, C. D., & McClelland, R. W. (1996). Introduction: Case management—everybody's doing it. In C. D. Austin and R. W. McClelland (Eds.), *Perspectives on Case Management Practice*. Milwaukee: Families International.

Austin, M. (1975). *The Florida human services task bank*. Florida Board of Regents.

Austin, M. (1978). *Professionals and paraprofessionals*. New York: Human Sciences Press.

Bachrach, A., Erwin, W., & Mohr, J. (1968). The control of eating behavior in an anorexic by operant conditioning techniques. In L. Ullman and L. Krasner (Eds.), *Case studies in behavior modification.* New York: Holt, Rinehart & Winston.

Bachrach, L. L. (1982). Young adult chronic patients: An analytic review of the literature. *Hospital and Community Psychiatry, 33.*

Bale, R. N., Miller, N., Luching, O., & Fitchner, C. (1980). Therapeutic communities vs. methadone maintenance. *Archives of General Psychiatry, 37.*

Bandura, A. (1977). *Social learning theories.* Englewood Cliffs, NJ: Prentice Hall.

Bandura, A. (1978). The self-system in reciprocal determinism. *American Psychologist, 33.*

Bandura, A. (1982). Self-efficiency mechanisms in human agency. *American Psychologist, 37.*

Bassuk, E., & Rubin, L. (1987). Homeless children: A neglected population. *American Journal of Orthopsychiatry, 52.*

Bateson, P. (1987). Biological approaches to the study of behavioral development. *International Journal of Behavioral Development, 10.*

Baum, A. S., & Burnes, D. W. (1993). *A nation in denial; The truth about homelessness.* Boulder, CO; Westview Press.

Bay, J., & Bay, C. (1973). Professionalism and the erosion of rationality in the health care field. *American Journal of Orthopsychiatry, 43.*

Bell, C. (1996). Treatment issues for African-American men. *Psychiatric Annals, 26.*

Berne, E. (1957). Ego states in psychotherapy. *American Journal of Psychotherapy, 11.*

Berne, E. (1966). *Principles of group treatment.* New York: Oxford University Press.

Bernstein, N. (1999, December 8). Deep poverty and illness found among homeless. *The New York Times.*

Beutler, L. E., & Harwood, T. M. (1995). Prescriptive psychotherapies. *Applied and Preventive Psychology, 4.*

Black, M. M., and Krishnakumar, A. (1998). Children in low-income, urban settings: Interventions to promote mental health and well-being. *American Psychologist, 53.*

Blair, N. (1999). Law, ethics, and the human service worker. In H. S. Harris and D. C.

Maloney (Eds.). *Human services: Contemporary issues and trends.* (2nd ed.). Boston: Allyn and Bacon.

Blake, R. (1985–86). Normalization and boarding homes: An examination of paradoxes. *Social Work in Health Care, 11.*

Blum, A. (1966). Differential use of manpower in public welfare. *Social Work, 11.*

Bokan, J. A., & Campbell, W. (1984). Indigenous psychotherapy in the treatment of a Laotian refugee. *Hospital and Community Psychiatry, 35.*

Bond, G. R., Salyers, M., & Fekete, D. (1996). *Illinois assertive community treatment project: Final report.* Springfield: Illinois Department of Mental Health and Developmental Disabilities.

Bornstein, R. F., & Masling, J. M. (1998). *Empirical perspectives on the psychoanalytic unconscious.* Washington, DC: American Psychological Association.

Bouchard, T. J., & Dorfman, D. D. (1995). Two views of the bell curve. *Contemporary Psychology, 40.*

Bowman, G., & Klopf, G. (1968). *Auxiliary school personnel: Their roles, training and institutionalization.* New York: Bank Street College of Education.

Braddock, D. (1992). Community mental health and mental retardation services in the United States: A comparative study of resource allocation. *American Journal of Psychiatry, 149.*

Braddock, D. (1997). Innovations in mental retardation: Historical and contemporary perspectives. In D. Biegel and A. Blum (Eds.)., *Innovations in Practice and Service Delivery with Vulnerable Populations across the Life Span.* New York: Oxford University Press.

Braddock D., & Hemp, R. (1999). DHD Forum: State of the states in developmental disabilities: Study update. *The Newsletter of the Institute on Disability and Human Development, 11.*

Braddock, D., Hemp, R., Bachelder, L., & Fujiura, G. (1995). *The state of the states in developmental disabilities* (4th ed.). Washington, DC: American Association on Mental Retardation.

Braginsky, B. M., Braginsky, D., & Ring, K. (1969). *Methods of madness: The mental hospi-*

tal as a last resort. New York: Holt, Rinehart & Winston.

Brantly, T. (1983). Racism and its impact on psychotherapy. *American Journal of Psychiatry, 140.*

Brawley, E. A. (1982). Bachelor's degree programs in the human services: Results of a national survey. *Journal of the National Organization of Human Service Educators, 4.*

Brawley, E. A. (1986). Paraprofessional social welfare personnel in international perspective: Results of a world-wide survey. *International Social Work, 29.*

Brown, W. F. (1974). Effectiveness of paraprofessionals: The evidence. *The Personnel and Guidance Journal, 53.*

Browning, P., Thorin, E., & Rhoades, C. (1984). A national profile of self-help/self-advocacy groups of people with mental retardation. *Mental Retardation, 22 .*

Buchanan, R. W. (1995). Clozapine: Efficacy and safety. *Schizophrenia Bulletin, 21.*

Bureau of Justice Statistics. (1999). *Bureau of Justice Statistics Fiscal Year 1998: At a glance.* Department of Justice, Washington, DC.

Byers-Lang, R. E. (1984). Peer counselors, network builders for elderly blind. *Journal of Visual Impairment and Blindness, 78.*

Caplan, G. (1964). *Principles of preventative psychiatry.* New York: Basic Books.

Castles, E. E. (1996). *We're people first: The social and emotional lives of individuals with mental retardation.* Westport, CT: Praeger.

Chaneles, S. (1987). Growing old behind bars. *Psychology Today, 21.*

Chapin, R. K. (1995). Social policy development: The strengths perspective. *Social Work: Journal of the National Association of Social Workers, 40.*

Chasnoff, I. J., & Schnoll, S. H. (1987). Consequences of cocaine and other drug use in pregnancy. In A. M. Washton and M. S. Gold (Eds.), *Cocaine: A clinician's handbook.* New York: Guilford Press.

CHIME. (1995). *Fundamentals of mental health and HIV/AIDS: The CHIME Project (CMHS HIV/AIDS) Illinois Mental Health Provider Education.* University of Illinois, Champaign, IL. CMHS grant #1T16SM19940-01.

Christmas, J. J., Wallace, H., & Edwards, J. (1970). New careers and mental health services: Fantasy or future? *American Journal of Psychiatry, 126.*

Church, G. J. (1990). The view from behind bars. *Time, 136.*

Cimmino, P. (1993). *Exactly what is human services? The evolution of a profession, academic discipline, and social science.* Bronx, NY: Council for Standards in Human Service Education Monograph Series.

Cimmino, P. (1999). Basic concepts and definitions of human services. In H. S. Harris & D. C. Maloney (Eds.), *Human services: Contemporary issues and trends.* (2nd ed.). Boston: Allyn and Bacon.

Citron, M., Solomon, P., & Draine, J. (1999). Self-help groups for families of persons with mental illness: Perceived benefits of helpfulness. *Community Mental Health Journal, 35.*

Clare, P. K., & Kramer, J. H. (1976). *Introduction to American corrections.* Boston: Holbrook Press.

Clubok, M. (1984). Four-year human service programs. *Journal of the National Organization of Human Service Educators, 6.*

Clubok, M. (1999). Human services as a career: Personal survival and professional growth. In H. S. Harris and D. C. Maloney (Eds.), *Human services: Contemporary issues and trends.* (2nd ed.). Boston: Allyn and Bacon.

Cogan, D. (1993, May 10). Personal communication.

Cohen, A. (1999). Empowerment: Toward a new definition of self-help. In H. S. Harris and D. C. Maloney (Eds.), *Human services: Contemporary issues and trends.* (2nd ed.). Boston: Allyn and Bacon.

Cohen, B. (1999). Intervention and supervision in strengths-based social work practice. *Families in Society: The Journal of Contemporary Human Services, 80.*

Cohen, R. E. (1987). The Armero tragedy: Lessons for mental health professionals. *Hospital and Community Psychiatry, 38.*

Coleman, J. (1956). *Abnormal psychology and modern life.* Chicago: Scott, Foresman and Co.

Collins, A. H. (1973). Natural delivery system: Accessible sources of power for mental health. *American Journal of Orthopsychiatry, 43.*

Corrigan, P. W. (1997). Behavior therapy empowers persons with severe mental illness. *Behavior Modification, 21.*

Corrigan, P. W., McCracken, S., & Mehr, J. (1995). *Practice guidelines for extended psychiatric residential care: From chaos to collaboration.* Springfield, IL: Charles C. Thomas.

Costa, C. (1975). *A comparative study of career opportunities of anti-poverty program graduates as first year teachers.* New York: New Careers Training Laboratory, Queens College.

Craighead, W. E., & Mercatoris, M. (1983). Mentally retarded residents as paraprofessionals: A review. *American Journal of Mental Deficiency, 78.*

Cross, T. L., & Bazron, B. J. (1996). *Training of trainers workshop on developing cultural competence.* Presentation at National Technical Assistance Center for Children's Mental Health at Georgetown University Child Development Center, Washington, DC.

Cross, T. L., Bazron, B. J., Dennis, K. W., & Isaacs, M. R. (1989). *Towards a culturally competent system of care.* Washington, DC: CASSP Technical Assistance Center, Georgetown University.

Cummings, J. L., & Jeste, D. V. (1999). Alzheimer's disease and its management in the year 2010. *Psychiatric Services, 50.*

Dangel, R. F., & Polster, R. A. (1988). *Teaching child management skills.* New York: Pergamon Press.

Danish, S. J., & Hauer, A. L. (1973). *Helping skills: A basic training program.* New York: Behavioral Publications.

Davis, D., Jemison, E., Rowe, M., & Sprague, D. (1984). Cluster homes: An alternative for troubled youths. *Children Today, 13.*

Dawkins, K., Liberman, J. A., Lewbowitz, B. D., and Hsiao, J. K. (1999). Antipsychotics: Past and future. *Schizophrenia Bulletin, 25.*

DeAngelis, T. (1990). Armenian earthquake survivors still suffer mental, physical pain. *APA Monitor, 21.*

DeAngelis, T. (1994). Youth take to the streets to escape family troubles. *Monitor* (American Psychological Association), 25.

DeLeon, G., & Schwartz, S. (1986). Therapeutic communities: What are the retention rates? *American Journal of Drug and Alcohol Abuse, 22.*

DeLeon, G., & Ziegenfuss, J. T. (Eds.). (1986). *Therapeutic communities for addictions: Readings in theory, research and practice.* Springfield, IL: Charles C. Thomas.

Demone, H., & Harshbarger, D. (Eds.). (1974). *A handbook of human service organizations.* New York: Behavioral Publications.

DiClemente, R. J. (Ed.). (1992). *Adolescents and AIDS: A generation in jeopardy.* Newbury Park, CA: Sage.

Drake, R. E., & Mueser, K. T. (1996a). Dual diagnosis of major mental illness and substance abuse, Vol. 2: Recent research and clinical implications. *New Directions for Mental Health Services, 70.*

Drake, R. E., & Mueser, K. T. (1996b). Editors' notes: Dual diagnosis of major mental illness and substance abuse, Vol. 2: Recent research and clinical implications. *New Directions for Mental Health Services, 70.*

Dubey, J. (1974). Confidentiality as a requirement of the therapist: Technical necessities for absolute privilege in psychotherapy. *American Journal of Psychiatry, 131.*

Duclos, M. A., & Gfroerer, M. (1999). Helping for alcohol and drug abuse. In H. S. Harris and D. C. Maloney (Eds.), *Human services: Contemporary issues and trends.* (2nd ed.). Boston: Allyn and Bacon.

Dumont, M. P. (1998). Us and them. *Readings: A Journal of Reviews and Commentary in Mental Health, 13.*

Durlak, J. A. (1979). Comparative effectiveness of paraprofessional and professional helpers. *Psychological Bulletin, 36.*

D'Zurilla, T. J. (1990). Current status of rational-emotive therapy. *Contemporary Psychology, 35.*

Eaton, W. W. (1986). *The sociology of mental disorders* (2nd ed.). New York: Praeger.

Edell Lopez, J. (1999). Child maltreatment and

abuse, the problem and human services. In H. S. Harris and D. C. Maloney (Eds.), *Human services: Contemporary issues and trends.* (2nd ed.). Boston: Allyn and Bacon.

Edelman, M. W. (1994). Introduction. In A. Sherman, *Wasting America's future: The Children's Defense Fund report on the costs of child poverty.* Boston: Beacon Press.

Edmonds, A., & Cauchon, R. (1994). Incidence of domestic abuse and its implications. *Public Welfare, 52.*

Emery, R. E., & Laumann-Billings, L. (1998). An overview of the nature, causes, and consequences of abusive family relationships: Toward differentiating maltreatment and violence. *American Psychologist, 53.*

Emrick, R. E. (1990). Self-help groups for former patients: Relations with mental health professionals. *Hospital and Community Psychiatry, 41.*

Ewalt, P. L. (1995). Editorial: Who cares for the children? *Social Work: Journal of the National Association of Social Workers, 40.*

Eysenck, H. (1966). *The effects of psychotherapy.* New York: International Science Press.

Eysenck, H. (1993). *Decline and fall of the Freudian empire.* New York: Viking-Penguin.

Eysenck, H., & Eysenck, M. (1985). *Personality and individual differences: A natural science approach.* New York: Plenum Press.

Fagnoni, C. M. (1999). *Statement on welfare reform: States' implementation progress and information on former recipients.* Washington, DC: U.S. General Accounting Office.

Fairweather, G. W., Sanders, D. H., Cressler, D. L., & Maynard, H. (1969). *Community life for the mentally ill: An alternative to institutional care.* Chicago: Aldine.

Fairweather, G. W., Sanders, D. H., & Tornatzky, L. G. (1974). *Creating change in mental health organizations.* Elmsford, NY: Pergamon Press.

Farberow, N. (1977). Mental health response in major disasters. *The Psychotherapy Bulletin, 10.*

Feringer, R., & Jacobs, E. (1987). Human services: Is it a profession. *The Link, 9.*

Fisher, W., Mehr, J., & Truckenbrod, P. (1974). *Human services: The third revolution in mental health.* Port Washington, NY: Alfred.

Follette, V. M., Ruzek, J. I., & Abueg, F. R. (Eds.). (1998). *Cognitive-behavioral therapies for trauma.* New York: The Guilford Press.

Forum on Child and Family Statistics. (1997). *America's children: Key indicators of well-being.* Washington, DC: Forum on Child and Family Statistics.

Fowers, B. J., & Richardson, F. C. (1996). Why is multiculturalism good? *American Psychologist, 51.*

Franklin, D. (1990). Hooked, not hooked: Why not everyone is an addict. *Health, 4.*

Franzini, L. R., & Grossberg, J. M. (1995). *Eccentric and bizarre behaviors.* New York: John Wiley.

Fraser, J. S. (1986). The crisis interview: Strategic rapid intervention. *Journal of Strategic and Systematic Therapies, 5.*

Freedman, J. (1993). *From cradle to grave: The human face of poverty in America.* New York: Atheneum.

Fried, M. (1964). Effect of social change on mental health. *American Journal of Orthopsychiatry, 34.*

Friedman, S. B., Alderman, E. M., Pantell, R. H., Saylor, C. F., & Sugar, M. (1995). *Psychosocial issues for children and families in disasters: A guide for the primary care physician.* Washington, DC: Substance Abuse and Mental Health Administration.

Frumkin, M., Imershein, A., Chackerian, R., & Martin, P. (1983). Evaluating state level integration of human services. *Administration in Social Work, 7.*

Fulla, S. (1998, Summer). New correctional programs will serve female inmates who are victims of abuse. *The Compiler: Illinois criminal justice information authority.*

Fullerton, S. (1999). Theories as tools and resources for helping. In H. S. Harris and D. C. Maloney (Eds.), *Human services: Contemporary issues and trends.* (2nd ed.). Boston: Allyn and Bacon.

Gage, R. W. (1976). Integration of human service delivery systems. *Public Welfare, 34.*

Galinsky, M. J., & Schopler, J. H. (1995). *Support groups: Current perspectives on theory and practice.* New York: Haworth Press.

Gallo, J. J., & Lebowitz, B. D. (1999). The epidemiology of common late life mental disorders in the community: Themes for the new century. *Psychiatric Services, 50.*

Garber, H. (1984). Comment: On Sommer and Sommer. *American Psychologist, 39.*

Garber, H., & Heber, F. R. (1977). The Milwaukee Project: Indications of the effectiveness of early interventions in preventing mental retardation. In P. Mittler (Ed.), *Research to practice in mental retardation* (Vol. 1). Baltimore, MD: University Park Press.

Garland, D. R. (1987). Residential child care workers as primary agents of family interventions. *Child and Youth Care Quarterly, 16.*

Gartner, A. (1971). *Paraprofessionals and their performance.* New York: Praeger.

Gartner, A. (1979). The effectiveness of paraprofessionals in service delivery. In S. Alley, J. Blanton, and R. E. Feldman (Eds.), *Paraprofessionals in mental health.* New York: Human Sciences Press.

Gartner, A., & Riessman, F. (1977). *Self-help in the human services.* San Francisco: Jossey-Bass.

Gartner, A., & Riessman, F. (1982). Self-help and mental health. *Hospital and Community Psychiatry, 33.*

Gaus, V., Steil, D., and Carberry, K. (1999). Grief counseling for mentally retarded adults: Two case studies. *The NADD Bulletin, 2.*

Gearan, A. (1999). Prison population reaches highest level ever in U.S. *USA Today,* March 15.

Geron, S., & Chassler, D. (1994). *Guidelines for case management practice across the long term continuum.* Report of the Robert Wood Johnson Grant to Connecticut Community Care. Bristol, CT. Boston, MA: Robert Wood Johnson Foundation

Getz, W., Wiessen, A., Sue, S., & Ayers, A. (1974). *Fundamentals of crisis counseling.* Lexington, MA: Lexington Books.

Gilson, S. F., & Levitas, A. (1987). Psychosocial crisis in the lives of mentally retarded people. *Psychiatric Aspects of Mental Retardation Reviews, 6.*

Giovanni, M. D. (1999). A human services credential in the next millenium. *The Link, 20.*

Godley, S. (1995). The Illinois MISA project: *A treatment system united for persons with mental illness and substance abuse.* Springfield, Il.: Illinois Department of Mental Health and Developmental Disabilities.

Goenjian, A. V., Weston, B., Steiner, L., & Marx, I. (1994). Posttraumatic stress disorder in elderly and younger adults after the 1988 earthquake in Armenia. *American Journal of Psychiatry, 151.*

Goffman, E. (1961). *Asylums: Essays on the social situation of mental patients and other inmates.* Garden City, NY: Doubleday Anchor.

Goldfried, M., & Davison, G. (1976). *Clinical behavior therapy.* New York: Holt, Rinehart & Winston.

Goldstein, M. Z. (1995). Maltreatment of elderly persons. *Psychiatric Services, 46.*

Gordon, J. (1965). Project Cause: The federal anti-poverty program and some implications of sub-professional training. *American Psychologist, 20.*

Gorman, C. (1997). The disease detective. *Time, 148*(29).

Gottesman, I. (1990). *Schizophrenia genesis: The origins of madness.* New York: W. H. Freeman.

Gould, K. H. (1995). The misconstruing of multiculturalism: The Stanford debate and social work. *Social Work: Journal of the National Association of Social Workers, 40.*

Grier, W. H., & Cobbs, P. M. (1968). *Black Rage.* New York: Basic Books.

Grimes, P. (1986). Youth suicide. *The Link, 8.*

Grob, G. (1994). *The mad among us: A history of the care of America's mentally ill.* New York: Free Press.

Grossinger, K. (1985). Organizing in the human service community. *Catalyst: A Socialist Journal of the Social Sciences, 5.*

Guerney, L., & Moore, L. (1983). Phone friend: A prevention-oriented service for latchkey children. *Children Today, 12.*

Gutheil, I. A. (1985). Sensitizing nursing home staff to residents' psychosocial needs. *Clinical Social Work Journal, 13.*

Guttesman, R. (1982). Due process and students' rights. *Social Work in Education, 4.*

Hahn, A. J. (1994). *The politics of caring: Human services at the local level.* Boulder, CO: Westview Press.

Haney, C., & Zimbardo, P. (1998). The past and the future of U.S. prison policy: Twenty-five years after the Stanford prison experiment. *American Psychologist, 53.*

Harper, R. (1960). *Psychoanalysis and psychotherapy: 36 systems.* Englewood Cliffs, NJ: Prentice Hall.

Harrington, M. (1962). *The other America.* New York: Macmillan.

Harris, H. S., & Maloney, D. C. (1999). *Human service: Contemporary issues and trends* (2nd ed.). Boston: Allyn and Bacon.

Hattie, J. A., Sharpley, C. R., & Rogers, H. (1984). Comparative effectiveness of professional and paraprofessional helpers. *Psychological Bulletin, 95.*

Hawkinshire, F. (1969). Training procedures for offenders working in community treatment programs. In B. Guerney (Ed.), *Psychotherapeutic agents: New roles for nonprofessionals, parents, and teachers.* New York: Holt, Rinehart & Winston.

Heckman, I. (1999). Going upstream: Prevention in human services. In H. S. Harris and D. C. Maloney (Eds.), *Human services: Contemporary issues and trends* (2nd ed.). Boston: Allyn and Bacon.

Henry, C. S. (1996). A human ecological approach to adolescent suicide. *Prevention Researcher, 3.*

Herr, S. (1983). *Rights and advocacy for retarded people.* Lexington, MA: Lexington Books.

Herrnstein, R. J., & Murray, C. (1994). *The bell curve: Intelligence and class structure in American life.* New York: Free Press.

Hersch, P. (1988). Coming of age on city streets. *Psychology Today, 22.*

Ho, D. (1999). The spread of HIV . . . and will we ever find a cure? *Time, 154.*

Hoaken, P. C. (1986). Psychiatry, civil liberty and involuntary treatment. *Canadian Journal of Psychiatry, 31.*

Hodge, M., & Giesler, L. (1997). *Case management practice guidelines for adults with severe and persistent mental illness.* Ocean Ridge, FL: National Association of Case Management.

Hogan, R. (1986). Gaining community support for group homes. *Community Mental Health Journal, 22.*

Hollingshead, A. V., & Redlich, F. C. (1965). Social stratification and psychiatric disorders. In O. Milton (Ed.), *Behavior disorders, perspectives, and trends.* Philadelphia: J. B. Lippincott.

Humphreys, K., & Rappaport, J. (1994). Researching self-help/mutual aid groups and organizations: Many roads, one journey. *Applied and Preventive Psychology, 3.*

Hurvitz, N. (1975). Peer self-help psychotherapy groups and the implications for psychotherapy. *Psychotherapy: Theory, Research, and Practice, 7.*

Iglehart, A. P., & Becarra, R. M. (1996). *Social services and the ethnic community.* Boston: Allyn and Bacon.

Jackson, D. (1957). The question of family homeostasis. *Psychiatric Quarterly Supplement, 31.*

James, V. (1979). Paraprofessionals in mental health: A framework for the facts. In S. Alley, J. Blanton, and R. E. Feldman (Eds.), *Mental health: Theory and practice.* New York: Human Sciences Press.

Johnson, L. C. (1983). Networking: A means of maximizing resources. *Human Services in the Rural Environment, 8.*

Johnson, M., Samberg, L., Calsyn, R., Blasinsky, M., Landow, W., & Goldman, H. (1999). Case management models for persons who are homeless and mentally ill: The access demonstration project. *Community Mental Health Journal, 35.*

Johnson, R. (1987). *Hard times: Understanding and reforming the prison.* Monterey, CA: Brooks/Cole.

Joint Commission on Mental Illness and Health. (1961). *Action for Mental Health.* New York: Basic Books.

Kalichman, S. C. (1998). *Understanding AIDS: A guide for mental health professionals.* (2nd ed.). Washington, DC: American Psychological Association Press.

Kanter, J. S. (1985). Case management of the young adult chronic patient: A clinical perspective. *New Directions for Mental Health Services, 27.*

Kanter, J. S. (1989). Clinical case management: Definition, principles, components. *Hospital and Community Psychiatry, 40.*

Kaplan, G. (1977). *From aide to teacher: The story of the career opportunities program.* Washington, DC: U.S. Government Printing Office.

Kaplan, J. S. (1998). *Beyond behavior modification: A cognitive-behavioral approach to behavior management in school.* (3rd ed.). Austin, TX: Pro-Ed.

Katz, A. H. (1981). Self-help and mutual aid: An emerging social movement? *Annual Review of Sociology, 7.*

Kazdin, A. E. (1982). The token economy: A decade later. *Journal of Applied Behavior Analysis, 15.*

Kazdin, A. E. (1992). Child and adolescent dysfunction and paths toward maladjustments: Targets for intervention. *Clinical Psychology Review, 12.*

Kempler, W. (1973). Gestalt therapy. In R. Corsini (Ed.), *Current psychotherapies.* Itasca, IL: F. E. Peacock.

Kennedy, J. F. (1961). *Statement by the president: National action to combat mental retardation.* Washington, DC: U.S. Government Printing Office.

Kermani, E. J., & Drob, S. L. (1987). Tarasoff decision: A decade later dilemma still faces psychotherapists. *American Journal of Psychotherapy, 41.*

Kestenbaum, S. E., & Bar-On, Y. (1982). Case aides: An answer for Israel. *Public Welfare, 40.*

Kiesler, C. A. (1982). Mental hospitals and alternative care: Noninstitutionalization as potential public policy for mental patients. *American Psychologist, 37.*

Kiesler, C. A. (1992). U.S. mental health policy: Doomed to fail. *American Psychologist, 47.*

Kihlstrom, J. F. (1999). [Review of the book *A tumbling ground for whimsies*]. APA Review of Books, 44.

Kittrie, N. N. (1971). *The right to be different: Deviance and enforced therapy.* Baltimore, MD: The Johns Hopkins Press.

Klein, D. F., & Wender, P. H. (1993). *Understanding depression: A complete guide to its diagnosis and treatment.* New York: Oxford University Press.

Kornetsky, C. (1976). *Pharmacology: Drugs affecting behavior.* New York: John Wiley & Sons.

Kramer, P. (1993). *Listening to Prozac: A psychiatrist explores antidepressant drugs and the remaking of the self.* New York: Viking-Penguin.

Krassner, M. (1986). Effective features of therapy from the healer's perspective: A study of Curanderismo. *Smith College Studies in Social Work, 56.*

Krause, N. (1987). Chronic financial strain, social support and depressive symptoms among older adults. *Psychology and Aging, 2.*

Kronick, R. (1986). What is human services: It is multidisciplinary and professional. *The Link, 8.*

Kronick, R. (1987). Professional development in human services. *The Link, 9.*

Kuno, E., Rothbard, A. B., & Sands, R. G. (1999). Service components of case management which reduce inpatient care for persons with serious mental illness. *Community Mental Health Journal, 35.*

Lakin, C. (1996). *Research on community integration of persons with mental retardation and related conditions: Current knowledge, emerging challenges and recommended future directions.* Washington, DC: National Institute on Disability and Rehabilitation Research.

Lamb, H. R. (1980). Therapist-case managers: More than brokers of services. *Hospital and Community Psychiatry, 31.*

Landon, J. W. (1986). *The development of social welfare.* New York: Human Sciences Press.

Lazarus, A. A. (1981). *The practice of multimodal therapy.* New York: McGraw-Hill.

LeFever, G. B., Dawson, K. V., and Morrow, A. L. (1999). The extent of drug therapy for attention deficit-hyperactivity disorder among children in public schools. *American Journal of Public Health, 89.*

Lemberg, R. (1984). Ten ways for a self-help group to fail. *American Journal of Orthopsychiatry, 54.*

Lieberman, M. A., & Borman, L. D. (1979). *Self-help groups for coping with crisis.* San Francisco: Jossey-Bass.

Lindemann, E. (1944). Symptomatology and management of acute grief. *American Journal of Psychiatry, 101.*

Linehan, M. M. (1993). *Cognitive-behavioral treatment of borderline personality disorder.* New York: Guilford Press.

Littleton, N. (1999). Personal qualities in a successful human services career. In H. S. Harris and D. C. Maloney (Eds.), *Human services: Contemporary issues and trends.* (2nd ed.). Boston: Allyn and Bacon.

Long, L. A. (1999). Human services for homeless people. In H. S. Harris and D. C. Maloney (Eds.), *Human services: Contemporary issues and trends* (2nd ed.). Boston: Allyn and Bacon.

Long, L. A., & Doyle, M. (1999). Human services: Necessary skills and values. In H. S. Harris and D. C. Maloney (Eds.), *Human services: Contemporary issues and trends.* (2nd ed.). Boston: Allyn and Bacon.

Lydersen, K. (1999, September 13). Settlement houses: Homes for justice. *Streetwise.*

Macht, J. (1986). What is human services? It is dynamic. *The Link, 8.*

Macht, J. (1999). Human services: history and recent influences. In H. S. Harris and D. C. Maloney (Eds.), *Human services: Contemporary issues and trends* (2nd ed.). Boston: Allyn and Bacon.

Maher, B. (1966) *Principles of psychopathology: An experimental approach.* New York: McGraw-Hill.

Maier, H. W. (1987). *Developmental group care of children and youth: Concepts and practices.* New York: Haworth Press.

Maisto, S. A. (1995). The abc's of researching AA. *Contemporary Psychology, 40.*

March, M. (1968). The neighborhood center concept. *Public Welfare, 26.*

Marcia, J. (1987). Empathy and psychotherapy. In N. Eisenberg and J. Strayer (Eds.), *Empathy and its development.* Cambridge: Cambridge University Press.

Maslow, A., & Mittelman, B. (1951). *Principles of abnormal psychology.* New York: Harper & Bros.

McAuliffe, W. E., & Ch'ien, J. M. (1986). Recovery training and self-help: A relapse prevention program for treated opiate addicts. *Journal of Substance Abuse Treatment, 3.*

McClam, T., & Woodside, M. R. (1989). A conversation with Dr. Harold McPheeters. *Human Service Education, 9.*

McClam, T., & Woodside, M. R. (1994). *Problem solving in the helping professions.* Pacific Grove, CA: Brooks/Cole.

McClelland, R. W., Austin, C. D., & Schneck, D. (1996). Practice dilemmas and policy implications in case management. In C. D. Austin and R. W. McClelland (Eds.), *Perspectives on case management practice.* Milwaukee: Families International.

McGrew, J. H., Wright, E. R., and Pescosolido, B. A. (1999). Closing of a state hospital: An overview and framework for a case study. *Journal of Behavioral Health Services and Research. 26.*

McKinney, W. L. (1999). People living with HIV and AIDS: The problem and human services. In H. S. Harris and D. C. Maloney (Eds.), *Human services: Contemporary issues and trends* (2nd ed.). Boston: Allyn and Bacon.

McPheeters, H. L. (1999). Policy, politics, and human services. In H. S. Harris and D. C. Maloney (Eds.), *Human services: Contemporary issues and trends* (2nd ed.). Boston: Allyn and Bacon.

McQuaide, S. (1983). Human service cutbacks and the mental health of the poor. *Social Casework, 64.*

Mehr, J. (1986). What is human services: It is whole-person focused. *The Link, 8.*

Mehr, J. (1999). Human services in the mental health arena: From institution to community. In H. S. Harris and D. C. Maloney (Eds.), *Human services: Contemporary issues and trends.* (2nd ed.). Boston: Allyn and Bacon.

Meichenbaum, D. (1977). *Cognitive-behavior modification: An integrated approach.* New York: Plenum.

Meltzoff, J., & Kornreich, M. (1970). *Research in psychotherapy.* New York: Atherton Press.

Mental Health News Alert. (1998). *1996 Mentally Retarded Persons Served.* Silver Spring, MD: CD Publications.

Meyer, H. (1969). Sociological comments. In C. Grosser, W. C. Henry, and J. G. Kelly (Eds.), *Nonprofessionals in the human services.* San Francisco: Jossey-Bass.

Michels, R. (1981). The right to refuse treatment: Ethical issues. *Hospital and Community Psychiatry, 32.*

Miller, A. D. (1985). Reinstitutionalization in retrospect. *Psychiatric Quarterly, 52.*

Miller, K., Fein, E., Howe, G. W., Gaudio, C. P., & Bishop, G. V. (1984). Time-limited, goal focused parent aide services. *Social Casework, 65.*

Minkoff, K. (1987). Beyond deinstitutionalization: A new ideology for the postinstitutional era. *Hospital and Community Psychiatry, 38.*

Moustakas, C. (1986). Being in, being for, and being with. *Humanistic Psychologist, 14.*

Mowrer, O. H. (1971). Peer groups and medication: The best therapy for professionals and laymen alike. *Psychotherapy: Theory, Research, and Practice, 8.*

Moxley, D. P. (1989). *The practice of case management.* Newbury Park, CA: Sage.

Mueser, K. T., Bond, G. R., Drake, R. E., & Resnick, S. G. (1998). Models of community care for severe mental illness: A review of research on case management. *Schizophrenia Bulletin, 24.*

Munoz-Kantha, M. (1999). Domestic violence, battered women and dimensions of the problem. In H. S. Harris and D. C. Maloney (Eds.), *Human services: Contemporary issues and trends* (2nd ed.). Boston: Allyn and Bacon.

Murray, B. (1995). Head Start sharpens focus on mental health. *Monitor: American Psychological Association, 26.*

Myers, D. (1994). *Disaster response and recovery: A handbook for mental health professionals.* Washington, DC: Substance Abuse and Mental Health Services Administration.

Myrdal, G. (1964). *An American dilemma* (2nd ed.). New York: McGraw-Hill.

Nader, K., Pynoos, R., Fairbanks, L., & Frederick, C. (1990). Children's PTSD reactions one year after a sniper attack at their school. *American Journal of Psychiatry, 147.*

Nadi, S., Nurnberger, J., & Gershon, E. (1984). Inherited trait marks depression. *Science, 845.*

Nardone, M. J., Tryon, W. W., & O'Connor, K. (1986). The effectiveness and generalization of a cognitive-behavioral group treatment to reduce impulsive/aggressive behavior for boys in a residential setting. *Behavioral and Residential Treatment, 1.*

NARF. (1983). Rehabilitation review. *National Association of Rehabilitation Facilities, 4.*

Nash, K. B., Lifton, N., & Smith, S. E. (1978). The paraprofessional: Selected readings. New Haven, CT: Advocate Press.

NASMHPD. (1999). *Preliminary FY 96 profiles information.* Alexandria, VA.: Research Institute of the National Association of State Mental Health Program Directors.

National Association of Social Workers. (1992). *NASW standards for social work case management.* Washington, DC: National Association of Social Workers.

National Institute of Mental Health. (1975). *Research in the service of mental health.* (D.H.E.W. Publication No. ADM 75–236.). Washington, DC: Superintendent of Documents.

Nebelkopf, E. (1986). The therapeutic community and human services in the 1980s. *Journal of Psychoactive Drugs, 18.*

Neisser, V., Boodoo, G., et al. (1996). Intelligence: Known and unknowns. *American Psychologist, 51.*

New Human Services Institute. (1975). *College programs for paraprofessionals.* New York: Human Sciences Press.

Newsome, B. L., & Newsome, M., Jr. (1983). Self-help in the United States: Social policy options. *Urban and Social Change Review, 16.*

Newton, J. (1988). *Preventing mental illness.* London: Routledge & Kegan Paul.

Niccum, K. J. (1999). Human service for older adults. In H. S. Harris and D. C. Maloney (Eds.), *Human services: Contemporary issues and trends.* (2nd ed.). Boston: Allyn and Bacon.

Nicks, T. L. (1985). Inequities in the delivery and financing of mental health services for ethnic minority Americans. *Psychotherapy: Theory/Research/Practice/Training, 22.*

NOHSE. (1994). Ethical standards of human service professionals. *National Organization for Human Service Education.* Web site, http://www.nohse.com.

NOHSE. (1996). The human services worker: A generic job description. *National Organization for Human Service Education.* Web site, http://www.nohse.com.

Novak, J. M. (1996). *Treatment protocol effectiveness study.* Washington, DC: Office of National Drug Policy.

Offer, D., & Sabshin, M. (Eds.). (1991). *The diversity of normal behavior: Further contributions to normatology.* New York: Basic Books.

Office of Applied Studies. (1999). *National household survey on drug abuse: Main findings 1997.* Washington, DC: Department of Health and Human Services.

Okpakus, S., Anderson, K., Silbulkin, A., Butler, J., & Bickman, L. (1997). The effectiveness of a multidisciplinary case management intervention on the employment of SSDI applicants and beneficiaries. *Psychiatric Rehabilitation Journal, 20.*

Orlans, H. (1982). *Human services coordination.* New York: Pica Press.

Paniagua, F. A. (1994). *Assessing and treating culturally diverse clients: A practical guide.* Thousand Oaks, CA: Sage.

Parad, H. J., & Resnik, H. L. P. (1975). The practice of crisis intervention in emergency care. In H. L. P. Resnik and H. Ruben (Eds.), *Emergency psychiatric care: The management of mental health crises.* Bowie, MD: Charles Press.

Parham, I. (1974, March). Constraints in implementing services integration goals—The Georgia experience. *Human services integration.* Washington, DC: American Society for Public Administration.

Parlin, A. W., & Grew, K. J. (1999). Human services in the schools: History and focus. In H. S. Harris and D. C. Maloney (Eds.), *Human services: Contemporary issues and trends* (2nd ed.). Boston: Allyn and Bacon.

Patterson, G. (1971). Behavioral intervention procedures in the classroom and in the home. In A. Bergin and S. Garfield (Eds.), *Handbook of psychotherapy and behavior change: An empirical analysis.* New York: Wiley.

Paul, G. (1967). Insight versus desensitization in psychotherapy, two years after termination. *Journal of Consulting Psychology, 31.*

Pearl, A., & Riessman, F. (1965). *New careers for the poor: The nonprofessional in human service.* New York: Free Press.

Pearlman, M. H., & Edwards, M. G. (1982). Enabling in the eighties: The client advocacy group. *Social Casework, 63.*

Perls, S. (1978). Paraprofessionals a decade later: What's in a name? *Hospital and Community Psychiatry, 29.*

Perls, S. (1979). A follow-up study of graduates of an associate-degree program for mental health workers. *Hospital and Community Psychiatry, 30.*

Petrie, R. D. (1984). Competence and curriculum. *Journal of the National Organization of Human Service Educators, 6.*

Petrie, R. D. (1986). Facilitating a working knowledge of community human service resources. *Journal of Humanistic Education and Development, 24.*

Petrie, R. D. (1999). Trends and challenges of cultural diversity. In H. S. Harris and D. C. Maloney (Eds.), *Human services: Contemporary issues and trends* (2nd ed.). Boston: Allyn and Bacon.

Phelan, J. C., & Link, B. C. (1999). Who are "the homeless"? Reconsidering the stability and composition of the homeless population. *American Journal of Public Health, 84.*

Pierce, R. L., & Pierce, L. H. (1996). Moving toward cultural competence in the child welfare system. *Children and Youth Services Review, 18.*

Pinderhughes, E. B. (1983). Empowerment for our clients and for ourselves. *Social Casework, 64.*

President's Panel on Mental Retardation (1962). *A proposed program for national action to combat mental retardation.* Washington, DC: U.S. Superintendent of Documents.

Price, R. H., Cowen, E. L., Lorion, R. P., & Ramos-McKay, J. (1988). *Fourteen ounces of prevention: A casebook for practitioners.* Washington, DC: American Psychological Association.

Program on Chronic Mental Illness. (1990, April). *National survey on public attitudes toward people with chronic mental illness.* Boston: The Robert Wood Johnson Foundation.

Prouty, R., & Lakin, K. C. (1995). *Residential services for persons with developmental disabilities: Status and trends through 1994.* Minneapolis: University of Minnesota, Research and Training Center on Community Living, Institute on Community Integration.

Purvis, A. (1997). The global epidemic. *Time, 148.*

Quinn, J. (1996). Foreword. In C. D. Austin and R. W. McClelland (Eds.), *Perspectives on case management practice.* Milwaukee: Families International.

Rapoport, L. (1962). The state of crisis: Some theoretical considerations. *The Social Service Review, 36.*

Rapp, C. A. (1993). Theory, principles, and methods of the strengths model of case management. In M. Harris and H. C. Bergman (Eds.), *Case management for mentally ill patients: Theory and practice.* Langhorne, PA: Harwood Academic Publishers.

Rapp, C. A. (1996). The active ingredients of effective case management: A research synthesis. In L. J. Giesler (Ed.), *Case management for behavioral managed care.* Cincinnati, OH: National Association of Case Management.

Rapp, C. A. (1997). *The strengths model: Case management with people suffering from severe and persistent mental illness.* London: Oxford University Press.

Rapp, C. A., & Chamberlin, R. (1985). Case management services for the chronically mentally ill. *Social Work, 30.*

Rapp, C. A., & Kisthardt, W. (1996). Case management with people with severe and persistent mental illness. In C. O. Austin and R. W. McClelland (Eds.), *Perspectives on case management practice.* Milwaukee: Families International.

Redlich, F. C., Hollingshead, A. B., Roberts, B. A., Robinson, H. A., Freedman, L. Z., & Myers, J. K. (1953). Social structure and psychiatric disorders. *American Journal of Psychiatry, 109.*

Reischauer, R. D. (1986). The prospects for welfare reform. *Public Welfare, 44.*

Reiss, C., Liner, L., Harrison, R., & Harrison, C. (1993). *The prevention of mental disorders: A national research agenda.* Washington, DC: National Institute of Mental Health.

Reiss, S. (1994). *Handbook of challenging behavior: Mental health aspects of mental retardation.* Worthington, OH: IDS Publishing.

Reppucci, N. D., & Saunders, J. T. (1983). Focal issues for institutional change. *Professional Psychology: Research and Practice, 14.*

Rhodes, M. (1998). Ethical challenges in social work: Comments for a special issue of *Families in Society* on ethics. *Families in Society: The Journal of Contemporary Human Services, 79.*

Riessman, F. (1965). The helper-therapy principle. *Social Work, 10.*

Riessman, F. (1979). Self-help. In S. Alley, J. Blanton, and R. E. Feldman (Eds.), *Parapro-* *fessionals in mental health.* New York: Human Sciences Press.

Riessman, F., & Carroll, C. (1995). *Redefining self-help: Policy and practice.* San Francisco: Jossey-Bass.

Riessman, F., & Miller, S. M. (1964). Social change versus the "psychiatric world view." *American Journal of Orthopsychiatry, 34.*

Riessman, F., & Popper, H. (1968). *Up from poverty: New career ladders for non-professionals.* New York: Harper & Row.

Rimland, B. (1969). Psychogenesis versus biogenesis: The issues and the evidence. In S. Plog and R. Edgerton (Eds.), *Changing perspectives in mental illness.* New York: Holt, Rinehart & Winston.

Rioch, M. (1966). Changing concepts in the training of therapists. *Journal of Counseling Psychology, 30.*

Rioch, M., Elker, C., Flint, A., Usdansky, B., Newman, R., & Silber, E. (1963). National Institute of Mental Health pilot study in training mental health counselors. *American Journal of Orthopsychiatry, 33.*

Rodriguez, B. M. (1996). From self to other: Communication across cultures. *Family Resource Coalition Report, 14.*

Rogers, C. (1942). *Counseling and psychotherapy.* Boston: Houghton.

Rogers, C. (1951). *Client-centered therapy: Its current practice, implications and theory.* Boston: Houghton Mifflin.

Rogers, C. (1957). The necessary and sufficient conditions of therapeutic personality change. *Journal of Consulting Psychology, 21.*

Rogers, C., Gendlin, E., Kiesler, D., & Louax, C. (1967). *The therapeutic relationship and its impact: A study of psychotherapy with schizophrenics.* Madison: University of Wisconsin Press.

Romanyshyn, J. M. (1971). *Social welfare: Charity to justice.* New York: Random House.

Rose, S. M., & Black, B. L. (1985). *Advocacy and empowerment: Mental health care in the community.* London: Routledge & Kegan Paul.

Rosel, N. (1983). The hub of a wheel: A neighborhood support network. *International Journal of Aging and Human Development, 16.*

Rossi, P. H. (1990). The old homeless and the new homelessness in historical perspective. *American Psychologist, 24.*

Rubenstein, L. S. (1986). Treatment of the mentally ill: Legal advocacy enters the second generation. *American Journal of Psychiatry, 143.*

Runyan, A. (1999). Helping services for individuals: Perspectives and skills. In H. S. Harris and D. C. Maloney (Eds.), *Human services: Contemporary issues and trends* (2nd ed.). Boston: Allyn and Bacon.

Rutan, J. S. (Ed.). (1992). *Psychotherapy for the 1990s.* New York: Guilford Press.

Rynearson, E. K. (1986). Psychological effects of unnatural dying on bereavement. *Psychiatric Annals, 16.*

Sabshin, M. (1989). Normality and the boundaries of psychopathology. *Journal of Personality Disorders, 3.*

Sakauye, K. M. (1986). A model for administration of electroconvulsive therapy. *Hospital and Community Psychiatry, 37.*

SAMHSA. (1996). *Trends in the incidence of drug use in the United States, 1919–1992.* Washington, DC: Substance Abuse and Mental Health Services Administration. Offices of Applied Studies.

SAMHSA. (1998). *HIV/AIDS programs.* Washington, DC: National Mental Health Services Knowledge Exchange Network, Center for Mental Health Services.

SAMHSA News. (1999). Service providers sensitized to mental health needs of clients with HIV. *SAMHSA News, 8.*

Sancilio, M. F. (1987). Peer interaction as a method of therapeutic intervention with children. *Clinical Psychology, 7.*

Santiago, J. M. (1993). Taking issue: Hispanic, Latino or Raza? Coming to terms with diversity. *Hospital and Community Psychiatry, 44.*

Sarason, S. B., Carroll, C. F., Maton, K., Cohen, S., & Lorentz, E. (1977). *Human services and resource networks.* San Francisco: Jossey-Bass.

Sarbin, T. (1968). Notes on the transformation of social identity. In L. M. Roberts, N. Greenfield, and M. Miller (Eds.), *Comprehensive mental health: The challenge of evaluation.* Madison: University of Wisconsin Press.

Satir, V. (1964). *Conjoint family therapy.* Palo Alto, CA: Science & Behavioral Books.

Sauber, S. R. (1983). *The human services delivery system.* New York: Columbia University Press.

Scheerenberger, R. C. (1983). *A history of mental retardation.* Baltimore, MD: Paul H. Brooks.

Scheff, T. (1984). *Being mentally ill: A sociological theory* (2nd ed.). Chicago: Aldine.

Scheffler, L. W. (1984). *Help thy neighbor.* New York: Grove Press.

Schensul, S. L., & Schensul, J. J. (1982). Self-help groups and advocacy: A contrast in beliefs and strategies. In G. H. Weber and L. M. Cohen (Eds.), *Beliefs and self-help: Cross cultural perspectives and approaches.* New York: Human Sciences Press.

Schneider-Corey, M., & Corey, G. (1989). *Becoming a helper.* Pacific Grove, CA: Brooks/Cole.

Schroeder, S. R., Schroeder, C. S., & Landesman, S. (1987). Psychological services in educational settings to persons with mental retardation. *American Psychologist, 42.*

Scott, J. E., & Dixon, L. B. (1995). Psychological interventions for schizophrenia. *Schizophrenia Bulletin, 21.*

Self-Help for the Widowed. (1975, Summer). *Innovations: Highlights of Evolving Mental Health Services, 2.*

Seligman, M. E. P. (1995). The effectiveness of psychotherapy: The *Consumer Reports* study. *American Psychologist, 50.*

Shanfield, S. B., Matthews, K. L., & Hetherly, V. (1993). What do excellent psychotherapy supervisors do? *American Journal of Psychiatry, 150.*

Shealy, C. N. (1995). From Boys' Town to Oliver Twist: Separating fact from fiction in welfare reform and out-of-home placement of children and youth. *American Psychologist, 50.*

Shodell, M. (1984). The clouded mind. *Science, 84.*

Shore, J. H., Vollmer, W. M., & Tatum, E. L. (1989). Community patterns of posttraumatic stress disorders. *Journal of Nervous & Mental Disease, 177.*

Silverman, L. (1976). Psychoanalytic theory: "The reports of my death are greatly exaggerated." *American Psychologist, 31.*

Simon, E. (1999). Field practicum: Standards, criteria, supervision, and evaluation. In H. S. Harris and D. C. Maloney (Eds.). *Human services: Contemporary issues and trends.* (2nd ed.). Boston: Allyn and Bacon.

Simoni, J., & Perez, L. (1995). Latinos and mutual support groups: A case for considering culture. *American Journal of Orthopsychiatry, 65.*

Slater, P. (1970). *The pursuit of loneliness: American culture at the breaking point.* Boston: Beacon Press.

Sloane, R. B., Staples, F. R., Yorkston, W., Cristol, A., & Whipple, K. (1975). *Behavior therapy versus psychotherapy.* Cambridge, MA: Harvard University Press.

Slovenko, R. (1973). *Psychiatry and the law.* Boston: Little, Brown.

Smith, M. L., Glass, G. V., & Miller, T. I. (1980). *The benefits of psychotherapy.* Baltimore, MD: The Johns Hopkins University Press.

Smith, N. K., & Meyer, A. B. (1981). Personal care attendants: Key to living independently. *Rehabilitation Literature, 42.*

Sobey, F. (1970). *The nonprofessional revolution in mental health.* New York: Columbia University Press.

Solomon, S. D., & Davidson, J. R. T. (1997). Trauma: Prevalence, impairment, service use, and cost. *Journal of Clinical Psychiatry, 58.*

Sosin, M., & Caulum, S. (1983). Advocacy: A conceptualization for social work practice. *Social Work, 28.*

Southern Regional Education Board. (1969). *Roles and functions for different levels of mental health workers.* Atlanta: Author.

Southern Regional Education Board. (1973). *The creation of a discipline: Middle level mental health workers.* Atlanta: Author.

Southern Regional Education Board. (1978). *Staff roles for mental health personnel: A history and rationale for paraprofessionals.* Atlanta: Author.

Southern Regional Education Board. (1979). *Mental health/human service worker activities: The process and the products.* Atlanta: Author.

Srole, L., Langer, T. S., Michael, S. T., Kirkpatrick, P., Opler, M. K., & Rennie, T. A. (1978). *Mental health in the metropolis: The midtown Manhattan study* (Rev. ed.). New York: New York University Press.

Stein, L. I., & Test, M. A. (1980). Alternatives to mental hospital treatment: I. Conceptual model, treatment program, and clinical evaluation. *Archives of General Psychiatry, 37.*

Steinberg, D. M. (1997). *The mutual-aid approach to working with groups: Helping people to help each other.* Northvale, NJ: Aronson.

Stephens, L., Wills, A., Leston, J., & Smith, B. (1987). Social networks as assets and liabilities in recovery from stroke by geriatric patients. *Psychology and Aging, 2.*

Stone, A. A. (1975). Overview: The right to treatment—Comments on the law and its impact. *American Journal of Psychiatry, 132.*

Stout, C. E., & Jongsma, A. E. (1998). *The continuum of care treatment planner.* New York: John Wiley & Sons.

Stroud, B. A. (1995). Case management in a system of care. In B. J. Friesen and J. Poertner (Eds.), *From case management to service coordination for children with emotional, behavioral, or mental disorders: Building on family strengths.* Baltimore: Paul Brooks.

Stroul, B. A. (1993). *Psychiatric crisis response systems: A descriptive study.* Washington, DC: Substance Abuse and Mental Health Administration.

Stroul, B. & Friedman, R. M. (1994). *A system of care for children & youth with severe emotional disturbances.* (Revised edition) Washington, DC: Georgetown University Child Development Center, CASSP Technical Assistance Center.

Strupp, H. H., & Hadley, S. W. (1979). Specific versus non-specific factors in psychotherapy: A controlled study of outcome. *Archives of General Psychiatry, 36.*

Styron, W. (1994, April 18). An interior pain that is all but indescribable. *Newsweek.*

Sue, D. W. (1992). The challenge of multiculturalism: The road less traveled. *American Counselor, 1.*

Sullivan, W. P. (1996). Beyond the twenty-eight day: Case management in alcohol and drug treatment. In C. D. Austin and R. W. McClelland (Eds.). *Perspectives on case management practice.* Milwaukee: Families International.

Sweitzer, H. F. (1999). Burnout: Avoiding the trap. In H. S. Harris and D. C. Maloney (Eds.), *Hu-*

man services: Contemporary issues and trends (2nd ed.). Boston: Allyn and Bacon.

Taylor, V. (1976). The delivery of mental health services in the Xenia tornado. (Unpublished doctoral dissertation, Ohio State University, Columbus, OH.)

Terr, L. C. (1981). Psychic trauma in children: Observations following the Chowchilla schoolbus kidnapping. *American Journal of Psychiatry, 138.*

Test, M. A. (1992). Training in community living. In R. P. Liberman (Ed.), *Handbook of psychiatric rehabilitation.* New York: Macmillan.

Thombs, D. L. (1999). *Introduction to addictive behavior* (2nd ed.). New York: Guilford Press.

Throits, P. (1986). Social support as coping assistance. *Journal of Consulting and Clinical Psychology, 54.*

Thyer, B. A. (Ed.). (1988). *Progress in behavioral social work.* New York: Haworth Press.

Torrey, E. F. (1989). Thirty years of shame: The scandalous neglect of the mentally ill homeless. *Policy Review, 48.*

Trappler, B., & Friedman, S. (1996). Posttraumatic stress disorder in survivors of the Brooklyn Bridge shooting. *American Journal of Psychiatry, 153.*

Trattner, W. I. (1986). *From poor law to welfare state: A history of social welfare in America* (3rd ed.). New York: Free Press.

Truax, C. B. (1969). *An approach toward training for the aide therapist: Research and implications.* Fayetteville, AR: Arkansas Rehabilitation Research and Training Center.

Truax, C. B., & Carkuff, R. R. (1967). *Toward effective counseling and psychotherapy.* Chicago: Aldine.

Uchitelle, L. (1999, October 1). Rising incomes lift 1.1 million out of poverty. *The New York Times.*

Umbricht, D., & Kane, J. M. (1995). Risperidone: Efficacy and safety. *Schizophrenia Bulletin, 21.*

U.S. Public Health Service. (1999). *The Surgeon General's call to action to prevent suicide.* Washington, DC: U.S. Public Health Service.

Van der Avort, A., & Van Harberden, P. (1985). Helping self-help groups: A developing theory. *Psychotherapy: Theory/Research/Practice/Training, 22.*

Vidaver, R. (1973). Developments in human services education and manpower. In H. Schulberg, F. Baker, and S. Roen (Eds.), *Developments in human services* (Vol. 1). New York: Behavioral Publications.

Vigoda, A. (1996, June 27). Risk reduced; Lifeline. *USA Today.*

Walker, C. E., Bonner, B. L., & Kaufman, K. L. (1987). *The physically and sexually abused child: Evaluation and treatment.* New York: Pergamon Press.

Walker, L. E. A. (1984). *The battered women syndrome.* New York: Springer.

Wallack, J. J. (1989). AIDS anxiety among health care professionals. *Hospital and Community Psychiatry, 40.*

Wallerstein, R. S. (1986). *Forty-two lives in treatment: A study of psychoanalysis and psychotherapy. The report of the Psychotherapy Research Project of the Menninger Foundation, 1954–1982.* New York: Guilford Press.

Wechsler, D. (1958). *The measurement and appraisal of adult intelligence.* Baltimore, MD: Williams & Wilkins.

Weil, M., & Karls, J. (1989). Key components in providing efficient and effective services. In M. Weil and J. Karls (Eds.), *Case management in human service practice.* San Francisco: Jossey-Bass.

Westermeyer, J. (1987). Cultural factors in clinical assessment. *Journal of Consulting and Clinical Psychology, 55.*

White, S. L. (1981). *Managing health and human service programs: A guide for managers.* New York: Free Press.

Whitman, D. (1990). The rise of the hyper-poor. *U.S. News and World Report, 109.*

Whittaker, J. K., Garbino, J., et al. (1983). *Social support networks: Informal helping in the human services.* New York: Aldine.

Wicks, R. (1974). *Correctional psychology.* San Francisco: Canfield Press.

Wilson, P. A. (1983). Towards more effective intervention in natural helping networks. *Social Work in Health Care, 9.*

Winarski, J. T. (1996). *Implementing interventions for homeless individuals with co-occurring mental health and substance use disorders: A*

PATH technical assistance package. Washington, DC: Center for Mental Health Services, SAMSHA, U.S. Department of Health and Human Services.

Wise, H. B. (1968). The family health worker. *American Journal of Public Health, 58.*

Withorn, A. (1998). No win . . . facing the ethical perils of welfare reform. *Families in Society: The Journal of Contemporary Human Services, 79.*

Wittman, M. (1972). The social welfare system: Its relation to community mental health. In S. Golann and C. Eisdorfer (Eds.), *Handbook of community mental health.* Englewood Cliffs, NJ: Prentice Hall.

Wolberg, L. R. (1977). *The technique of psychotherapy* (3rd ed.). New York: Grune & Stratton.

Wolpe, J. (1961). The Systematic desensitization treatment of neurosis. *Journal of Nervous and Mental Disorders, 132.*

Wood, A. (1974). *Deviant behavior and control strategies.* Lexington, MA: D. C. Heath.

Woodside, M., & McClam, T. (1998). *Generalist case management: A method of human services delivery.* Pacific Grove, CA: Brooks/Cole.

Woody, R. H., & Associates. (1984). *The law and the practice of human services.* San Francisco: Jossey-Bass.

Yalom, I. D. (1985). *The theory and practice of group psychotherapy* (3rd ed.). New York: Basic Books.

Yates, A. (1970). *Behavior therapy.* New York: John Wiley & Sons.

Youngblood, G. S., & Bensberg, G. J. (1983). *Planning and operating group homes for the handicapped.* Lubbock, TX: Research and Training Center in Mental Retardation.

Youngstrom, N. (1990). Seriously mentally ill need better tracking. *APA Monitor, 21.*

Zarit, S. H. (1980). *Aging and mental disorders.* New York: Free Press.

Zigler, E. (1985). Assessing Head Start at 20: An invited commentary. *American Journal of Orthopsychiatry, 55.*

Zigler, E. (1999). Comment: Head start is not child care. *American Psychologist, 54.*

Zimbardo, P. (1970). The human choice: Individuation, reason and order versus deindividuation, impulse and chaos. In D. Levine (Ed.), *Nebraska Symposium on Motivation, 1969.* Lincoln: University of Nebraska.

Zingale, D. D. (1985). The importance of empathic responding in the psychotherapeutic interview. *International Social Work, 28.*

Zlotnick, C., Kronstadt, D., & Klee, L. (1999). Essential case management services for young children in foster care. *Community Mental Health Journal, 35.*

Zlotnik, J. L. (1996). Case management in child welfare. In C. D. Austin and R. W. McClelland (Eds.), *Perspectives on case management practice.* Milwaukee: Families International.

Index